Transnational Terrorist Groups and International Criminal Law

Attacks by network-based transnational terrorist groups cause on average 25,000 deaths every year worldwide, with the law enforcement agencies of some states facing many challenges in bringing those responsible to justice. Despite various attempts to codify the law on transnational terrorism since the 1930s, a crime of transnational terrorism under international law remains contested, reflecting concerns regarding the relative importance of prosecuting members of transnational terrorist groups before the International Criminal Court. This book critically examines the limits of international criminal law in bringing members of transnational terrorist groups to justice in the context of changing methods of warfare, drawing from human rights, sociology, and best practices in international criminal justice.

Drawing on organisational network theory, Anna Marie Brennan explores the nature of international crimes and assesses the potential for the International Criminal Court to prosecute and investigate alleged crimes perpetrated by members of transnational terrorist groups, paying particular attention to their *modus operandi* and organisational structure. This book argues that because of the network-based organisational structure of some transnational terrorist groups, achieving justice for victims will prove challenging, in the context of the relationship between the commanders and the subordinate members of the group requiring a re-evaluation of accountability mechanisms at the international level.

In advancing an innovative perspective on the accountability of members of transnational terrorist groups, and in offering solutions to current challenges, the book will be of great interest and use to academic, practitioners, and students engaged in the study of terrorism, the ICC, or international humanitarian law.

Anna Marie Brennan is a senior lecturer in law at the University of Waikato in New Zealand. Her interests are in international criminal justice, international humanitarian law, non-state armed groups, and responsibility.

Routledge Research in International Law

For a full list of titles in this series, visit https://www.routledge.com/Routledge-Research-in-International-Law/book-series/INTNLLAW

Available:

Unilateral Acts
A History of a Legal Doctrine
Betina Appel Kuzmarov

Regional Developmentalism Through Law
The Use of Law to Support the Effective Establishment of an African Economic Community
Jonathan Bashi Rudahindwa

China's One Belt One Road Initiative and Private International Law
Poomintr Sooksripaisarnkit and Sai Ramani Garimella

Transnational Terrorist Groups and International Criminal Law
Anna Marie Brennan

The EU Social Market Economy and the Law
Theoretical Perspectives and Practical Challenges for the EU
Delia Ferri and Fulvio Cortese

Confronting Cyberespionage Under International Law
Oğuz Kaan Pehlivan

Russian Discourses on International Law
Sociological and Philosophical Phenomenon
P. Sean Morris

Transnational Terrorist Groups and International Criminal Law

Anna Marie Brennan

Routledge
Taylor & Francis Group
LONDON AND NEW YORK

First published 2019
by Routledge
2 Park Square, Milton Park, Abingdon, Oxon OX14 4RN

and by Routledge
52 Vanderbilt Avenue, New York, NY 10017

First issued in paperback 2020

Routledge is an imprint of the Taylor & Francis Group, an informa business

British Library Cataloguing in Publication Data
A catalogue record for this book is available from the British Library

Library of Congress Cataloging in Publication Data
Names: Brennan, Anna Marie, author.
Title: Transnational terrorist groups and international criminal law / Anna Marie Brennan.
Description: New York: Routledge, 2018. | Series: Routledge research in international law | Includes bibliographical references and index.
Identifiers: LCCN 2018013035 | ISBN 9781138291904 (hardback)
Subjects: LCSH: Terrorism -Prevention -Law and legislation. | Transnational crime -Prevention. | International criminal law.
Classification: LCC KZ7220 .B74 2018 | DDC 345/.02317 -dc23
LC record available at https://lccn.loc.gov/2018013035

ISBN 13: 978-0-367-58810-6 (pbk)
ISBN 13: 978-1-138-29190-4 (hbk)

Typeset in Galliard
by Taylor & Francis Books

Contents

Acknowledgements

I would like to make a special thank you to my supervisors, Professor Siobhan Mullally and Dr Fiona Donson who provided helpful feedback and guidance throughout my PhD. Both my supervisors' patience, encouragement, and support made this monograph possible, they always made me welcome to chat to them about it, and I cannot thank them enough for the help and guidance they have given me.

I would also like to thank my examiners Professors Javaid Rehman and Caroline Fennell, who took the time to read the thesis, challenged me during my viva, and provided insightful observations on the future direction of my research. Thanks to all the staff at UCC Faculty of Law, particularly Ms Veronica Calnan and Mr Pat Rice, for their assistance. I would also like to express my gratitude to Dr Padraig MacAuliffe for his advice during the authoring process. I am also grateful for the support of my fellow PhD candidates. Thanks to my family, particularly my parents, who continually provided support and encouragement throughout my PhD. I would also like to extend my gratitude to Katie Carpenter and Olivia Manley at Routledge who guided and supported me through the authoring and copy-editing process.

My PhD research was kindly funded by the President James Slattery Prize and Gold Meal in Law and a Faculty of Law PhD Fellowship at University College Cork and an Irish Research Council Postgraduate Fellowship. In The Hague, I would like to thank Mark Dillon at the International Criminal Court for his advice and assistance. Thank you to all the interns and practitioners I worked with in The Hague. I would like to especially thank the judges I spoke to and I hope what I have written a monograph which will make a strong contribution to the field.

A special thanks to Judge Sylvia Steiner who allowed me to work alongside her on the Jean Pierre Bemba Gombo trial at the International Criminal Court; and to Peter Robinson who allowed me to work on the defence team of Radovan Karadžić at the UN International Criminal Tribunal for the Former Yugoslavia. Both are a source of inspiration in their tireless devotion to the pursuit of international justice.

During the time between the completion of my PhD and finishing this book I was fortunate to work alongside Alex Batemsith, Michael Dougan, Eleanor

Drywood, Kanstantin Dzehtsiarou, Seamus Bryne, Michelle Farrell, and Vassilis Tzevelekos who all broadened my perspective and approach to transnational terrorist groups and international criminal law. I really appreciate their advice, support, and comments which helped to ground this book in reality.

Abbreviations

AFRC	Armed Forces Revolutionary Council
DRC	Democratic Republic of Congo
ETA	Euskadi ta Askatasuna
FDLR	Forces démocratiques pour la libération du Rwanda
FPLC	Patriotic Forces for the Liberation of Congo
HVO	Croatian Defence Council
ICC	International Criminal Court
ICCPR	International Covenant on Civil and Political Rights
ICJ	International Court of Justice
ICL	International Criminal Law
ICRC	International Committee of the Red Cross
ICTR	International Criminal Tribunal for Rwanda
ICTY	International Criminal Tribunal for the Former Yugoslavia
IHL	international humanitarian law
ILC	International Law Commission
IMT	International Military Tribunal
IRA	Irish Republican Army
ISIS	Islamic State of Iraq and Syria
JCE	Joint Criminal Enterprise
LRA	Lord's Resistance Army
MILF	Moro Islamic Liberation Front
OAU	Organisation of African Unity
OIC	Organisation of the Islamic Conference
RUF	Revolutionary United Front
SAARC	South Asia Association for Regional Cooperation
SCSL	Special Court for Sierra Leone
SPIN	Segmented Polycentric Ideologically Integrated Network
STL	Special Tribunal for Lebanon
UK	United Kingdom
UN	United Nations
UNCM	Uniform Code of Military Justice
UNITA	National Union for the Total Independence of Angola
UOC	Union of Congolese Patriots
US	United States
WUO	Weather Underground Organization

1 Introduction

The Islamic State of Iraq and Syria (ISIS) has caused considerable loss of life, bodily injury, and destruction of property and infrastructure in the Middle East since its emergence in 2013.[1] Indeed, the Office of the United Nations High Commissioner for Human Rights estimates that between January 2014 and October 2015, 18,802 civilians were killed and more than 36,245 civilians were injured by ISIS and its associated groups in Iraq alone.[2] The threat posed by ISIS has caused major upheaval for other states as well.[3] Faced with ongoing terrorist attacks by ISIS militants returning from fighting in Syria and Iraq, the United Kingdom has elevated its terrorist threat level from 'substantial' to 'severe' and has also put additional security measures in place.[4]

In June 2014, the United States launched Operation Inherent Resolve in Iraq and Syria in an attempt to curb the threat posed by ISIS and also immobilise its de facto headquarters, access to territory and vital resources.[5] Although the cumulative

1 Samuel Smith, 'UN Report on ISIS: 24,000 Killed, Injured by Islamic State; Children Used as Soldiers, Women Sold as Sex Slaves' (*CP World*, 9 October 2014) available at: www.christianpost.com/news/un-report-on-isis-24000-killed-injured-by-islamic-state-children-used-as-soldiers-women-sold-as-sex-slaves-127761 (date accessed: 14 March 2018).

2 UN Human Rights Office of the High Commissioner for Human Rights and the UN Assistance Mission for Iraq, *Report on the Protection of Civilians in Armed Conflict in Iraq: 6 July–10 September 2014* (Geneva, 2014) at p. i, available at: www.ohchr.org/Documents/Countries/IQ/UNAMI_OHCHR_POC_Report_FINAL_6July_10September2014.pdf (date accessed: 14 March 2018).

3 Ian Traynor, 'Major Terrorist Attack Is "Inevitable" as ISIS Fighters Return, says EU officials' (*The Guardian*, 25 September 2014) available at: www.theguardian.com/world/2014/sep/25/major-terrorist-attack-inevitable-isis-eu (date accessed: 14 March 2018).

4 'Terrorism Laws: "Time is Right" for New Police Powers' (*BBC News*, 24 November 2014) available at: www.bbc.co.uk/news/uk-30173238 (date accessed: 14 March 2018) (no author name provided). See also Emma Thomas, 'Security Tightened for Remembrance Sunday after Four Arrested for Terror Plot' (*Express*, 8 November 2014) available at: www.express.co.uk/news/uk/532964/Security-tightened-for-Remembrance-Sunday-after-four-arrested-for-terror-plot (date accessed: 14 March 2018).

5 Staff writer, 'Obama Admits: We "Underestimated" ISIS Threat' (*Al Arabiya News*, 29 September 2014) available at: http://english.alarabiya.net/en/News/middle-ea

expenditure on this operation has exceeded $14.3 billion so far,[6] the US administration believes that this is the most pragmatic approach to deal with the threat posed by ISIS considering the highly deterritorialised and decentralised nature of their activities.[7] So when it was alleged that former detainees of the US detention centre in Guantánamo Bay joined ISIS upon their release, major criticism arose not only about the capacity of states to protect civilians from harm but also their ability to prosecute members of these groups for alleged crimes.[8] Such concerns reflect the dilemma that states such as the United States and the United Kingdom face when determining how best to deal with attacks by transnational terrorist groups and also raises questions whether international criminal law (ICL) could overcome any of these challenges.

Of course, the United States and the United Kingdom are not the only states facing serious threats by transnational terrorist groups. States such as Afghanistan, Australia, Belgium, Bulgaria, Cameroon, France, India, Kenya, Lebanon, Malaysia, Nigeria, Pakistan, the Philippines, Spain, and Turkey have all had to deal with the tragic consequences of terrorist attacks.[9] In particular, the National Consortium for the Study of Terrorism and Responses to Terrorism in the United States estimates that attacks by transnational terrorist groups in 2016 killed approximately 34,676 people worldwide.[10] In contrast to terrorist groups of the 1960s, 1970s,

st/2014/09/29/-We-underestimated-ISIS-admits-Obama.html (date accessed: 14 March 2018).

6 US Department of Defense, 'Operation Inherent Resolve: Targeted Operations to Defeat ISIS' available at: www.defense.gov/OIR (date accessed: 14 March 2018).

7 Ibid.

8 Tom Burridge, 'Spain Arrests Eight in "ISIS Cell"' (*BBC News*, 16 June 2014) available at: www.bbc.co.uk/news/world-europe-27865046 (date accessed: 14 March 2018).

9 Barney Henderson, 'Mumbai 26/11: Five Years On: City Still Feels Scars of Devastating Terrorist Attack' (*The Telegraph*, 26 November 2013) available at: www.fas.org/sgp/crs/natsec/RL33110.pdf (date accessed: 14 March 2018); Jamela Alindogan, 'Battle for Control of Kampung Tanduo' (*Al Jazeera*, 25 February 2013) available at: http://blogs.aljazeera.com/blog/asia/battle-control-kampung-tanduo (date accessed: 14 March 2014); Jon Boone, 'Islamabad Court Suicide Attacks Strikes Terrorism Blow in Pakistani Capital' (*The Guardian*, 3 March 2014) available at: www.theguardian.com/world/2014/mar/03/islamabad-court-suicide-attack-terrorism-pakistani-capital (date accessed: 14 March 2018); Maria Ressa, 'Philippines' Evolving Terrorism Threat' (*CNN*, 1 February 2011) available at: http://edition.cnn.com/2011/OPINION/01/31/maria.ressa.bus.bombing (date accessed: 14 March 2018). For further commentary on the 9/11 attacks in the US, see National Commission on Terrorist Attacks upon the United States, *The 9/11 Commission Report* (2004) at p. 316, available at: http://govinfo.library.unt.edu/911/report/911Report_Ch9.pdf (date accessed: 14 March 2018). Unpublished data on hospital visits in the aftermath of the attacks indicate that thousands of people were treated for inhalation injuries, musculoskeletal injuries burns, and eye injuries. For more on this point, see US Government Accountability Office, 'September 11: Health Effects in the Aftermath of the World Trade Center Attack' (8 September 2004) at p. 7, available at: www.gao.gov/new.items/d041068t.pdf (date accessed: 14 March 2018).

10 National Consortium for the Study of Terrorism and Responses to Terrorism, 'Overview: Terrorism in 2016' (August 2017) available at: www.start.umd.edu/pubs/START_GTD_OverviewTerrorism2016_August2017.pdf (date accessed: 14 March 2018).

and 1980s, the contemporary terrorist group is a looser, more fragmented entity, which mirrors developments in technology and has the capacity to exert considerable global reach and influence.[11] Modern technology not only provides transnational terrorist groups with the capacity to conduct attacks in more than one state, it also enables them to disseminate their ideology and messages of terror and intimidation on a worldwide stage.[12] In November 2015, for example, it was with great horror that the international community watched the Paris attacks unfold on the television and internet.[13] As a result, transnational terrorist groups can utilise modern technology not only to increase the impact of their attacks and instil fear in civilian populations that further attacks will occur but also to disseminate their ideology and recruit new members.[14]

Transnational terrorist groups also constitute a polymorphic threat because they have the capacity to carry out both large-scale attacks and more isolated strikes.[15] Members are often indistinguishable from the civilian population and function autonomously in network-based cells. This in turn poses a challenge for states with limited resources to investigate their activities and bring them to justice.[16] So the question arises about what role, if any, ICL can play in bringing members of these groups to justice especially since transnational terrorist groups egregiously subvert the law. Transnational terrorist groups also complicate the interconnection between the state and the individual upon which the Westphalian concept of international law is based.[17] As a result, they are able to perpetrate far-reaching violence across state borders while also evading responsibility.[18]

11 For instance, the 'war' on terror has arguably enhanced the status of transnational terrorists on the international plane. See Mary-Ellen O'Connell, 'Enhancing the Status of Non-State Actors through a Global War on Terror?', *Columbia Journal of Transnational Law* 43 (2005) 435–458.

12 Boaz Ganor, 'Terrorism as a Strategy of Psychological Warfare', in Y. Danieli et al. (eds), *The Trauma of Terrorism: Sharing Knowledge and Shared Care: An International Handbook* (Haworth Press, 2013) p. 34.

13 Ivano Bongiovanni, 'Brussels Airport Attacks are not just a matter of Airport Security' (*The Conversation*, 23 March 2016) available at: https://theconversation.com/brussels-airport-attacks-are-not-just-a-matter-of-airport-security-56736 (date accessed: 14 March 2018).

14 Vincent-Joel Proulx, *Transnational Terrorism and State Accountability: A New Theory of Prevention* (Hart, 2012), p. 3.

15 Ibid.

16 Ibid. See also Mark Osiel, *The End of Reciprocity: Terror, Torture, and the Law of War* (Cambridge University Press, 2009).

17 Andrea Bianchi (ed.), *Enforcing International Law Norms against Terrorism* (Hart, 2004); Jean-Christophe Martin, *Les règles internationales relatives à la lutte contre le terrorisme* (Bruylant, 2006); Pierre Klein, 'Le droit international à l'épreuve du terrorisme', *Recueil des cours* 321 (2006) 203; Pablo Antonio Fernández-Sánchez (ed.), *International Legal Dimension of Terrorism* (Nijhoff, 2009). The emergence of transnational terrorism also generated international legal scholarship prior to 9/11: see Rosalyn Higgins and Maurice Flory (eds), *Terrorism and International Law* (Routledge, 1997).

18 Tal Becker, *Terrorism and the State: Rethinking the Rules of State Responsibility* (Hart, 2006), p. 1. See also generally Klejda Mulaj (ed.), *Violent Non-State Actors in World Politics* (Columbia University Press, 2010).

In many states, there is a swift and impressive response by law enforcement authorities to such attacks.[19] The incidents are investigated; suspects are charged and subsequently prosecuted before the courts.[20] However, a small number of states have not been as effective in bringing members of these groups to justice for their role in the planning and perpetration of alleged terrorist attacks.[21] For instance in states, such as Libya,[22] Mali,[23] Yemen,[24] Afghanistan,[25] and Nigeria,[26] the authorities have faced challenges due to widespread corruption or armed conflict, in regulating the activities of transnational terrorist groups and putting their members on trial for alleged criminal acts. Consequently, these states are not in the position to effectively investigate the alleged criminal behaviour of transnational terrorist groups or initiate criminal proceedings against them. The lack of an effective criminal justice system in some of these jurisdictions means that victims of attacks by transnational terrorist groups have no legal redress and the civilian population is left vulnerable to further attacks.

On the other hand, states which have tried to hold members of transnational terrorist groups accountable have faced insurmountable challenges in doing so.[27] For example, the United States has faced criticism for failing to observe the due process rights of suspected members of transnational terrorist groups during trial while others have been disparaged for adopting other mechanisms other than the criminal justice system to deal with terrorist attacks such as

19 Craig Allen, 'Armed Groups and the Law', in Jeffrey Norwitz (ed.), *Armed Groups: Studies in National Security, Counterterrorism and Counterinsurgency* (US Naval College, 2008) p. 94.

20 See generally Mahmoud Cherif Bassiuouni, 'Legal Control of International Terrorism: A Policy-Oriented Assessment', *Harvard International Law Journal* 43(1) (2002) 83–103.

21 See generally Detlev Vagts, 'Which Courts Should Try Persons Accused of Terrorism', *European Journal of International Law* 14(2) (2003) 313–326.

22 Madeline Morris, 'Arresting Terrorism: Criminal Jurisdiction and International Relations', in Andrea Bianchi and Yasmin Naqvi (eds), *Enforcing International Law Norms against Terrorism* (Hart, 2004) p. 65.

23 J. Netto, F. Sevenzo, and D. Simon, 'Gunmen Attack Mali Luxury Resort, at Least 2 Dead' (*CNN*, 19 June 2017) available at: http://edition.cnn.com/2017/06/18/africa/urgent–gunfire-heard-at-mali-tourist-resort/index.html (date accessed: 14 March 2018).

24 J. Sharp, 'Yemen: Background and US Relations' (CRS Report for Congress, July 2010), p. 3. See generally Eugene Kontorovich, '"A Guantanamo on the Sea": The Difficulty of Prosecuting Pirates and Terrorists', *California Law Review* 98(1) (2010) 243–275; Chris Downes, 'Targeted Killings in an Age of Terror: The Legality of the Yemen Strike', *Journal of Conflict and Security Law* 9(2) (2004) 277–294.

25 Brett Shumate, 'New Rules for a New War: The Applicability of the Geneva Conventions to Al Qaeda and Taliban Detainees in Afghanistan', *New York International Law Review* 18 (2005) 1–98.

26 See generally Salihu Niworu, 'Boko Haram Sects: Terrorists or a Manifestation of the Failed Nigerian State', *Journal of Politics and Law* 6(2) (2013) 245–250.

27 Allen (n. 19), p. 94.

prolonged detention of suspects without trial.[28] Moreover, states that have a well-functioning legal system have faced logistical challenges in trying defendants accused of terrorist offences.[29] Assembling the evidence necessary to achieve a conviction from locations outside the state's jurisdiction is only achieved with the cooperation of the international community.[30] Not all states are willing to cooperate with such requests and some states are not able to offer any assistance whatsoever for a variety of reasons including the lack of a functioning justice system and limited financial resources to carry out investigations and bring prosecutions.[31]

This is not the first time the international community has recognised the fundamental challenges in holding members of transnational terrorist groups accountable for terrorist attacks. In the aftermath of the assassination of King Alexander I of Yugoslavia and Mr Louis Bathou, the Foreign Minister of the French Republic, in Marseilles on 9 October 1934, by Yugoslav militants operating from Hungary, the League of Nations drafted a Convention for the Prevention and Punishment of Terrorism which provided the international community with its first global approach, and corresponding legal framework, for responding to terrorist attacks.[32] The Convention required states to criminalise and prosecute acts of transnational terrorism but also provided the possibility of prosecuting such

28 Harold Koh, 'The Case against Military Commissions', *American Journal of International Law* 96 (2002) 337–344; Laura Dickinson, 'Using Legal Process to Fight Terrorism: Detentions, Military Commissions, International Tribunals and the Rule of Law', *South California Law Review* 75 (2001) 1407–1492; Fleur Johns, 'Guantanamo Bay and the Annihilation of the Exception', *European Journal of International Law* 16(4) (2005) 613–635; Daryl Mundis, 'The Use of Military Commissions to Prosecute Individuals Accused of Terrorist Acts', *American Journal of International Law* 96(2) (2002) 320–328; Scott Silliman, 'On Military Commissions', *Case Western Reserve Journal of International Law* 34 (2004) 529–540.

29 Allen (n. 19), p. 94.

30 Ibid.

31 Ibid.

32 League of Nations, 'Committee of Experts for the Codification of International Criminal Law, Replies of Governments', League of Nations Doc. C.196.M.70.1927. V, at 221. Convention for the Prevention and Punishment of Terrorism 1937 (League Convention 1937), in International Conference Proceedings on the Repression of Terrorism, Geneva, 1–16 November 1937, League of Nations Doc. C.94.M.47.1938. V (League of Nations Archives Geneva: Council Members Docs, Vol. 1103), Annex I, p. 5. For further analysis of this Convention, see Ben Saul, 'The Legal Response of the League of Nations to Terrorism', *Journal of International Criminal Justice* 4(1) (2006) 78–102; Henri Donnedieu de Vabres, 'La repression internationale du terrorisme – Les conventions de Genève' (16 November 1937), *Revue de droit international et législation comparée* 62 (1938) 45; Geoffrey Marston, 'Early Attempts to Suppress Terrorism: The Terrorism and International Criminal Court Conventions of 1937', *British Yearbook of International Law* 73 (2002) 293–313; Peter Kovacs, 'La Société des Nations et son action après l'attentat contre Alexandre, roi de Yougoslavie, *Journal of the History of International Law* 6 (2004) 65–77; J. G. Starke, 'The Convention for the Prevention and Punishment of Terrorism', *British Yearbook of International Law* 19 (1938) 214; Francis Walters, *A History of the League of Nations* (Oxford University Press, 1969), p. 599. Bogdan Zlataric, 'History of International

acts before an international criminal court.[33] The creation of an international criminal jurisdiction was meant to ensure that there was no impunity for terrorist attacks even in situations where the state in which the terrorist attack occurred was unable to prosecute. However, due to the political situation in Europe in the 1930s, the League of Nations Convention on the Prevention and Punishment of Terrorism never came into force.[34] International efforts to repress terrorism through the development of an international criminal mechanism were quickly forgotten with the arrival of the Second World War and the dissolution of the League of Nations itself.[35]

Following the completion of the Nuremberg Trials, terrorism was for a second time included as a crime in the Draft Code of Offences against the Peace and Security of Mankind.[36] However, between 1954 and 1981, work on the Draft Code was impeded due to deadlock on a definition of aggression.[37] In the interim, the international community's concern about terrorism grew following an upsurge in terrorist attacks in the 1960s and 1970s.[38] In an effort to address this activity, states ratified a number of international treaties in an attempt to suppress terrorist attacks. These international treaties compelled states to criminalise terroristic activity and to extradite or prosecute alleged offenders.[39] The purpose of such measures was to ensure that transnational terrorist groups could not manipulate the limitations of any one state's jurisdictional boundaries and sought to ensure that suspects were brought to justice.[40] The treaties sought to fill the jurisdictional loophole that an international criminal court might have filled.[41] However, as this book will elaborate, international treaties have not been entirely successful in responding to transnational terrorist groups due to their

Terrorism and Its Legal Control', in Mahmoud Cherif Bassiouni (ed.), *International Terrorism and Political Crimes* (Charles C. Thomas, 1975), p. 481.

33 League of Nations (n. 32).

34 Joseph Lambert, *Terrorism and Hostages in International Law: A Commentary on the Hostages Convention 1979* (Grotius, 1990), p. 29.

35 For further commentary on the dissolution of the League of Nations see Hans Kelsen, *The Law of the United Nations: A Critical Analysis of its Fundamental Problems* (Law Book Exchange, 2000), p. 595.

36 Article 2(6) of the Draft Code adopted in 1954 defined the offence of terrorism as '[t]he undertaking or encouragement by the authorities of a State of terrorist activities in another State, or the toleration by the authorities of a State of organized activities calculated to carry out terrorist acts in another State'. Report of the International Law Commission covering the work of Its Sixth Session, UN Doc. A/2693 (1954), 151.

37 UN General Assembly Resolution 36/106 (1981).

38 Alona Evans, 'The Apprehension and Prosecution of Offenders: Some Current Problems', in Alona Evans and John Murphy (eds), *Legal Aspects of International Terrorism* (American Society of International Law, 1978), p. 493.

39 Rohan Gunaratna, *Inside Al Qaeda: Global Network of Terror* (Hurst, 2002).

40 Ibid.

41 Report of the UN High-Level Panel on Threats, Challenges and Change, 'A More Secure World: Our Shared Responsibility', UN Doc. A/59/565 (2004), 2 December 2004, p. 18.

failure to keep pace with the continuously evolving methods utilised by them to carry out attacks.[42]

When the Draft Code was resuscitated in the 1990s, terrorism was again left on the sideline because of continuing wrangling on a general comprehensive definition of terrorism and whether it should include the behaviour of non-state actors, state actors, or both.[43] Nevertheless, the International Law Commission (ILC) in its draft statute for an international criminal court in 1994 included terrorism as a crime within the subject matter jurisdiction of the international criminal court.[44] In order to sidestep continuing debate on state-sponsored terrorism and self-determination, the ILC included certain terrorism offences in its draft statute and utilised the approach adopted by international treaties on terrorism to define both the *actus reus* and the *mens rea* of the proposed crime.[45] However, in doing so it circumvented the challenging issue of a comprehensive definition of terrorism.[46]

Locating attacks by transnational terrorist groups within the expansive framework of ICL – especially with its special emphasis on crimes perpetrated in armed conflict situations – would make certain that prosecutions of suspected members of transnational terrorist groups take place in a setting that is appreciative of the interaction between the criminalisation of transnational terrorism and international law. It would also ensure that individuals suspected of terrorist offences would be prosecuted where states were unwilling or unable to do so. Thus, the International Criminal Court (ICC) could have a deterrent effect on future potential terrorist attacks. However, prosecutions for transnational terrorism have thus far been left to the purview of domestic courts. Even though the ILC's proposal to prosecute terrorism before the ICC has not been fully abandoned, the current situation remains that states shoulder the primary responsibility to curb transnational terrorist attacks by prosecuting suspects through their domestic courts.[47]

The international treaties which require states to prosecute members of transnational terrorist groups are broadly based on the League of Nations Terrorism Convention 1937 and tackle a specific manifestation of terrorism and address the

42 See p. 79 of this book.

43 See Report of the International Law Commission on the work of Its Forty-Fifth Session, UN Doc. A/48/10 (1993), p. 28 (para. 150); Report of the International Law Commission on the work of Its Forty-Eighth Session, UN Doc. A/51/10 (1996), p. 16 (para. 46); Kimberley Trapp, *State Responsibility for International Terrorism* (Oxford University Press, 2011), pp. 252–256.

44 Report of the International Law Commission (n. 43).

45 See Report of the International Law Commission on the work of Its Forty-Sixth Session, UN Doc. A/49/10 (1994), Article 20(e) and Appendix II.

46 ICC Report of the Working Group on the Review Conference, ICC Res. 8/20, app. III, ICC ASP/8/20 (November 2009); Resolution E of the Final Act of the United Nations Diplomatic Conference of Plenipotentiaries on the Establishment of an International Criminal Court, UN Doc. A/CONF.183/10, 17 July 1998.

47 There are of course hybrid international courts which have been created purely for the purposes of prosecuting acts of terrorism, but these are exceptional, for instance the Special Tribunal for Lebanon (STL).

criminal law enforcement duties of states.[48] However, the methods utilised by transnational terrorist groups to carry out attacks have continued to evolve despite the international community's best efforts to suppress their activities through international instruments. As a result, international instruments have only been able to prohibit specific types of terroristic activity and have failed to address the ever-changing methods utilised by transnational terrorist groups to carry out attacks.

ICL still has a key role to play in suppressing terrorism where states are unwilling or unable for whatever reason to bring suspected members of transnational terrorist groups to justice. Impunity is in conflict with the preamble of UN General Assembly Resolution 64/2010 which 'stress[es] the need to ensure accountability for all violations of international humanitarian law and international human rights law in order to prevent impunity'.[49] In particular, authoritative non-binding international instruments assert that states have an obligation to prosecute individuals suspected of carrying out terrorist acts.[50] Most notably, UN Security Council Resolution 1373 (2001) which was passed in the aftermath of the 9/11 attacks obliges states to 'deny safe haven to those who finance, plan, support, or commit terrorist acts, or provide safe havens'[51] and 'ensure that any person who participates in the financing, planning, preparation or perpetration of terrorist acts or in supporting terrorist acts is brought to justice'.[52]

International law already obliges states to prosecute individuals for international crimes. For example, Article 6 of the Genocide Convention 1948 provides that individuals 'charged with genocide . . . shall be tried by a competent tribunal of the state in the territory of which the act was committed'.[53] However, the Geneva Conventions go even further by providing that every state must:

> search for persons alleged to have committed, or to have ordered to have committed, such grave breaches, and shall bring such persons, regardless of their nationality, before its own court. It may also, if it prefers, and in accordance with the provisions of its own legislation, hand such persons over for trial to another High Contracting Party.[54]

48 There are currently 13 international conventions and protocols addressing various manifestations of terrorism (including hijackings, ship-jacking, hostage taking, crimes against internationally protected persons, terrorist bombings, and acts of nuclear terrorism). A full list of the international terrorism suppression conventions and protocols can be found at: www.un.org/terrorism/instruments.shtml

49 UN General Assembly Resolution 64/10 (2010).

50 See generally Stefano Betti, 'The Duty to Bring Terrorists to Justice and Discretionary Prosecution', *Journal of International Criminal Justice* 4(5) (2006) 1104–1116.

51 UN Security Council Resolution 1373 of 28 September 2011 and UN Security Council Resolution 1540 of 28 April 2004.

52 Ibid.

53 Article 6 of the Genocide Convention 1948.

54 Article 49 of the First Geneva Convention 1949.

The Preamble of the Rome Statute reiterates this stance affirming that, 'the most serious crimes of concern to the international community as a whole must not go unpunished and that their effective prosecution must be ensured by taking measures at the national level and by enhancing international cooperation'.[55]

The 1993 Principles for the Protection and Promotion of Human Rights through Action to Combat Impunity which were adopted by the UN Commission on Human Rights defined impunity as the failure to provide 'appropriate penalties' for the individual affected by the breach in question.[56] Attacks by transnational terrorist groups have evolved over time but the dilemma on how to bring them to justice where states are unwilling or unable to do so has remained the same. As a result, where states are unwilling or unable to prosecute members of transnational terrorist groups, ICL, in particular the Rome Statute of the ICC, could have a key role to play in ensuring that a culture of impunity does not persist in states which have failed to bring members of these groups to justice. However, the sufficiency of the ICC's role in prosecuting members of transnational terrorist groups must be comprehensively examined to decipher whether their attacks come within the current wording of the Rome Statute.

A Aim and approach

It is hoped that this book can contribute new insights into international criminal justice by addressing three interconnected questions regarding the implications of holding members of network-based transnational terrorist groups accountable before the ICC for their role in the planning and perpetration of attacks, and the extent to which they can be brought to justice under the Rome Statute, namely:

1 Can attacks by network-based transnational terrorist groups be classified as international crimes under the current wording of the Rome Statute?
2 To what extent can members of the network-based transnational terrorist group be held accountable for crimes committed by the group before the ICC?
3 If the answer to the above two questions is no, can ICL be adapted or reformed through case law and practice to bring members of network-based transnational terrorist groups to justice or are the structures of ICL limited by a continuing Westphalian legacy and state-centred concept of international law?

Underpinning these three questions are broader meta-questions regarding the challenges of prosecuting members of network-based transnational terrorist groups under the current wording of the Rome Statute. Hence, this book will probe the limits of ICL in bringing members of these types of groups to justice in the context of changing methods of warfare.

Drawing on organisational network theory, as developed by Max Weber, one of the founders of sociology, and the more recent writings of Nitin Nohria and

55 Preamble, Rome Statute of the International Criminal Court.
56 UN Commission on Human Rights Resolution 2003/72 (25 April 2003).

Ekaterina Stepanova, this book will initially consider how the Rome Statute applies to network-based transnational terrorist groups.[57] To answer this question, it is necessary to break it down into two parts, namely: can attacks by transnational terrorist groups constitute a crime under the Rome Statute? And how does the Rome Statute apply to members of transnational terrorist groups in light of their network-based organisational structure? By doing so, this book investigates the gaps in ICL concepts to date and highlights the limited development of accountability mechanisms before the ICC for members of network-based entities. The organisational structure of the transnational terrorist group has direct implications for how the Rome Statute applies to its members, both in the context of the relationship between the commanders and the subordinate members of the group and the extent to which they can be held accountable for their role in the planning and perpetration of attacks.

This book will show that while holding members of non-state armed actors such as armed opposition groups accountable under the Rome Statute has been relatively straightforward, the accountability of members of a transnational terrorist group in particular the high-ranking members has the potential to be far more problematic in view of the ambiguous organisational structure of the group. The ICC has thus far only prosecuted individuals who are members of state and non-state armed actors with a clear-cut hierarchical organisational structure.[58] Hence, it has not yet had to consider the application of ICL to members of armed groups which have a network-based organisational structure. In particular, this book will demonstrate that the Rome Statute is particularly difficult to apply to leaders of transnational terrorist groups because they may not hold a formal command position in the group and as a result are unable to assert control over their subordinates within the meaning of the Rome Statute because of the fragmented network-based structure of the group.

Over time, organisational studies has expanded beyond business organisational models.[59] Research in organisational studies is now focused on the prevalence of network models of organisations such as clans, civic movements, and political protest movements.[60] Though useful, this work has only recently started to map the prevalence of network organisational features in terrorist groups. As a result, the study of network-based transnational terrorist groups is still in its infancy and has thus far been overlooked by legal scholars. It follows that the organisational

57 Ekaterina Stepanova, *Terrorism in Asymmetrical Conflict: Ideological and Structural Aspects* (Oxford University Press, 2008), p. 127; Nitin Nohria et al. (eds), *Networks and Organizations: Structure, Form and Action* (Harvard Business School, 1992); Max Weber, *The Theory of Social and Economic Organisation* (Free Press, 1947); Haridimos Tsoukas and Christian Knudsen (eds), *The Oxford Handbook of Organisation Theory* (Oxford University Press, 2005).

58 See generally Liesbeth Zegveld, *The Accountability of Armed Opposition in International Law* (Cambridge University Press, 2002).

59 For a general overview of organisational theory, see Tsoukas and Knudsen (n. 57) and Stepanova (n. 57).

60 Ibid.

structure of the transnational terrorist group has direct implications for how the Rome Statute applies to attacks by transnational terrorist groups, both in the context of the relationship between the commanders and the subordinate members of the group and the extent to which they can be held accountable for their role in the planning and perpetration of attacks.

It is well established that the jurisdiction of the ICC is only invoked where a state is unwilling or unable to prosecute individuals suspected of committing international crimes, while one of the fundamental purposes of the Court is 'to put an end to impunity . . . thus to contribute to the prevention of . . . crimes'.[61] Nevertheless, the legal framework for prosecuting transnational terrorism as a crime under international law is far from settled despite the work of the ILC and the recent Interlocutory Decision of the STL.[62] The diverse sources and nature of legal instruments addressing transnational terrorism suggest that the international community is engaged in a process of norm creation, elaboration, and interpretation reflecting the need for legal clarity on the existence of a crime of transnational terrorism under international law. Despite this, there is an extremely limited body of international law which deals with the prosecution of network-based transnational terrorist groups.

Nonetheless, the social and cultural impacts of terrorist attacks are wide-ranging, and are key subjects of study for criminologists, social scientists, penologists, and psychologists to name just a few; while international relations and politics play a fundamental role in the analysis and development of their criminal accountability.[63] Moreover, cross-cutting these professional and academic sources are reports and research from numerous non-governmental organisations and international organisations on terrorist attacks such as Amnesty International, Human Rights Watch, the Stockholm International Peace Research Institute, and the United Nations Human Rights Council.[64]

61 Preamble of the Rome Statute (n. 57).

62 *Interlocutory Decision on the Applicable Law: Terrorism, Conspiracy, Homicide, Perpetration, Cumulative Charging* (Appeals Chamber) STL-11–01/I, 16 February 2011; Report of the International Law Commission on the Work of Its Forty-Fifth Session, UN Doc. A/48/10 (1993), p. 28 (para. 150); Report of the International Law Commission on the Work of Its Forty-Eighth Session, UN Doc. A/51/10 (1996), p. 19 (para. 46).

63 Paul Walkinson, *Terrorism and the Liberal State* (Halstead, 1997); John Bell, *A Time of Terror: How Democratic Societies Respond to Revolutionary Violence* (Basic Books, 1978); Philip Heymann, *Terrorism and America: A Common-Sense Strategy for a Democratic Society* (MIT Press, 1998); Jeffrey Ross and Ted Gurr, 'Why Terrorism Subsides: A Comparative Study of Canada and the United States', *Comparative Politics* 21(4) (1989) 405–426, p. 408.

64 See for example Human Rights Watch, 'Lives Destroyed: Attacks on Civilians in the Philippines' (July 2007) available at: www.hrw.org/reports/2007/07/30/lives-destroyed (date accessed: 30 December 2017); Amnesty International, 'Syrian Activists Held on Spurious Terrorism Charges Face Prolonged Detention' (June 2013) available at: www.amnesty.ie/news/syrian-activists-held-spurious-%E2%80%98terrorism%E2%80%99-charges-face-prolonged-detention (date accessed: 14 March 2018); UN Human Rights Council, Supporting Victims of Terrorism (2008) available at: www.

Situating my overall findings within the framework of international criminal justice and the simultaneous implications of prosecuting terrorist attacks before the ICC, this book will argue that the accountability of transnational terrorist groups under ICL can be best described and analysed from a sociolegal approach which analyses the case law and practice of the ICC as it relates to transnational terrorist groups and employs organisational theory to critically analyse the potential of the Court to achieve its aims and objectives as they apply to this type of group. Context for this analysis is provided by an exploration of the traditionally marginal role of terrorist attacks in the ICL sphere and how this position has evolved over time. This discussion includes, in particular, the greater prominence that the crime of terrorism has acquired through the jurisprudence of the International Criminal Tribunal for the Former Yugoslavia (ICTY) and the STL.[65]

In particular, sociolegal research is used to identify, analyse, and synthesise the content and application of ICL to transnational terrorist groups in particular the principle of individual criminal responsibility, the doctrine of command responsibility, and the concept of transnational terrorism as a crime. It highlights the challenges and gaps in how ICL applies to transnational terrorist groups with complex organisational structures and uncovers how ICL has up until now only dealt with armed groups with well-defined hierarchical organisational structures. It also identifies whether the ICC would face challenges in prosecuting members of network-based transnational terrorist groups such as ISIS and advances a solution to those challenges.

Goldstone and Simpson are of the view that the legal framework of the ICC can sufficiently prosecute such terrorist attacks.[66] However, an examination of the organisational network theory propounded by Weber and its application to transnational terrorist groups tells a different story and reveals the difficulty in applying the principle of individual criminal responsibility when prosecuting members of transnational terrorist groups under ICL.[67] Since the transnational terrorist group is a relatively new phenomenon in the international arena, it is important to take into consideration the structure and organisation of these groups. An examination of their structure and organisation is useful for determining whether the Rome Statute is in need of reform. Hence, this approach provides a better insight into the shortcomings of the Rome Statute in the prosecution of transnational terrorist groups by taking into account extralegal factors such as the network-based

ohchr.org/Documents/Press/UN_Report_on_Supporting_Victims_of_Terrorism.pdf (date accessed: 14 March 2018); Gerry Simpson, 'Terrorism and the Law: Past and Present International Approaches', *Stockholm International Peace Research Institute Yearbook* (2003) 23 available at: www.sipri.org/yearbook/2003/files/SIPRIYB03E1.pdf (date accessed: 14 March 2018).

65 See further *Prosecutor* v. *Galić*, IT-98–29-T, Judgment, 5 December 2003; *Interlocutory Decision on the Applicable Law: Terrorism, Conspiracy, Homicide, Perpetration, Cumulative Charging* (Appeals Chamber) STL-11–01/I, 16 February 2011.

66 Richard Goldstone and Janine Simpson, 'Evaluating the Role of the International Criminal Court as a Legal Response to Terrorism', *Harvard Human Rights Journal* 16 (2003) 13–26.

67 See further Stepanova (n. 57), p. 127; Weber (n. 57).

structure of the transnational terrorist group and the challenges in holding its members accountable under ICL.

Two main analytical methods are used to achieve this: the comparison of sociological and legal theories on transnational terrorist groups and the application of these theories to prosecuting members of transnational terrorist groups under ICL.[68] Since the concept of the transnational terrorist group was first identified in sociology; sociological and social policy literature on the aims and purposes of the transnational terrorist group is reviewed to assess whether the transnational terrorist group is indeed a new phenomenon in the international arena or merely a wing of an already established armed opposition group.[69] This aspect of the methodology is designed to address the first research question as it clarifies the organisational structure of the transnational terrorist group in the context of how armed attacks are planned and perpetrated.

While attempting to draw on sociology to enhance the accountability of the transnational terrorist groups before the ICC this analytical method respects the boundaries between the disciplines of sociology and law, rather than attempting to make a new contribution to sociological knowledge. This methodology benefits the book by helping to shape the research questions and also makes certain that this book can produce a reasoned and articulate argument that the ICC is not an effective mechanism for holding transnational terrorist groups and their members accountable under ICL.

B Contribution to knowledge

When researching the international criminal justice system, ICL writers most frequently document the doctrinal legal development of the core international crimes and the fundamental legal principles such as the doctrine of command responsibility and the doctrine of joint criminal enterprise.[70] Additionally, criminologists

68 Nigel Gilbert, 'Research, Theory and Method', in N. Gilbert (ed.), *Researching Social Life* (Sage 2001, 2nd edn), pp. 21–40; Otto Kahn-Freund, 'Comparative Law as an Academic Subject', *Law Quarterly Review* 82 (1966) 40–61, p. 43.

69 Louise Richardson (ed.), *The Roots of Terrorism* (Routledge, 2006); Christian Davenport, 'Human Rights and the Democratic Proposition', *Journal of Conflict Resolution* 43(1) (1999) 92–116; Ted Gurr, 'The Political Origins of State Violence and Terror: An Theoretical Analysis', in M. Stohl and G. Lopez (eds), *Governments Violence and Repression: An Agenda for Research* (Greenwood Press, 1986), p. 62; Charles Russell and Bowman Miller, 'Profile of a Terrorist', *Terrorism* 1(1) (1977) 17–34, p. 18; Neil Livingstone, *The War against Terrorism* (Heath Lexington, 1982), p. 43; Michael Stohl, 'Is the Past Prologue: Terrorists and WMD', *International Studies Review* 7(1) (2005) 146–148; Ethan de Mesquita, 'Conciliation, Counterterrorism and Patterns of Terrorist Violence', *International Organization* 59(1) (2005) 145–176; Jack Goldstone, 'Towards a Fourth Generation of Revolutionary Theory', *Annual Review of Political Science* 4(1) (2001) 139–187.

70 For further commentary, see Roy Lee et al. (eds), *The International Criminal Court: Elements of Crimes and Rules of Procedure and Evidence* (Transnational, 2001); Elies van Sliedregt, *Individual Criminal Responsibility in International Law* (Oxford University Press, 2012); Ciara Damgaard, *Individual Criminal Responsibility for Core*

and penologists analyse the application of ICL to state armed forces and non-state armed actors with well-defined hierarchical organisational structures but ignore organisations which are network based.[71] This emphasis is often reflected in the leading textbooks on ICL and few texts exist on the issue of accountability for transnational terrorist attacks before the ICC.[72] Although Roberta Arnold has examined the classification of terrorist attacks as an international crime under the Rome Statute she has not considered this question in light of the emerging jurisprudence of the ICC nor the network-based organisational structure of these actors.[73]

Sassóli has called for further research on the application of ICL to transnational terrorist groups that engage in terroristic activity, arguing that

> [Commentators] . . . agree that more specific rules are needed to combat international terrorism in relation to law enforcement, international criminal law, jurisdiction, and cooperation in criminal matters. Some have been adopted . . . [o]thers are still needed.[74]

International Crimes (Springer, 2008); Stefano Manacorda, 'The Principle of Individual Criminal Responsibility: A Conceptual Framework', *Journal of International Criminal Justice* 5 (2007) 913–915; Jordan Paust, 'Individual Criminal Responsibility for Human Rights Atrocities and Sanction Strategies', *Texas International Law Journal* 33 (3) (1999) 631–641.

71 For further commentary, see Antonio Cassese, 'Terrorism as an International Crime', in Andrea Bianchi and Yasmin Naqvi (eds), *Enforcing International Law Norms Against Terrorism* (Hart, 2004), p. 211; Steven Ratner and Jason Abrams, *Accountability for Human Rights Atrocities in International Law: Beyond the Nuremburg Legacy* (Oxford University Press, 2001); Manisuli Ssenyonjo, 'Accountability of Non-State Actors in Uganda for War Crimes and Human Rights Violations: Between Amnesty and the International Criminal Court', *Journal of Conflict and Security Law* 10(3) (2005) 405–434; Denise Plattner, 'The Penal Repression of Violations of International Humanitarian Law Applicable in Non-International Armed Conflicts', *International Review of the Red Cross* 30 (278) (1990) 409–420, p. 414; Andres Franco, 'Armed Non-State Actors', in David Malone (ed.), *The UN Security Council: From Cold War to the 21st Century* (Lynne Rienner, 2004), p. 117.

72 For further reading see for example, Roberta Arnold, *The ICC as a New Instrument for Repressing Terrorism* (Transnational, 2004); Antonio Cassese, *International Law* (Oxford University Press, 2008); Kriangsak Kittichaisaree, *International Criminal Law* (Oxford University Press, 2001); Robert Cryer et al. (eds), *An Introduction to International Criminal Law and Procedure* (Cambridge University Press, 2010); Guenael Mettraux, *The Law of Command Responsibility* (Oxford University Press, 2009); Jean de Preux et al., *Commentary on the Additional Protocols of 8 June 1977 to the Geneva Conventions of 12 August 1949* (International Committee of the Red Cross, 1987); Alexander Zahar and Goran Sluiter, *International Criminal Law* (Oxford University Press, 2008); Anthony Aust, *Handbook on International Law* (Cambridge University Press, 2010, 2nd edn); Gerhard Werle, *Principles of International Criminal Law* (TMC Asser Press, 2005); James Crawford (ed.), *I. Brownlie: Principles of International Law* (Oxford University Press, 2012, 8th edn).

73 Arnold (n. 72).

74 Marco Sassóli, 'Transnational Armed Groups and International Humanitarian Law' (HPCR Occasional Paper Series 2006), p. 27.

Unfortunately, this call has gone unanswered and much of the literature on transnational terrorist groups continues to be concerned with demonstrating the seriousness of their criminal behaviour and how states have responded to such criminal acts.[75] It also analyses how its costs and damages dwarf those of conventional or ordinary crime.[76] In addition, this body of work does not acknowledge that many of these groups have a network-based organisational structure which could have major implications for prosecuting members before the ICC.

There is useful sociological literature on transnational terrorist groups. However, it has tended to be preoccupied with the causes underlying attacks by transnational terrorist groups and the reasons for their formation.[77] In particular, globalisation, economic deprivation, and political instability have all been posited as reasons for their formation.[78] However, the extent of even this research should not be overemphasised, given that it has only recently considered the personality traits of individuals who are most likely to become members of transnational terrorist groups.[79] Organisational theory not only offers a unique perspective on the

75 Julio Barboza, 'Liability: Can We Put Humpty-Dumpty Together Again?', *Chinese Journal of International Law* 1 (2002) 499–526, p. 500; Rene Värk, 'State Responsibility for Private Armed Groups in the Context of Terrorism', *Juridica International* 11 (2006) 184–193, p. 184; Alan Nissel, 'Tal Becker, *Terrorism and the State: Rethinking the Rules of State Responsibility* (Hart, 2006)', *Journal of International Criminal Justice* 5 (2007) 245–249, p. 245.

76 See for example Bruno Frey et al., 'Calculating Tragedy: Assessing the Costs of Terrorism', *Journal of Economic Surveys* 21(1) (2007) 1–24; Todd Sandler and Kevein Siqueira, 'Global Terrorism: Deterrence versus Pre-Emption', *Canadian Journal of Economics* 39(4) (2006) 1370–1387.

77 William Eubank and Leonard Weinberg, 'Terrorism and Democracy: Perpetrators and Victims: Terrorism and Political', *Violence* 13(1) (2001) 155–164; Hsinchun Chen et al., 'Analysing Terrorist Networks' (2005) (3495) *Intelligence and Security Informatics Lecture Notes in Computer Science* 287–304.

78 Ted Gurr, 'The Political Origins of State Violence and Terror: A Theoretical Analysis', in M. Stohl and G. Lopez (eds), *Governments Violence and Repression: An Agenda for Research* (Greenwood Press, 1986), p. 62; Peter Kurrild-Klitgaard, Mogens Justesen, and Robert Klemmensen, 'The Political Economy of Freedom, Democracy and Transnational Terrorism', *Public Choice* 128 (2006) 289–315; Atin Basuchoudhary and William Shughart, 'On Ethnic Conflict and the Origins of Transnational Terrorism', *Defence and Peace Economics* (2010) 10; Brian Burgoon, 'On Welfare and Terror: Social Welfare Policies and Political-Economic Roots of Terrorism', *Journal of Conflict Resolution* 50(2) (2008) 176–203; Andreas Freytag, Jens Krüger, Daniel Meierrieks, and Friedrich Schneider, 'The Origins of Terrorism: Cross-Country Estimates on Socio-Economic Determinants of Terrorism' (University of Paderborn CIE Working Paper 2009–01, 2008); Alan Krueger and Jitka Maleckova, 'Education, Poverty and Terrorism: Is there a Causal Connection?', *Journal of Economic Perspectives* 17(4) (2003) 119–114.

79 Jerrold Post, *The Mind of the Terrorist: The Psychology of Terrorism from the IRA to Al-Qaeda* (Palgrave Macmillan, 2007); Tim Krieger and Daniel Meierricks, 'What Causes Terrorism?', *Public Choice* 147 (2011) 3–27; David Ronfeldt, 'Al-Qaeda and Its Affiliates: A Global Tribe Waging Segmental Warfare?', *First Monday* 10 (3) (2005) available at: http://firstmonday.org/issues/issue10_3 (date accessed: 14 March 2018); Louis Beam, Leaderless Resistance, *The Seditionist* 12 (1992) available at www.

application of the Rome Statute to transnational terrorist groups and the extent to which its members can be brought to justice before the ICC but also highlights how transnational terrorist groups challenge the traditional state-centric concept of international law.

In particular, the distinctive contribution of this book is not in its analysis of the nature of terrorist attacks but rather in its examination of the legal framework underlying the ICC and how it applies to transnational terrorist groups with network-based organisational structures. The book analyses the curious feature of the current legal regime of the ICC which does not include a crime of transnational terrorism within its subject-matter jurisdiction, but instead can potentially prosecute terroristic activity as genocide, a crime against humanity, or a war crime. International criminal justice is not a new field of inquiry, but it has long been monopolised by academics commentating on the application of the Rome Statute to state and non-state armed actors with a clear-cut hierarchical command structure.[80]

With regard to transnational terrorist groups, lawyers have benefited enormously from the work done by researchers in the social sciences. In particular, Max Weber, the father of sociology, whose work has dominated the literature on organisational theory for the best part of the twentieth century, focused almost exclusively on markets as an organisational model partially as a result of the longevity of his studies but also because of his insights and proficiency.[81] Only recently has organisational studies moved beyond business organisational models to consider the prevalence of network organisational features in terrorist groups.[82]

The first research project on transnational terrorist groups was established in 2005 by the Program on Humanitarian Policy and Conflict Research at Harvard University.[83] Only very recently have legal scholars discussed the application of international law to transnational terrorist groups.[84] Nevertheless, despite its slow start, the study of transnational terrorist groups is becoming more prevalent. Geffrey Corn and Jensen Talbot have written extensively on the regulation of attacks

louisbeam.com/leaderless.htm (date accessed: 14 March 2018); Jeffrey Kaplan, 'Leaderless Resistance', *Terrorism and Political Violence* 9(3) (1997) 80–95; Simson Garfinkel, 'Leaderless Resistance Today' (2004) 8 (3) *First Monday* available at: http://firstmonday.org/issues/issue8_3 (date accessed: 14 March 2018); Alex Schmid, 'Terrorism and Democracy', *Terrorism and Political Violence* 4(4) (1992) 14–25; Peter Bernholz, 'International Political System, Supreme Values and Terrorism', *Public Choice* 128 (2006) 221–231; Daniel Arce and Todd Sandler, 'An Evolutionary Game Approach to Fundamentalism and Conflict', *Journal of Institutional and Theoretical Economics* 159 (2003) 132–154.

80 See generally Zegveld (n. 58).

81 Weber (n. 57).

82 For a general overview of organisational theory, see Tsoukas and Knudsen (n. 57) and Stepanova (n. 57).

83 Harvard University, Program on Humanitarian Policy and Conflict Research, Research Project on Transnational Armed Groups and International Law, available at: www.hsph.harvard.edu/world-map/research_project/transnational-and-non-state-armed-groups-legal-and-policy-responses (date accessed: 14 March 2018).

84 Mohammad-Mahmoud Ould Mohamedou, 'Al-Qaida: une guerre non linéaire', *Revue interdisciplinaire de sciences sociales* 3(2) (2005) 130–170, p. 130.

by transnational terrorist groups under international humanitarian law (IHL).[85] However, this sudden surge of interest in transnational terrorist groups lacks any contextual analysis of their organisational structure. This book provides that foundation. It is the first dedicated examination of the practicalities and operable outlook of holding members of network-based transnational terrorist groups accountable before the ICC for their role in carrying out attacks. As such it represents a significant contribution to knowledge. It also provides an interesting study of the ICC at a critical stage in the development of its jurisprudence. The rich sociological analysis of the network organisational structure of transnational terrorist groups and how this impacts upon the application of the Rome Statute to its members is also of considerable significance.

C Book structure

This book consists of eight chapters. Chapter 2 develops the theoretical basis of the book, from the perspective of organisational theory, by examining how the evolution of many transnational terrorist groups from an organisation with a hierarchical command structure into a network-based group has enabled them to carry out more highly coordinated terrorist attacks in more than one jurisdiction. An examination of the structure and organisation of the transnational terrorist group is central to any consideration of the accountability of its members for their role in the perpetration of international crimes, linked as it is to the direct imposition of accountability if ICL is violated. Drawing on the seminal writings of Max Weber and the more recent work of David Ronfeldt, Ekaterina Stepanova, and Louis Beam, I bring organisational theory to the field of ICL to highlight the limits of accountability mechanisms before the ICC in bringing members of transnational terrorist groups to justice. The organisational theory discussed in Chapter 1 will be used in subsequent chapters to evaluate the extent to which the ICC fulfils its mandate to prosecute the crime of most concern to the international community.

Chapter 3 considers whether terrorist attacks constitute an international crime within the current subject-matter jurisdiction of the ICC. Underpinning this discussion will be an examination of the constituent elements of each crime with reference to the recent jurisprudence of the ICC and the ad hoc tribunals to determine whether terrorist attacks by transnational terrorist groups can be classified as either a war crime, crime against humanity, or genocide under the Rome Statute. The analysis conducted in this chapter highlights the challenges involved in classifying terrorist attacks as international crimes under the Rome Statute as well as the likely evidentiary obstacles for the Office of the Prosecutor at the ICC.

Chapter 4 proceeds to elaborate the basis for amending the Rome Statute to include a crime of transnational terrorism in light of the recent pronouncement of the Appeals Chamber of the STL. Unsurprisingly, the existence of a crime of

85 Geoffrey Corn and Eric Talbot, 'Transnational Armed Conflict: A "Principled" Approach to the Regulation of Counter-Terror Combat Operations', *Israel Law Review* 42(1) (2009) 46–79.

terrorism under ICL is widely contested. Perhaps, the Appeals Chamber's decision is merely a cog in the development process of an international crime of transnational terrorism? The definition of transnational terrorism laid down by the Appeals Chamber satisfies the *Tadić* criteria which must be fulfilled in order for particular conduct to constitute an international crime.[86] Nevertheless, the ICC does not have jurisdiction over transnational terrorism. Drawing on organisational theory, the chapter concludes by outlining the constituent elements of this emerging crime of transnational terrorism to decipher whether an amendment of the Rome Statute is needed to incorporate it as a crime within the subject jurisdiction of the ICC.

Building on the analysis in the previous chapters on the classification of terrorist attacks as an international crime Chapter 5 addresses a central research question of this book, namely to what extent can individual members of network-based transnational terrorist groups be held accountable for crimes committed by the group before the ICC? In doing so, this chapter examines how the doctrine of command responsibility applies to leaders of transnational terrorist groups. Even though the doctrine of command responsibility applies to both peacetime and wartime situations, the doctrine may not apply in the same way to both contexts because the evidence necessary to prove its elements in one context may not be sufficient to prove the elements in the other context. So, a duty which may be binding on a commander during peacetime may not be binding upon him/her in an armed conflict situation. For example, leaders of transnational terrorist groups have a duty to ensure that subordinates do not attack civilians during armed conflict situations. However, it is questionable whether he or she has the same duty with respect to terrorist attacks perpetrated during non-armed situations. The ICC would have to determine whether the duty to safeguard and protect civilians from harm during terrorist attacks which the leader of the group has allegedly violated is indeed binding upon him or her in the context of the relevant charges.

Utilising organisational theory, the chapter will address the challenge in applying the doctrine of command responsibility to transnational terrorist groups due to their lack of a centralised command to govern the conduct of its network cells and to take action to prevent crimes. This difficulty will be considered against the backdrop of the jurisprudence of the ICC, the ICTY, and the International Criminal Tribunal for Rwanda. The chapter concludes by addressing the claims that because of the high turnover of the high-ranking members of transnational terrorist groups applying the doctrine of command responsibility to successor commanders is too cumbersome.

While this initial assessment argues that bringing leaders of transnational terrorist groups to justice before the ICC under the doctrine of command responsibility is problematic, Chapter 6 considers the extent to which subordinate members of transnational terrorist groups can be held accountable under Article 25 for their role in the planning and perpetration of terrorist attacks in pursuance of a common criminal policy. Fundamental issues underpinning their accountability

86 *Prosecutor* v. *Tadić, Decision on the Defence Motion for Interlocutory Appeal on Jurisdiction*, Case No. IT-94-I, 2 October 1995, para. 94.

under Article 25 including the controversial control theory of co-perpetration as developed by the Pre-Trial Chamber in *Prosecutor* v. *Lubanga* and *Prosecutor* v. *Katanga and Chui* is discussed in light of organisational theory, before the chapter concludes with an examination of the challenges in applying this new doctrine to members of transnational terrorist groups.

Chapter 6 assesses the overall effectiveness to the ICC to deliver justice to the victims of attacks by transnational terrorist groups. The chapter's main finding that the ICC may not be the most effective accountability mechanism for prosecuting terrorist attacks perpetrated in non-armed conflict situations does not preclude the finding that it would be an efficient mechanism to prosecute terrorist attacks committed in armed conflict situations, whether they are committed by non-state armed actors such as network-based transnational terrorist groups or state armed forces. Similarly, even though the crime of terrorism is not currently included in the subject-matter jurisdiction of the ICC, the potential exists for the crystallisation of such a crime through an amendment of the Rome Statute although this is very unlikely to happen. Until a definition of terrorism is adopted by the Assembly of State Parties, it is noteworthy that terrorist attacks by transnational terrorist groups can only be prosecuted before the ICC as either a war crime or crime against humanity depending on the factual situation, thus reflecting the flexibility of the wording of the Rome Statute. Simultaneously, a consideration of the doctrine of command responsibility and the emerging principle of co-perpetration provide the basis for examining whether the ICC would be an effective accountability mechanism for holding members of transnational terrorist groups to justice. Organisational theory provides the best method of analysing the application of the Rome Statute to network-based transnational terrorist groups and can also be used to highlight the challenges in prosecuting them. It also facilitates a discussion of the implications of the emerging case law of the ICC in particular the Trial Chamber's judgments in both the *Katanga* and *Lubanga* cases for the accountability of subordinate members of transnational terrorist groups who have only played a minor role in the planning or perpetration of an attack.

Building on the analysis in the previous chapters on the difficulties in prosecuting individual members before the ICC Chapter 7 probes the practicalities in pursuing the accountability of the transnational terrorist group as a collective entity under ICL. The contested legal status of non-state armed groups suggests that it is difficult for international lawyers to conceptualise their accountability as a collective entity under ICL. Legal approaches to the issue have thus far failed to resolve the problem, and although the literature on ICL suggests that the individual should bear the most responsibility for international crimes, this is not a completely satisfying position with regard to non-state armed groups. This chapter bridges this gap by contending that systems theory may bolster our analysis on the need for an accountability model for collective entities like transnational terrorist groups under ICL. If the theory is correct, a non-state armed group is not always reducible to the individuals who supposedly comprise it. Rather, it is a complex system that lacks a linear connection with its individual members. Thus, complexity theory is inconsistent with the basic premise of ICL that the individual as such is the most appropriate bearer of responsibility since the divide between the collective entity and its members in the distribution of criminal responsibility may never be overcome. The argument developed in this chapter is that these insights highlight the need for an accountability mechanism for transnational terrorist groups as a collective entity under ICL.

Chapter 8 concludes the book by drawing together the key themes in the previous chapters to assess the overall potential of the ICC to investigate and prosecute crimes committed by transnational terrorist groups. The chapter has four main findings: accountability for members of transnational terrorist groups before the ICC will be limited; no crime of transnational terrorism exists under ICL; applying the principle of individual criminal responsibility to individual members of transnational terrorist groups will be exceedingly difficult; and there is thus a need for an accountability model to pursue collective entities like transnational terrorist groups under ICL instead. The chapter finishes by making a number of recommendations on the potential investigation and prosecution of members of these groups before the ICC in the future.

2 The network-based structure of transnational terrorist groups

An analysis of their effectiveness in perpetrating terrorist attacks

A Introduction

Building on decades of religious, philosophical, and religious thought, the past 20 years has seen the emergence of a wide range of non-state armed actors. Some commentators contend that the emergence of the transnational terrorist group is the result of factors such as globalisation and economic deprivation. Indeed, Krieger and Meierricks contend that '[i]f individuals are incited by an existing global order that is perceived as "unfair" . . . [transnational terrorist groups will] find support by building on related grievances in the source countries of terrorism'.[1] Yet little is known about the structure and organisation of transnational terrorist groups and how the core principles of ICL in particular the principle of individual criminal responsibility apply to them in view of this organisational structure. As noted by the Program on Humanitarian Policy and Conflict Research at Harvard University transnational terrorist groups are 'irregular, not easily recognizable [and] difficult to respond to'.[2]

Until recently, there was a lack of research mapping the organisational structure of transnational terrorist groups. This has arguably led to an imprecise analysis in the legal literature of how ICL applies to members of transnational terrorist groups. If this is indeed the case, should the Rome Statute be adapted to include entities that do not have a clear-cut hierarchical organisational structure to ensure that all potential crimes are prosecuted? Or, alternatively can the subject-matter jurisdiction of the ICC be reformed through case law and practice without the need for an amendment? There is a need for clarity on the precise organisational structure of transnational terrorist groups to ascertain how the Rome Statute applies to them. As a counterpart to Stepanova's belief that transnational terrorist groups have a network-based organisational structure, there is a risk that the ICC

1 Tim Kreiger and Daniel Meierricks, 'What Causes Terrorism?', *Public Choice* 147 (2011), p. 8.
2 Harvard University Program on Humanitarian Policy and Conflict Research, *Transnationality, War and the Law: A Report on a Roundtable on the Transformation of Warfare, International Law and the Role of Transnational Armed Groups* (Harvard University, 2006), p. 10.

would face insurmountable challenges in prosecuting members of such groups.[3] So would the network-based organisational structure of the transnational terrorist group impede the prosecution of its members before the ICC?

It is not possible within the confines of this book to examine in detail the origins and conceptual basis for transnational terrorist groups in general. However, as this book will argue that the ICC is not an effective accountability mechanism for prosecuting attacks perpetrated by transnational terrorist groups, it is necessary to understand the organisational structure of the transnational terrorist group and the connected concerns regarding the extent to which their attacks can be classified as an international crime under the Rome Statute. Furthermore, it is important to distinguish between a transnational terrorist group with a network-based organisational structure and a transnational terrorist group with a clear-cut hierarchical organisational structure to facilitate an examination of the application of the Rome Statute in the context of terrorist attacks. As the ICC has not yet prosecuted a member of a transnational terrorist group for their role in the planning and perpetration of a terrorist attack, the argument that is advanced over the course of this chapter is that because some transnational terrorist groups have a network-based organisational structure securing the successful prosecution of their members will be problematic. This is for a myriad of reasons including the fact that the prosecution may face additional challenges in producing evidence to support its hypothesis that the accused participated in the perpetration of the terrorist attack.

On the basis of this understanding, key questions that need to be asked are: how are transnational terrorist groups structured and how are they different from other non-state armed actors such as armed opposition groups? As described in Chapter 1, this book argues that a clear conception of the organisational structure of the transnational terrorist group provides the best basis for analysing how the Rome Statute applies to crimes perpetrated by transnational terrorist groups, both in the context of the relationship between the commanders and the subordinate members of the group and the extent to which they can be held accountable for their role in the planning and perpetration of attacks. So, while there have been a range of authoritative statements from academics, non-governmental organisations, and some governments, we cannot yet say definitively that the ICC would be an effective accountability mechanism for prosecuting attacks by transnational terrorist groups.

Nevertheless, as set out further in Chapters 5–7, I propose that the doctrine of command responsibility and the doctrine of co-perpetration can only be applied to organisations with a well-defined organisational structure.[4] So an analysis of the organisational structure of transnational terrorist groups is pivotal for determining how the core principles of ICL apply to members of these groups. Yet, the organisational structure of transnational terrorist groups which conduct attacks has thus far not been explored in the field of international criminal justice. Carlos Marighella provides a useful account of how these types of groups are structured

3 Ekaterina Stepanova, *Terrorism in Asymmetrical Conflict: Ideological and Structural Aspects* (Oxford University Press, 2008), pp. 127ff.

4 See p. 151 of this book.

which in turn can facilitate an analysis of how the Rome Statute applies to transnational terrorist groups.[5] Drawing on Max Weber's organisational theory this chapter will investigate the organisational structure of the transnational terrorist group in light of Marighella's theory of urban guerrilla warfare. It will then briefly examine how the structure of transnational terrorist groups is different to other non-state armed actors such as armed opposition groups whose members are currently being investigated and prosecuted before the ICC.

B The conceptualisation of the network-based terrorist group

One of the first transnational terrorist groups can be traced back to the writings of Herodotus in 500 BC who remarked how the nomadic tribes in the Anatolian Peninsula, the Caucasus region, and Central Asia preferred not to engage in armed conflict with the state armed forces of the empires in the Greek islands preferring instead to perpetrate once-off sporadic attacks.[6] In more recent times politically inspired nationalist movements were organised transnationally in an attempt to challenge the political and institutional order of states.[7] In particular, in the nineteenth and twentieth centuries, the Irish nationalist movement operated transnationally as Fenian groups in Ireland, Great Britain, the United States, and Australia.[8] Numerous other nationalist movements operated in the Hapsburg and Ottoman Empires such as the Young Bosnians, the Inner Macedonian Revolutionary Organisation, the Greek and Albanian nationalist movements, and the Young Ottomans.[9] This 'pattern of transnational political mobilization accompanied by violence continued throughout the twentieth century in the form of transnationally organised anti-imperial, anti-colonial and separatist nationalist movements'.[10] Even though their 'ideology was nationalism their strategies were

5 See generally Stepanova (n. 3), p. 127; Max Weber, *The Theory of Social and Economic Organisation* (Free Press, 1947); Carlos Marighella, *Mini-Manual of the Urban Guerrilla* (Paladin Press, 1975).

6 See generally George Rawlinson (ed.), *The History of Herodotus: Vol. 3 (Book 4)* (Appleton, 1885).

7 David Rapport, 'The Fourth Wave: September 11 and the History of Terrorism', *Current History* (2001) 419; Audrey Cronin, 'Behind the Curve: Globalisation and International Terrorism', *International Security* 27(3) (2002–2003) 30–58.

8 See generally Leon O'Broin, *Revolutionary Underground: The Story of the Irish Republican Brotherhood: 1858–1924* (Gill & Macmillan, 1976), R. V. Comerford, *The Fenians in Context: Irish Politics and Society: 1848–82* (Wolfhound Press, 1985); Eric Hobsbawm, *The Age of Capital: 1848–1875* (Vintage, 1996).

9 See generally Sukru Hanioglu, *The Young Turks in Opposition* (Oxford University Press, 1995).

10 Fiona Adamson, 'International Terrorism, Non-State Actors, and Transnational Political Mobilization: A Perspective from International Relations', in T. Biersteker et al. (eds), *International Law and International Relations: Bridging Theory and Practice* (Routledge, 2006) 79–82, p. 81 The Algerian and Palestinian nationalist movements are two prime examples. For further commentary on the Algerian nationalist movement, see John Reudy, *Modern Algeria: The Origins and Development of a Nation* (Indiana University Press, 2005, 2nd edn), pp. 114ff. For further commentary on the

transnational . . . these movements operated internationally and used political violence and terrorism to pursue their goals'.[11]

From the 1960s until the late 1980s, transnational terrorist groups were predominantly motivated by anti-racism, nationalism, separatism, and Marxist ideology.[12] However, since the attacks by Al-Qaeda in the United States in September 2001, researchers have been perplexed by the underlying organisational structure of transnational terrorist groups. In 2003, the then German Chancellor, Gerhard Schröder, contended that 'to address the root causes of terrorism and insecurity . . . we must ensure social and material but also cultural security'.[13] In recent times, the argument has been made that transnational terrorist groups have emerged as a result of social grievances.[14] However, beyond this relatively recent research on the reasons for the formation of transnational terrorist groups little is understood about their underlying organisational structure and how they conduct attacks.

Since the 1960s, some non-state armed actors have utilised a network-based organisational structure to perpetrate sporadic terrorist attacks.[15] One prominent example is the Irish Republican Army (IRA) which still operates in the Republic of Ireland, the United Kingdom, and continental Europe and has utilised a network-based organisational structure since the 1970s.[16] Before the 1970s, the group was organised into regional brigades and battalions which emulated the well-defined command structure of state armed forces. However, over time a network of smaller self-directed cells was assembled to carry out attacks in conjunction with traditional battalions which were preserved to support the autonomous cells.[17] This organisational structure has bolstered the increasingly complex communication capacity of the IRA which has enabled the group to strengthen the effusive

Palestinian nationalist movement, see generally Wendy Pearlman, *Violence, Non-Violence and the Palestinian National Movement* (Cambridge University Press, 2011).

11 Adamson (n. 10); see generally Mary Kaldor, *New and Old Wars: Organised Violence in a Global Era* (Stanford University Press, 1999).

12 See generally Paul Wilkinson, *Terrorism and the Liberal State* (Macmillan, 1986); Bruce Hoffman, 'The Confluence of International and Domestic Trends in Terrorism', *Terrorism and Political Violence* 9(2) (1997) 1, p. 2.

13 Address by Gerhard Schröder Chancellor of the Federal Republic of Germany at the Fifty-Eighth Session of the United Nations General Assembly (New York, 24 September 2003) available at: www.un.org/webcast/ga/58/statements/germeng030924.htm (date accessed: 14 March 2018).

14 Colin Beck, 'The Contribution of Social Movement Theory to Understanding Terrorism', *Sociology Compass* 2 (2008) 1565–1581, p. 1568. See generally Doug McAdam, *Political Process and the Development of Black Insurgency: 1930–1970* (University of Chicago Press, 1982); see also Ted Gurr, *Why Men Rebel* (Princeton University Press, 1970), p. 24 who advances this proposition.

15 Examples of such groups include the Palestine Liberation Organization and the Popular Front for the Liberation of Palestine.

16 Jerrold Post, *The Mind of the Terrorist: The Psychology of Terrorism from the IRA to Al-Qaeda* (Palgrave Macmillan, 2007), p. 39.

17 Brendan O'Brien, *Long War: IRA and Sinn Féin 1985 to Today* (Syracuse University Press, 1999).

effect of their terrorist attacks notwithstanding the simple and somewhat ingenuous methods utilised to conduct them.

This realignment of the organisational structure of the IRA was necessary for the group to achieve its long-term strategy and also 'a way out of the stalemate that had resulted from the inability of each side of the armed confrontation to achieve a decisive military success'.[18] So the modification to the organisational structure of the IRA enabled the cells to carry out highly coordinated terrorist attacks.[19] However, the introduction of network-based cells at the lowest level of the organisation did not fundamentally change the overall hierarchical command structure of the group. So, the IRA continued to have both a hierarchical and network-based organisational structure.

The impetus for the development of the network-based structure of the IRA was the Brazilian Marxist revolutionary, Carlos Marighella who developed the concept of 'urban guerrilla warfare' as a method of overthrowing the authoritarian political institution of the state in order to bring about social change.[20] Marighella posited that an armed group will not accomplish its aims and objectives if it cannot sufficiently defend itself from the superior military power of the state.[21] In contrast to Che Guevara, who asserted that guerrilla warfare should only take place in rural settings, Marighella propositioned that urban areas with high population density were the prime locations for attacks by terrorist groups.[22] Even though Marighella's theory did not address the transnational aspects of urban guerrilla warfare it was so highly respected that it was applied by a number of non-state armed groups including the Basque ETA separatists, the IRA, Greek N17, the Red Army Faction, the Weather Underground Organization (WUO), and Direct-Action France.[23]

18 Stepanova (n. 3), p. 103.
19 Ibid.
20 See generally Marighella (n. 5).
21 Ibid.
22 For more on this point, see John Williams and Carlos Marighella, 'The Father of Urban Guerrilla Warfare', *Terrorism* 12(1) (1989) 1; see also more generally, Ernesto Guevara, *Guerrilla Warfare* (University of Nebraska Press, 1985).
23 Louise Richardson (ed.), *The Roots of Terrorism* (Routledge, 2006); Christian Davenport, 'Human Rights and the Democratic Proposition', *Journal of Conflict Resolution* 43(1) (1999) 92–116; Ted Gurr, 'The Political Origins of State Violence and Terror: A Theoretical Analysis', in M. Stohl and G. Lopez (eds), *Governments Violence and Repression: An Agenda for Research* (Greenwood Press, 1986), p. 62; Paul Walkinson, *Terrorism and the Liberal State* (Halstead, 1997); John Bell, *A Time of Terror: How Democratic Societies Respond to Revolutionary Violence* (Basic Books, 1978); Philip Heymann, *Terrorism and America: A Common-Sense Strategy for a Democratic Society* (MIT Press, 1998); Ian Ross and Ted Gurr, 'Why Terrorism Subsides: A Comparative Study of Canada and the United States', *Comparative Politics* 21(4) (1989) 408; Charles Russell and Bowman Miller, 'Profile of a Terrorist', *Terrorism* 1(1) (1977) 18; Neil Livingston, *The War against Terrorism* (Heath Lexington, 1982), p. 43; Michael Stohl, 'Is the Past Prologue: Terrorists and WMD', *International Studies Review* 7(1) (2005) 146; Ethan de Mesquita, 'Conciliation, Counterterrorism and Patterns of Terrorist Violence', *International Organization* 59(1) (2005) 146; Jack Goldstone,

Deeply cognisant of the asymmetrical character of hostilities between insurgents and state armed forces,[24] Marighella hypothesised that a non-state armed actor will fail to accomplish its aims and objectives if it cannot sufficiently defend itself against the superior military resources of the state.[25] In his own words, 'defensive action means death for . . . [armed groups]' because '[they] are inferior to the enemy'.[26] So to counterbalance the asymmetrical nature of hostilities with the state some non-state armed groups developed innovative offensive strategies which did not prioritise the acquisition of territory or the defence of a particular base or location but instead sporadic attacks on state infrastructure and civilian populations.[27] The paradox was that 'the urban guerrilla, although weaker . . . [was] nevertheless the attacker'[28] and difficult for the state to neutralise.[29]

According to Marighella, this 'attack and retreat' strategy could only be effectively accomplished by an organisation without a strict hierarchical command structure. Attacks by non-state armed actors against the state were recognised by Marighella as the most asymmetrical form of urban guerrilla warfare requiring particular determination to execute.[30] So in order for an armed group to successfully commit attacks he suggested that they should abandon their strict hierarchical command structure,[31] and instead be composed of independent self-governing cells linked to one another by a centralised command and shared ideology.[32] Since the centralised command of the non-state armed actor should be the focal coordinator of the group's attacks the autonomous activity of each cell would enable 'mobility, and flexibility, as well as versatility and a command of any situation'.[33]

Furthermore, Marighella believed that to be most effective the group should be 'organized in small groups . . . of no more than four or five'.[34] Even though each member of the group must be self-sufficient, group interconnection was essential.[35] To be most effective the general strategy of the group had to be planned and coordinated by the centralised leadership. However, Marighella also expressed the importance of avoiding 'old-type hierarchy' and 'rigidity in the organization . . . to permit the greatest possible initiative on the part of the . . . [small] group'.[36] The consequence, in his view, was 'an indestructible network of small groups . . .

'Towards a Fourth Generation of Revolutionary Theory', *Annual Review of Political Science* 4(1) (2001) 139.

24 Marighella (n. 5), p. 16.
25 Ibid.
26 Ibid.
27 Ibid.
28 Ibid.
29 Ibid.
30 Ibid, p. 32.
31 Ibid. p. 16
32 Ibid.
33 Ibid., p. 22.
34 Ibid., p. 11.
35 Ibid.
36 Ibid., p. 13.

that function simply and practically with a general command that also participates in the attacks'.[37] In order for a cell to become part of the network it is not enough for the cell to have the same ideology as the network; it must also conduct terrorist attacks.[38] So '[a]ny single urban guerrilla who wants to establish a firing group and begin action can do so and thus become part of the organization'.[39] The requirement to conduct attacks in order to become an integral part of the urban guerrilla movement is very similar to the manner in which cells of modern transnational terrorist groups such as Al-Qaeda and Jemaah Islamiyah have emerged. Indeed, it is this 'method of action [which] eliminates the need for knowing who is carrying out which actions, since there is free initiative and the only important point is to increase substantially the volume of urban guerrilla activity'.[40]

C Modern organisational network theory and transnational terrorist groups

Marighella's theory of urban guerrilla warfare has directly fed into modern organisational network theory[41] which posits that the organisational structure of some armed groups is network based rather than hierarchical in nature. Even though organisational theory initially studied markets as an organisational model, over time it has expanded beyond business models to include clans, associations, and networks.[42] Beck has defined a network as a number of individuals that 'exist in independent operational cells linked by connections between just a few key operatives'.[43] In line with Marighella's theory, Beck suggests that the 'more informal, flexible and fragmented is the organizational structure of such a group and the more network elements it incorporates, the greater are its comparative advantages in an asymmetrical confrontation with a state'.[44] However, Beck's supposition can be challenged on the basis that a transnational terrorist group, even if its organisational structure is to a significant degree network based, arguably still needs 'a minimum set of hierarchical features' in order to successfully carry out a terrorist attack.[45] A network lacks this hierarchical structure and although the cells are interconnected they are also autonomous and are not required to comply with formal orders from commanders.[46] Thus, the capacity of the transnational terrorist group to successfully perpetrate international crimes can

37 Ibid., p. 14.
38 Ibid.
39 Ibid.
40 Ibid., p. 14.
41 Stepanova (n. 3), p. 127.
42 See generally Weber (n. 5); Haridimos Tsoukas and Christian Knudsen (eds), *The Oxford Handbook of Organisation Theory* (Oxford University Press, 2005).
43 Beck (n. 14), p. 1572.
44 Stepanova Note 3, p. 26.
45 Ibid., p. 129.
46 Ibid.

be brought it into question if it lacks the organisational structure necessary to ensure that the subordinate cells comply with orders issued by command.

Nevertheless, network-based transnational terrorist groups have a distinct advantage over armed groups with a clear-cut hierarchical command structure when carrying out attacks. The lack of a hierarchical command structure and a centralised leadership exercising direct control over subordinates enables them to change their modus operandi quite easily and thus complicates the task of state authorities to prevent attacks and prosecute members of these groups.[47] At the same time, the difference between transnational terrorist groups with a network-based organisational structure and groups with a hierarchical command structure is not as clear-cut as previously thought.

Modern organisations are complex and dialectical with hybrid structures containing both network and hierarchical characteristics. In addition, the organisational structure of such groups can evolve over time from 'a relatively loose organization balancing hierarchical and network features, such as . . . al-Qaeda, to a more decentralized movement'[48] such as Jemaah Islamiyah. Even though this decentralised organisational form has preserved 'multi-level coordination' and some hierarchical features[49] its decentralised network-based structure makes transnational terrorist groups 'more flexible, more mobile, better adapt to changing circumstances and are more stable during system shocks and at times of crisis'.[50]

Moreover, the network structure of the transnational terrorist group is exemplified by 'the effective, multi-level coordination of multiple cells' activities exercised through generally formulated strategic guidelines'.[51] These cells 'lack direct operational links but still manage to act and see themselves as part of the same . . . [transnational] movement'.[52] So the organisational structure of transnational terrorist groups is uniquely different to the organisational structure of both state armed forces and armed opposition groups which have a clear-cut hierarchical structure which enables subordinates to receive orders from the central command. So, for a transnational terrorist group to constitute a network all of its constituent cells must regard themselves as part of the wider network and be prepared to act as a network.

The major difference between armed opposition groups that operate within the territorial boundaries of a state and transnational terrorist groups which have the capacity to operate in more than one state is the capricious level of connection between network and hierarchical characteristics. Indeed, network characteristics will have a more significant role in the success of a transnational terrorist group which carries out attacks than a localised armed opposition group. However,

47 Ibid.
48 Ibid., p. 131.
49 See generally Manuel Castells, *The Information Age; Economy, Society and Culture: Vol. 1: The Rise of the Network Society* (Blackwell, 2000, 2nd edn).
50 Stepanova (n. 3), p. 128.
51 Ibid., p. 26.
52 Ibid.

because they have a network organisational structure transnational terrorist groups face difficulties making strategic political–military decisions because network cells may not have the capacity to communicate effectively with each other.[53] So transnational terrorist groups lack the organisational structure necessary to ensure that decisions are implemented by the cells. Even though the 'multiple cells form a network . . . their basic ideological proximity may not suffice to impose upon them strong and stable mutual obligations to engage in violent activity, especially in the form of . . . [armed attacks] against civilians'.[54] Since transnational terrorist groups are composed of a nebulous and multilayered network structure containing loosely coordinated cells they lack the central hierarchical command structure necessary to concretely pinpoint which individuals within the group orders and plans terrorist attacks.

For example, Al-Qaeda has evolved from an organisation with a centralised command to a devolved system of network cells that is very similar to a business franchise. Each of the cells in Al-Qaeda impart the same ideology and strategy devised by its commanders and also use the name Al-Qaeda as a trademark even though they are not firmly concomitant to the group. So the Al-Qaeda movement is similar to a segmented, polycentric, ideologically integrated network (SPIN) such as a civil rights group or social protest movement.[55] The polycentric construction of Al-Qaeda suggests that the group does not have a central governance mechanism but still has a number of commanders. In particular, Stepanova notes that the 'network structure [groups like Al-Qaeda] indicates that its various segments, leaders and central nodes are integrated into a network by means of structural, ideological and personal links'.[56] So the integrating dynamism of a transnational terrorist group would appear to be its ideology. Indeed, through the use of 'modern means of communication, shared ideology helps connect the fragmented, dispersed, isolated or informally interlinked elements of modern networks'.[57]

Nevertheless, the idea that the cells of a transnational terrorist group share the same ideology can be challenged on the ground that cells may be formed in different political contexts and may be located in more than one state. If this is the case it is difficult to understand how these cells are able to carry out effective and coordinated terrorist attacks if they do not have a unifying belief system? The high number of attacks carried out by some transnational terrorist groups would suggest that considerable intra-organisational coherence is required when planning

53 Stepanova (n. 3), p. 132.

54 Ibid.

55 For further reference, see Luther Gerlach, 'Protest Movements and the Construction of Risk', in B. Johnson and V. Costello (eds), *The Social and Cultural Construction of Risk: Essays on Risk Selection and Perception* (Reidel, 1987), p. 103; Luther Gerlach and Virginia Hine, *People, Power, Change: Movements of Social Transformation* (Bobbs-Merrill, 1970).

56 Stepanova (n. 3), p. 134.

57 Ibid., p. 134. See also Jialun Qin et al., 'Analysing Terrorist Networks', *Intelligence and Security Informatics Lecture Notes in Computer Science* 3495 (2005) 287–304.

and perpetrating such attacks. So the absence of a central leadership within the majority of transnational terrorist groups compels the network cells 'to resort to various consultative and consensus-building mechanisms in the decision-making process' which closely resembles tribal organisational systems.[58]

Indeed, Ronfeldt, a leading theorist on network-based organisations, has described some modern-day transnational terrorist groups as a 'global clan waging segmental warfare'.[59] The individual cells of some transnational terrorist groups are not established on impersonalised networks but instead on familial and close-kin relationships.[60] The major decisions within the group are determined by consensus following a period of consultation with the most experienced clan members.[61] However, Ronfeldt's theory still does not explain the organisational model of violence adopted by transnational terrorist groups because it fails to acknowledge the central role of ideology in binding the cells together. His theory merely hypothesises that the clan provides the basis for the network characteristics of transnational terrorist groups.

Thus, Ronfeldt's theory emasculates the role of ideology as the dynamic force for the transnational terrorist group. Arguably, modern transnational terrorist groups require a high level of ideological integration in order to successfully carry out attacks. Indeed, the network-based structure of these groups can be regarded as a projection of this ideology. At the same time, some transnational terrorist groups are not a strict network[62] and like armed opposition groups and state armed forces may exhibit some hierarchical characteristics. For example, ISIS which has allegedly perpetrated grave international crimes during the armed conflicts in Syria and Iraq but also isolated sporadic attacks in Belgium, France, Spain, and the UK, has both a centralised command and network cells.[63] Stepanova is of the view that this type of structure enables transnational terrorist groups like ISIS 'to reinforce their comparative strengths and compensate for their mutual weaknesses'.[64] However, this hybrid structure does not sufficiently explain how self-governing cells orchestrate terrorist attacks in an effective and coordinated manner in keeping with the overall strategy developed by the group's leaders.

Beam has proposed an alternative theory of leaderless resistance to explain how transnational terrorist groups coordinate terrorist attacks in numerous states.[65] Leaderless resistance is a strategy initially developed by animal liberation groups such as the Animal Rights Militia and neo-Nazi groups such as Stormfront, Aryan

58 Stepanova (n. 3), p. 135.
59 David Ronfeldt, 'Al-Qaeda and Its Affiliates: A Global Tribe Waging Segmental Warfare?', *First Monday* 10(3) (2005) available at: http://firstmonday.org/issues/issue10_3 (date accessed: 14 March 2018).
60 Stepanova (n. 3), p. 135.
61 Ibid.
62 Ibid.
63 Ibid.
64 Ibid., p. 140.
65 Louis Beam, 'Leaderless Resistance', *The Seditionist* 12 (1992) available at www.louisbeam.com/leaderless.htm (date accessed: 14 March 2018); Jeffrey Kaplan, 'Leaderless Resistance', *Terrorism and Political Violence* 9(3) (1997) 80.

Nations, and the Hammerskins. There is no explicit communication between the network cells, so they lack a bidirectional command link. Nevertheless, they still have the capacity to act in pursuance of a common goal.[66] Although leaderless resistance has been utilised by many right-wing extremist groups it is arguably not an effectual organisational model to describe transnational terrorist groups because it is often a device utilised as a last-ditch effort to prolong violence where there is very little public support for the aims and objectives of the group.[67]

Beam's theory also does not explain how an organisation would implement its strategic aims and objectives without a centralised system of direct control. In any event, attacks by transnational terrorist groups are a high-cost exercise.[68] The group needs considerable resources if it plans to carry out more than one attack and sustain a prolonged campaign. Beck notes that a fundamental problem for collective movements such as transnational terrorist groups is gaining access to the resources necessary to carry out terrorist attacks.[69] If the strategy of the group is to carry out attacks such as suicide bombings in more than one state, then the group also requires the regular recruitment of members who are willing to carry out attacks in order to achieve the aims and objectives of the transnational terrorist group. The Izz ad-Din al-Qassam Brigades in the Gaza Strip and the transnational terrorist group ISIS have had little difficulty in overcoming this challenge and thus undermines Beck's conclusion.

In this way, transnational terrorist groups can be compared to 'modern social movement organizations – a highly professionalized core that directs and manages attacks, assembles resources, and provides overall leadership to a broader base of supporters'.[70] So transnational terrorist groups such as ISIS have been able to conduct attacks over a prolonged time period because they are composed of network cells that 'are likely constrained and enabled by the same dynamics of resources and organizations as social movements'.[71] Since some transnational terrorist groups do not have a formal hierarchical structure like state armed forces they are instead organised as networks comprising numerous cells. Each cell has a specific function in the network despite the fact that it lacks a direct operational link with a central command. The cell is also a constituent part of the transnational terrorist group and performs its specific function in keeping with the overall objectives of the group. The distinct advantage of structuring transnational terrorist groups into network cells is that they are not only difficult to detect by law enforcement and can operate with relative anonymity amongst the civilian population they can also conduct sporadic attacks swiftly and efficiently as was the case with attacks by ISIS in Paris in November 2015.

66 Kaplan (n. 65), p. 81.
67 Simon Garfinkel, 'Leaderless Resistance Today', *First Monday* 8(3) (2004) available at: http://firstmonday.org/issues/issue8_3 (date accessed: 14 March 2018).
68 Beck (n. 14), p. 1569.
69 Ibid.
70 See generally Nitin Nohria et al. (eds), *Networks and Organizations: Structure, Form and Action* (Harvard Business School, 1992); Beck (n. 14), p. 1569.
71 Ibid.

D Conclusion

This chapter has shown there is considerable divergence of opinion on the organisational structure of transnational terrorist groups. The concept of the transnational terrorist group remains a highly contested issue, and determining what constitutes a 'transnational terrorist group' from either a legal or non-legal perspective can be challenging. Yet, despite the ongoing debate, no one would contest that the structure and organisation of such groups is very different to other types of non-state armed actors such as armed opposition groups which enables them to evolve quite easily. Indeed, some transnational terrorist groups have a network-based organisational structure composed of cells which for the most part operate independently of one another. This complicates the task of law enforcement authorities responsible for investigating the behaviour of transnational terrorist groups and bringing their members to justice.

The lack of a centralised command within some transnational terrorist groups means that the cells resort to consensus decision-making in formulating the overall policy and ideology of the group. As a result, it can be difficult to determine who within the transnational terrorist group orders the terrorist attack and physically plans and perpetrates it. This is further complicated by the fact that some transnational terrorist groups have a hybrid organisational structure containing both network and hierarchical organisational features. As a result, network cells can perpetrate attacks in an impromptu manner without receiving formal orders from the centralised command. This in turn can lead to evidential difficulties in determining whether such attacks constitute an international crime. Therefore, it is now necessary to turn to the question of whether attacks by a transnational terrorist group can be classified as an international crime under the Rome Statute.

3 The classification of attacks by transnational terrorist groups as a crime under the Rome Statute

A Introduction

Building on centuries of religious, philosophical, and legal thought, the past 70 years has seen the formal creation, elaboration, and enforcement of a wide range of international criminal law (ICL) principles. Some may argue that the onward march of ICL is a foregone conclusion.[1] As proclaimed in the preamble of the Rome Statute 'the most serious crimes of concern to the international community as a whole must not go unpunished and . . . their effective prosecution must be ensured by taking measures at the national level and by enhancing international cooperation'.[2] Yet globally, the mechanisms, frameworks and implementation of ICL have often been sporadic, ad hoc and compliance is more likely once it has been violated than the observance.

As noted by Kofi Annan, the International Criminal Court (ICC) represents 'a gift of hope to future generations, and a giant step forward in the march towards universal human rights and the rule of law . . . [It] is an achievement which . . . nobody would have thought possible'.[3] If this is the case, is there an on-going requirement to recognise new or novel international crimes within the Rome Statute to ensure that all potential harms are proscribed, or alternatively should efforts focus on existing well-established crimes to ensure they can be applied to new or novel situations? Moreover, can the ICC truly fulfil its mandate to deter international crime if the Rome Statute does not adequately address non-state armed actors that have evolved from a strict hierarchical command structure to a more fragmented entity with a network-based organisational structure?

As a counterpart to Kofi Annan's belief in the need to reinforce accountability mechanisms for international crimes, one must also highlight the risk that the

1 Fedric Mégret, 'The Case for a General International Crime against the Environment', in S. Jodoin and M. Cordonier Segger (eds), *Sustainable Development, International Criminal Justice and Treaty Implementation* (Cambridge University Press, 2013) 50, p. 54.

2 Preamble of the Rome Statute of the International Criminal Court.

3 UN press release, 'Secretary-General says establishment of International Criminal Court is major step toward universal human rights, rule of law' (L/2890, 20 July 1998), available at: www.un.org/News/Press/docs/1998/19980720.l2890.html (date accessed: 14 March 2018).

inclusion of a crime of terrorism within the Rome Statute would further politicise the ICC.[4] Nevertheless, terrorism continues to be a grave threat to international peace and security and a matter of serious concern to the international community. So, would the explicit inclusion of a crime of terrorism within the subject-matter jurisdiction of the ICC alleviate the difficulties in prosecuting members of network-based transnational terrorist groups or is the creation of such a crime an example of the international legal and humanitarian elite redefining the problem of transnational terrorist groups into the prevailing international consensus of how such crimes should be prosecuted?

It is not possible within the confines of this book to examine in detail the development and conceptual basis for ICL in general. However, as I will argue that the ICC would not be an efficient accountability mechanism for prosecuting attacks perpetrated by transnational terrorist groups, it is still necessary to understand if their acts constitute an international crime within the current wording of the Rome Statute. Furthermore, it is important to distinguish between terrorist attacks in armed conflict situations and non-armed conflict situations to facilitate an examination of the application of the Rome Statute to transnational terrorist groups.

Since the ICC has not yet prosecuted a member of a transnational terrorist group for their role in the planning and perpetration of an attack, the argument that I will advance over the course of this chapter is that even though terrorist attacks can be classified as a war crime if they occur during an armed conflict situation they cannot be easily classified as a crime against humanity in view of the challenges in proving they were widespread and systematic attacks committed in pursuance of an organisational policy. As Michael Scharf and Michael Newton have noted:

> the effort to achieve international consensus on the inclusion of a specific crime against humanity of 'terrorism' would introduce a whole new level of uncertainty and politicizations into the existing legal structures and definitions. The effort could therefore undermine the fundamental human rights of the perpetrator and the efficacy of existing prohibitions and punitive forums.[5]

4 See generally Hans Köchler, *Global Justice or Global Revenge?: The ICC and the Politicisation of International Criminal Justice* (Khartoum: World Conference for International Justice, 6 April 2009); Bartram Brown, 'The Politicization of International Criminal Law', available at: www.kentlaw.edu/faculty/bbrown/classes/IntlOrgSp07/CourseDocs/IVOnthePoliticizationofInternationalCriminalLaw.pdf (date accessed: 14 March 2018); Gene Lyons, David Baldwin, and Donald McNemar, 'The Politicization Issue in the UN Specialized Agencies', in D. Kay (ed.), *The Changing United Nations: Options for the United States* (Praeger, 1977) 85, pp. 85–86; Robert Keohane and Joseph Nye, 'World Politics and the International Economic System', in C. Bergsten (ed.), *The Future of the International Economic Order: An Agenda for Research* (Lexington Books, 1973) 115–179, p. 117; Bartram Brown, 'U.S. Objections to the Statute of the International Criminal Court: A Brief Response', *New York University Journal of International Law and Policy* 31 (1999) 855–891, pp. 871–873.

5 'Terrorism and Crimes against Humanity', in L. Sadat (ed.), *Forging a Convention for Crimes against Humanity* (Cambridge University Press, 2011) 262–278, p. 278.

In spite of this, debate on the utilisation of the ICC to prosecute terrorist attacks as a crime against humanity has continued. As noted by Roberta Arnold in 2004:

> Although terrorism was excluded as a specific provision from the ICC Statute, there are several elements suggesting that it may nevertheless be prosecuted under the heading of crimes against humanity. In particular, it could be addressed as the sub-offence of murder, torture, deportation, or forcible transfer of population, imprisonment or other severe deprivation of physical liberty in violation of fundamental rules of international law, persecution, enforced disappearance, and, more general, as an inhumane act pursuant to Article 7(1)(k).[6]

On the basis of this understanding, key questions that need to be asked are: can attacks by transnational terrorist groups in non-armed conflict situations be classified as an international crime under the Rome Statute? Has a customary crime of transnational terrorism crystallised in international law?

Drawing on my findings in Chapter 2, this chapter will argue that the drafters of the Rome Statute focussed solely on state and non-state armed actors with a strict hierarchical chain of command and did not take into consideration entities with a network-based organisational structure. Thus, for a terrorist attack to be classified as an international crime under the Rome Statute we need to establish whether such attacks fulfil the constituent elements of each crime with reference to the recent jurisprudence of the ICC. This chapter will contend that we have not yet reached the stage in ICL where we can categorise attacks by transnational terrorist groups in either an armed conflict situation or a non-armed conflict situation as a crime within the subject matter jurisdiction of the ICC. So, while there have been a range of authoritative statements from academics, non-governmental organisations, and some governments we cannot yet say that the classification of terrorist attacks as an international crime has passed into the realm of general international law or the corpus of ICL.

Nevertheless, as set out further in Chapter 4, this book proposes that a customary crime of transnational terrorism in non-armed conflict situations is beginning to emerge in international law. Indeed, the emergence of this crime could perhaps facilitate the prosecution of members of transnational terrorist groups before the ICC if the Rome Statute was amended accordingly. As examined in Chapter 5, the doctrine of command responsibility can only be applied to state and non-state actors with a clear chain of command between the leader and the subordinates. So, in network-based transnational terrorist groups it is hard to ascertain whether there is a leader who has the capacity to exercise effective

6 *The Prosecution of Terrorism as a Crime against Humanity* (Max-Planck-Institut für ausländisches öffentliches Recht und Völkerrecht, 2004) 979, p. 999, available at: www.zaoerv.de/64_2004/64_2004_4_a_979_1000.pdf (date accessed: 14 March 2018).

control over his or her subordinates. However, before considering this question this chapter will evaluate the categorisation of attacks by transnational terrorist groups as an international crime. This chapter begins by briefly examining the categorisation of attacks by transnational terrorist groups as an act of genocide under Article 6 of the Rome Statute. The chapter will subsequently examine the categorisation of terrorist attacks as a war crime and a crime against humanity.

B Genocide

Article II of the Genocide Convention 1948 defines genocide as including acts of killing or causing serious bodily harm or mental harm with the intent to destruct a national, ethical, racial or religious group or members of that group.[7] Genocidal acts clearly incur individual criminal liability and can be perpetrated during peacetime as well as during armed conflict.[8] Originally, genocide was included in the same category as crimes against humanity in Article 6(c) of the Charter of the Nuremburg Tribunal. However, both crimes have now been separated despite the considerable overlap between them.[9]

Article IV of the Genocide Convention 1948 clearly stipulates that the support of a government is not required for the perpetration of genocide.[10] Therefore individuals 'committing genocide or any other acts enumerated in Article III shall be punished, whether they are constitutionally responsible rulers, public officials or private individuals'.[11] From a simple analysis of this provision, it is clear that members of transnational terrorist groups can incur criminal accountability under this Convention.[12] The UN Secretary General's Report on Minimum Humanitarian Standards which concluded that genocide, as provided for in the Genocide Convention, can be 'committed by non-State agents' supports this view.[13] In addition, the definition of genocide in Article 4 of the Statute of the International Criminal Tribunal for the Former Yugoslavia (ICTY) and Article 2 of the Statute

7 Antonio Cassese, 'Terrorism as an International Crime', in A. Bianchi and Y. Naqvi (eds), *Enforcing International Law Norms Against Terrorism* (Hart, 2004) 213–225, p. 213.

8 Article 1 of the Genocide Convention 1948. For further reference, see Paola Gaeta, 'Génocide d'état et responsabilité pénale individuelle', *Revue de droit international public* 111 (2007) 272. On state responsibility for acts of genocide, see Antonio Cassese, 'On the Use of Criminal Law Nations in Determining State Responsibility for Genocide', *Journal of International Criminal Justice* 5 (2007) 875–887.

9 For further reference, see Steven Ratner and Jason Abrams, *Accountability for Human Rights Atrocities in International Law: Beyond the Nuremburg Legacy* (Oxford University Press, 2001), p. 27.

10 Article IV of the Genocide Convention 1948.

11 Ibid.

12 Liesbeth Zegveld, *The Accountability of Armed Opposition Groups under International Law* (Cambridge University Press, 2002), p. 109.

13 United Nations Secretary General, *Report on Minimum Humanitarian Standards*, 5 January 1998, paras 62–63.

of the International Criminal Tribunal for Rwanda (ICTR) is a carbon copy of the definition set out in the Genocide Convention.[14]

The Rome Statute reiterates this same definition in Article 6 which provides that:

> For the purpose of this Statute, 'genocide' means any of the following acts committed with intent to destroy, in whole or in part, a national, ethnical, racial or religious group, as such:
> (a) Killing members of the group;
> (b) Causing serious bodily or mental harm to members of the group;
> (c) Deliberately inflicting on the group conditions of life calculated to bring about its physical destruction in whole or in part;
> (d) Imposing measures intended to prevent births within the group;
> (e) Forcibly transferring children of the group to another group.[15]

Therefore, the Rome Statute leaves open the possibility of prosecuting members of transnational terrorist groups for the commission of genocide. Nevertheless, despite the fact that many attacks by transnational terrorist groups can involve the perpetration of the *actus reus* of the crime of genocide it is improbable that such attacks are perpetrated with the requisite *mens rea* which is 'the intent to destroy, in whole or in part, a national, ethnical, racial or religious group'.[16] At the same time this does not mean that attacks by transnational terrorist groups could never be defined as an act of genocide. However, it is highly improbable that 'the offence of genocide would be used in an indictment against individuals suspected of commissioning or carrying out terrorist attacks'.[17] The reason for this is that the vast majority of terrorist groups lack the resources necessary to perpetrate this category of crime.[18]

14 See further Article 4 of the Statute of the International Criminal Tribunal for the Former Yugoslavia adopted on the 25 May 1993 by UN Security Council Resolution 827 (1993) and Article 2 of the Statute of the International Criminal Tribunal for Rwanda (ICTR) adopted on the 8 November 2004 by UN Security Council Resolution 944, as amended.

15 Article 6 of the Rome Statute of the International Criminal Court.

16 Fiona de Londras, 'Terrorism as an International Crime', in W. Schabas and N. Bernaz (eds), *Routledge International Book of Criminal Law* (Routledge, 2010) 167–180, p. 171.

17 Ibid.

18 However, ISIS would appear to be a group which has allegedly committed the crime of genocide. See for instance Samira Shackle, 'Yazidis in Iraq: The Genocide is Ongoing' (*Al Jazeera*, 7 November 2017) available at: www.aljazeera.com/news/2017/11/yazidis-iraq-genocide-ongoing-171105064140012.html (date accessed: 14 March 2018); Erin Dooley and Kirit Radia, 'ISIS is clearly responsible for genocide, Tillerman says' (ABC News 15 August 2010), available at: http://abcnews.go.com/International/isis-respondible-genocide-tillerson/story?id=49231365 (date accessed: 14 March 2018); Kathleen Harris, 'Canada on Track to Resettle 1200 Victims of ISIS Genocide, Sexual Slavery' (*CBC News*, 26 October 2017), available at: www.cbc.ca/news/politics/yazidi-isis-victims-canada-1.4369673 (date accessed: 14 March 2018).

C War crimes

Article 8(2)(b)(i) of the Rome Statute provides that '[i]ntentionally directing attacks against the civilian population as such or against individual civilians not taking direct part in hostilities' constitutes a war crime.[19] Since the phrase 'hostilities' is a rather convoluted concept to define, the adoption of the phrase 'armed conflict' in the Geneva Conventions was supposed to ensure that these instruments would only apply to wars in the conventional sense. Indeed, the prevailing view is that an armed conflict situation has two main features: (i) the presence of two or more organised armed groups and; (ii) their participation in hostilities of considerable intensity.[20] This resembles the definition of armed conflict laid down by the ICTY in *Prosecutor* v. *Tadić.* [21] Here, the Appeals Chamber stated that 'an armed conflict exists whenever there is a resort to armed force between States or protracted armed violence between governmental authorities and organised armed groups or between such groups within a State'.[22] Both requirements must be satisfied before a violent situation can be classified as an armed conflict situation. Parties to an armed conflict will be held individually criminally accountable for breaches of Common Article 3 and Additional Protocol II to the Geneva Conventions.

This can be readily inferred from the decision of the ICTY in the *Prosecutor* v. *Furundžija* where it was held that:

> The treaty and customary rules referred to above [Common Article 2 and Additional Protocol II] impose obligations upon States and other entities in an armed conflict, but first and foremost address themselves to the acts of individuals, in particular to State officials or more generally, to officials of a party to the conflict or else to individuals acting at the instigation or with the consent or acquiescence of a party to the conflict. Both customary rules and treaty provisions applicable in time of armed conflict prohibit any act of torture. Those who engage in torture are personally accountable at the criminal level of such acts.[23]

19 Article 8(2)(b)(i) of the Rome Statute; see also Article 15 of Additional Protocol I and Article 13 of Additional Protocol II to the Geneva Conventions. Antonio Cassese defines war crimes as 'serious violations of customary or treaty rules belonging to the corpus of the international humanitarian law of armed conflict'. Antonio Cassese, *International Criminal Law* (Oxford University Press, 2008), p. 81.

20 International Law Association Use of Force Committee, Initial Report on the Meaning of Armed Conflict in International Law (2008), available at: www.ila-hq.org/en/committees/index.cfm/cid/1022 (date accessed: 14 March 2018).

21 *Prosecutor* v. *Tadić*, IT-94–1-A, Appeal Judgment, 15 June 1999.

22 Ibid., para. 70.

23 *Prosecutor* v. *Furundžjia*, IT-95–17/1-T, Judgment, 10 December 1998, para. 140. Analogous evidence to this effect can also be found in both the statute and the case law of the ICTR. For further analysis, see Article 4 of the Statute of the ICTR. As regards case law, see *Prosecutor* v. *Rutaganda*, ICTR-96-3-T, Judgment, 6 December 1999, para. 88.

So, it would seem that an attack by a transnational terrorist group will constitute a war crime if it occurs during an 'armed conflict' situation. In fact, individuals have previously been prosecuted and found guilty of participating in terroristic conduct during an armed conflict situation. In *Prosecutor* v. *Galić*, for example, the accused was found guilty under Article 3 of the ICTY Statute for violations of the laws or customs of war relating to the shelling and sniping of the civilian population in Sarajevo with the intent to spread terror among civilians.[24] The ICTY classified the offence as a 'crime of terror against the civilian population'.[25] However, the question whether the Tribunal had jurisdiction *ratione materiae* to consider the issue was undertaken 'only to the extent relevant to the charge in this case'.[26] The Tribunal examined the elements of an international crime as formulated in the *Tadić* case to determine whether it had jurisdiction over the crime of terror[27] and concluded that the crime was entrenched in Article 51 of Additional Protocol I to the Geneva Conventions.[28]

Since the crime was a treaty-based rule and a grave infringement of international humanitarian law (IHL) an individual could be held accountable for violating it.[29] The ICTY heard submissions that the crime of terror could only be perpetrated if attacks were purposely aimed at the civilian population with the intent to spread terror among the general civilian population.[30] All these particular constituent elements were established with respect to *Galić* who was subsequently convicted of war crimes in respect of the spread of terror among the general civilian population. So, a member of a transnational terrorist group could be prosecuted under Article 8(2)(b)(i) of the Rome Statute if there is evidence to indicate that the transnational terrorist group intentionally made civilians the target of the attack. However, in order for an attack by a transnational terrorist group to constitute a war crime it must occur during an armed conflict situation. So, the question remains whether hostilities between a state and a transnational terrorist group can be classified as an international or non-armed conflict situation? As we will see in Chapters 5–7 this question has a significant bearing on the responsibility of members of transnational terrorist groups for war crimes before the ICC.

1 Classifying hostilities with a transnational terrorist group as an international or non-international armed conflict

Transnational terrorist groups can be participants in both international and non-international armed conflicts under IHL.[31] Common Article 2 to the Geneva Conventions as supplemented by Additional Protocol I provides that an

24 *Prosecutor* v. *Galić*, IT-98-29-T, Judgment, 5 December 2003.
25 Ibid., para. 87.
26 Ibid., para. 96.
27 Ibid., para. 97.
28 Ibid., para. 109.
29 Ibid., paras 127 and 129.
30 Ibid., paras 133 and 135.
31 See generally, Ben Saul, 'Terrorism and International Humanitarian Law', in B. Saul (ed.), *Research Handbook on International and Terrorism* (Edward Elgar, 2014), ch. 13.

international armed conflict exists under IHL where there is protracted violence between two or more states.[32] As a result, the legal classification of a violent situation as an international armed conflict is dependent on states engaging in violence against each other or where a state uses irregular armed forces against other states as outlined in Article 4(2) of the Third Geneva Convention 1949.[33] The provision refers to 'organised resistance movements', 'militias' and 'volunteer corps' but also includes non-state armed actors such as insurgents, guerrillas, paramilitaries, private military corporations and terrorists. So, what is pivotal is whether pursuant to Article 4(2) all hostilities against the armed forces or the territory of one state are under the direction or control of another state.

Consequently, if the transnational terrorist group does not belong to a state within the meaning of Article 4 of the Third Geneva Convention, members would be classified as civilians under Article 51 of Additional Protocol I.[34] So, the law of international armed conflict does not regulate transnational terrorist groups that do not receive support from a state in the form of weapons and training. Thus, transnational terrorist groups can only be targeted by states in a military action 'for such time as they take a direct part in the hostilities'.[35] The perpetration of an attack by a transnational terrorist group cannot be categorised as a war crime when at the time of the initial attack there was not yet an armed conflict situation. Since the transnational terrorist group is not obliged to comply with the law of international armed conflict in their initial terrorist attack against the state this attack cannot be classified as a war crime.

Classifying hostilities involving transnational terrorist groups as a non-international armed conflict situation is much more uncomplicated. Common Article 3 to the Geneva Conventions as supplemented by Additional Protocol II was drafted on the premise that non-international armed conflicts were principally conventional civil wars by rebel groups fighting against government forces within the territorial boundaries of that state. In the aftermath of the 9/11 attacks there was much uncertainty whether the conflict classification scheme of IHL was sufficient to regulate the challenges of contemporary armed conflicts waged by a state against a transnational terrorist group. The United States Supreme Court took a straightforward approach in *Hamdan* v. *Rumsfeld* [36] by concluding that Common Article 3 applies to any armed conflict not occurring between two states

32 Common Article 2 to the Geneva Conventions. Although Article 1(3) of Additional Protocol I cites this provision, Article 1(4) widens the scope of application to national liberation wars.

33 Geneva Convention Relative to the Treatment of Prisoners of War (Third Geneva Convention), adopted 12 August 1949, 75 UNTS 135 (entered into force 21 October 1950).

34 Article 4 of the Third Geneva Convention.

35 Article 51 (3) of Additional Protocol I to the Geneva Conventions.

36 *Hamdan* v. *Rumsfeld,* 548 US 557 (2006) available at: www.supremecourt.gov/opinions/boundvolumes/548bv.pdf (date accessed: 14 March 2018)

irrespective of the location it takes place.[37] The conflict between the United States and Al-Qaeda in Afghanistan was consequently classified as a non-international armed conflict situation. The Supreme Court thus dismissed the United States government's contention that the 'war against terror' in Afghanistan fell into a legal void in IHL, as neither an international armed conflict nor a non-international armed conflict.[38] Instead, it expanded the 'minimum humanitarian protections of [C]ommon [A]rticle 3 . . . to non-citizen "terrorists" on a foreign battlefield'.[39]

Since on the facts of the case it was not necessary for the court to deliberate on whether there was a distinct international armed conflict between the United States and the government of Afghanistan (the Taliban), the predominant view was that this was the case.[40] The armed conflict ended upon the establishment of an autonomous Afghan government, which subsequently became embattled in a non-international conflict with the vestiges of the Taliban and Al-Qaeda. The *Hamdan* decision nevertheless can be challenged for not taking into consideration the widely accepted *Tadić* criteria of intensity and organisation in ascertaining the existence of a non-international conflict situation under Common Article 3 to the Geneva Conventions. It also did not consider whether Common Article 3 assumes that the non-state armed actor has the capacity to comply with IHL in view of their complex structure and organisation.[41] The court's classification of the armed conflict situation between a state and a non-state armed actor on the territory of another state as a non-international armed conflict is odd given that the state is engaging in combat operations on foreign soil.

Nevertheless, the correct categorisation of the situation ultimately depends on how Common Article 2 and Common Article 3 of the Geneva Conventions should be construed in light of one another. Common Article 2 clearly states that an international conflict is one arising 'between two or more of the High Contracting Parties'.[42] The Supreme Court in the *Hamdan* case understood this to imply that in order for a situation to be classified as an international armed conflict the hostilities must occur between the armed force of two or more states and this would seem to be the majority understanding of the provision.[43] Another view is that the phrase also includes situations where one state conducts hostilities against a transnational terrorist group on the territory of another state without the latter's permission. Pursuant to this approach, such situations are categorised as an international armed conflict between two High Contracting Parties, rather than a non-international armed conflict between a state and a

37 Ibid., pp. 628–631. On this point, see also Jelena Pejic, 'The Protective Scope of Common Article 3: More than Meets the Eye', *International Review of the Red Cross* 93 (881) (2011) 189, p. 195.

38 *Hamdan* v. *Rumsfeld*, 415 F.3d33 (DC Cir. 2005), rev'd, 126 S. Ct. 2749 (2006).

39 Saul (n. 31), p. 6.

40 Ibid.

41 Andrea Bianchi and Yasmin Naqvi, *International Humanitarian Law and Terrorism* (Hart, 2011), pp. 106–107.

42 Common Article 2 to the Geneva Conventions.

43 Hamdan (n. 36), pp. 41–42.

transnational terrorist group. In particular, Common Article 2 specifically refers to armed conflict between 'High Contracting Parties' namely, the legal entity of the state and its territory and is therefore not limited to armed conflict between state armed forces.[44]

The question is whether a lack of permission by the state to allow foreign state armed forces into its territory to conduct combat operations against a transnational terrorist group is sufficient to establish an international armed conflict situation within the meaning of Common Article 2. The hostilities in 2006 between Israel and Hezbollah in Lebanon has exasperated this classification dilemma. No hostilities took place between Israeli and Lebanese armed forces since the Lebanese government did not exert control over Hezbollah and also did not give permission for Israel's incursion.[45] However, since Israel's military objective was to weaken and destabilise Hezbollah it conducted attacks not only against its bases and equipment in southern Lebanon but also on civilian infrastructure with a dual purpose such as airfields, bridges, ports, and roads.[46] These targets were also geographically scattered throughout Lebanon far from active hostilities.

Human Rights Watch concluded that Israel's incursion into Lebanon constituted a non-international armed conflict situation.[47] However, the Rule of Law in Armed Conflict Project at the Geneva Academy of International Law was of the view that Israel's attack on Lebanese civilian infrastructure transmuted the hostilities into an international armed conflict situation.[48] This view is rather inept in light of the difficulties in ascertaining the exact moment the hostilities evolved from a non-international armed conflict to an international one. Other commentators have suggested that the lack of consent from the Lebanese government for Israeli forces to conduct an incursion into its territory is sufficient to classify the hostilities as international in character.[49] While this latter classification of Israel's operation in Lebanon is to be favoured the vast majority of states do not launch costly and time consuming operations in the territory of another state to defeat the perceived threat of transnational terrorist groups to its own civilian population

44 Ibid.

45 For further academic commentary on the classification of the hostilities, see Geoffrey Corn, 'Hamdan, Lebanon and the Regulation of Hostilities: The Need to Recognise a Hybrid Category of Armed Conflict', *Vanderbilt Journal of Transnational Law* 40 (2) (2007) 295–355.

46 'Israeli Airplanes Hit Beirut Suburb' (CNN, 14 July 2006), available at: http://edition.cnn.com/2006/WORLD/meast/07/13/mideast (date accessed: 14 March 2018).

47 Human Rights Watch, 'Civilians under Assault: Hezbollah's Rocket Attacks on Israel in the 2006 War' (August 2007), pp. 21–22.

48 'Rule of Law in Armed Conflicts Project' (Geneva Academy of International Humanitarian Law and Human Rights, 13 June 2012), available at: www.geneva-academy.ch/RULAC/qualification_of_armed_conflict.php (date accessed: 14 March 2018).

49 See for example Iain Scobbie, 'Lebanon 2006', in E. Wilmshurst (ed.), *International Law and the Classification of Armed Conflicts* (Oxford University Press, 2012) 387, p. 401.

and territory. Since a sizeable proportion of terrorist attacks do not occur in an armed conflict paradigm they cannot be classified as a war crime within the meaning of the Rome Statute. So, perhaps they can instead be classified as a crime against humanity?

D Crimes against humanity

The UN High Commissioner for Human Rights, Mary Robinson, stated at the U. S. Institute of Peace in 2001 that the 9/11 attacks by Al-Qaeda on the United States constituted a crime against humanity.[50] An examination of the definition of crimes against humanity contained in Article 7 of the Rome Statute together with the elements of the crime contained in Appendix 3 to the Statute suggests that terrorist attacks can be classified as 'murder' and 'inhumane acts' if 'committed as part of a widespread or systematic attack directed against the civilian population'.[51] The statement of the UN High Commissioner was of course a supposition given that the ICC cannot exercise jurisdiction over crimes which occurred prior to the coming into force of the Rome Statute in July 2002. Nevertheless, similar attacks occurring after this date could be classified as a crime against humanity.

Article 7(2)(a) of the Rome Statute provides that crimes against humanity are preconditioned on the perpetration of an attack on a civilian population 'pursuant to or in furtherance of a State or organisational policy to commit such attack'.[52] Furthermore, the Explanatory Memorandum of the Rome Statute in its summary of Article 7 defines crimes against humanity as:

> particularly odious offenses in that they constitute a serious attack on human dignity or grave humiliation or a degradation of one or more human beings; they are not isolated or sporadic events, but are part either of a government policy (although the perpetrators need not identify themselves with this policy) or of a wide practice of atrocities tolerated or condoned by a government or a de facto authority. However, murder, extermination, torture, rape,

50 Kevin Boyle, *A Voice for Human Rights: Mary Robinson* (University of Philadelphia Press, 2006), p. 331. In the weeks following the 9/11 attacks, academics also used this term to describe the atrocities. See further: Mark Drumbl, 'Judging the 11 September Terrorist Attack', *Human Rights Quarterly* 24 (2002) 323–360; Antonio Cassese, 'Terrorism Is also Disrupting Some Crucial Legal Categories of International Law', *European Journal of International Law* 12 (2001) 993–1001, p. 995; Nico Schrijver, 'Responding to International Terrorism: Moving the Frontiers of International Law for "Enduring Freedom"'?, *Netherlands International Law Review* 49 (2001) 271–291; Roderico Andreu-Gueran, 'Terrorisme et droits de l'homme', *Review of the International Commission of Jurists* (2002) 31; Mahmoud Bassiouni, 'Legal Control of International Terrorism: A Policy-Oriented Assessment', *Harvard International Law Journal* 43 (2002) 83–104.

51 Article 7 of the Rome Statute of the International Criminal Court; see also Appendix 3 to the Rome Statute of the International Criminal Court.

52 Article 7 of the Rome Statute.

> political, racial, or religious persecution and other inhumane acts reach the threshold of crimes against humanity only if they are part of a widespread or systematic practice.[53]

The classification of an attack by a transnational terrorist group as a crime against humanity necessitates the execution of one or more of the acts listed above as part of a 'widespread or systematic attack against the civilian population and pursuant to a policy or plan'.[54] So attacks must constitute 'acts of policy, not sporadic acts of wayward individual soldiers'.[55]

Peter Burns notes that the reference to a state or organisational policy in Article 7 introduces 'an extremely cryptic element' to crimes against humanity.[56] In view of contradictory case law and discord in the literature, important questions, such as whether non-state actors such as transnational terrorist groups can commit crimes against humanity remain controversial. While the Nuremburg Trials initially categorised crimes against humanity as acts committed by a government against civilians, it seems there is no longer a requirement that government involvement be a prerequisite to convert a straightforward crime into a crime against humanity.[57] None of the ad hoc criminal tribunals mention the necessity for governmental action.[58] In particular, the ICTY in *Prosecutor* v. *Dragon Nikolić* held that there is no link whatsoever between the perpetration of crimes against humanity and the

53 Commentary on the Rome Statute of the International Criminal Court; see also Article 7 of the Rome Statute; Cassese (n. 19), p. 250.

54 Kriangsak Kittichaisaree, *International Criminal Law* (Oxford University Press, 2001), p. 91.

55 Zegveld (n. 12), p. 107; see also *Prosecutor* v. *Akayesu*, ICTR-96-4-T, 2 September 1998, para. 565. For further analysis, see Leslie Green, *The Contemporary Law of Armed Conflict* (Manchester University Press, 1993), chs 2, 18, and 19. See also Burrus Carnahan, 'Lincoln, Lieber and the Laws of War: The Origins and Limits of the Principle of Military Necessity', *American Journal of International Law* 92 (1998) 213–231.

56 Peter Burns, *Aspect of Crimes Against Humanity and the International Criminal Court: Paper for the Symposium on the International Criminal Court* (Beijing, February 2007) available at: www.icclr.law.ubc.ca/Site%20Map/ICC/AspectofCrimesAgainstHumanity.pdf (date accessed: 14 March 2018).

57 Zegveld (n. 12), p. 107. For further reference on the Nuremburg Trials, see Cassese (n. 19), pp. 103–109. For further commentary on the evolution of the concept of crimes against humanity, see generally Ratner and Abrams (n. 9), p. 46. See also Jean Garven, 'Les crimes l'humanité', *Recueil des cours* 76 (1950–1951) 433–607; James Brand, 'Crimes against Humanity and the Nuremburg Trials', *Oregon Law Review* 28 (1949) 93–119. The first modern effort to attribute individual responsibility for crimes against humanity occurred in the aftermath of the First World War. For further analysis on this point, see Commission on the Responsibility of the Authors of the War and on Enforcement of Penalties Report Presented to the Preliminary Peace Conference, 19 March 1919, as reprinted in *American Journal of International Law* 14 (1920) 95. For further analysis, see Green (n. 55), chs 2, 18, and 19; Carnahan (n. 55).

58 Ibid.

state[59] so at first glance it would seem that attacks by transnational terrorist groups could be classified as crimes against humanity under Article 7 of the Rome Statute.[60]

However, Mahmoud Cherif Bassiouni who chaired the drafting committee of the Rome Statute argues to the contrary observing that crimes committed by non-state actors do not fall within the subject matter jurisdiction of the ICC. In particular, he noted that:

> [c]ontrary to what some advocates advance, Article 7 does not bring a new development to crimes against humanity, namely, its applicability to non-state actors. If that were the case, the mafia, for example, could be charged with such crimes before the ICC, and that is clearly neither the letter nor the spirit of article 7. The questions arose after 9/11 as to whether a group such as al-Qaeda, which operates on a worldwide basis and is capable of inflicting significant harm in more than one state, falls within this category. In this author's opinion, such a group does not qualify for inclusion within the meaning of crimes against humanity as defined in Article 7 . . . The text clearly refers to state policy, and the words 'organisational policy' . . . do not refer to the policy of an organization, but the policy of a state. It does not refer to non-state actors.[61]

William Schabas suggests that 'crimes against humanity may in some circumstances be committed by non-state actors'.[62] However, he qualifies this suggestion by contending that all prosecutions before international criminal courts and tribunals:

> have involved offenders acting on behalf of a State and in accordance with a State policy, or those acting on behalf of an organization that was State-like in its attempts to exercise control over territory and seize political power, such as the Republika Srpska.[63]

As a result, he concludes that:

> Dictionary definitions consider an organization to comprise any organized group of people, such as a club, society, trade union, or business. Surely the

59 For further reference, see *Prosecutor* v. *Nikolic Review of the Indictment Pursuant to Rule 61 of the Rules of Procedure and Evidence*, IT-94-2-R61, Judgment, 20 October 1995, para. 26. The ICTY restated this view in the *Tadić* case. For further reference, see *Prosecutor* v. *Tadić*, IT-94-1-T, Opinion and Judgment, 7 May 1997, para. 654.

60 For further reference on the Nuremburg Trials, see Cassese (n. 19), pp. 103–109. For further commentary on the evolution of the concept of crimes against humanity, see generally Ratner and Abrams (n. 9), p. 46.

61 *The Legislative History of the International Criminal Court* (Brill/Martinus Nijhoff, 2005), pp. 151–152.

62 *An Introduction to the International Criminal Court* (Cambridge University Press, 2017), p. 97.

63 'State Policy as an Element of International Crimes', *Journal of Criminal Law and Criminology* 98 (2008) 953–982, p. 954.

> drafters of the Rome Statute did not intend Article 7 to have such a broad scope, given that previous case law concerning crimes against humanity, and all evidence of national prosecutions for crimes against humanity, had concerned State supported atrocities. If they really meant to include any type of organization, such as a highly theoretical 'organization' of two people, why did they put these words in at all? The biggest problem for the proponents of the broad view is their inability to explain how the term organization is to be qualified.[64]

Peter Burns has a completely different opinion in his interpretation of Article 7(2)(a). He observes that organisational policy 'can undoubtedly include state organs and will extend to para-military units of a state, organized rebel groups within a state, or even unorganized rebel groups so long as there is a sufficient core that develops such a policy for the group'.[65]

Even though the statutes of the ad hoc tribunals do not explicitly contain a state or organizational policy requirement, the case law suggests that non-state actors can in certain circumstances commit crimes against humanity.[66] Trial Chamber II in the *Tadić* case at the ICTY noted that:

> [t]he traditional conception was, in fact, not only that a policy must be present but that the policy must be that of a State, as was the case in Nazi Germany . . . While this may have been the case during the Second World War, and thus the jurisprudence followed by courts adjudicating charges of crimes against humanity based on events alleged to have occurred during this period, this is no longer the case . . . [T]he law in relation to crimes against humanity has developed to take into account forces which, although not those of the legitimate government, have de facto control over, or are able to move freely within, defined territory.[67]

The Trial Chamber's judgment concluded that 'although a policy must exist to commit these acts, it need not be the policy of a State'.[68]

The three judges of ICC Pre-Trial Chamber II in the *Kenyatta* case also agreed that non-state actors can in theory be classified as an organisation under Article 7 (2)(a) of the Rome Statute.[69] The underlying reasoning for their conclusion was that if the drafters of the Rome Statute had intended to exclude non-state actors, they would not have inserted the word 'organization' into Article 7(2)(a).[70]

64 Ibid., p. 972.
65 Burns (n. 56), p. 11.
66 Cassese (n. 19), p. 116.
67 *Tadić* Opinion and Judgment (n. 59), para. 654.
68 Ibid., para. 655.
69 *Decision Pursuant to Article 15 of the Rome Statute on the Authorization of an Investigation into the Situation in the Republic of Kenya*, ICC-01/09, 31 March 2010, para. 45.
70 Ibid., para. 92.

However, Judge Kaul and the two majority judges disagreed about the criteria non-state actors must fulfil in order to satisfy the organisational requirement. The majority concluded that:

> With regard to the term 'organizational', the Chamber notes that the Statute is unclear as to the criteria pursuant to which a group may qualify as an 'organization' for the purposes of article 7(2)(a) of the Statute. Where some have argued that only State-like organizations may qualify, the Chamber opines that the formal nature of a group and level of its organization should not be the defining criterion. Instead, as others have convincingly put forward, a distinction should be drawn on whether a group has the capability to perform acts which infringe on basic human values.[71]

It is still unclear how this criterion is different from the criteria thus far applied by the pretrial chambers, namely that Article 7(2)(a) includes 'groups of persons who govern a specific territory' and 'any organisation with the capacity to commit a widespread or systematic attack against a civilian population'.[72]

However, unlike these previous cases, the majority of Pre-Trial Chamber II in the *Kenya Investigation Authorisation Decision* expands on what factors must be taken into consideration when ascertaining whether a non-state actor has the capacity to violate basic human rights values:

> (i) whether the group is under a responsible command, or has an established hierarchy; (ii) whether the group possesses, in fact, the means to carry out a widespread or systematic attack against a civilian population; (iii) whether the group exercises control over part of the territory of a State; (iv) whether the group has criminal activities against the civilian population as a primary purpose; (v) whether the group articulates, explicitly or implicitly, an attention to attack a civilian population; (vi) whether the group is part of a larger group, which fulfils some or all of the abovementioned criteria.[73]

Judge Kaul disagreed with the majority, observing that not any group with the power to violate basic human rights values can be classified as an organisation under Article 7(2)(a), but only those that are state-like in character.[74]

71 Ibid., para. 90.

72 *Prosecutor* v. *Germain Katanga and Mathieu Ngudjolo Chui, Decision on the Confirmation of Charges*, ICC-01/04–01/07, 30 September 2008, para. 396; *Prosecutor* v. *Jean-Pierre Bemba Gombo, Decision Pursuant to Article 61(7)(a) and (b) of the Rome Statute on the Charges of the Prosecutor Against Jean-Pierre Bemba Gombo*, ICC-01/05-01/08, 15 June 2009, para. 81.

73 *Kenya Investigation Authorization Decision* (n. 69), para. 93.

74 *Dissenting Opinion of Judge Kaul Appended to the Decision Pursuant to Article 15 of the Rome Statute on the Authorization of an Investigation into the Situation in the Republic of Kenya*, ICC-01/09-19-Corr, 31 March 2010, para. 66.

He underpins this interpretation with a number of arguments. First, he questions the application of the ICC's jurisprudence on this issue because non-state actors in previous cases such as *Prosecutor* v. *Jean Pierre Bemba Gombo* were 'military-like organized armed groups in the context of an armed conflict not of an international character who over a prolonged period of time allegedly committed crimes according to a policy'.[75] Second, Judge Kaul asserted that 'the juxtaposition of the notions of "State" and "organization" in Article 7(2)(a) of the Statute are an indication that even though the constitutive element of statehood need not be established those "organizations" should partake of some characteristics of a State'.[76] Third, utilising a contextual reading of Article 7(2)(a), he contends that the preamble of the Rome Statute should be interpreted as directing the ICC 'to avoid a "banalisation or trivialization" of the crimes contained in the Statute', which supports calibrating a high threshold for the term 'organization'.[77] Finally, Judge Kaul utilises a teleological construal of Article 7(2)(a).[78] He reflects that the concept of crimes against humanity was pioneered by the international community in the aftermath of the Second World War to address 'mass crimes committed by sovereign States against the civilian population, sometimes the State's own subjects, according to a State plan or policy, involving large segments of the State apparatus'.[79]

Judge Kaul argued that such crimes should be differentiated from other crimes because they 'represent an intolerable threat against the peace, security and well-being of the world, indeed a threat for humanity and fundamental values of mankind'.[80] He further added that:

> [c]rimes of this nature and magnitude were made possible only by virtue of an existing State policy followed in a planned and concerted fashion by various segments of public power targeting parts of the civilian population who were deprived totally and radically of their basic fundamental rights. It was not (only) the fact that crime had been committed on a large scale but the fact that they were committed in furtherance of a particular (inhumane) policy. Consequently, it was felt that the threat emanating from such state policy is so fundamentally different in nature and scale that it concerned the entire international community. In other words, the presence of a policy element elevated those crimes to the international level.[81]

He concluded by noting that 'historic experience demonstrates that it is, exactly and above all, the phenomenon of a State adopting either formally or

75 Ibid., para. 48; see also *Prosecutor* v. *Jean Pierre Bemba Gombo, Decision on the Confirmation of Charges*, ICC-01/05-01/08-424, 15 June 2009.
76 *Dissenting Opinion* (n. 74), para. 51.
77 Ibid., para. 55.
78 Ibid., para. 56.
79 Ibid., paras 59 and 61.
80 Ibid.
81 Ibid., para. 60.

in practice a policy to attack a civilian population, which leads to this very grave; if not enormous risk and threat of mass crimes and mass victimization'.[82]

By distinguishing 'between international crimes and human rights infractions; between international crimes and ordinary crimes; between those crimes subject to international jurisdiction and those punishable under domestic penal legislation',[83] Judge Kaul discounts from the Rome Statute crimes committed by non-state actors that do not have state-like features.[84] In doing so, he outlined the characteristics that are indicative of a state-like armed group:

> (a) a collectivity of persons; (b) which was established and acts for a common purpose; (c) over a prolonged period of time; (d) which is under responsible command or adopted a certain degree of hierarchical structure, including, as a minimum, some kind of policy level; (e) with the capacity to impose the policy on its members and to sanction them; and (f) which has the capacity and means available to attack any civilian population on a larger scale.[85]

Judge Kaul also considered when the acts of individuals can be linked to an organisation:

> For the purposes of attribution, the acts of the members of the 'organization' must be linked to the 'organization'. Several factors may be indicative. A specific collectivity of persons with some kind of policy level and hierarchical structure, the capacity to impose the policy on its members and to sanction them, induces a particular relationship between the policy level of that 'organization' and its members. Generally, any of the acts of a member of that 'organization' will be ascribed to the 'organization'. Further, any such act of an individual that following such a policy, is condoned by the policy-making level of the 'organization' may be attributable. The attribution may also be ascertained in the event that members of the 'organization' use the means of the 'organization' to attack any civilian population.[86]

Determining whether terrorist attacks by individual members can be linked to an organisation will be difficult in the context of transnational terrorist groups. As discussed in Chapter 2 of this book, some transnational terrorist groups are structured into network cells, which may have a tenuous link to the overall group.[87] As a result, it is difficult to ascribe the acts of an individual member

82 Ibid., para. 61.
83 Ibid., para. 65.
84 Ibid., para. 52.
85 Ibid., para. 51.
86 Ibid., para. 69.
87 See p. 27 of this book.

or cell to the 'organisation'. Indeed, network cells of some transnational terrorist groups do not receive any direct orders and carry out attacks autonomously without using the 'means of the organisation'.[88]

Overall, the majority of the judges in the *Kenya Investigation Authorisation Decision* made a distinction between groups that have the capability to perpetrate acts that violate fundamental human rights values and those do not. Conversely, Judge Kaul stressed that only non-state actors with a state-like nature fulfil the requirement of an organisation under Article (2)(a) of the Rome Statute. Classifying attacks by network-based transnational terrorist groups that are not state-like as a crime against humanity under the Rome Statute would be difficult in light of the jurisprudence of the ICC. In particular, it would be difficult for the prosecution to prove that a transnational terrorist group is a collectivity and established to achieve a common purpose due to their fragmented organisational structure. For example, the main group of ISIS operating in Iraq and Syria would appear to have a hierarchical structure but outside of these territories the group appears to be organised in network cells, which operate independently of the main group. As considered in Chapter 2 of this book, it would be difficult for the prosecutor to prove that the centralised command of the main group has the capacity to impose a policy on the members of these network cells.

1 Determining what constitutes a 'policy' to commit crimes against humanity

The definition of a 'policy' to commit terrorist attacks is also highly contested.[89] One can start with the basic premise set out in the Elements of Crimes Addendum to the Rome Statute, which provides that a policy to attack 'requires that the State or organization actively promote or encourage such an attack against a civilian

88 Ibid.

89 Article 7(2)(a) of the Rome Statute of the International Criminal Court. See also Mahnoush Arsanjani, 'The Rome Statute of the International Criminal Court', *American Journal of International Law* 93 (1999) 22–43, p. 31, where he notes that the phrase 'organisational policy' applies to non-state actors. However, see also Marcello Di Filippo, 'Terrorist Crimes and International Co-operation: Critical Remarks on the Definition and Inclusion of Terrorism in the Category of International Crimes', *European Journal of International Law* (2008) 533–570, p. 567; Matt Halling, 'Push the Envelope Watch It Bend: Removing the Policy Requirement and Extending Crimes against Humanity', *Leiden Journal of International Law* (2010) 827–845, p. 833; Leila Sadat, 'Emerging from the Shadow of Nuremberg: Crimes against Humanity in the Modern Age' (Washington University, St. Louis Legal Studies Research Paper, 2012), pp. 84–92; Gerhard Werle and Boris Burghardt, 'Do Crimes against Humanity Require the Participation of a State or a "State-like" Organization?', *Journal of International Criminal Justice* (2012) 1151–1170, p. 1167; Yann Jurovics, 'Article 7: Crimes contre l'humanité', in J. Fernandez and X. Pacreau (eds), *Statut de Rome de la cour pénale international: commentaire article par article* (Pedone, 2012) 417–478, p. 464; Charles Jalloh, 'What Makes a Crime against Humanity a Crime Against Humanity', *American University International Law Review* (2013) 381–441, pp. 416–417.

population'.[90] Yet at the Rome Conference, numerous states including the permanent members of the UN Security Council expressed concern about the 'widespread or systematic' test for determining whether an act constitutes a crime against humanity.[91] While some delegations at the Rome Conference were of the view that disparate and isolated crimes could not be categorised as an attack[92] other delegations suggested that the 'widespread or systematic' test could be adopted so long as isolated and disparate crimes were not included in the definition of an 'attack'.[93]

The Rome Conference was not the only occasion the over-inclusiveness of the 'widespread or systematic' test was questioned. ICTY Trial Chamber II in the *Tadić* case and the International Law Commission's (ILC) Draft Code of Crimes 1996 also noted this problem and proposed that the term 'policy' should not be described as including attacks that are 'isolated, random acts of individuals'.[94] Likewise, the Trial Chamber compared the 'policy' element with the conditions laid down by the ILC in its Draft Code of Crimes 1996 and stated that an attack must be 'instigated or directed by a Government or by any organization or group'.[95] Both the ICTY Trial Chamber and the ILC designated this element as supplementary to the 'widespread or systematic' test.[96]

The Trial Chamber in the *Tadić* case also stressed that the 'policy need not be formalized and can be deduced from the way in which the acts

90 The Elements of Crimes are reproduced from the *Official Records of the Assembly of States Parties to the Rome Statute of the International Criminal Court, First Session, New York, 3–10 September 2002* (United Nations Publication, Sales No. E.03.V.2 and corrigendum), part II.B. The Elements of Crimes adopted at the 2010 Review Conference are replicated from the *Official Records of the Review Conference of the Rome Statute of the International Criminal Court, Kampala, 31 May–11 June 2010* (International Criminal Court Publication, RC/11), p. 5.

91 Harmen von Hebel and Darryl Robinson, 'Crimes within the Jurisdiction of the Court', in R. Lee (ed.), *The International Criminal Court: The Making of the Rome Statute* (Martinus Nijhoff, 1999) 92–103, pp. 92–98. See also Phylilis Hwang, 'Defining Crimes against Humanity in the Rome Statute of the International Criminal Court', *Fordham International Law Journal* 22 (1998) 457–504.

92 *Report of the Preparatory Committee on the Establishment of an International Criminal Court*, vol. II (Compilation of proposals), UN GAOR, 51st session, Supp. No. 22A, UN Doc. A/51/22 (1996).

93 Ibid.

94 *Tadić* Opinion and Judgment (n. 59), para. 653.

95 Ibid., para. 655; ILC Draft Code of Crimes against the Peace and Security of Mankind, A/RES/51/160 of 16 December 1996, p. 47 (Article 18), available at http://legal.un.org/ilc/texts/instruments/english/draft%20articles/7_4_1996.pdf (date accessed: 14 March 2018)

96 Ibid. See also *Tadić* Opinion and Judgment (n. 59), para. 653. The Canadian delegation at the Rome Conference proposed that Article 7(2)(a) of the Rome Statute should be explicitly based on the findings of the Trial Chamber in the *Tadić* case and the ILC Draft Code of Crimes. See further Darryl Robinson, 'Defining Crimes against Humanity at the Rome Conference', *American Journal of International Law* 93 (1999) 43–57.

occur'.[97] However, the Trial Chamber in *Prosecutor* v. *Blaškić* went even further by stating that this policy need not have been devised at the highest levels of the organisation.[98] Besides endorsing that the plan 'need not necessarily be declared expressly or even stated clearly and precisely'[99] the decision in the *Blaškić* case also listed a number of factors from which the policy element could be implied including the scale of the particular acts and the repetition of those acts.[100] In the wake of the ICTY decision in *Prosecutor* v. *Kunarac*, the ICTR and the Special Court for Sierra Leone (SCSL) have also held that the policy element is not obligatory.[101] However, the decision in the *Blaškić* case still provides a valuable guide for the ICC on the content of the policy element.[102]

97 *Tadić* Opinion and Judgment (n. 59), para. 653. The case, *Prosecutor* v. *Kupreškić* also confirmed that 'the policy need not be explicitly formulated' (IT-95–16-T, Judgment, 14 January 2000, para. 551). See also *Prosecutor* v. *Kordić and Čerkez*, IT-95-14/2-T, Judgment, 26 February 2001, para 181. The draft Elements of Crimes initially contained a provision specifying that a policy to commit crimes could be implied from the way in which the attacks occurred. However, it was deleted from the final draft because it was deemed unnecessary. See further Roy Lee et al. (eds), *The International Criminal Court: Elements of Crimes and Rules of Procedure and Evidence* (Transnational Publishers, 2001), p. 77. Delegations from Canada and Germany were of the view that '[t]he existence of a policy may be inferred on the basis of the available evidence as to the facts and circumstances. It is not necessary to prove that a policy has been formally adopted'. See more on this point, see UN Doc. PCNICC/1999/WGEC/DP.36, 23 November 1999.

98 *Prosecutor* v. *Blaškić*, IT-95-14-T, Judgment, 3 March 2000, para. 205.

99 Ibid., para. 204.

100 Ibid. Other tribunals have affirmed these factors. For example, SCSL held that a policy can be inferred from the way in which attacks occur. In particular, the SCSL in *Prosecutor* v. *Fofana and Kondewa*, SCSL-04-14-A, Appeal Judgment, 28 May 2008, para. 307 concluded that '[i]n view of these findings of fact taken as a whole, the Appeals Chamber is of the view that the criminal conduct against those civilians was neither random nor isolated acts but was rather perpetrated pursuant to a common pattern of targeting the civilian population'. See also the decisions of the ICTR in *Prosecutor* v. *Akayesu*, ICTR-96-4-T, Judgment, 2 September 1998, para. 508; *Prosecutor* v. *Rutaganda*, ICTR-96-3-T, Judgment, 6 December 1999, para. 68; *Prosecutor* v. *Musema*, ICTR-96-13-T, Judgment, 27 January 2000, para. 204 which affirmed that a policy needs to be formally adopted.

101 *Prosecutor* v. *Kunarac*, IT-96-23/1-A 12, Appeal Judgment, 12 June 2002, para. 98; *Prosecutor* v. *Semanza*, ICTR-97-20-T, Judgment, 15 May 2003, para. 329; CDF Case Note 100.

102 The 1994 Commission on Experts, which was established pursuant to UN Security Council Resolution 780 on crimes in the former Yugoslavia, acknowledged that the policy element can be inferred from the circumstances in which the crimes occurred. In particular, the Commission noted that '[t]here is sufficient evidence to conclude that the practices of "ethnic cleansing" were not coincidental, sporadic or carried out by disorganized groups or bands of civilians who could not be controlled by the Bosnian-Serb Leadership'. Even more importantly the Commission concluded that '[i]t should not be accepted at face value that the perpetrators are merely uncontrolled elements, especially not if these elements target almost exclusively groups also otherwise discriminated against and persecuted. Unwillingness to manage, prosecute and

This interpretation of the policy requirement has also found support in domestic criminal courts, which have acknowledged that a policy can be inferred from the circumstances surrounding the perpetration of the attacks.[103] For example, in *Prosecutor* v. *Mitar Rašević and Savo Todović*, the Court of Bosnia and Herzegovina, applying a legal provision identical to the wording of Article 7(2) of the Rome Statute, specified a number of factors from which a policy to commit an attack could be inferred such as:

> concerted action by members of an organization or State; distinct but similar acts by members of an organization or State; preparatory acts prior to the commencement of the attack; prepared acts or steps undertaken during or at the conclusion of the attack; the existence of political, economic or other strategic objectives of a State or organization furthered by the attack; and in the case of omissions, knowledge of an attack or attacks and wilful failure to act.[104]

However, as seen in the previous section international criminal tribunals continuously make a distinction between crimes that have state or organisational support and crimes that are sporadic and haphazard.[105]

Due to an inclination to combine the 'policy' and 'systematic' elements of crimes against humanity, the differences between the two elements under Article 7 were not examined. The ICC must apply its own pertinent law and therefore any examination of the approach adopted by other international tribunals is ancillary. In particular, Article 21(1)(a) of the Rome Statute clearly states that the Court shall apply '[i]n the first place, the Statute, Elements of Crimes and its Rules of Procedure and Evidence'.[106] With regard to transnational terrorist groups the

punish uncontrolled elements may be another indication that these elements are, in reality, but a useful tool for the implementation of a policy of crime against humanity.' For further reference, see *Final Report of the Commission of Experts Established Pursuant to Security Council Resolution 780 (1992)*, UN Doc. S/1994/674, 27 May 1994, paras 84–85 and 142.

103 The Argentine case *Cámara Nacional de Apelaciones en lo Criminal y Correccional Federal de Buenos Aires (C.Fed), 9/12/1985, 'Causa No. 13/84 (Juicio a las Juntas Militares)', Sentencia* 9 December 1985, Second Part, para. 3(c), available at www.derechos.org/nizkor/arg/causa13/cap20.html (date accessed: 14 March 2018). See also the Guatemalan case *Tribunal de Alto Riesgo A, Sentencia* C-01076-2011-00015 (Rios Montt, Rodriguez Sanchez), 2 May 2011, Folio 697.

104 *Prosecutor* v. *Mitar Rašević and Savo Todović*, Court of Bosnia and Herzegovina, 28 February 2008, Case No. X-KR/06/275, available at www.legal-tools.org/en/doc/6a28b5 (date accessed: 14 March 2018). See also the Guatemalan case of *Tribunal de Alto Riesgo A, Sentencia* C-01076-2011-00015 (Rios Montt, Rodriguez Sanchez) 2 May 2011, Folio 697, available at: http://paraqueseconozca.blogspot.com (date accessed: 30 December 2014); judgment pending appeal against the dismissal of a defence motion to excuse two judges: Corte de Constitucionalidad, 20 May 2013, available at: www.right2info.org/resources/publications/constitutional-court-judgment-5.20.2013 (date accessed: 14 March 2018).

105 See p. 50 of this book.

106 Article 21(1)(a) of the Rome Statute of the International Criminal Court.

definition of the term 'policy' is ambiguous because it can have both formalistic and non-formalistic undertones. The term can be regarded as formalistic because it refers to a strategy or plan that is officially adopted. However, it can also be regarded as non-formalistic as it constitutes a 'course of action adopted as expedient'.[107] Both elements are difficult to prove in the context of attacks by transnational terrorist groups because as discussed in Chapter 2 some transnational terrorist groups have a network-based organisational structure and thus lack a centralised command to formulate a policy for the overall group.[108] Even though the network cells may have a common goal they often operate under their own direction.[109] So it is difficult to establish whether the overall transnational terrorist group has adopted or even formulated a policy to conduct attacks. Consequently, it will be inherently difficult for the ICC to prosecute members of transnational terrorist groups for crimes against humanity.

Moreover, the decision of Pre-Trial Chamber I in *Prosecutor* v. *Laurent Gbagbo* also illustrates the dangers of equating 'policy' with evidence of 'systematic' terrorist attacks.[110] Gbagbo, the former President of the Ivory Coast, currently stands trial as an indirect perpetrator of crimes against humanity, namely murder, sexual crimes, and persecution. These acts were allegedly perpetrated by the Ivorian Defence and Security Forces and pro-Gbagbo youth militia and mercenaries following the presidential election.[111] The prosecutor's case focused almost exclusively on four particular incidents where more than 294 crimes were committed against civilians. In mid 2013, Pre-Trial Chamber I, by a majority, concluded that the evidence presented by the Prosecutor was insufficient to prove the allegations and ordered an adjournment of the confirmation hearing to allow the Office of the Prosecutor more time to document and present further evidence.[112] In an attempt to prove the policy element the prosecution presented a considerable amount of direct evidence such as witness statements, videos and photographs of the alleged crimes in addition to indirect evidence. Even though public statements by pro-Gbagbo political leaders as well as internal instructions were also presented as evidence[113] the majority of the Pre-Trial Chamber requested

107 *Oxford English Dictionary* (Oxford University Press, 2012, 2nd edn), vol. XII, at p. 27.

108 See p. 32 of this book.

109 Ibid.

110 *Prosecutor* v. *Laurent Gbagbo, Decision Adjourning the Hearing on the Confirmation of Charges pursuant to Article 61(7)(c)(i) of the Rome Statute,* ICC-02/11-01/11, 3 June 2013.

111 For further reference, see 'Document Amendé de Notification des Charges', ICC-02/11-01/11-184-AnxI-Red, paras 21, 37, 40, 44, 50, and 81–84 (available in French only), 13 July 2012. See also *Prosecutor* v. *Laurent Gbagbo, Amicus Curiae Observations of Professors Robinson, de Guzman, Jalloh and Cryer,* ICC-02/11-01/11, 9 October 2013, available at: www.icc-cpi.int/iccdocs/doc/doc1662514.pdf (date accessed: 14 March 2018).

112 *Gbagbo* (n. 110).

113 For example, see 'Document Amendé' (n. 111), paras 21, 37, 40, 44, 50, 81–84.

supplementary evidence concerning meetings at which the policy to attack protestors was implemented.

In particular, the Pre-Trial Chamber sought to know:

> [h]ow, when and by whom the alleged policy/plan to attack the 'pro-Outtara civilian population' was adopted, including specific information about meetings at which this policy/plan was allegedly adopted, as well as how the existence and content of this policy/plan was communicated or made known to members of the 'pro-Gbagbo forces' once it was adopted.[114]

The Pre-Trial Chamber also requested evidence about the organisation and structure of the Ivorian Defence and Security Forces and the youth militia groups as well as the manner in which they operated.[115] The majority of the Pre-Trial Chamber was of the opinion that the policy element must satisfy stringent evidential requirements. The difficulty with this approach is that it suggests a rigid formula for determining the policy element because the Pre-Trial Chamber specifically requested evidence of the meetings at which the policy was implemented and the communication of this policy to the pro-Gbagbo forces.[116]

Thus, the Pre-Trial Chamber can be criticised for being too cautious about the type of conduct from which the policy element can be inferred. The Pre-Trial Chamber was hesitant about the conclusions it was asked to infer from the presented evidence and as a result requested additional evidence that the inner political circle of Gbagbo adopted a formal policy to orchestrate attacks against civilians. Since it overlooked that a policy will nearly always be inferred from the manner in which the acts took place, the Pre-Trial Chamber's request is contradictory to the jurisprudence of the ICTY, the ICTR, and the SCSL which have time and again declared that a policy need not be formally adopted and can be deduced from the way in which the attacks occurred.[117]

Instead, the Pre-Trial Chamber could have easily implied the policy from the improbability that more than 294 crimes perpetrated by pro-Gbagbo forces against anti-Gbagbo protestors happened by chance. Categorising the crimes as individual acts perpetrated without any state or other organisational involvement is illogical. Essentially, the Pre-Trial Chamber attributed the same meaning to the terms 'policy' and 'systematic'.[118] By requesting direct evidence of the formal adoption of a policy by pro-Gbagbo forces the Chamber undermined the relationship between Articles 7(1) and (7)(2)(a) of the Rome Statute.[119]

114 *Gbagbo* (n. 110), para. 44.
115 Ibid.
116 Ibid.
117 *Prosecutor* v. *Kunarac*, IT-96–23/1-A 12, Appeal Judgment, 12 June 2002, para. 98; *Prosecutor* v. *Semanza*, ICTR-97–20-T, Judgment, 15 May 2003, para. 329; CDF Case Note 100, para. 307.
118 Article 7 of the Rome Statute of the International Criminal Court.
119 Ibid.

The case, *Prosecutor* v. *Callixte Mbarushimana*, also illustrates the difficulty in applying the Pre-Trial Chamber's interpretation of the policy element to transnational terrorist groups.[120] Pre-Trial Chamber I refused to confirm the charges against Mbarushimana because it was not satisfied that he was personally responsible for war crimes perpetrated by subordinate members of the Forces démocratiques de libération du Rwanda (FDLR), pursuant to Article 25 of the Rome Statute.[121] The most striking aspect of the Pre-Trial Chamber's decision is that the majority held that the accused's responsibility for crimes against humanity had not been established.[122] The Prosecutor adopted the same strategy in the *Gbagbo* case by presenting direct and indirect evidence to infer the policy element of the alleged crime. This evidence included written records and witness testimony that there were orders to attack civilians and a report of a UN Special Rapporteur on the tactics of the FDLR.[123] Despite this compelling evidence the majority of the Pre-Trial Chamber was not satisfied that there was a policy to attack civilians.[124]

Regrettably, the Chamber considered each piece of direct evidence of policy individually rather than examining all the evidence together. However, the most frustrating aspect of its decision is the contradictory finding that the FDLR did not direct any attack against civilians even though it stated earlier in its decision that this had in fact occurred.[125] Following its examination of whether there was sufficient evidence of war crimes, the majority affirmed:

> that the FDLR soldiers were directly ordered to take revenge on both civilians and soldiers, as the name of the operation, i.e. 'eye for an eye', also suggests. The orders for the attack were clear: 'everything which has breath shouldn't be there at all'. Orders were given: 'destroy everything because everybody who was considered as [their] enemy', 'we don't want to hear anything, anybody there, anything in Busurungi', and 'everything that moves should be killed'. The soldiers were then expected to kill anyone they met because

120 *Prosecutor* v. *Callixte Mbarushimana, Decision on the Confirmation of Charges*, ICC-01/04-01/10, 16 December 2011, para. 295.

121 Ibid. See also *Prosecutor* v. *Callixte Mbarushimana, Judgment on the Appeal of the Prosecutor against the Decision of Pre-Trial Chamber I of 16 December 2011 entitled 'Decision on the Confirmation of Charges'*, ICC A.Ch. ICC-01/04-01/10 OA 4, 30 May 2012, available at: www.icc-cpi.int/iccdocs/doc/doc1420080.pdf (date accessed: 14 March 2018)

122 *Prosecutor* v. *Callixte Mbarushimana* (n. 120)

123 *Mbarushimana Confirmation Decision* (n. 121), paras 242–267. Former members of the FDLR testified that they were ordered 'to carry out attacks that will make the civilian population suffer', to 'set fire to houses without regard for the civilians "because the civilians were our enemies as well" and that "everything that has breath shouldn't be there at all" meaning that the village would have to be annihilated' (paras 248–250).

124 Ibid., para. 265.

125 Ibid.

everything in the village, and to 'annihilate the whole place . . . as a sign to . . . Congolese'.[126]

The evidence also showed that:

> even after the FARDC and Mai Mai were chased away, civilians were killed by being directly fired upon, cut into pieces with hooks and machetes or burnt alive inside their homes. Witness 561 saw several corpses of civilians, including women and children. Witness 683 saw civilians being slaughtered and about forty dead bodies lying in the village; the burnt bodies were too many to count. Witness 562 saw civilians being killed with machetes or burned in houses after the Congolese soldiers had been chased away from the village . . . Witness 562 . . . [also] saw around thirty-five or forty corpses of civilians, including women and children, some of which were burnt, cut into pieces or with skulls broken . . . Witness 650 counted seventy-nine bodies of adults and children who had been burnt alive in their houses, had gunshot wounds or had been cut with machetes.[127]

On the face of it, these acts would fulfil the requirements of Article 7(2)(a). The governmental or organizational policy requirement can be readily implied from the recurring attacks by the FDLR on villages. In fact, the Pre-Trial Chamber noted that the purpose of the attacks was to target civilians.[128]

One rationale for the Pre-Trial Chamber's findings in both the *Gbagbo* and *Mbarushimana* cases is that it may have been persuaded by the notion that 'policy' involves conduct that is more substantial than the issuance of orders to subordinates such as the adoption of a formal strategy by the high command of the group. This view is compelling because the Chamber's finding that the subordinates of the group in each case were ordered to carry out attacks on civilians should have been clear evidence of such a policy. The Pre-Trial Chamber's reluctance in both the *Mbarushimana* and *Gbagbo* cases to declare there was a policy to attack civilians is unusual in light of the case law of the ad hoc tribunals.[129] The only justification for the Chamber's approach is its concern with the clandestine rationale for the attacks on civilians.[130]

126 Ibid., para. 144.
127 Ibid., para. 149.
128 Ibid., para. 151.
129 *Prosecutor* v. *Kunarac,* IT-96-23/1-A 12, Appeal Judgment, 12 June 2002, para. 98; *Prosecutor* v. *Semanza*, ICTR-97–20-T, Judgment, 15 May 2003, para. 329; CDF Case Note 100, para. 307.
130 For example, in the *Mbarushimana Confirmation Decision* (n. 121), paras 243 and 245–246 the prosecution argued that the objective of the FDLR in attacking civilians was to bring about a 'humanitarian catastrophe'. However, the Pre-Trial Chamber at paras 250–251 and 254 was of the view that the attacks were simply reprisals on the civilian population to force them to flee their homes.

However, when an organisation carries out attacks on civilians they are classified as a crime against humanity regardless of the underlying reasons for them. The killings were not indiscriminate or unplanned but were directed by an armed group thereby satisfying the requirements of the policy element. By establishing in the *Mbarushimana* case, for example, that the FDLR intentionally attacked civilians the majority of the Pre-Trial Chamber had in reality fulfilled the requirements to establish that the FDLR carried out the acts pursuant to a policy. It is therefore difficult to rationalise the Pre-Trial Chamber's decision not to confirm the charges against *Mbarushimana*. Perhaps the Pre-Trial Chamber was of the view that there could only be one purpose for the policy? Then again, multiple different purposes do not diminish the fact that the FDLR did indeed have a policy to specifically target civilians during attacks. One hypothesis is that the Pre-Trial Chamber thought attacks carried out for revenge could not be regarded as crimes against humanity.[131] Nevertheless, the judiciary has confused the criteria for determining crimes against humanity with the criteria for determining the crime of genocide by examining whether there was a special intent to destroy a group.[132]

Alternatively, the Pre-Trial Chamber should have applied the precise wording of Article 7 by accepting that the policy element can be implied from the manner in which the alleged crimes occurred. This would have been in keeping with the jurisprudence of the ad hoc tribunals.[133] Although, one could contend that the ICC should not consider the jurisprudence of these bodies because the Rome Statute provides its own unique regulatory framework Article 7 still denotes the general and well-established principles of ICL and indeed echoes customary international law.[134] Indeed, the ICC is permitted to consider the approaches adopted by international tribunals and national courts for two reasons. First, the principle of systemic integration laid down in Article 31(3)(c) of the Vienna Convention on the Law of Treaties provides that 'any relevant rule of international

131 However, see the Dissenting Opinion of Judge Monageng, ICC-01/04-01/10-465-Red, para. 17 where she noted that retaliatory attacks do not change the fact that there was a clear policy to attack civilian populations. Indeed, there seems to be a growing emphasis in ICC jurisprudence on the criteria states and organisations should use to select the victims of their international crimes.

132 Article 6 of the Rome Statute of the International Criminal Court. Once the judiciary determines that the civilians were killed intentionally the next issue is whether these killings stemmed from genocidal intent or some other reason. The Pre-Trial Chamber's decisions in both the *Gbagbo* case and the *Mbarushimana* case applied a special intent requirement for determining whether there was a policy to carry out crimes against humanity. Applying the special intent approach to allegations of crimes against humanity has led to some bizarre decisions in domestic jurisdictions. For example, the US District Court of Northern California in *Bowoto* v. *Chevron Corporation*, 2007 US Dist. LEXIS 59374 (US District Court, Northern California), pp. 31 and 32 ruled that there were no crimes against humanity because the individuals were targeted because they were 'oil protestors' and not because they were civilians.

133 See Article 21 of the Rome Statute of the International Criminal Court.

134 See further *Report of the Preparatory Committee on the Establishment of an International Criminal Court*, vol, I, UNGAOR, 55th session, Supp. No. 22, A/51/22 (1996), paras 51–54.

law' must be taken into consideration in order to fully appreciate the wider legal situation.[135] Article 21 (1)(b) of the Rome Statute also provides that the ICC must not only consider international treaties but also 'principles and rules of international law'.[136] As already noted above the jurisprudence of the ICTY, ICTR, and the SCSL demonstrates that a policy can be implied from the manner in which the acts were committed. Indeed, the purpose of the policy element is to exclude random crimes committed by individuals who are not a part of a criminal plan.

The judiciary in the Pre-Trial Chamber of the *Gbagbo* case and the *Mbarushimana* case should have followed the general principles and rules of international law as clearly stated in Article 21 (1)(b) of the Rome Statute and paid closer attention to the jurisprudence of other international tribunals and national courts when applying Article 7 of the Rome Statute. Indeed, the Chamber's requests for direct evidence of a policy were completely impractical. The conclusion that Article 7 only applies to crimes if they are committed pursuant to a policy and approved at the highest levels of the organisation will have major consequences for holding members of transnational terrorist groups accountable before the ICC because when they plan and perpetrate terrorist attacks against civilians they often purposely avoid creating an evidential footprint. In addition, as discussed in Chapter 2 because of the various types of transnational terrorist groups which carry out attacks it is difficult to assume that only groups with a formal hierarchical structure can commit such acts.[137]

E Conclusion

The conceptual and operational development of the ICC set out above has been fundamentally influenced by the jurisprudence of other international courts and tribunal for the past 70 years. Modern views on international crime, like many areas of international law were redefined at the end of the Second World War. The horrors of the war along with Hiroshima and the Holocaust traumatised an already dazed international community into fundamental advances in international legal protections. The Nuremberg Trials, the International Military Tribunal for the Far East, the ICTY, and the ICTR formed the basis for bringing individuals to justice for international crimes of the gravest concern to the international community while the ratification of the Rome Statute led to the foundation of the ICC, the first permanent court to address international crimes. While the

135 Article 31(3) (c) of the Vienna Convention on the Law of Treaties. See also International Law Commission, Fragmentation of International Law: Report of the Study Group, UN Doc. A/CN.4/L.682, 13 April 2006, paras 410–423.

136 Article 21 (1)(b) of the Rome Statute of the International Criminal Court. For further analysis of Article 21, see Margaret de Guzman, 'Article 21', in O. Trifterrer (ed.), *Commentary on the Rome Statute of the International Criminal Court: Observers' Notes, Article by Article* (Hart, 2008, 2nd edn) 701–748, pp. 707–8.

137 See p. 31 of this book. For further commentary on this point, see Jalloh (n. 89), 381–441.

jurisprudence of the ad hoc tribunals as well as the wording of Article 8 clearly propounds the view that attacks by transnational terrorist groups will constitute a war crime if they are perpetrated in an armed conflict situation the theoretical underpinnings of Article 8 can be challenged in light of the reality that the vast majority of attacks by transnational terrorist groups are perpetrated in non-armed conflict situations.

Prosecuting members of transnational terrorist groups on the grounds of crimes against humanity will be difficult because as identified in Chapter 2 they are composed of network cells that do not directly communicate with each other. As a result, it could be difficult for the prosecution to prove that there was a policy to carry out terrorist attacks. Evidence of recurrent attacks of a significant scale as well as evidence of public statements, prior warnings and statements during attacks is the type of evidence from which the ad hoc international tribunals and domestic courts have implied this policy element. Once the prosecution produces compelling evidence of 'widespread or systematic' attacks as well as the policy element, the threshold for 'attack' under Article 7(2)(a) of the Rome Statute is satisfied. However, the jurisprudence of the ICC illustrates a disquieting propensity to suffuse the policy element with requirements that are not within the Rome Statute. Indeed, the ICC Pre-Trial Chamber appears to be imposing unrealistic conceptions of the policy element which will exclude many definitive cases of crimes against humanity by transnational terrorist groups. If these problems are not addressed, it will make the ICC an incongruous mechanism for prosecuting crimes against humanity cases against members of these groups.

The judiciary of the ICC needs to urgently reconsider the relationship between Articles 7(1) and 7(2)(a) and the objective of the policy element. The best solution is for the judiciary to correct its approach through its jurisprudence by either, a Pre-Trial, Trial or Appeals Chamber decision when the opportunity arises. However, the Appeals Chamber has to date not corrected the problem despite having had the opportunity to do so.[138] Thus, the other course of action would be to amend the Elements of Crimes to stipulate the precise components of the policy element.[139] Although, this course of action should not be taken nonchalantly the problem is so extreme that the alternative approach of allowing the judiciary to correct the jurisprudence through a future decision is unfeasible. The judiciary, for the moment, are of the firm view that there must be direct evidence of the policy element and that this cannot be inferred from the circumstances in which the attacks occurred. As a result, the prosecution of members of transnational terrorist groups on the ground of crimes against humanity will be exceedingly difficult in light of their interpretation of the policy element in the *Gbagbo* and *Mbarushimana* cases.

138 *Prosecutor* v. *Callixte Mbarushimana* (n. 121). For more commentary on the Appeal Chamber's decision, see generally Ruth Frolich, '*Prosecutor* v. *Callixte Mbarushimana*: Judgment on the Appeal of the Prosecutor against the Decision of Pre-Trial Chamber I of 16 December 2011 Entitled "Decision on the Confirmation of Charges": Introductory Note', *International Legal Materials* 52(2) (2013) 417.

139 The Elements of Crimes (n. 90), Part II.B.

This chapter has shown there is considerable divergence of opinion both within international legal thought and across disciplines such as international law and international relations. The classification of attacks by transnational terrorist groups under the current wording of the Rome Statute remains a highly contested area, and determining what constitutes an 'international crime' from either a legal or non-legal perspective can be challenging. Yet, despite the ongoing debate, no one would contest that attacks by transnational terrorist groups constitute a significant challenge for both international politics and international law. Therefore, it is necessary to now turn to the question of whether a customary crime of transnational terrorism has emerged in international law in light of an interlocutory decision of the Special Tribunal for Lebanon in 2011 and how it could be prosecuted before the ICC.

4 The evolution of an international crime of transnational terrorism

A Introduction

The past 30 years has seen the formal creation, elaboration, and enforcement of a wide range of international treaties prohibiting specific types of terrorism. Some may argue that the need for an amendment of the Rome Statute to include a crime of transnational terrorism is a foregone conclusion.[1] As proclaimed by the Dutch delegation during the 8th session of the Assembly of State Parties to the ICC in 2009, terrorism is a threat to international peace and security and international accountability is essential when states with jurisdiction are unwilling or unable to prosecute suspects of terrorist attacks.[2] Yet globally, the mechanisms, frameworks, and implementation of international treaties designed to tackle terrorism have often been sporadic, ad hoc, and unenforceable. There has not been a lack of treaties designed to suppress terroristic activity, but instead a lack of implementation of existing international treaties.[3] If this is the case, is there a need for the Assembly of State Parties to amend the Rome Statute to ensure that it can be applied to new types of situations?

As a counterpart to Goldstone and Simpson's belief that the legal framework of the ICC can sufficiently prosecute attacks by transnational terrorist groups, there is a risk that classifying terrorism as an international crime under the current wording of the Rome Statute could complicate its ability to respond to its own internal

1 For further academic commentary on this point, see Kathleen Maloney-Dunn, 'Humanizing Terrorism through International Criminal Law: Equal Justice for Victims, Fair Treatment of Suspects, and Fundamental Human Rights at the ICC', *Santa Clara Journal International Law* 8 (2010) 69–86, p. 74; Matthew Lippman, 'The New Terrorism and International Law', *Tulsa Journal of Comparative and International Law* 10 (2003) 297, p. 354; Eric Bales, 'Torturing the Rome Statute: The Attempt to Bring Guantanamo's Detainees within the Jurisdiction of the International Criminal Court', *Tulsa Journal of Comparative and International Law* 16 (2009) 173–191, p. 188.

2 Assembly of State Parties to the Rome Statute of the International Criminal Court, 8th Session at Annex II, at paras 40–51 and Annex I, at para. 41, ICC Doc. ICC-ASP/8/20 (18–26 November 2009).

3 See generally Nico Schrijver, 'Responding to International Terrorism: Moving the Frontiers of International Law for "Enduring Freedom"', *Netherlands International Law Review* 48(3) (2001) 271–291.

weaknesses and contradictions.[4] So would the explicit recognition of a customary crime of transnational terrorism enhance the accountability of members of transnational terrorist groups before the ICC or is the creation of such a crime an example of the international legal elite redefining the problem of transnational terrorist groups in order for them to fit into the prevailing international consensus on how such problems should be resolved?

It is not possible within the confines of this chapter to examine in detail the development and conceptual basis for customary international law in general.[5] However, the chapter will discuss whether a customary crime of transnational terrorism exists in international law, but in order to do so it is necessary for the following section to analyse the processes that lead to the evolution of the legal concept of terrorism and the connected concerns regarding the proliferation of an international crime of terrorism. The subsequent section discusses whether there is a substantial difference between the customary crime of transnational terrorism laid down by the STL,[6] and the prohibitions on terrorist attacks in international treaties which posit that states must bring individuals responsible for terrorist attacks to justice.

As the international legal framework surrounding the criminalisation of attacks by transnational terrorist groups contains both explicitly binding normative obligations and also a wealth of non-binding resolutions that are difficult to enforce, this chapter concludes that the Rome Statute does not adequately capture the metamorphic nature of transnational terrorist groups and their crimes. Thus, an amendment of the Rome Statute is needed to bring members of transnational terrorist groups to justice before the ICC where states are unwilling or unable to

4 See generally Richard Goldstone and Janine Simpson, 'Evaluating the Role of the International Criminal Court as a Legal Response to Terrorism', *Harvard Human Rights Journal* 16 (2003) 13–26.

5 Among the voluminous writings by lawyers on the topic, see Anthony D'Amato, *The Concept of Custom in International Law* (Cornell University Press, 1971); Michael Akehurst, 'Custom as a Source of International Law', *British Yearbook of International Law* 47 (1974–1975) 1–53, pp. 38–42; Hersch Lauterpacht, *The Development of International Law by the International Court* (Cambridge University Press, 1958), pp. 368–393; Jorg Kammerfhofer, 'The Uncertainty in the Formal Source of International Law: Customary International Law and Some of Its Problems', *European Journal of International Law* 15 (2004) 523–553; International Law Association, 'Statement of Principles Applicable to the Formation of General Customary International Law', in *Report of the Sixty-Ninth Conference*, London, 2000, p. 713; Ian MacGibbon, 'Customary International Law and Acquiescence', *British Yearbook of International Law* 33 (1957) 115–145, p. 131; Myres McDougal et al., *Studies in World Public Order* (Yale University Press, 1960), p. 763; Ted Stein, 'The Approach of the Different Drummer: The Principle of the Persistent Objector in International Law', *Harvard International Law Journal* 26 (1985) 457–482; Jonathan Charney, 'The Persistent Objector Rule and the Development of Customary International Law', *British Yearbook of International Law* 56 (1985) 1–24; James Crawford, *I. Brownlie:, Principles of International Law* (Oxford University Press, 2012, 8th edn), p. 22.

6 *Interlocutory Decision on the Applicable Law: Terrorism, Conspiracy, Homicide, Perpetration, Cumulative Charging* (Appeals Chamber) STL-11-01/I, 16 February 2011, para. 1.

investigate and prosecute them. On the basis of this understanding, the key question that needs to be asked is: has transnational terrorism become a crime under international law? And, if so, what is the legal basis for such a determination?

Criticism of the interlocutory decision by the Appeals Chamber of the STL reveals considerable opposition to the existence of such a crime.[7] Therefore, for a crime of transnational terrorism to exist we must get to a stage where a process of interactions and interpretations between and within states has led to the internalisation of the crime into both domestic and international legal frameworks. This chapter will contend that this stage has not yet been reached at the international level in regard to a specific crime of transnational terrorism. So, while there has been a range of statements from academics, the STL, and some governments, plus examples of state practice, we cannot yet say definitively that a crime of transnational terrorism has passed into the realm of general international law or the corpus of international criminal law.

Nevertheless, it is proposed in this chapter that the broad range of existing law and practice relating to the prevention and response to terrorist attacks by transnational terrorist groups, both in armed conflict and non-armed conflict situations, is evidence that a customary crime of transnational terrorism will eventually crystallise in international law. Indeed, the emergence of this crime would be in parallel with previous practice at the ICTY on the crime of terrorism in armed conflict situations. As examined in Chapter 5, leaders of transnational terrorist groups will be held criminally responsible under the doctrine of command responsibility if they knew or had reason to know that their subordinates committed or were about to commit international crimes.[8] However, because of the network-based organisational structure of many of these groups it can be hard to discern whether the leader ordered the attacks or failed to prevent and punish them.[9] So the concept of transnational terrorism has a significant bearing on the application of the Rome Statute to members of these groups in light of their organisational structure.

Yet, as with many international legal instruments a proposed amendment of the Rome Statute to include a crime of terrorism would highlight the need for a definition of terrorism in the Elements of Crimes Addendum or indeed the statute itself. As will be seen in Chapters 5 and 6, an amendment would also provide much needed clarification on how the doctrine of command responsibility and the doctrine of co-perpetration apply to network-based transnational terrorist groups. I will now briefly examine the development of the legal concept of transnational terrorism to understand why an amendment of the Rome Statute is needed, before examining why a customary crime of transnational terrorism has not yet emerged in international law in the context of the global system for responding to

7 For example, see Ben Saul, 'Legislating from a Radical Hague: The United Nations Special Tribunal for Lebanon Invents an International Crime of Transnational Terrorism', *Leiden Journal of International Law* 24 (2011) 677–700.

8 See pp. 107–110 of this book.

9 See p. 28 of this book.

attacks by transnational terrorist groups. I will then briefly propose the constitute elements of a crime of transnational terrorism if the Rome Statute were amended.

B The evolution of the legal concept of terrorism

There is little consensus concerning what conduct constitutes an act of terrorism.[10] This has made it difficult to adopt an international convention to criminalise acts of transnational terrorism that includes a legally binding, all-inclusive definition of the term.[11] Indeed, Stern contends that '[h]undreds of definitions of terrorism are offered in the literature. Some focus on the perpetrators, others on their purposes, and still others on their techniques.'[12] By and large an unlawful act will only be classified as terroristic 'in all circumstances . . . when it is said to have been directed at a particular purpose or, in other words, to have a particular motive'.[13]

The objective of transnational terrorism is 'to cause fear, death, serious bodily injury and property damage to a person, group or general population in order to force a government or international organisation to perform or refrain from performing a particular act'.[14] So it is the perpetration of attacks with the purpose to provoke fear in the civilian population in order to attain a particular political objective, which differentiates them from ordinary criminal acts such as mass murder. Both acts entail the same action and outcome; bringing about the death of numerous individuals by unlawful means. Conversely, the label of terrorism raises acts that would normally be dealt with under ordinary law, to something that is required to be dealt with under special law.[15] This is because if a person 'has a political, ideological or religious motivation, it is thought that the deterrent effect generally associated with the criminal law is less likely to have an impact on prospective offenders'.[16]

10 See generally, Ben Saul, *Defining Terrorism in International Law* (Oxford University Press, 2008); Antonio Cassese, 'Terrorism as an International Crime', in A. Bianchi and Y. Naqvi (eds), *Enforcing International Law Norms Against Terrorism* (Hart, 2004) 213–225, p. 213.

11 Fiona de Londras, 'Terrorism as an International Crime', in W. Schabas and N. Bernaz (eds), *Routledge International Book of Criminal Law* (Routledge, 2010), p. 167.

12 Jessica Stern, *The Ultimate Terrorist* (Harvard University Press, 1999), p. 11; UN Security Council Resolutions 731 (1992) and 1624 (2005).

13 de Londras (n. 11), p. 168.

14 Anna Brennan, 'Investigating the Accountability of Transnational Armed Groups under International Law for Armed Attacks', *Boolean* 2 (2011), p. 6, available at: http://publish.ucc.ie/boolean/2011/00/Brennan/02/en (date accessed: 14 March 2018).

15 Conor Gearty, 'The Super-Patriotic Fervour of the Moment', *Oxford Journal of Legal Studies* 28(1) (2008) 183–200, p. 189.

16 Ibid.; Anna Brennan, 'The Difficulties in Defining Terrorism under International Law' (Human Rights in Ireland Blog, 11 October 2011), available at http://humanrights.ie/criminal-justice/the-difficulties-in-defining-terrorism-under-international-law (date accessed: 14 March 2018).

Accordingly, some commentators have called for efforts to formulate a generally accepted definition of terrorism to be abandoned in favour of a more practical approach whereby terrorism would be recognised as an international crime without a precise definition.[17] This is precisely the position adopted by the UN Security Council which has developed its own counter-terrorism mechanism without incorporating a definition of terrorism.[18] Regardless of this pragmatic outlook, it must be emphasised that the lack of a definition of terrorism presents additional difficulties when terrorism is described as a threat to international peace and security.[19] Permitting states to determine what conduct constitutes terrorism creates legal ambiguity which makes the precise scope of the state's obligation to prosecute suspected members of terrorist groups unclear.

Despite these conceptual challenges the UN has endeavoured to develop a universally acceptable definition of terrorism. In 2005, a UN panel proposed the following definition:

> any action, in addition to actions already specified by the existing conventions on aspects of terrorism, the Geneva Conventions and Security Council resolutions 1566 (2004) that is intended to cause death or serious bodily harm to civilians or non-combatants, when the purpose of such an act, by its nature and context, is to intimidate a population, or to compel a Government or an international organization to do or to abstain from doing any act.[20]

However, it was subsequently rejected by UN member states because it incorporates an ambiguous reference to 'civilians or non-combatants' which implicitly refers to wartime terminology which has major implications under IHL since the majority of terrorist attacks occur during non-armed conflict situations. In addition, the definition goes further than the description of the term in UN Security Resolution 1566 (2004) because it clearly states that it is 'in addition to' the acts already listed in the Resolution. The UN Special Rapporteur on counter-terrorism has criticised this approach and has advocated a more precise definition restricted to the cumulative characteristics set out in Resolution 1566 (2004).[21]

Nevertheless, the UN made further progress on the definition of terrorism at the World Summit in 2005 where the Outcome Document, which was universally

17 Report of the Sub-Commission Special Rapporteur on Terrorism and Human Rights, *Specific Human Rights Issues: New Priorities, in particular Terrorism and Counter-Terrorism*, UN Doc. E/CN.4/Sub.2/2004/40 (2004) at para. 30; see also the Rapporteur's 1997 Report, UN Doc. E/CN.4/Sub.2/1997/28.

18 UN Security Council Resolution 1373 (2001); Brennan (n. 17).

19 Michael Lawless, 'Terrorism: An International Crime', *International Journal* 63(1) (2007/2008) 139, p. 147.

20 UN Secretary General, *In Larger Freedom: Towards Development, Security and Human Rights for All*, UN Doc. A/59/2005 (21 March 2005), para. 91.

21 Report of the UN Special Rapporteur on the Promotion and Protection of Human Rights while Countering Terrorism, Martin Scheinin, *The Protection and Promotion of Human Rights While Countering Terrorism*, UN Doc. E/CN.4/2006/098 (2005), para. 36.

endorsed by world leaders, included an 'unqualified condemnation of terrorism'.[22] Efforts by the UN to develop a definition of terrorism that will be accepted by all member states are currently ongoing in the Comprehensive Convention of International Terrorism.[23] However, this has also reached a stumbling block due to concerns about the precise scope of the right to self-determination including whether it includes a right to use force and engage in wars of national liberation.[24] As a result, attempts by the international community to reach consensus on a definition of terrorism have thus far been futile.

C The emergence of a customary crime of transnational terrorism

On 14 February 2005, 21 people including the former Prime Minister of Lebanon, Rafiq Hariri, were killed when a vehicle, containing explosives, was blown up in close proximity to his motorcade.[25] The UN and the government of Lebanon negotiated an agreement to establish the STL to investigate and prosecute the individuals allegedly responsible for the act.[26] In contrast to the ICC and the ad hoc international tribunals which have been established to date, the STL is unique because the crime of transnational terrorism is included in its subject-matter jurisdiction.[27] The first case to come before the Appeals Chamber was submitted by the Pre-Trial Chamber in January 2011. The Appeals Chamber was asked, to consider, *inter alia*, three questions concerning the crime of transnational terrorism. In particular:

i Whether the Tribunal should apply international law in defining the crime of terrorism;
ii (ii) If so, how the international law of terrorism should be reconciled with any difference in the Lebanese domestic crime of terrorism; [and]
iii (iii) In either case what are the objective and subjective elements of the crime of terrorism to be applied by the Tribunal.[28]

22 Ibrahim Gambari, 'A Multilateral Response to Terrorism', in *Commonwealth Ministers Reference Book* (Henley Media Group, 2006), available at: www.un.org/terrorism/docs/gambari_med-final.pdf (date accessed: 14 March 2018).
23 UN General Assembly Resolution 63/129, UN Doc. A/RES/63/129 (29 January 2009).
24 Report of the Sub-Commission Special Rapporteur on Terrorism and Human Rights, Specific Human Rights Issues: New Priorities, in particular Terrorism and Counter-Terrorism, UN Doc. E/CN.4/Sub.2/2004/40 (2004) at para. 30; see also the Rapporteur's 1997 report, UN Doc. E/CN.4/Sub.2/1997/28.
25 *BBC News*, 'Beirut Blast "Was Suicide Attack"' (15 February 2005), available at: www.newsvote.bbc.co.uk/mpapps/pagetools/print/news.bbc.co.uk/2/hi/middle_east/4266587.stml (date accessed: 14 March 2018).
26 Bardo Fassbender, 'Reflections on the International Legality of the Special Tribunal for Lebanon', *Journal of International Criminal Justice* 5(5) (2007) 1091–1105, p. 1093.
27 Article 2(1)(a) of the Statute of the Special Tribunal for Lebanon, adopted pursuant to UN Security Council Resolution 1664 (2006) of 29 March 2006.
28 *Order on Preliminary Questions Addressed to the Judges of the Appeals Chamber pursuant to Rule 68, paragraph (G) of the Rules of Procedure and Evidence* STL- I I-O1/I, 21 January 2011.

Thirty days after the submission was lodged, the Appeals Chamber delivered a unanimous decision that there is a customary crime of transnational terrorism under international law.[29]

Relying on international law to interpret the Lebanese Criminal Code the Appeals Chamber devised a definition of transnational terrorism containing three distinct elements:

a the perpetration of a criminal act (such as murder, kidnapping, hostage-taking, arson, and so on), or threatening such an act;
b the intent to spread fear among the population (which would generally entail the creation of a public danger) or directly or indirectly coerce a national or international authority to take some action, or to refrain from taking it; and
c when the act involves a transnational element.[30]

The special intent requirement, *dolus specialis*, could include conduct that does not result in terror. The Appeals Chamber appears to have laid down a bifurcated special intent standard necessitating two alternative *mens rea* standards:

> (i) an intent to spread fear amongst the population (which would generally entail the creation of public danger) *or* (ii) directly or indirectly coerce a national or international authority to take some action, or to refrain from taking it.[31]

Where these two standards do not intersect the second standard has the potential to be over-inclusive and encompass conduct that would not normally be regarded as transnational terrorism such as civil protests.[32] So this broad standard could be used as a tool for governments to subdue political opponents. The Appeals Chamber has tried to sidestep any criticism of its approach by contending that the standard is not important since, 'a terrorist generally coerces by spreading fear [and the] two articulations of the special intent required for the crime of terrorism, in practical terms, largely overlap with each other'.[33] The 'means' part of the definition was interpreted too broadly by the Appeals Chamber. Lebanese courts have repeatedly asserted that the list under Article 314 of the Lebanese Criminal Code is not all-inclusive. Any additional means of conducting a terrorist attack not contained in Article 314 must be similar to the means that are laid down in the provision.

The Appeals Chamber's definition inflates the 'means' requirement of 'acts that cause public danger' to also include other behaviour such as 'murder, kidnapping,

29 For further academic commentary, see Matthew Gillet and Mathias Schuster, 'Fast-Track Justice: The Special Tribunal for Lebanon Defines Terrorism', *Journal of International Criminal Justice* 9 (2011) 989–1020.
30 *Interlocutory Decision* (n. 6), para. 85.
31 Ibid.
32 Ibid., para. 223 (emphasis in original text).
33 Ibid.

hostage taking, arson and so on'.[34] The use of the phrase 'and so on' at the end of the phrase suggests that the term 'means' is open-ended.[35] Since the Appeals Chamber noted that 'the expansive judicial interpretation of potential ambiguities is not merely a remote hypothesis'[36] in combination with the two-pronged intent standard, the fluid definition of terrorism implies that it is possible for crimes committed during political protests such as common assault to fall within the definition of terrorism propounded by the Appeals Chamber. As Guillet and Schuster note 'political protests in support of dissidents like Aung San Suu Kyi of Myanmar could possibly fall within this definition if they involved criminal conduct'.[37] Thus, the distinctive criminal character of terrorism is watered down leading to the possible exploitation of the offence.

By expanding the principle of *dolus specialis* and the means requirement, the Appeals Chamber has broadened the definition of terrorism and incorporated conduct that was previously not considered terrorism under Article 314 of the Lebanese Criminal Code. Nevertheless, this broader definition of terrorism can be contested since it violates the principle of *nullum crimen sine lege*. Pursuant to this principle, an individual can only be punished for an act that was criminalised by law at the time the act was committed. In other words, the accused must be aware that particular conduct is illegal.[38] The Appeals Chamber blatantly rejected this argument on the grounds that the crime of terrorism was already established in international law at the time the terrorist attacks occurred.[39]

The final aspect of the definition which requires consideration is the transnational element. Ventura is of the view that this element has 'a far greater impact than simply to distinguish between international and domestic terrorism'.[40] However, the Appeals Chamber did not explain the parameters of this transnational element since it only requires a 'connection of perpetrators, victims or means . . . across two or more countries' or 'a significant impact [on] international peace and security'.[41] The definition should have included an additional requirement namely the condemnation of the act by the international community. Ventura notes that:

> it would be an odd result to, on the one hand, rely on international condemnation of and attention to terrorism to extract the requirement of a transnational element, and on the other hand, not to demand similar international attention or condemnation (such as a Security Council or

34 *Interlocutory Decision* (n. 6), para. 85.
35 Ibid.
36 Guillet and Schuster (n. 29), p. 1010.
37 Ibid., p. 1011.
38 Interlocutory Decision (n. 6), para. 131.
39 Ibid.
40 Manuel Ventura, 'Terrorism According to the STL's Interlocutory Decision on the Applicable Law', *Journal of International Criminal Justice* 9 (2011) 1021–1042, p. 1024.
41 *Interlocutory Decision* (n. 6), para. 90.

General Assembly Resolution) when seeking to satisfy this same element in a particular case.[42]

This also raises a number of human rights considerations. Article 15 of the International Covenant on Civil and Political Rights (ICCPR) provides for a principle of legality in that '[n]o one shall be held guilty of any criminal offence on account of any act or omission which did not constitute a criminal offence, under national or international law, at the time it was committed'.[43]

Providing that the definition of terrorism existed at the time of the commission of the criminal offence 'states would only need to . . . add a transnational element to their existing definitions (provided they include the other two identified elements) in order to be able to prosecute persons retroactively'.[44] This accordingly requires the identification of the precise date as to when the emergence of the customary crime of terrorism occurred. Unfortunately, the Appeals Chamber did not consider when precisely the crime emerged.

D Sources of law relied upon by the STL Appeals Chamber to deduce a customary crime of transnational terrorism

The most contentious aspect of the interlocutory decision is the conclusion of the Appeals Chamber that a customary crime of transnational terrorism has emerged in international law. The finding came after almost 50 years of deadlock in negotiations that had sought to agree on a comprehensive definition of the crime.[45] The Appeals Chamber relied on a vast array of evidence to support its conclusion including UN Security Council and General Assembly resolutions, domestic criminal law, case law, and international treaties. Following an analysis of these sources, it concluded that even though variances in definitions of terrorism remained, these had not hindered the emergence of the customary crime of transnational terrorism.[46]

1 National law

The Appeals Chamber endeavoured to infer a customary crime of transnational terrorism from national law.[47] Although an analysis of national laws may impart considerable evidence of state practice and *opinio juris*, on their own they were not satisfactory evidence of custom.[48] Following an examination of the laws of 37

42 Ventura (n. 40), p. 1024.
43 Article 15 of ICCPR.
44 Ventura (n. 40), p. 1025.
45 For more commentary on these negotiations, see Michael Sharf, 'Defining Terrorism as the Peacetime Equivalent of War Crimes: Problems and Prospects', *Case Western Reserve Journal of International Law* 36 (2004) 359–374, pp. 360–65.
46 *Interlocutory Decision* (n. 6), para. 97.
47 Ibid., para. 88.
48 *Lotus (France* v. *Turkey)* at 96 (Separate Opinion of Judge Altamira); Karol Wolfke, *Custom in Present International Law* (Martinus Nijhoff, 1993, 2nd edn), p. 148.

states[49] the Appeals Chamber determined that national laws, 'consistently define terrorism in similar, if not identical terms to those used in international instruments'.[50] In light of the considerable number of national laws which prohibit terrorism an in-depth examination of the national laws considered by the Appeals Chamber lays bare the incomplete nature of its analysis.

First, it did not make a distinction between national laws that address domestic terrorism and national laws that address transnational terrorism. Only the national laws of Argentina,[51] Belgium,[52] Ecuador,[53] France,[54] Finland,[55] Germany,[56] India,[57] Jordan,[58] Mexico,[59] the Netherlands,[60] New Zealand,[61] Pakistan,[62] Panama,[63] Peru,[64] the Philippines,[65] the Seychelles,[66] Saudi

49 The national laws considered were those of Argentina, Australia, Austria, Belgium, Brazil, Canada, Chile, Columbia, Ecuador, Egypt, France, Finland, Germany, India, Iran, Iraq, Jordan, Mexico, the Netherlands, New Zealand, Pakistan, Panama, Peru, Philippines, Russian Federation, Saudi Arabia, Seychelles, South Africa, Sweden, Tunisia, United Arab Emirates, United Kingdom, United States, and Uzbekistan.

50 *Interlocutory Decision* (n. 6), para. 91.

51 Article 213ter of the Argentinian Penal Code.

52 Article 137(1) of the Belgian Criminal Code.

53 Articles 158, 159, and 160.1 of the Ecuadorian Criminal Code.

54 Article 421-1 of the French Penal Code states that 'Constituent des actes de terrorisme, lorsqu'elles sont intentionnellement en relation avec une entreprise individuelle ou collective ayant pour but de troubler gravement l'ordre public par l'intimidation ou la terreur, les infractions suivantes: (I) les atteintes volontaires à la vie'.

55 Pursuant to s. 34(a) of the Criminal Code particular crimes will be classified as terrorism where they are committed 'with terrorist intent and in a manner that is likely to cause serious harm to a State or to an international organization'.

56 *Stra/gesetzbuch* [Criminal Code] 4 July 2009, *Bundesgesetzblall* [Federal Law Gazette] 1 3322, as amended, s. 129(a), para. 2.

57 See further s. 4 of the Unlawful Activities (Prevention) Amendment Act 2008, No. 35.

58 Jordan has stated that it amended its definition of terrorism in 2001 in order to comply with UN Security Council Resolution 1373 (2001). See *Report to the Counter-Terrorism Committee* (Jordan), 24 March 2006, S1200612 12, p. 1. Terrorism is criminalised in Article 148 of the Jordanian Criminal Code.

59 *Código Penal Federal* [CPF], as amended by *Diario Oficial de la Federación* [DO], 20 August 2009, Article 139.

60 See further Article 1(D) of the Crimes of Terrorism Act, 24 June 2004.

61 See s. 5 of the Terrorism Suppression Act 2002, 2002 SNZ No. 34 which defines terrorism.

62 See s. 6 of the Anti-Terrorism Act 1997 as amended by Ordinance No. XXXIX of 2001, Act 11 of 2005, and Ordinance No. XXI of 2009; National Public Safety Commission, *Anti-Terrorism Manual* (National Police Bureau, 2008) which traces the recent development of Pakistan's terrorism laws, available at: www.unodc.orgltldblpdflPakistan_Anti-terrorism_Manual_2008.pdf (date accessed: 14 March 2018).

63 Article 287 of the Panamanian Criminal Code.

64 Article 2 of Decree Law No. 25475.

65 Section 3 of the Human Security Act 2007, Rep. Act No. 9372.

66 See further s. 2 of the Prevention of Terrorism Act 2004. The Supreme Court of the Seychelles in *Republic* v. *Doh* (26 July 2010) summarised the definition of terrorism at para. 37 as involving 'indiscriminate violence with the *objective of influencing governments or international organizations* for *political ends*' (emphasis in original).

Arabia,[67] Sweden,[68] the Russian Federation,[69] the United States,[70] and Uzbekistan[71] concerning transnational terrorism should have been taken into consideration by the Appeals Chamber.[72] In particular, the Appeals Chamber noted that the transnational element

> will typically be a connection of perpetrators, victims, or means used across two or more countries, but it may also be a significant impact that a terrorist act in one country has on another – in other words, when it is foreseeable that a terrorist attack that is planned and executed in one country will threaten international peace and security, at least for neighbouring countries.[73]

The rationale for this element is to discount from the definition of transnational terrorism 'those crimes that are purely domestic, in planning, execution, and direct impact'.[74] However, domestic terrorist attacks can be just as serious as transnational terrorist attacks in terms of civilian deaths and property damage.[75] The 'exclusion of the transnational element from the domestic crime of terrorism, as defined by most countries' criminal codes, does not detract from the essential communality of the concept of terrorism in international and domestic criminal law'.[76] However, the exclusion allows states to increase their investigative powers and accountability mechanisms and to define serious crimes as terrorism which may not have a transnational element.[77]

The second criticism of the Appeal Chamber's approach to national laws is that it relied on domestic definitions of terrorism adopted for both criminal purposes

67 See *Report to the Counter-Terrorism Committee* (Saudi Arabia), 26 December 2001, S/200111294, p. 5. According to an Interpol document, the Kingdom's Council of Senior Religious Scholars issued a statement on terrorism in which it declared that: 'bloodshed, the violation of honour, the theft of private and public property, the bombing of dwellings and vehicles and the destruction of installations are, by the consensus of Muslims, legally forbidden because they violate the sanctity of the innocent, destroy property, security and stability and take the lives of peaceable human beings in their homes and at their work'. Under sharia law, crimes of terrorism are included in crimes of hirabah. Such crimes warrant the highest penalties as set forth by the Quran, available at: www.interpol.intlpubliclbioterrorism/nationallawslSaudiArabia (date accessed: 14 March 2018).

68 Law (2003: 148) on the crime of terrorism.

69 Article 3 of the Federal Law, No. 35-FZ of 6 March 2006 on Counteraction against Terrorism.

70 18 USC §2331.

71 Pursuant to Article 155 of the Criminal Code, as amended by the Law of the Ruz. No. 254–11, 29 August 2001.

72 In particular see the national laws of Argentina, Belgium, Brazil, Ecuador, France, Finland, Germany, Iran, Jordan, New Zealand, Pakistan, Panama, Peru, the Philippines, Seychelles, Saudi Arabia, Sweden, Russian Federation, and Uzbekistan.

73 *Interlocutory Decision* (n. 6), para. 90.

74 Ibid. For example, the Oklahoma City bombing of 1995 and ETA bombings in Spain.

75 Ibid.

76 Ibid.

77 Ibid.

and non-criminal purposes, when only the former should have been taken into consideration.[78] States use different definitions of terrorism in civil, administrative, and criminal law.[79] These definitions are inherently inconsistent with each other and do not support the conclusion that state practice is unanimously consistent on the definition of terrorism.[80] Third, the Appeals Chamber relied on a number of national laws that breach international human rights law for, 'being too [broad and] vague to satisfy the principle of legality and freedom from retroactive criminal punishment'.[81]

Indeed, many of the definitions do not comply with Article 15 of the ICCPR.[82] In particular, in his 2005 report the UN Special Rapporteur on the Protection and Promotion of Human Rights and Fundamental Freedoms while Countering Terrorism, Michael Schenin, noted alleged human rights violations by states such as Uzbekistan concerning the due process rights of individuals accused of terrorist offences during trial.[83] So the reliance by the STL Appeals Chamber on these national laws to substantiate its conclusion that a customary crime of transnational terrorism exists under international law is curious to say the least when such laws are a violation of the ICCPR.

Furthermore, the Special Rapporteur noted in his 2010 report that '[t]he adoption of overly broad definitions of terrorism carried the potential for deliberate misuse of the term – including as a response to claims and social movements of indigenous peoples – as well as unintended human rights abuses'.[84] The Special Rapporteur also added that failure to restrict domestic counter-terrorism laws poses 'the risk that . . . such laws will offend the principles of necessity and proportionality that govern the permissibility of any restriction'.[85] It can be thus

78 For examples, see s. 4 of the Unlawful Activities (Prevention) Amendment Act 2008, No. 35 (India); Article 3 of the Federal Law No. 35-FZ of 6 March 2006 on Counteraction against Terrorism (Russian Federation).

79 Nico Keijzer, 'Terrorism as a Crime', in W. Heere (ed.), *Terrorism and the Military: International Legal Implications* (Asser Press, 2003) 115–132, p. 121.

80 For instance, different definitions of terrorism are employed in the United States by the CIA, Defense Department, the FBI, and the State Department, as considered in *Flaow* v. *Iran* (1998) F Supp. 1, DDC 17.

81 Ben Saul, 'Amicus Curiae Brief – The Notion of Terrorist Acts', 14 February 2011, para. 41; Defence Office Submissions at para. 101; STL Factsheet, 'The Special Tribunal's standards of justice, including principles of due process, will be based on the highest international standards of criminal justice as applied in other international tribunals', available at: www.un.org/apps/news/infocus/lebanon/tribunal/factsheet.shtml (date accessed: 14 March 2018); Special Tribunal for Lebanon Rules of Evidence and Procedure, Rule 3(B) which states that '[a]ny ambiguity . . . shall be resolved by the adoption of such interpretation as is considered to be the most favourable to any relevant suspect or accused in the circumstances then under consideration'. See generally Saul (n. 7).

82 Report of the Special Rapporteur (n. 21), paras 27–28, 45–47, 56, and 62.

83 Ibid., para. 33. Scheinin also mentioned at paras 22 and 24 the alleged human rights violations by states such as the United States, the United Kingdom, and Jordan.

84 Ibid., para. 26.

85 Ibid.

inferred that 'the Appeal Chamber's punitive impulse to enlarge criminal liability for terrorism appears to overshadow its concern for human-rights considerations'.[86] By classifying the unlawful definitions of states such as Jordan[87] and the United Arab Emirates[88] as reflective of a universal comprehensive definition, the Appeals Chamber could be accused of encouraging and providing legitimacy to states to convict political opponents of terrorist offences.[89]

Finally, and perhaps most importantly, even where states do define the term 'terrorism' in their criminal law there are major discrepancies between the definitions. Ben Saul's analysis of state reports to the UN Counter-Terrorism Committee demonstrates clear and unequivocal evidence of these wide and varying differences.[90] For example he concluded that 87 countries did not have legislation defining the crime of terrorism or indeed terrorist offences while 46 states had basic definitions of terrorism and 48 states had multifactorial definitions of terrorism.[91] Instead of containing 'peripheral variations' as suggested by the Appeals Chamber, there are significant differences between the approaches adopted by states to defining terrorism.[92] Research conducted by both Weinberg *et al.* and Schmid and Jongman identifies between 73[93] and 106[94] variations in the definitions of terrorism adopted by states. Having analysed the 37 national laws utilised by the Appeals Chamber a significant incongruence in the definitions is clear. So, the lack of harmony in these laws can hardly support the conclusion that there is a comprehensive, universal definition of terrorism grounded on state practice.

2 UN Security Council Resolutions 1373 and 1566

The STL Appeals Chamber was of the strong view that the widespread condemnation of terrorism by the UN Security Council justifies the criminalisation of the offence under international law.[95] Even though UN Security Council

86 Saul (n. 7), p. 684.
87 Article 148 of the Jordanian Criminal Code.
88 Decree by Federal Law No. I of 2004 on Combating Terrorist Offences.
89 *Interlocutory Decision* (n. 6), para. 93.
90 See also the Global Survey of the Implementation of Security Council Resolution 1373 (2001) by Member States (2011), available at: www.un.org/en/sc/ctc/docs/2011-globalsurvey1373.pdf (date accessed: 14 March 2018) which provides at p. 86 that 'vague or overly broad definitions of terrorist offences continue to pose a challenge to effective implementation of resolution 1373 (2001)'.
91 Saul (n. 7), p. 684.
92 For further general commentary, see Ben Saul, 'The Curious Element of Motive in Definitions of Terrorism: Essential Ingredient or Criminalizing Thought?', in A. Lynch, E. MacDonald, and G. Williams (eds), *Law and Liberty in the War on Terror* (Federation Press, 2007) pp. 28–38.
93 Leonard Weinberg, Ami Perdzhur, and Sivan Hirsch-Hoefler, 'The Challenge of Conceptualizing Terrorism', *Terrorism and Political Violence Journal* 16 (2004) 777–794.
94 See generally Alex Schmid and Albert Jongman, *Political Terrorism: A New Guide to Actors, Authors, Concepts, Databases, Theories and Literature* (North Holland, 2005).
95 *Interlocutory Decision* (n. 6), para. 104.

resolutions were widely cited by the Appeals Chamber in support of its decision, such resolutions, albeit adopted under Chapter VII of the UN Charter, do not strictly produce new international law. Instead, they impose normative duties on UN member states pursuant to the UN Charter.[96]

However, since September 11, 2001 the UN Security Council has passed a number of binding and quasi-legislative resolutions aimed at combating terrorism in general.[97] The first UN Security Council resolution to proclaim 'a widespread stand on and a shared view to terrorism',[98] was Resolution 1373 (2001).[99] It affirmed transnational terrorism as a threat to 'international peace and security'[100] and imposed binding obligations on all UN member states to criminalise terrorist acts in domestic legislation

> All States shall ensure that any person who participates in the financing, planning, preparation or perpetration of terrorist acts or in supporting terrorist acts is brought to justice and ensure that, in addition to any other measures against them, such terrorist acts are established as serious criminal offences in domestic laws and regulations and that the punishment duly reflects the seriousness of such terrorist acts.[101]

96 Marc de Brichambaut, 'The Role of the United Nations Security Council in the International Legal System', in Michael Byers (ed.), *The Role of International Law in International Politics* (Oxford University Press, 2001) 269–276, p. 269. Among the voluminous writing by lawyers and political scientists on the topic of the UN Security Council's lawmaking role in relation to terrorism, see Rosa Giles-Carnero, 'Terrorist Acts as Threats to International Peace and Security', in P. Fernández-Sanchez, *International Legal Dimension of Terrorism* (Martinus Nijhoff, 2009) 55–71, p. 55; Jean Allain, 'The Legacy of Lockerbie: Judicial Review of the Security Council Actions or the First Manifestations of "Terrorism" as a Threat to International Peace?', *Indian Journal of International Law* 44(1) (2004) 74–112; Valeria Santori, 'The UN Security Council's (Broad) Interpretation of the Notion of the Threat to Peace in Counter-Terrorism', in G. Nesi (ed.), *International Cooperation in Counter-Terrorism: The United Nations and Regional Organisations in the Fight against Terrorism* (Ashgate, 2006) 89–111; Alexander Marschik, 'The Security Council's Role: Problems and Prospects in the Fight against Terrorism', in G. Nesi (ed.), *International Cooperation in Counter-Terrorism: The United Nations and Regional Organisations in the Fight against Terrorism* (Ashgate, 2006) 69–80; Paul Szasz, 'The Security Council Starts Legislating', *American Journal of International Law* 96(4) (2002) 901–905; Eric Rosand, 'Resolutions 1373 and the CTC: The Security Council's Capacity-Building', in G. Nesi (ed.), *International Cooperation in Counter-Terrorism: The United Nations and Regional Organisations in the Fight against Terrorism* (Ashgate, 2006) 81–88.

97 Eric Rosand, 'Security Council Resolution 1373, the Counter-Terrorism Committee and the Fight against Terrorism', *American Journal of International Law* 97 (2003) 333–341; Stefan Talmon, 'The Security Council as World Legislature', *American Journal of International Law* 96 (2005) 175–193; Jane Stromseth, 'The Security Council's Counter-Terrorism Role: Continuity and Innovation', *ASIL Proceedings* 97 (2003) 41.

98 *Interlocutory Decision* (n. 6), para. 92.

99 UN Security Council Resolution 1373 (28 September 2001).

100 Ibid.

101 Ibid., at para. 2(a).

However, the resolution did not attempt to define the term 'terrorism' for the purpose of domestic criminalisation, which permitted states to adopt their own legislative definitions. This led to the inconsistent implementation of the resolution with many states adopting definitions to suit their own political agendas.

As noted in the previous subsection, Security Council resolutions did not include a definition of terrorism until the passing of Resolution 1566 (2004) by which time the majority of UN member states had already criminalised terrorism.[102] This resolution provided a non-binding definition of terrorism, and so states were permitted to retain their own definitions.[103] Even though the common description of terrorism as a threat to international peace and security is noteworthy,[104] the resolutions do not assign universal jurisdiction to states to prosecute individuals suspected of carrying out terrorism offences.[105] In view of the range of different approaches adopted by states in defining the term, Security Council resolutions essentially constitute, 'soft law guide-posts',[106] suggesting the path for the development of the law on terrorism. However, in time, the Security Council's repetitive references to terrorism may gain normative importance for the development of the customary law of terrorism.

3 Case law

Pursuant to Article 38(1)(d) of the Statute of the International Court of Justice (ICJ) judicial decisions constitute an ancillary mechanism for ascertaining international legal rules.[107] As a result, case law may represent convincing evidence of a customary law norm.[108] Even though the STL Appeals Chamber relied on a number of judgments from domestic courts to support its conclusion that there is a crime of transnational terrorism in international law, all the judgments impart different definitions of the term. Nevertheless, the Appeals Chamber referenced nine judgments to support its conclusion.[109] Saul argues that a detailed examination of the cases reveals that the Appeals Chamber, 'misread, exaggerated, or

102 See p. 66 of this book.
103 UN Security Council Resolution 1566 (8 October 2004).
104 UN Security Council Resolutions 731 (1992), para. 2; 748 (1992), para. 7; 1044 (1996), p. 2; 1054 (1996), p. 2; 1070 (1996), p. 2; 1189 (1998), p. 1; 1193 (1998), p. 1; 1267 (1999), p. 1; 1368 (2001), para. 1; 1390 (2002), p. 2; 1455 (2003), p. 1; 1511 (2003), p. 1; 1526 (2004), p. 1 refers to terrorism as a threat to international peace and security.
105 Robert Kolb, 'Universal Criminal Jurisdiction in Matters of International Terrorism: Some Reflections on Statutes and Trends in Contemporary International Law', *Revue hellénique droit international* 1 (1997) 43–88, p. 77; Rosand (n. 97).
106 Oscar Schachter, 'The Quasi-Judicial Role of the Security Council and the General Assembly', *American Journal of International Law* 58 (1964) 960–965, p. 964.
107 Article 38(1)(d) of the ICJ Statute.
108 Antonio D'Amato, *The Concept of Custom in International Law* (Cornell University Press, 1971), p. 43.
109 *Interlocutory Decision* (n. 6), para. 100.

misinterpreted every one of those decisions'.[110] For instance, the Appeals Chamber cited the Canadian Supreme Court decision in *Suresh* v. *Canada* to substantiate its conclusion that national courts have recognised the existence of a crime of terrorism under international law.[111] But the Appeals Chamber failed to mention the Canadian Supreme Court's finding that 'there is no single definition that is accepted internationally'.[112] So the Appeal Chamber's misinterpretation of the decision is erroneous, to say the least.

Based on the development of state practice as evidenced by the judicial decisions of domestic courts, specific offences of terrorism such as hijacking, that have attained customary status[113] do not substantiate the argument that a comprehensive universal definition of terrorism has been agreed upon. The only case that clearly suggests that terrorism has developed into a customary crime is the Italian case of *Bouyahia Maher Ben Abdelaziz et al.* [114] Since the Supreme Court of Cassation judgment only provided a definition of the term terrorism and not transnational terrorism, it is completely at odds with the definition formulated by the STL Appeals Chamber. In particular, the Italian court required the additional element of a 'political, religious or ideological motivation in accordance with generally accepted international standards', in order for the conduct in question to constitute terrorism.[115] The court noted that without this particular element the conduct would not be classified as terrorism because it did not possess the element that transmutes ordinary criminal offences into the special crime of terrorism.[116]

The Appeals Chamber was of the view that incongruities in state practice on the inclusion of an additional element of ideological, political, religious or racial motive in the definition of terrorism have 'not yet been so broadly and consistently spelled out and accepted as to rise to the level of customary law . . . [I]t remains to be seen whether one day it will emerge as an additional element of the international crime of terrorism'.[117] The Appeals Chamber therefore dismissed this requirement as an element of the definition it adopted. In doing so, the Appeal Chamber's approach is questionable because it invoked the judgment as supportive of its conclusion of the existence of a customary crime of terrorism.

110 Saul (n. 7), p. 691.
111 *Suresh* v. *Canada (Minister for Immigration and Citizenship)* [2002] 1 SCR 3; *Interlocutory Decision* (n. 6), para. 86.
112 Ibid., pp. 53 and 94. The judge went on to state at p. 94 that 'one searches in vain for an authoritative definition'.
113 *Interlocutory Decision* (n. 6), para. 100. See also David Freestone, 'International Cooperation against Terrorism and the Development of International Law Principles of Jurisdiction', in K. Higgins and M. Flory (eds), *Terrorism and International Law* (Routledge, 1997), p. 50.
114 Judgment of 11 October 2006 Corte di Cassazione.
115 Ibid., para 2.1.
116 *Interlocutory Decision* (n. 6), paras 90–91 and 113.
117 Ibid., para. 106.

The Appeals Chamber also did not discuss a number of influential domestic judgments that directly contradict it[118] and merely consigned them to a single footnote.[119] It also completely ignored the judgment of the ICTY in *Prosecutor* v. *Galić*, which concluded that 'terrorism has never been singly defined under international law'.[120] Indeed, the Appeals Chamber only cited cases which were indicative of a customary crime of terrorism:

> In recent years courts have reached concordant conclusions about the elements of an international criminal of terrorism . . . Judicial decisions stating instead that no generally accepted definition of terrorism exists are far and few between, and their number diminished each year.[121]

It also overlooked a number of decisions that did not corroborate its conclusion. It ignored the US Court of Appeals' decision in *U.S.* v. *Yousef* [122] where the defendants were charged with conspiracy to bomb 12 aircraft in the Philippines which were bound for the United States. In reaching its decision, the US Court of Appeals for the 2nd Circuit considered whether there was universal jurisdiction over terrorism under customary international law. The court ruled that universal jurisdiction only applied to a 'limited set of crimes that cannot be expanded judicially', and determined that there is, 'no international consensus on the definition of terrorism or even its proscription'.[123] Taking into consideration the 'strenuous disagreement between states about what actions do or do not constitute terrorism'[124] the Court determined that terrorism 'is a term as loosely deployed as it is powerfully charged'.[125]

The Appeals Chamber also relegated two other significant cases to the footnotes of its interlocutory decision.[126] The first case was the Indian Supreme Court decision in *Madan Singh* v. *State of Bihar* where it was held that there needed to be consensus on the definition of terrorism before agreement on 'any meaningful international countermeasure[s]' could be reached.[127] In particular, Judge Arijit Pasayat indicated that the failure of the international community to reach consensus on a definition of terrorism has highlighted the difficulties in criminalising it.[128] The second case relegated to the footnotes was the French Court of Cassation judgment in the *Gaddafi* case which ruled that terrorism was not an

118 Defence Office's Submissions Pursuant to Rule I 76bis (B), STL-II-OIII, 31 January 2011, paras 98–101.
119 *Interlocutory Decision* (n. 6), para. 127.
120 *Prosecutor* v. *Galić*, IT-98–29, Judgment, 5 December 2003, fn. 150.
121 *Interlocutory Decision* (n. 6), para. 100.
122 *US* v. *Yousef et al.* 327 F 3d 56, US Court of Appeal, 2nd Circuit, 4 April 2003.
123 *Interlocutory Decision* (n. 6), para. 51.
124 *Yousef* (n. 122), pp. 106–108.
125 Ibid.
126 *Madan Singh* v. *State of Bihar* [2004] INSC 225 (2 April 2004) and *Gaddafi* 125 ILR 490 (2001) (Court of Cassation, France).
127 *Madan Singh* (n. 126), p. 500 (per Judge Arijit Pasayat).
128 Ibid.

international crime for the purposes of removing a head of state from office.[129] By not referring to these cases, the Appeal Chamber's conclusion that there is a body of jurisprudence which supports the emergence of a customary crime of terrorism can be challenged.

4 International and regional conventions and treaties

The Appeals Chamber was of the view that, 'most of the regional and multilateral conventions regarding terrorism incorporate into their definition of terrorism the specific offences criminalised in a long line of terrorism-related conventions'.[130] At the time, the UN had drafted approximately 13 international legal instruments that sought to tackle certain terrorist acts.[131] The Appeals Chamber held that these instruments corroborate the argument that there is a customary crime of terrorism.[132] However, each international treaty was drafted specifically because states could not agree on a definition of terrorism. The Appeals Chamber ignored

129 *Gaddafi* (n. 126). There is extensive academic commentary on the *Gaddafi* case: Salvatore Zappalá, 'Do Heads of State in Office Enjoy Immunity from Jurisdiction for International Crimes? The Ghaddafi Case before the French Cour de Cassation', *European Journal of International Law* 12(3) (2001) 595–612.

130 *Interlocutory Decision* (n. 6), para. 140.

131 Convention on Offences and Certain Other Acts Committed on Board Aircraft, 14 September 1963, entered into force 4 December 1969; Convention for the Suppression of Unlawful Seizure of Aircraft, 16 December 1970, entered into force 14 October 1971; Convention for the Suppression of Unlawful Acts against the Safety of Civil Aviation, 23 September 1971, entered into force 26 January 1973; Convention on the Prevention and Punishment of Crimes against Internationally Protected Persons, including Diplomatic Agents, 14 December 1973, entered into force 20 February 1977; International Convention against the Taking of Hostages, 17 November 1979, entered into force 3 June 1983; Convention on the Physical Protection of Nuclear Material, 26 October 1979, entered into force 8 February 1987; Convention for the Suppression of Unlawful Acts Against the Safety of Maritime Navigation, 10 March 1988, entered into force 1 March 1992; Protocol for the Suppression of Unlawful Acts against the Safety of Fixed Platforms Located on the Continental Shelf, 10 March 1988, entered into force 1 March 1992; Protocol for the Suppression of Unlawful Acts of Violence at Airports Serving International Civil Aviation, Supplementary to the Convention for the Suppression of Unlawful Acts against the Safety of Civil Aviation, 24 February 1988, entered into force 6 August 1989; Convention on the Marking of Plastic Explosives for the Purpose of Detection, 1 March 1991, entered into force 21 June 1998; International Convention for the Suppression of Terrorist Bombings, 15 December 1997, entered into force 23 May 2001; International Convention for the Suppression of the Financing of Terrorism, 9 December 1999, entered into force 10 April 2002; International Convention for the Suppression of Acts of Nuclear Terrorism, 13 April 2005, entered into force 7 July 2007; International Covenant on Civil and Political Rights, 16 December 1966, entered into force 23 March 1976; Council of Europe, European Convention for the Protection of Human Rights and Fundamental Freedoms, as amended by Protocols Nos. 11 and 14, 4 November 1950, entered into force 3 September 1953.

132 *Interlocutory Decision* (n. 6), para. 140.

the fact that none of these legal instruments contain a clear-cut definition of terrorism or create an international crime of terrorism *per se*.

Indeed, the Special Rapporteur on the Promotion and Protection of Human Rights and Fundamental Freedoms while Countering Terrorism noted that '[n]one of the 13 anti-terrorism conventions contains a comprehensive definition of the term "terrorism". Rather, the Conventions are operational in nature and confined to specific subjects.'[133] Thus, the treaties can only address specific types of terroristic activity. The UN Sub-Commission on the Promotion and Protection of Human Rights stated that because there is no international definition of terrorism 'the initial characterisation of an activity as "terrorist" is made by the domestic legal system'.[134] So there is very little evidence to support the finding of the Appeals Chamber that the treaties and conventions are evidence of an emerging customary rule of terrorism.

Regional treaties also contain diverse and contradictory definitions of terrorism. In particular the Inter-American Commission's Report on Terrorism and Human Rights asserts that '[i]n defining the parameters of members states' obligations, it must be recognized that to-date there has been no consensus on a comprehensive international legal definition of terrorism'.[135] Chapter II of the report states that '[a]t best . . . it may be said that the international community has identified certain acts of violence that are generally considered to constitute particular forms of terrorism'.[136] An initial construal of regional treaties shows a significant difference in how they have defined the term.[137] For example, the Inter-American Convention against Terrorism 1971 and the Organization of American States Convention to Prevent and Punish Acts of Terrorism Taking the Form of Crimes against Persons and Related Extortion that are of International Significance 2002 only focus on particular types of terroristic activity.[138] On the other hand, treaties such as the Council of Europe Convention on the Suppression of Terrorism 1977 do not create any offences whatsoever.[139]

133 Report of the Special Rapporteur (n 21), paras 37–38, 40–41.

134 United Nations Commission on Human Rights Sub-Commission on the Promotion and Protection of Human Rights, *Specific Human Rights Issues: New Priorities in Particular Terrorism*, 8 August 2003, p. 49. The Commission also noted at p. 23 that 'the efforts and initiatives taken in the framework of the United Nations indicate very clearly that almost universally insurmountable difficulties that, to this very day, stand in the way of formulating a single, acceptable general definition of the crime of "terrorism"'.

135 Inter-American Commission on Human Rights, *Report on Terrorism and Human Rights* (OEA/Ser.L/V/II.116, 2002).

136 Ibid.

137 Saul (n. 7), p. 677.

138 Organization of American States Convention to Prevent and Punish Acts of Terrorism Taking the Form of Crimes against Persona and Related Extortion that Are of International Significance 2002 and the Inter-American Convention against Terrorism 1971.

139 Council of Europe Convention on the Suppression of Terrorism, 1977. In addition, see South Asia Association for Regional Cooperation (SAARC) Regional Convention

Although some treaties include broad definitions of terrorism[140] other conventions recategorise ordinary criminal offences as terrorism.[141] Indeed, many of the regional treaties have not received much state support. For example, only one-quarter of OIC members have become parties to the OIC Convention on Combating International Terrorism. Even where states have become parties to these conventions they have not influenced state practice whatsoever.[142] Thus, it is very difficult to conclude that regional treaties are evidence that a customary crime of terrorism has emerged in international law.

5 UN General Assembly resolutions

The impact of terroristic activity has resounded in the UN General Assembly since the 1970s. The most noteworthy General Assembly resolution is the 1994 Declaration on Measures against International Terrorism which stated that 'criminal acts intended or calculated to provoke a state of terror in the general public, or group of persons or particular persons for political purposes are in any circumstance unjustifiable'.[143] This resolution is significant because the UN General Assembly was able to agree on a political definition of terrorism for the first time ever. It defined terrorism as:

> [c]riminal acts intended or calculated to provoke a state of terror in the general public, a group of persons or particular persons for political purposes are in any circumstances unjustifiable, whatever the consideration of a political, philosophical, ideological, racial, ethnic, religious or any other nature that may be invoked to justify them.[144]

General Assembly resolutions can convey a general consensus generating an expectation of compliance, which in time could become binding as a customary norm.[145] The predominant indicator that the 1994 Declaration has attained

on Suppression of Terrorism 1987 and the Commonwealth of Independent States Treaty on Cooperation in Combating Terrorism 1999.

140 Arab Convention for the Suppression of Terrorism, 1998; Organisation of the Islamic Conference (OIC) Convention on Combating International Terrorism; Organisation of African Unity (OAU) Convention on the Prevention and Combating of Terrorism, 1999; EU Framework Decision on Combating Terrorism, 2002.

141 Article 1(2) of the Arab Convention, 1998; Article 1(2) of the OIC Convention, 1999; Shanghai Cooperation Organization Convention on Combating Terrorism, Separatism and Extremism, 2001; Council of Europe Convention on the Prevention of Terrorism, 2005; SAARC Additional Protocol to the 1987 Convention, 2004; African Union Protocol to the 1999 Convention, 2004.

142 For instance, the OAU Convention on the Prevention and Combating of Terrorism, 1999 does not appear to have been ratified by many African states.

143 UN General Assembly 1994 Declaration on Measures against International Terrorism.

144 Ibid., para. 3.

145 Robert Jennings and Arthur Watts (eds), *Oppenheim's International Law* (Longman, 1992, 9th edn), p. 45.

customary status is that it was adopted without a vote. This implies that there was consensus among states to apply its provisions and this has since been repeated in a number of subsequent resolutions.[146]

A number of factors tempered the application of the 1994 Declaration. Even though every member of the UN sanctioned the declaration, the preamble underlines the need to develop and collate the law on terrorism gradually over time.[147] This is further supported by the fact that numerous member states have persistently called for the design of a legal definition of terrorism.[148] However, the adoption of the 1994 Declaration by consensus does not necessarily mean that states were unanimous on the need to develop a definition of terrorism but instead that there was an absence of opposition.[149] In addition, UN General Assembly resolutions adopted by consensus do not mean universal support of their provisions, because member states may not object on the grounds that the instrument is non-binding upon them.[150] The 1994 Declaration and the subsequent declarations upholding it illustrate that UN member states are still deeply divided on the definition of terrorism despite Security Council resolutions expressing a 'clear sign of deep concern regarding the problem'.[151] The 1996 Supplement to the 1994 Declaration supports the idea that the definition was not meant to be of any legal significance.[152] It gave the job of drafting a definition to the UN General Assembly's Ad Hoc Committee on Negotiating a Comprehensive Convention on Terrorism.[153]

146 See for example UN General Assembly Resolutions: A/RES/49/60 Annex (1994), para. 3; A/RES/64/118 (2009), para. 4; A/RES/63/129 (2008), para. 4; A/RES/62/71 (2007), para. 4; A/RES/61/40 (2006), para. 4; A/RES/60/43 (2005), para. 2; ARES159146 (2004), para. 2; A/RES/58/81 (2003), para. 2; A/RES/57/27 (2002), para. 2; ARES156188 (2001), para. 2; A/RES/55/158 (2000), para. 2; A/RES/54/1 10 (1999), para. 2, A/RES/53/108 (1998), para. 2; A/RES/52/165 (1997), para. 2; ARES/51/210 (1996), para. 2; A/RES/50/53 (1995), para. 2.

147 Preamble to the 1994 Declaration, para. 12.

148 XIV Ministerial Conference, Final Doc., Durban, 17–19 August 2004, paras 98, 99, 101–102, and 104; XIII Conference of Heads of State or Government, Final Doc., Kuala Lumpur, 25 February 2003, paras 105–106, 108, and 115; XIII Ministerial Conference, Final Doc., Cartagena, 8–9 April 2000, paras 90–91; OIC Resolutions 6/31-LEG (2004), para. 5; OIC, Islamic Summit Conference (10th session), Final Communiqué, Malaysia, 16–17 October 2003, para. 50.

149 Erik Suy, 'The Meaning of Consensus in Multilateral Diplomacy', in R. Akkerman, P. Van Krieken, and C. Pannenborg (eds), *Declarations on Principles: A Quest for Universal Peace* (Springer, 1977) 259–272, p. 272.

150 Peter Van Krieken, *Terrorism and the International Legal Order* (Asser Press, 2002), p. 121.

151 *Legality of the Threat or Use of Nuclear Weapon (Opinion)* [1996] ICJ Rep. 226 Advisory Opinion, para. 71.

152 Declaration to Supplement the 1994 Declaration on Measures to Eliminate International Terrorism, 1996.

153 See further the Mandate of the Ad Hoc Committee Established by General Assembly Resolution 51/210 of 17 December 1996, available at: www.un.org/law/terrorism (date accessed: 14 March 2018).

However, the Ad Hoc Committee has not been able to agree on a definition of terrorism since its foundation in 1996. The STL Appeals Chamber held that there is a 'large measure of approval' within the Ad Hoc Committee on the definition of terrorism.[154] This is a rather odd conclusion since the Committee itself reported in 2011 that delegations had still not agreed upon a definition of terrorism.[155] The Appeal Chamber's decision seems to have overlooked the fact that the Ad Hoc Committee, despite extensive negotiations for over 15 years, has not reached consensus on a definition of the term. The UN Draft Treaty is the best evidence yet that there is a lack of consistent state practice on the definition of terrorism.

E Classifying the customary crime of transnational terrorism as an international crime

On the basis of the above analysis, can we deduce that there is a crime of transnational terrorism under international criminal law? Many academics have rejected this possibility by simply maintaining that such a crime does not exist at the international level.[156] Other academics have only expressed criticism about certain aspects of the definition laid down by the STL Appeals Chamber without denunciating it outright. Instead, they have contended that the Chamber's interlocutory decision is part of the development process of a new customary rule.[157]

There is a clear distinction between fundamental international crimes and treaty-based crimes.[158] Since the latter are essentially transnational offences and their criminalisation is laid down in international treaties and conventions they can only be enforced by states at the national level.[159] On the other hand, international crimes are binding on individuals thereby imposing individual criminal responsibility. Ambos is of the view that, 'terrorism is a "special" transnational offence that may come closer to a true international crime than "ordinary" transnational offences'.[160] The reasoning underlying this contention is based on the *Tadić* criteria, namely the three criteria that must be fulfilled in order for the act to constitute a crime under international law.[161] These criteria are as follows:

154 *Interlocutory Decision* (n. 6), para. 88.
155 Report of the Ad Hoc Committee established by the General Assembly Resolution 51/210 of 17 December 1996, *Fifteenth Session Report A/66/37* (2011).
156 Gilbert and Schuster (n. 29), p. 1002. See also Michael Sharf, 'Special Tribunal for Lebanon Issues Landmark Ruling on Definition of Terrorism and Modes of Participation' (4 March 2011) *ASIL Insights*, available at: www.asil.org/insights110304.cfm (date accessed: 14 March 2018); Stefan Kirsch and Anna Oehmichen, 'Judges Gone Astray', *Durham Law Review* 1 (2011) 32, p. 40.
157 Ibid. See also: Kai Ambos, 'Judicial Creativity at the Special Tribunal for Lebanon: Is There a Crime of Terrorism under International Law?, *Leiden Journal of International Law* 24 (2011) 655–675, p. 657.
158 Ibid.
159 Ibid.
160 Ibid.
161 Ibid.

1 the respective underlying prohibition (primary norm) must be a part of international law;
2 a breach of this prohibition must be particularly serious, namely it must affect important universal values; and
3 the breach must entail individual criminal responsibility in its own right, namely independently of any criminalization in domestic criminal law.[162]

Even though the STL Appeals Chamber applied the same criteria in its interlocutory decision, it did not specify that the criteria originated from the *Tadić* case. The definition of transnational terrorism formulated by the Appeals Chamber arguably fulfils the first two criteria. In particular, the Chamber noted that the act in question 'needs to be regarded by the world community as an attack on universal values . . . or on values held to be of paramount importance in that community'.[163]

Referring to the concept of international custom laid down by the ICJ in the *Continental Shelf* cases[164] the Appeals Chamber noted there was:

> settled practice concerning the punishment of acts of terrorism . . . when committed in time of peace; in addition, this practice is evidence of a *belief* of States that the punishment of terrorism responds to a social necessity and is hence obligatory by the existence of a rule requiring it.[165]

The Chamber further noted that this customary rule imposed duties on states:

> to refrain from engaging through their officials and agents in acts of terrorism . . . [and] to prevent and repress terrorism, and in particular to prosecute and try persons on its territory or in territory under its control who are allegedly involved in terrorism.[166]

Despite the Chamber's finding of a customary rule prohibiting transnational terrorism and the consequent duties of states to prevent and suppress terrorist attacks, it is an entirely different matter to infer from this prohibition an international crime of transnational terrorism. Indeed, the Appeals Chamber recognised that 'the existence of a customary rule outlawing terrorism does not

162 *Prosecutor* v. *Tadić, Decision on the Defence Motion for Interlocutory Appeal on Jurisdiction*, Case No. IT-94-I, 2 October 1995, para. 94; Ambos (n. 157), p. 670.
163 *Interlocutory Decision* (n. 6), para. 91.
164 *North Sea Continental Shelf Cases (Federal Republic of Germany* v. *Denmark and the Netherlands)* [1969] 3 ICJ 3, paras 76–77. It was held at paras 76–77 that 'not only must the acts concerned amount to a settled practice, but they must also be such, or be carried out in such a way, as to be evidence of a belief that this practice is rendered obligatory by the existence of a rule of law requiring it'.
165 *Interlocutory Decision* (n. 6), para. 102 (emphasis in original text).
166 Ibid.

automatically mean that terrorism is a criminal offence under international law'.[167]

Relying on the decision of the ICTY Appeals Chamber in the *Tadić* case[168] the STL Appeals Chamber was of the view that 'to give rise to individual criminal liability at the international level it is necessary for a violation of the international rule to entail the individual criminal responsibility of the person breaching the rule'.[169] Essentially 'individual criminal liability at the international level' assumes the 'individual criminal responsibility' of the wrongdoer.[170] However, this is a *petitio principii* because it bases a conclusion on an assumption that needs to be proved as much as the conclusion itself. This argument is a fallacy because a presumption and a conclusion cannot be equated with one another. Instead, the Appeals Chamber should have taken an alternative approach and stated that the standards laid down in the *Tadić* case, which intended to espouse violations of international humanitarian law in both international and non-international armed conflicts by also criminalising the latter,[171] should be utilised to determine whether the prohibition of terrorism has led to the development of an international crime of terrorism.

The Appeals Chamber did not adopt this approach but instead described the criteria for ascertaining the existence of such a crime.[172] It held that 'the intention to criminalise the prohibition must be evidenced by statements of government officials and international organisations, as well as by punishment for such violations by national courts'.[173] The Appeals Chamber concluded that an examination of these factors will determine whether states seek to criminalise violations of the international rule.[174] In paragraph 104 of the interlocutory decision the Appeals Chamber set forth the evidence supporting its conclusion that a customary crime of terrorism exists under international law. Interestingly, it found that the 'formation process of the international criminalisation of terrorism is similar to that of war crimes'.[175] Following an analysis of the criminalisation of war crimes from the Versailles Treaty of 1919 to the Nuremberg Trials the Appeals Chamber concluded that:

> the domestic criminalisation of breaches of international humanitarian law led to the international criminalisation of those breaches and the formation of rules of customary international law authorising or even imposing their punishment.[176]

167 Ibid., para. 103.
168 *Tadić* (n. 162), para. 94.
169 *Interlocutory Decision* (n. 6), para. 103.
170 Ibid.
171 *Tadić* (n. 162), para. 94.
172 Ibid.
173 Ibid., paras 128–137.
174 *Interlocutory Decision* (n. 6), para. 103.
175 Ibid., para. 104.
176 Ibid.

Similarly, the criminalisation of terrorist attacks initially began at the domestic level 'with many countries of the world legislating against terrorist acts and bringing to court those allegedly responsible for such acts'.[177]

The more persuasive view is that transnational terrorism is a serious treaty-based crime which is closely akin to core international crimes. International criminal law as it is currently framed makes a clear distinction between treaty-based crimes and core international crimes.[178] The difference being that treaty-based crimes are transnational offences that can only be implemented by states at the national level. International treaties and conventions merely provide for the criminalisation and suppression of terrorist acts at the national level by state parties[179] and do not impose individual criminal responsibility. In contrast, core international crimes create this type of criminal responsibility with the additional:

> correlative right of international enforcement by a supranational institution (such as the ICC) or by states, independent of domestic criminalization and traditional jurisdictional links (replacing territoriality, nationality, and the protective principle by universal jurisdiction stricto senso).[180]

This difference has from time to time been given expression in international instruments. A comparison of both the Genocide Convention 1948 and the UN Convention against Torture and Other Cruel, Inhuman or Degrading Treatment or Punishment 1987 illustrates this point quite well.[181]

177 Ibid.

178 Claus Kress, 'International Criminal Law', in R. Wolfman (ed.), *The Max Planck Encyclopaedia of Public International Law* (2008), online edition, available at www.mpwpil.com, paras 6ff. (date accessed: 14 March 2018); Robert Cryer and Elizabeth Wilmhurst, 'Introduction: What Is International Criminal Law?', in R. Cryer et al. (eds), *An Introduction to International Criminal Law and Procedure* (Oxford University Press, 2010) 1–21, pp. 4–5; Paola Gaeta, 'International Criminalisation of Prohibited Conduct', in A. Cassese (ed.), *The Oxford Companion to International Criminal Justice* (Oxford University Press, 2009) 63–74, p. 69; David Luban, 'Fairness to Rightness: Jurisdiction, Legality, and the Legitimacy of International Criminal Law', in S. Besson and J. Tasioulas (eds), *The Philosophy of International Law* (Oxford University Press, 2010) 569–588, p. 572; Marko Milanović, 'Is the Rome Statute Binding on Individuals? (And Why Should We Care)', *Journal of International Criminal Justice* 9(1) (2011) 25–52, p. 28.

179 For instance, Article 4 of the International Convention for the Suppression of Terrorist Bombings, UN Doc. A/RES/52/164 (1997), 2149 UNTS 256 states that '[e]ach State Party shall adopt such measures as may be necessary: (a) To establish as criminal offences under its domestic law the offences set forth in article 2 of this Convention; (b) To make those offences punishable by appropriate penalties which take into account the grave nature of those offences.' See also Elizabeth Wilmhurst, 'Transnational Crimes, Terrorism and Torture', in R. Cryer et al. (eds), *An Introduction to International Criminal Law and Procedure* (Cambridge University Press, 2010, 2nd edn), pp. 335–336 and 344; Gaeta (n. 178), p. 63.

180 Kress (n. 178), para. 10.

181 See further the Convention on the Prevention and Punishment of the Crime of Genocide, 1948 (hereafter the Genocide Convention 1948) and the UN Convention

Article 1 of the Genocide Convention 1948 states that '[t]he Contracting Parties confirm that genocide, whether committed in time of peace or in time of war, is a crime under international law which they undertake to prevent and to punish'.[182] On the other hand, Article 4(1) of the UN Convention against Torture and Other Cruel, Inhuman or Degrading Treatment or Punishment 1987 provides that '[e]ach State Party shall ensure that all acts of torture are offences under its criminal law'.[183] However, these provisions do not completely settle the issue because it can always be contended, as the Appeals Chamber does, that a crime that was initially treaty based can attain the categorisation of an international crime by way of customary international law.[184] The prohibition against torture, for example, has gained *jus cogens* status[185] and must therefore be regarded in the same manner as the *jus cogens* prohibition against genocide.[186] This imparts support for the opinion of the Institute of International Law that torture is no longer a mere transnational crime but a core international crime. Indeed, Article 1 of the Institute's 2009 Resolution on Immunity and International Crimes provides that torture should be classified alongside genocide, crimes against humanity, and war crimes as 'serious crimes of international law'.[187] Similarly many international conventions emphasise that terrorist acts are 'a matter of grave concern to the international community as a whole',[188] and as

against Torture and Other Cruel, Inhuman or Degrading Treatment or Punishment 1987.

182 Article 1 of the Genocide Convention 1948.

183 Article 4(1) of the Convention against Torture and Other Cruel, Inhuman or Degrading Treatment or Punishment, GA Res. 39/46 of 10 December 1984, 1465 UNTS 85.

184 Ibid.

185 *Prosecutor* v. *Furunzija*, IT-95–17/I-T (ICTR), Judgment of 10 December 1998, paras 153–157.

186 *Case Concerning the Application of the Convention on the Prevention and Punishment of the Crime of Genocide* (*Bosnia and Herzegovina* v. *Serbia and Montenegro*), Judgment of 26 February 2007, ICJ, para. 161.

187 Article I of the 2009 Institute's Resolution on Immunity and International Crimes (Institute of International Law). For further analysis on this resolution, see Annyssa Bellal, 'The 2009 Resolution of the Institute of international Law on Immunity and International Crimes', *Journal of International Criminal Justice* 9 (2011) 227.

188 Convention for the Suppression of Unlawful Acts against the Safety of Maritime Navigation, UN Doc. A/RES/584 (1988), 1678 UNTS 201; International Convention for the Suppression of the Financing of Terrorism, UN Doc. A/RES/54/109 (1999), 39 ILM 270. See also Convention for the Suppression of Unlawful Seizure of Aircraft, 16 December 1970, 860 UNTS 106; Convention for the Suppression of Unlawful Acts against the Safety of Civil Aviation, 23 September 1971, 974 UNTS 178; Protocol for the Suppression of Unlawful Acts of Violence at Airports Serving International Civil Aviation, supplementary to the Convention for the Suppression of Unlawful Acts against the Safety of Civil Aviation, 23 September 1971, 1589 UNTS 474; Convention on the Prevention and Punishment of Crimes against Internationally Protected Persons, 14 December 1973, 1035 UNTS 168; Convention on the Physical

a result 'give prevalence to judicare (prosecute) over dedere (extradite) obligations'.[189]

If these criteria are applied to attacks by transnational terrorist groups, the first and second criteria are fulfilled. At paragraph 91 of its interlocutory decision, the Appeals Chamber stated that the 'domestic offence needs to be regarded by the world community as an attack on universal values . . . or on values held to be of paramount importance in that community'.[190] However, the application of the third criterion warrants further examination. The Appeals Chamber recognises that the international criminalisation of a domestic crime necessitates that:

> the States and intergovernmental organisations, through their acts and pronouncements, sanction this attitude by clearly expressing the view that the world community considers the offence at issue as amounting to an international crime.[191]

This is closely akin to the view above that international criminalisation must be clearly avowed by the law. However, the declaration that transnational terrorism is a crime under international law is clearly non-existent. Moreover, the fact that transnational terrorism is not included as a core crime under the Rome Statute and that it has hitherto not been conceivable to implement a comprehensive international convention on terrorism[192] is evidence which suggests the contrary, that attacks by transnational terrorist groups in non-armed conflict situations are not yet recognised as a distinct crime under international law.[193]

Ambos notes that the Appeals Chamber's finding of a 'special treatment of terrorism as compared to other transnational offences only demonstrates that terrorism is a "special" transnational offence that may come closer to a true international crime than "ordinary" transnational offences'.[194] The fact that attacks by transnational terrorist groups fulfil the first and the second criteria laid down by the ICTY illustrates that such attacks are situated somewhere on the spectrum between a treaty-based criminal offence and an international crime within the remit of the Rome Statute. Since transnational terrorism cannot at present be classified as an international crime it would seem that it is slowly moving towards such a

Protection of Nuclear Material, 26 October 1979, 1456 UNTS 125; International Convention against the Taking of Hostages, of 17 December 1979, 1316 UNTS 206.

189 Ambos (n. 157), p. 669. See for example Article 5(2) of the International Convention against the Taking of Hostages, 17 December 1979, 1316 UNTS 206.

190 *Interlocutory Decision* (n. 6), para. 91.

191 Ibid., para. 91.

192 Report of the Ad Hoc Committee Established by UN General Assembly Resolution 51/210, A/58/37 (2003); Decision, para. 88.

193 This is the prevailing view in the literature as well: Ambos (n. 164), p. 670; Institute of International Law (n. 194), which also does not incorporate terrorism as a 'serious crime under international law'. Antonio Cassese argues that some extreme forms of international terrorism constitute international crimes: Cassese (n. 178), p. 12; Gaeta (n. 178), p. 69; Wilmhurst (n. 179), p. 338; Cryer and Wilmhurst (n. 178), p. 4.

194 Ibid., p. 671.

classification. Thus, an examination of the constituent elements of this emerging crime is imperative for determining how the Rome Statute could be amended to respond to terrorist attacks by transnational terrorist groups.

F The constituent elements of the customary crime of transnational terrorism

1 The actus reus

UN Security Council Resolution 1566 (2004),[195] UN General Assembly resolutions,[196] and the draft Comprehensive Convention on Terrorism[197] all state that the only objective element of terrorism is criminal conduct causing or threatening to cause harm to life and property.[198] All of the national laws analysed by the Appeals Chamber contained this objective element.[199] Many domestic laws also criminalise any acts in the planning and preparation of a terrorist attack.[200] Some UN treaties and conventions have gone even further and criminalised particular terrorist acts such as plane hijackings and attacks on diplomatic staff.[201] Moreover, these conventions necessitate a transnational element.[202] For example, Article 3 of the Terrorist Bombing Convention specifies that the Convention 'shall not apply where the offence is committed within a single State, the alleged offender and the victims are nationals of that State'.[203] However, this element is not a component of the definition of transnational terrorism but is instead a jurisdictional rule that restricts the application of the Convention to terrorist attacks with a transnational dimension.[204] The Appeals Chamber reaches the same conclusion affirming that this element 'goes not to the definition of terrorism'.[205] However, the analysis of the Appeals Chamber is ambiguous.[206] It is not clear how the transnational element forms a part of the customary crime pronounced by the Appeals Chamber if it is not a part of the definition of the crime.[207]

195 *Interlocutory Decision* (n. 6), para. 88.
196 Ibid.
197 Ibid.
198 Ibid.
199 *Interlocutory Decision* (n. 6), para. 91.
200 See for example Chapter II Part I of the Terrorist Act (UK) 2006.
201 See further Article 1(a) of the Hijacking Convention, which prohibits people from unlawfully seizing and exercising control over the aircraft and Article 2(1) of the Diplomatic Agent Conventions, which prohibits 'murder, kidnapping or other attack, violent attack upon the official premises'.
202 Wilmhurst (n. 179), p. 344.
203 Article 3 of the International Convention for the Suppression of Terrorist Bombings, UN Doc. A/RES/52/164 (1997), 2149 UNTS 256.
204 Ibid.
205 *Interlocutory Decision* (n. 6), para. 89.
206 Ibid.
207 *Interlocutory Decision* (n. 6), para. 111.

The additional qualification that the crime must constitute 'a threat to the stability of society of the State' is not corroborated by the Appeals Chamber's decision and arguably confounds both the objective and subjective elements of the crime.[208] The Appeals Chamber does not make any distinction whatsoever between the two elements in its decision because what it describes as objective is actually subjective. In general, the effect of a terrorist attack on a state or civilian population is examined with reference to the special intent requirement.[209] The sources of law relied upon by the Appeals Chamber show that the customary crime of transnational terrorism has only one objective element which is the physical act of causing or threatening to cause serious death, injury, or property damage.[210] The physical act component is on a parallel with the first part of the Appeals Chamber's customary norm.[211] However, on the basis of the sources of law relied upon by the Appeals Chamber this objective element is so general that it does not comply with the principle of legality.[212]

2 Mens rea

The Appeals Chamber is of the view that the customary crime of transnational terrorism has a dual *mens rea* element. First, that the accused must have acted with a general intent to perpetrate the physical elements of the act, and, second, had a special intent to spread fear among the civilian population and compel state authorities to perform or refrain from performing a particular act.[213] With reference to general intent, if the definition of transnational terrorism refers to an act which is not listed as a crime in domestic criminal law the object of reference of the *mens rea* is deficient. The sources of law relied upon by the Appeals Chamber refer to both a general special intent 'to cause a state of terror'[214] and a superior special intent which 'require[s] a particular political or ideological purpose' such as 'the purpose of coercing a state, or international organisation to do or refrain from doing something'.[215] So the first part of the Chamber's definition which refers to a general special intent

208 Ibid.
209 See further Article 1 of the European Council, *Framework Decision on Combating Terrorism*, 13 June 2002, (2002/475/JHA) which provides that '[e]ach Member State shall take the necessary measures to ensure that the intentional acts . . . where committed with the aim of . . . seriously destabilising or destroying the fundamental political, constitutional, economic or social structures of a country or an international organisation, shall be deemed to be terrorist offences'.
210 On this point see further Wilmhurst (n. 179), p. 344.
211 *Interlocutory Decision* (n. 6), paras 85 and 111.
212 Ambos (n. 157), p. 673.
213 *Interlocutory Decision* (n. 6), para. 85.
214 Article 314 of the Lebanon Criminal Code.
215 Antonio Cassese, 'The Multifaceted Criminal Notion of Terrorism in International Law', *Journal of International Criminal Justice* 4 (2006) 933–958, p. 957.

has a firm grounding in customary international law, whereas the second part of the definition denoting a superior intent does not.

The Appeals Chamber was of the view that the special intent element could be derived 'from an underlying political or ideological purpose'.[216] Indeed, the Chamber does not refer to superior special intent in its interlocutory decision. Instead, it refers to an 'underlying political or ideological purpose' specifically the motivation of the wrongdoer for carrying out the terrorist attack.[217] Although, some individuals may have this superior intent when they carry out an attack, others may simply carry out attacks to fulfil ordinary criminal objectives under the facade of a political or ideological purpose. So, the question arises whether the political or ideological purpose should form a part of the definition of transnational terrorism at all.

The Appeals Chamber held that 'it remains to be seen whether one day it [the said purpose requirement] will emerge as an additional element of the international crime of terrorism'.[218] But the Appeals Chamber's finding is contradictory because at paragraph 98 of its interlocutory decision it notes that the sources of laws relied upon suggest that motives should not be included in the definition of transnational terrorism.[219] So the Appeals Chamber appears to confuse the meaning of the terms 'intent' and 'motive' and fails to recognise that the 'reason why a perpetrator performed a certain act, is irrelevant to his intent'.[220] A motive can 'only be taken into account at the sentencing stage as a mitigating or aggravating factor'.[221] States can include the motive within the *mens rea* element of the crime of transnational terrorism in particular the political or ideological purpose underlying the attack in their domestic criminal law.[222] Although the Appeals Chamber may have been contemplating this when it included the intent and motive element in the definition, the *mens rea* element of the crime requires clarification especially if the Assembly of State Parties is to include transnational terrorism as a crime within the subject matter jurisdiction of the ICC.

G Challenges in prosecuting the customary crime of terrorism at the ICC

The role of the ICC in prosecuting the customary crime of terrorism is likely to be limited. As discussed in Chapter 3, the jurisdiction of the court is restricted to genocide, war crimes, and crimes against humanity and does not contain a crime of terrorism.[223] Classifying terrorism as a war crime under the Rome Statute

216 *Interlocutory Decision* (n. 6), para. 106.
217 Ibid.
218 *Interlocutory Decision* (n. 6), para. 106.
219 Ibid., para. 98.
220 Ambos (n. 157), p. 675.
221 Ibid.
222 Ibid.
223 Articles 6–8 of the Rome Statute.

requires the fulfilment of elements that are very different to those of the customary crime of transnational terrorism developed by the STL. However, this customary crime is unlikely to be included in the jurisdiction of the ICC. Despite proposals to amend the Rome Statute to include the crime of terrorism, these have been repeatedly rejected for two reasons.[224]

First, as discussed in section B of this chapter there is a 'lack of a definition of terrorism, since the 13 counter-terrorism conventions defined a multitude of acts that constituted terrorism'.[225] Second, there is the possibility that inserting a crime of terrorism would lead to politicisation of the ICC.[226] Indeed, amending the Rome Statute to include the crime of transnational terrorism in the same way as the crime of aggression was dismissed because it was thought that 'the analogy could not easily be drawn as a degree of consensus had already existed on the definition of the crime of aggression . . . while no such definition of terrorism as yet existed'.[227] It was also believed that the procedure for amending the Rome Statute should only be used 'in very exceptional circumstances' and 'should not become the norm'.[228] Nevertheless, Resolution E of the Final Act of the United Nations Diplomatic Conference of Plenipotentiaries on the Establishment of an International Criminal Court stated that the Assembly of State Parties could amend the Rome Statute at a later stage to include the crime of terrorism.[229]

Indeed, in the run-up to the Kampala Review Conference of the Rome Statute in 2010 the Bureau on the Review Conference reported a number of proposed amendments.[230] The Netherlands suggested the inclusion of terrorism as a crime in the Rome Statute. Denunciating terroristic activity as one of the 'most serious threats to international peace and security'[231] the Netherlands asserted that this behaviour was a 'serious crime of concern to the international community'.[232] It was proposed that the amendment of the Rome Statute to include the crime of terrorism would fortify counter-terrorism measures at the international level despite the absence of an internationally accepted definition of the term. The

224 Assembly of State Parties (n. 2), at 40–51 and Appendix III at 65–66. The International Law Commission has recommended the amendment of the Rome Statute to include the crime of terrorism. See further Article 20 of the ILA Draft Statute for an International Criminal Court, available at: http://untreaty.un.org/ilc/texts/instruments/english/draft%20articles/7_4_1994.pdf (date accessed: 14 March 2018).

225 Assembly of State Parties (n. 2), para. 45.

226 Ibid., para. 46.

227 Ibid.

228 Ibid., para. 49.

229 Resolution E of the Final act of the United Nations Diplomatic Conference of Plenipotentiaries on the Establishment of an International Criminal Court, UN Doc. A/CONF.183/10, 17 July 1998.

230 Report of the Bureau on the Review Conference, Doc. ICC-ASP/8/43/Add.1, 10 November 2009.

231 Proposal of Amendment by the Netherlands, UN Doc. CN723.2009.Treaties-5 (29 October 2009), available at: www.adh-geneva.ch/RULAC/news/NetherlandsCN723EN.pdf (date accessed: 14 March 2018).

232 Ibid.

Dutch proposal sought to defer the ICC's jurisdiction over the crime of terrorism until a definition of the term and the specific elements of the crime had been agreed.[233] However, despite reaffirming their denunciation of terroristic activity, the delegations of the Credentials Committee, which held two sessions in 2009, concluded that an amendment of the Rome Statute to include the crime of terrorism was premature.[234]

Bearing in mind the definitions of terroristic activity laid down in approximately 13 counter-terrorism instruments, the plenipotentiaries emphasised the need for a clear all-inclusive definition backed by the UN.[235] However, in view of the risk of the politicisation of the term 'terrorism', delegates of the Review Conference viewed the proposed amendment as a barrier to negotiations and concluded that terroristic activity was already criminalised under existing articles of the Rome Statute.[236] Indeed, the Report of the Working Group on the Review Conference noted that the Assembly of State Parties 'should strive for universality of the Court, which could be hindered by entering into negotiations on terrorism'.[237] Cases concerning transnational terrorism are often politicised and the ICC needs the support of states to ensure the enforcement of its decisions and the execution of its arrest warrants. Diplomats believed that there was little value in establishing a working group to draft a definition of terrorism in order to facilitate an amendment of the Rome Statute.[238] As a result, at the ICC Review Conference in 2010, proposed amendments to include the crime of terrorism in the Rome Statute were not considered.[239]

Ten months after the STL's interlocutory decision, during the 10th session of the Assembly of State Parties, the Working Group on Amendments again dismissed a proposal from the Netherlands to insert a crime of terrorism into the Rome Statute.[240] Even though the interlocutory decision of the STL Appeals Chamber may persuade some delegations in time that a definition of transnational terrorism is beginning to emerge the possibility of the subject-matter jurisdiction of the ICC being expanded to include a crime of terrorism in the future is unlikely. Indeed, without providing any reasoning for its

233 Proposed Art. 5(3), Proposal of Amendment by the Netherlands (n. 231).
234 Ibid.
235 Ibid.
236 Ibid.
237 Report of the Working Group on the Review Conference (2009), para. 46.
238 Report of the Credentials Committee, ICC-ASP/8/20, paras 44–49, available at: www.icc-cpi.int/iccdocs/asp_docs/ASP8/OR/OR-ASP8-Vol.1-ENG.Annexes.pdf (date accessed: 14 March 2018).
239 §3, ICC-ASP/8/Res.6, 26 November 2009, see Resolutions adopted by the Assembly of State Parties at 35, available at: www.icc-cpt.int/iccdocs/asp_docs/ASP8/OR/OR-ASP8-Vol.I-ENG.Part.II.pdf (date accessed: 14 March 2018). See also The Hague Justice Portal, 'ICC Review Conference Concludes in Kampala', available at: www.haguejusticeportal.net/smartsite.html?id=11779 (date accessed: 14 March 2018).
240 Assembly of State Parties, 10th session, New York, OR (ICC-ASP/10/32), vol. 1 (*Report on the Working Group on Amendments*), 9–21 December 2011, p. 17.

conclusion, the Leiden Policy Recommendations deduced that it is not only improbable but also 'undesirable, that the Rome Statute of the International Criminal Court will be amended to include terrorism as a specifically articulated crime'.[241]

H Conclusion

There is considerable divergence of opinion both within international legal thought and across disciplines such as international law and international relations about the existence of an international crime of transnational terrorism. The creation and enforcement of a crime of transnational terrorism under international law remains a highly contested area, and determining what constitutes 'terrorism' from both a legal and non-legal perspective can be challenging. Yet despite the ongoing attempts to define the term, few would contest that the ICC should play an important role in the prosecution of members of transnational terrorist groups where states are unwilling to do so. Such prosecutions would potentially have a deterrent effect by sending a message to transnational terrorist groups that even though some states may be unwilling or unable to investigate and prosecute their crimes there is a judicial mechanism at international level with the necessary resources to do so. Therefore, it is now necessary to turn to the question of how international criminal law applies to members of transnational terrorist groups from the application of the doctrine of command responsibility to the ICC's understanding of the principle of individual criminal responsibility which claims there is a doctrine of co-perpetration.

241 Nico Schrijver and Larissa van den Herik, *Leiden Policy Recommendations on Counter-Terrorism and International Law* (Grotius Centre for International Legal Studies, 2010), p. 8 contended that 'domestic states should cooperate to eradicate terrorism to the fullest extent possible based on the unequivocal condemnation of all acts, methods, and practices of terrorism as criminal and unjustifiable committed wherever and by whoever'.

5 Applying the doctrine of command responsibility under Article 28 of the Rome Statute

The dilemma of successor commanders

A Introduction

The extent to which leaders of transnational terrorist groups can be held accountable before the ICC is examined in this chapter to determine whether the doctrine of command responsibility applies to terrorist attacks perpetrated in non-armed conflict situations. The role of the leader is essential to ensure that the transnational terrorist group complies with international law. However, if the leader either authorises or fails to punish or prevent the commission of attacks, subordinate members will be able to continue the perpetration of crimes.

This chapter explores the application of the doctrine of command responsibility to leaders of transnational terrorist groups, which carry out terrorist attacks in non-armed conflict situations. The accountability of the leader should be differentiated from the accountability of the subordinate members of the group because the former can be held responsible for the crimes of the latter even though the former may not have ordered the crimes. The subordinate members of the group can only be held accountable for the crimes they commit themselves. State armed forces have a well-defined three-tier chain of command. At the lowest level of the chain of command, the subordinate members who planned and perpetrated the crime can be held accountable. At the next level of the chain of command, leaders can be held accountable. The highest level of criminal accountability can hold the state responsible, on the grounds that it is answerable for the acts committed by its agents.

As discussed in Chapter 2, the difficulty with network-based transnational terrorist groups is that they do not all have a defined chain of command like most state and non-state armed forces, and as a result it is exceedingly difficult for the centralised command to govern the activities of the network cells. The difficulty prosecuting leaders under Articles 25 and 28 of the Rome Statute will be examined with reference to not only the jurisprudence of the ICC but also the ICTY and the ICTR. The criteria required to establish the accountability of the leader will be examined in light of the network organisational structure of the transnational terrorist group. The superior–subordinate relationship is central to this examination, because to establish command responsibility there must be evidence that the leader exercised control or authority over the subordinate members. The leader must also have knowledge that his subordinates had or were about to commit a crime. Since the network cells of the group are based in different states the centralised command may not have knowledge about their activities. The hybrid organisational structure of the transnational terrorist group is considered in detail to analyse whether this is an effective criterion in prosecuting leaders.

Leaders of transnational terrorist groups have a duty to take all reasonable measures to prevent the commission of attacks by his/her subordinates. They also have a duty to punish subordinates for their role in the commission of such acts. This chapter will examine the challenges faced by the leader in fulfilling these duties with particular reference to successor commanders. As a result, it may be difficult for the leader to oversee the activities of each cell and take steps to prevent international crimes. This chapter will explore claims that these duties are particularly onerous for successor leaders who can be held accountable for failing to punish subordinates for crimes they committed before he/she took up a command position. In view of the high turnover of the commanders of the transnational terrorist group, this chapter will analyse the sufficiency of the doctrine of command responsibility in bringing successor leaders to justice. Even though the goal of international criminal justice is to combat impunity, the application of the doctrine of command responsibility to successor commanders of transnational terrorist groups is perhaps erroneous.

B The scope of application of the doctrine of command responsibility to attacks by transnational terrorist groups

Although the majority of cases concerning the doctrine of command responsibility have related to armed conflict situations, a strong argument can be made that the doctrine also applies to situations where no armed conflict situation exists. In the ICTY case, *Prosecutor* v. *Hadžihasanović*, defence counsel questioned the view that the doctrine of command responsibility could apply to non-international armed conflict situations.[1] In particular, defence counsel argued that the doctrine originated in Additional Protocol I to the Geneva Conventions and that, therefore, its scope of application was limited to international armed conflicts.[2]

However, the Trial Chamber dismissed these submissions stating that the doctrine of command responsibility is in principle applicable to both international and non-international armed conflicts.[3] The fact that:

1 *Prosecutor* v. *Hadžihasanović*, IT-01-47-AR72, Article 7(3) Appeal Chamber Decision, 16 July 2003, paras 11ff.

2 Ibid.

3 Ibid. See also *Prosecutor* v. *Orić*, IT-03-68-T, Judgment, 30 June 2006, para. 291; *Prosecutor* v. *Brđanin*, IT-99-36-T, Judgment, 1 September 2004, para. 27; *Prosecutor* v. *Halilović*, IT-01-48-T, Judgment, 16 November 2005, para. 55, where the Trial Chamber held that Article 7(3) of the ICTY Statute 'is applicable to all acts referred to in Articles 2 to 5 thereof and applies to both international and non-international armed conflicts'. See also *Prosecutor* v. *Boškoski*, IT-04-82-T, Judgment, 10 July 2008, para. 404 and the 'Report of the International Commission of Inquiry on Darfur to the

> Additional Protocol II, unlike Additional Protocol I, did not provide for specific provisions concerning commanders' obligations to prevent and punish the crimes of their subordinates could not be read in such a way as to execute the application of that doctrine in the context of internal armed conflict.[4]

The ICTY Appeals Chamber was of the view that when customary international law recognises that a war crime can be perpetrated by a member of an organised armed force, it also acknowledges that a commander can be held criminally accountable for such a crime on the basis of the doctrine of command responsibility.[5]

> Thus the fact that it was in the course of an internal armed conflict that a war crime was about to be committed or was committed is not relevant to the responsibility of the commander; that only goes to the characteristics of the particular crime and not to the responsibility of the commander. The basis of the commander's responsibility lies in his obligations as commander of troops making up an organised military force under his command, and not in the particular theatre in which the act was committed by a member of that military force.[6]

It remains unclear whether the doctrine of command responsibility also applies to violent situations, which fall short of being categorised as an armed conflict situation. This issue is especially important to explore because the vast majority of attacks perpetrated by transnational terrorist groups occur during peacetime. The Trial Chamber in the *Hadžihasanović* case has suggested *obiter dicta* that the doctrine of command responsibility applies to both armed conflict and peacetime situations.[7] Without providing any legal basis to support its finding the Trial Chamber noted that 'the doctrine has been recognized as applying to offences committed either within or in the absence of an armed conflict'.[8]

In *Hilao* v. *Estate of Marcos*, a group of Philippine citizens brought a damages claim against the former President of the Philippines, Ferdinand Marcos, for torture committed by the military and paramilitary forces under his command during his 14-year rule.[9] The United States Court of Appeals for the 9th Circuit, held that '[t]he principle of "command responsibility" that holds a superior responsible for the actions of subordinates appears to be well accepted in U.S. and

United Nations Secretary-General Pursuant to Security Council Resolution of 18 September 2004', 25 January 2005, para. 560.

4 Guenael Mettraux, *The Law of Command Responsibility* (Oxford University Press, 2009), p. 96.

5 *Hadžihasanović* (n. 1), para. 18.

6 Ibid., para. 20.

7 Ibid., para. 93 (v).

8 Ibid.

9 *Hilao* v. *Estate of Marcos*, 103 F.3d 767 (9th Cir. 1996).

international law in connection with acts committed in wartime'.[10] The Court of Appeals further noted that:

> [t]he United States has moved towards recognising similar 'command responsibility' that occurs in peacetime, perhaps because the goal of international law regarding the treatment of noncombatants in wartime – 'to protect civilian populations and prisoners from brutality', Yamashita, 327 U.S. at 15 – is similar to the goal of international human-rights law.[11]

Mettraux is of the view that since the doctrine of command responsibility stems from international humanitarian law it only applies to armed conflict situations.[12] Indeed, the ad hoc tribunals have only thus far charged leaders for their role in criminal conduct occurring during an armed conflict situation.[13] In principle, the doctrine of command responsibility applies to both crimes against humanity and genocide which need not be perpetrated during an armed conflict.[14]

Neither the Rome Statute nor the statutes of ad hoc tribunals state that the doctrine of command responsibility only applies to armed conflict situations. Indeed, Judge David Hunt, in his separate and partially dissenting opinion in the Appeals Chamber decision in the *Hadžihasanović* case citing with approval the decision of the ICTY Appeals Chamber on the *Interlocutory Appeal Challenging Jurisdiction in Relation to Command Responsibility*, noted that the principle of command responsibility applies, 'to whatever situation reasonably falls within the application of the principle'.[15] So the doctrine of command responsibility would seem to apply to non-armed conflict situations even if customary international law does not mandate it.[16]

Even though the doctrine of command responsibility applies to both peacetime and wartime situations, the doctrine may not apply in the same way to both contexts because the evidence necessary to prove its elements in one context may not be sufficient to prove the elements in the other context.[17] The inference of

10 Ibid., p. 777.

11 Ibid. For further reference, see also *Jane Doe et al.* v. *Lui Qi et al.* 349 F. Supp. 2d 1258 (2004), p. 1330, where it was held that '[w]hile these cases and statutes have involved war or war-like contexts', the Ninth Circuit noted that the 'United States has moved towards recognizing similar "command responsibility" for torture that occurs in peacetime, perhaps because the goal of international law regarding the treatment of non-combatants in wartime – to protect civilian populations and prisoners . . . from brutality is similar to the goal of international human rights law'.

12 Mettraux (n. 4), pp. 97–98.

13 Ibid.

14 Anna Brennan, 'The Accountability of Leaders of Armed Opposition Groups under International Law', *The Hague Yearbook of International Law* (2010) 223, p. 245.

15 See the separate dissenting opinion of Judge David Hunt, *Hadžihasanović* (n. 1), para. 8.

16 Mettraux (n. 4), p. 98.

17 Ibid.

knowledge that subordinates have either committed or are about to commit crimes may be more straightforwardly drawn in peacetime:

> where the absence of the mayhem that generally accompanies warfare makes the circulation and the acquisition of information a more likely occurrence than would be the case where the [subordinates] . . . and their commanders are involved in the thick of war.[18]

Similarly, an inference of effective control may be more easily made during peacetime where there are no ongoing hostilities, because combat activities tend to make communication between the commander and his/her subordinates more difficult. This ineffective communication between the superior and his subordinate could lead to subordinates failing to follow the orders of his/her commander.

Although the doctrine of command responsibility applies to attacks committed by members of transnational terrorist groups during peacetime the classification of the situation surrounding the commission of the offences as a peacetime situation may lead to the application of a different legal regime. This could 'provide for different kinds of duties and obligations – as well as competencies – for military commanders and other superiors'.[19] A duty which may be binding on a commander during peacetime situations may not be binding upon him/her in an armed conflict situation. For example, leaders of transnational terrorist groups have a duty to ensure that subordinates do not attack civilians during armed conflict situations. However, it is questionable whether he/she has the same duty with respect to terrorist attacks perpetrated during non-armed situations. The ICC would have to determine whether the duty to safeguard and protect civilians from harm during terrorist attacks is indeed binding upon the alleged leader of the transnational terrorist group in the context of the relevant charges. In determining this question, it would also be necessary for the ICC to examine the criteria for

18 Ibid.

19 Ibid. Indeed, the question arises as to whether the duties which would be binding upon a commander in the context of an international armed conflict would be equally binding upon him/her in a non-international armed conflict situation. See *Hadžihasanović* (n. 1), para. 12. For further academic commentary on this particular point, see Hans Gasser, 'Armed Conflict within the Territory of a State', in W. Haller et al. (eds), *Im Dienst and der Gemeinschaft* (Helbing und Lichtenhahn, 1989), p. 225. At p. 29 Gasser notes that: 'It would be erroneous, for legal and political reasons, to read too much into that treaty [Additional Protocol II]. A particular danger must be mentioned specifically: the temptation to conclude from a (written) provision applicable to international armed conflicts (e.g. an article of Protocol I) that the same obligation therefore exists (although unwritten) for internal armed conflicts. As States have chosen to distinguish between two separate types of armed conflicts, with their distinct systems of law, conclusions by analogy are not sufficient to support the existence of a customary law rule. Any attempt to "create" new obligations in this way for internal armed conflict must be resisted . . . Their legal status is completely different, by decision of the international "legislator".' This statement does not, however, preclude the existence of common principles which have found their way into both legal regimes.

determining the accountability of transnational terrorist groups. The aim of the next section will be to analyse the definitive criteria for establishing the accountability of leaders of transnational terrorist groups before the ICC to determine what obstacles there would be for the Office of the Prosecutor in bringing them to justice.

C The command responsibility of leaders of transnational terrorist groups

There are two types of command responsibility under international law. The first type entails accountability for specifically ordering violations of international norms. This kind of responsibility is also referred to as direct responsibility because of the positive instruction given by the leader to subordinates.[20] The other form of command responsibility consists of a, 'superior's responsibility for a subordinate's unlawful conduct that was not directly based on a specific superior order'.[21] Command responsibility essentially consists of omission because it entails a 'failure in a duty to exercise due diligence in order to prevent a specific unlawful act or to repress unlawful conduct'.[22]

1 Ordering the commission of crimes

There was no recognition of the criminal accountability of command leaders of non-state armed actors for ordering the commission of crimes until very recently.[23] All contracting state parties under the 1949 Geneva Conventions are required to impose criminal sanctions on individuals who order violations of the Conventions. However, these provisions only apply to armed conflicts between states. The legal practice of domestic courts with regard to the implementation and adoption of the Rome Statute has significantly altered this situation.[24] These courts along with the decisions handed down by the ICTY and the ICTR verify that leaders of non-state armed actors can be held criminally responsible for ordering crimes.[25]

In particular, Article 4 of the ICTR Statute provides that the tribunal has the authority to prosecute individuals suspected of ordering crimes in contravention to Common Article 3 and Additional Protocol II of the Geneva

20 See generally Steven Ratner and Jason Abrams, *Accountability for Human Rights Atrocities in International Law: Beyond the Nuremberg Legacy* (Oxford University Press, 2001), p. 15.

21 Liesbeth Zegveld, *The Accountability of Armed Opposition Groups in International Law* (Cambridge University Press, 2002), p. 111.

22 Ibid.

23 For general commentary on this point, see Geneva Call, *Seeking Rebel Accountability: Report of the Geneva Call Mission to the Moro Islamic Liberation Front (MILF) in Central Mindanao, Philippines 3–8 April 2002* (Geneva Call Monograph No. 1, August 2002).

24 Zegveld (n. 21), p. 115.

25 Ibid.

Conventions.[26] On the other hand, Article 25 of the Rome Statute does not describe the type of armed conflict to which it should be applied.[27] In fact, the provision does not refer to the term 'armed conflict' whatsoever. Article 25(3)(b) merely states that an individual who ordered the commission of a crime will be held responsible for ordering that crime.[28] Moreover, the reference in Article 25 to 'a person' and the reference in Article 28 to a 'military commander or person' imply that the provisions apply to both members of state armed forces and members of non-state armed actors. So, Article 25 applies to leaders of both state armed forces and non-state armed groups in both armed conflict and peacetime situations.

This construal of Article 25(3)(b) is based on several key decisions handed down by both the ICTY and the ICTR.[29] Although none of the decisions specifically deal with leaders of armed groups accused of ordering the commission of crimes, statements to this effect can be readily found in the jurisprudence of both the ICTY and the ICTR. For example, in *Prosecutor* v. *Tadić*, the accused was acting on the authority of Republika Srpska, an armed group operating in Bosnia and Herzegovina.[30] During the proceedings, the tribunal classified the armed conflict between the Bosnian Serbs and the Republic of Bosnia Herzegovina and Bosnian Croat armed forces as a non-international armed conflict.[31] The Tribunal held that ordering the commission of crimes as laid down in Article 7 of the

26 For further analysis, see Article 4 of the ICTR Statute.

27 Ibid., Article 25.

28 Ibid., Article 25(3)(b).

29 *Prosecutor* v. *Zejnil Delalić, Zdravko Mucić, Hazim Delić, Esad Landžo*, IT-96-21-T, Judgment, 16 November 1998, para. 346. See also the following ICTY Judgments: *Prosecutor* v. *Aleksovski*, IT-95-14/1-T, Judgment, 25 June 1999, paras 69ff.; concurring Appeals Chamber (24 March 2000), paras 69–77; *Prosecutor* v. *Blaskić*, IT-95-14-T, Judgment, 3 March 2000, paras 289ff.; concurring Appeals Chamber (29 July 2004), para. 484; *Prosecutor* v. *Kordić and Čerkez*, IT-95-14/2-T, Judgment, 26 February 2001, paras 401ff.; partly reversed by the ICTY Appeals Chamber (17 December 2004) but no change with regard to the requirements for superior/command responsibility (para. 827); *Br⊠anin* (n. 3), para. 275; *Prosecutor* v. *Strugar*, IT-01-42-T, Judgment, 31 January 2005, para. 358; *Halilović* (n. 3), paras 55ff. (confirmed by the Appeals Chamber on 16 October 2007); *Prosecutor* v. *Limaj et al.*, IT-03-66-T, Judgment, 30 November 2005, paras 520ff.; *Prosecutor* v. *Hadžihasanović/Kubura*, IT-01-47-T, Judgment, 15 March 2006, paras 76ff.; *Orić* (n. 3), para. 294 (confirmed by the Appeals Chamber on 3 July 2008, para. 18); *Prosecutor* v. *Mrkšić, Radić and Šlji-van⊠anin*, IT-95-13/1-T, Judgment, 27 September 2007, para. 558; *Prosecutor* v. *Boskoski* and *Tarculovski*, IT-04-82-T, Judgment, 10 July 2008, para. 406, *Prosecutor* v. *Delić*, IT-04-83-T, Judgment, 15 September 2008, para. 56. For the ICTR: *Prosecutor* v. *Akayesu*, ICTR-96-4-T, Judgment, 2 September 1998, paras 486ff.; *Prosecutor* v. *Kayishema and Ruzindana*, ICTR- 95-1-T; ICTR-96-10-T, Judgment, 21 May 1999, paras 208–31; *Prosecutor* v. *Rutaganda*, ICTR-96-3-T, Judgment, 6 December 1999, paras 31ff.; *Prosecutor* v. *Bagilishema*, ICTR-95-1A-T, Judgment, 7 June 2001, para. 38; *Prosecutor* v. *Kajelijeli*, ICTR-98-44A-T, Judgment, 1 December 2003, paras 754–782; *Prosecutor* v. *Semanza*, ICTR-97-20-T, Judgment, 15 May 2003, paras 375–407.

30 *Prosecutor* v. *Tadić*, Case No. IT-94-1-T, paras 574–575.

31 *Prosecutor* v. *Tadić*, IT-94-1-A, Appeal Judgment, 15 July 1999, para. 166.

Statute is illegal during non-international armed conflict and also a violation of customary norms.[32]

The Rome Statute has followed the same approach. As will be seen in the next chapter of this study, Article 25(3)(b) of the Statute provides that a person will be held accountable for a crime within the legal authority of the court if that person orders 'the commission of such a crime which in fact occurs or is attempted'.[33] The term 'person' would suggest that Article 25(3)(b) applies to both agents of the state and members of armed groups. It is reasonable to assume that because 'Article 25 establishing [that] individual criminal responsibility is of a general nature, applicable to all substantive crimes in the Statute', Article 25(3)(b) is applicable to leaders of transnational terrorist groups.[34] In conclusion, the practice of the ICTY and the ICTR along with the Rome Statute suggests that leaders of transnational terrorist groups can be held individually criminally accountable for ordering their subordinates to commit crimes.

2 The principle of command responsibility proper

Additional Protocol 1 to the Geneva Conventions, which only applies to international armed conflict situations, was the only treaty provision which recognised that commanders could be held criminally liable for crimes committed by subordinates which they did not order on the basis that they should have prevented such acts. The provision specifies that:

> [t]he fact that a breach of the Conventions or of this Protocol was committed by a subordinate does not absolve his superiors from penal or disciplinary responsibility, as the case may be, if they knew, or had information which should have enabled them to conclude in the circumstances at the time, that he was committing or was going to commit such a breach and if they did not

32 *Tadić* (n. 30), paras 666–669. *Prosecutor* v. *Furundžija* also provides evidence of this. Here, the accused was a commander of a special unit of the HVO (Croatian Defence Council) military police which was founded by the self-proclaimed Bosnian Croats within Bosnia and Herzegovina. It was held by the ICTY that an individual who orders the commission of a crime such as torture is an active participant in the crime and on that basis is responsible. For further analysis, see *Prosecutor* v. *Furundžija*, IT-95-17/1-T, Judgment, 10 December 1998, paras 187, 253, and 254. It is interesting to note that the Tribunal did not examine whether the armed conflict was international or internal in character, nor the legal status of the accused. Zegveld is of the view that the implication of this is that 'the ordering of the commission of crimes, whether by leaders of state armies or armed opposition groups, is prohibited in internal conflicts as well as international ones' (n. 21), p. 113. It may be argued that this conclusion is in line with resolutions issued by the United Nations Security Council. For further reference, see UN Security Council Resolution 1193 (28 August 1998), para. 12.

33 Article 25(3)(b) of the Rome Statute.

34 Zegveld (n. 21), p. 114.

> take all feasible measures within their power to prevent or repress the breach.[35]

During international armed conflicts the doctrine of command responsibility principally applies to organised state armies. In turn, the 'relationship between the superior and the subordinate in state armies normally involves direct subordination in a clearly and formally organised hierarchy'.[36]

Consequently, the International Committee of the Red Cross (ICRC) Commentary on Article 87 of Additional Protocol 1 to the Geneva Conventions provides that:

> [t]he first duty of a military commander, whatever his rank, is to exercise command. For this purpose the relationship between ranks and responsibilities are, as a general rule, exactly determined within armed forces, and the authority of each of the different levels of the hierarchy is precisely defined. It is under these conditions that the armed forces can be submitted to a regime of internal discipline . . . This regime is inseparable from the status of armed forces . . . The disciplinary system must ensure, in particular, compliance with the rules of international law applicable in armed conflict.[37]

However, the superior–subordinate relationship in the context of transnational terrorist groups is much more complex than that of state armed forces. This is because these groups have a more complex organisational structure than other state armed forces and other non-state armed actors such as armed opposition groups.[38] As explored in Chapter 2, transnational terrorist groups comprise a multilayered network structure containing loosely coordinated cells and they lack the central hierarchical command structure needed to pinpoint which individuals within the group orders and plans attacks.[39]

In contrast to Additional Protocol 1 to the Geneva Conventions, the provisions laid down in Article 28 of the Rome Statute may be applied to both international and non-international armed conflict situations and to non-armed conflict situations. In particular, Article 28 (b) states that a leader will be held accountable for the criminal acts of subordinates under his effective control where:

> (i) The superior either knew, or consciously disregarded information which clearly indicated, that the subordinates were committing or about to commit such crimes;

35 Additional Protocol 1 to the Geneva Conventions.
36 Zegveld (n. 21), p. 115.
37 Jean de Preux et al., *Commentary on the Additional Protocols of 8 June 1977 to the Geneva Conventions of 12 August 1949* (International Committee of the Red Cross, 1987), pp. 1017–1018.
38 Zegveld (n. 21), p. 115.
39 See p. 31 of this book.

(ii) The crimes concerned activities that were within the effective responsibility and control of the superior; and

(iii) The superior failed to take all necessary and reasonable measures within his or her power to prevent or repress their commission or to submit the matter to the competent authorities for investigation and prosecution.[40]

So, Article 28 expands the application of the doctrine of command responsibility for failing to prevent or punish crimes committed by subordinates to superiors of transnational terrorist groups. In particular, the provision acknowledges the responsibility of 'a military commander or person effectively acting as a military commander' for omitting to prevent or punish the commission of offences by subordinates.

If one does not agree with the classification of leaders of transnational terrorist groups as 'commanders' under Article 28(1), these individuals are in any event included under the phrase 'persons effectively acting as a military commander'.[41] Moreover, since crimes against humanity can also be perpetrated in non-armed conflict situations and the provisions on individual criminal accountability pertain to all major crimes, it would be logical to conclude that a leader of a transnational terrorist group may be held accountable for acts of omission under Article 28 of the Rome Statute.[42] It is immaterial whether the accused is a leader of a transnational terrorist group or a commander of a state army.[43]

D The criteria for establishing the accountability of leaders of transnational terrorist groups

1 Establishing a superior–subordinate relationship

The primary criterion for fulfilling the doctrine of command responsibility is establishing that there is a relationship between the superior and the

40 Article 28 of the Rome Statute.

41 Ibid.

42 It is also interesting to note the stance of the ICTY in relation to this issue. In *Aleksovski* (n. 29) the accused was in charge of a detention facility which imprisoned Bosnian Muslims. Counsel for the accused argued that the principle of command responsibility did not apply in this particular case. It was specifically argued at para. 74 that the doctrine did not apply because it only applied to cases concerning international armed conflict, whereas the conflict in this particular case was non-international in nature. The ICTY appears to have rejected this argument. In particular, it was held at para. 76 that 'any person acting de facto as a superior may be held responsible under Article 7(3)' of the Statute. To be more specific, it would seem that the Tribunal found the fact that the conflict was internal rather than international in nature to be completely irrelevant. Even more importantly, the Tribunal had no regard for the legal status of the accused and whether he was a member of an armed group or a state actor. While it may be argued that the accused was a member of an armed group, the Tribunal did not openly state this its judgment.

43 For further academic commentary, see Jordan Paust, 'Superior Orders and Command Responsibility', in M. Bassiouni (ed.), *International Criminal Law* (Transnational, 1986), vol. III, p. 80.

subordinate.[44] The rationale for imposing criminal sanctions on leaders of transnational terrorist groups for crimes committed by their subordinates is that the leader has the authority to control their acts.[45] However, an analysis of the case law of the ad hoc international tribunals illustrates that the chief stumbling block for the application of the doctrine of command responsibility to transnational terrorist groups is the superior–subordinate relationship.[46]

The ICTY and the ICTR have modified the element of authority and control to the practical realities of armed groups and their leaders.[47] It is the effective control over the subordinates and 'the ability and duty to prevent or stop the commission of crimes by the subordinates, which entails – when such a duty is breached – the criminal responsibility of the superior'.[48] Article 7(3) of the ICTY Statute and Article 6(3) of the ICTR Statute refer to commanders as 'superiors'.[49] However, Article 28 of the Rome Statutes provides very little guidance on the relationship necessary between command leaders and their subordinates to establish accountability. An examination of the wording of Article 28 indicates that the accused need not have held a formal command position within the transnational terrorist group. In particular, the use of the term 'superior' in Article 28(b) encompasses individuals who hold a position of authority established on the presence of *de facto* powers of control.[50]

This interpretation of Article 28 finds support in the jurisprudence of the ICTY and the ICTR. For example, in the *Prosecutor* v. *Kayishema* case, it was held by the ICTR that the Tribunal was 'under a duty, pursuant to Article 6(3), to consider the responsibility of all individuals who exercised effective control, whether that control be de jure or de facto'.[51] In addition, the ICTY Trial Chamber in the *Čelebići* case applied the standard of actual authority to command structures that were not obvious from formal authorisation:

44 For further analysis, see Allison Danner and Jenny Martinez, 'Guilty Associations: Joint Criminal Enterprise, Command Responsibility, and the Development of International Criminal Law', *California Law Review* 93 (2005) 75–169.

45 For further analysis, see Rodney Dixon, 'Prosecuting the Leaders: The Application of the Doctrine of Superior Responsibility before the United Nations International Criminal Tribunals for the Former Yugoslavia and Rwanda', in A. Vogelaar et al. (eds), *The Commander's Responsibility in Difficult Circumstances: NL Arms Netherlands Annual Review of Military Studies* (Gianotten, 1998), p. 109; Ratner and Abrams (n. 20), p. 132.

46 Beatrice Bonafe, 'Command Responsibility between Personal Culpability and Objective Liability: Finding a Proper Role for Command Responsibility', *Journal of International Criminal Justice* 5(3) (2007) 599–618, p. 608.

47 Ibid.

48 Ibid.

49 There does not appear to be any clear definition of 'superior' in international law. However, it should be borne in mind that since the Second World War it has been recognised that a superior does not need to be a military leader. For further reference, see *The Roechling Case*, 14 CCL No. 10 Trials 1111–16.

50 Ibid.

51 *Kayishema* (n. 29), para. 122.

> a position of command is indeed a necessary precondition for the imposition of command responsibility. However, this statement must be qualified by the recognition that the existence of such a position *cannot be determined by reference to formal status alone*. Instead, the factor that determines liability for this type of criminal responsibility is the *actual possession, or non-possession, of powers of control over the actions of subordinates*. [52]

To prove that a superior–subordinate relationship existed between the accused and the persons who carried out the criminal act, there must be compelling evidence that the accused exercised effective control over the subordinates, 'in the sense of having the material ability to prevent and punish the commission of these offences'.[53]

Even though the *Čelebići* case involved state actors the same principle would apply to leaders of non-state armed actors. For example, in *Prosecutor* v. *Aleksovski*, the ICTY Trial Chamber held that the application of the doctrine of command responsibility is not limited to superiors who are legally authorised to order subordinates in a definite military chain of command.[54] The Tribunal in particular stated that 'the decisive criterion in determining who is a superior according to customary international law is not only the accused's formal legal status, but also his ability . . . to exercise control'.[55] Therefore, in cases concerning leaders of transnational terrorist groups the critical factor in determining the existence of a superior–subordinate relationship is not whether the accused holds a formal command position within the group but whether he/she is capable of asserting control over his/her subordinates.[56]

This is because the organisational structure of the group may be disorganised, so it may be unclear whether the leader occupies a formal command position. The

52 *Čelebići* (n. 29), paras 302, 303, and 370 (emphasis added).

53 Ibid., para. 378. See also Bonafe (n. 46), p. 609, who states that 'the adoption of the effective control criterion excludes that the mere influence of the superior over the subordinates suffices for finding a superior–subordinate relationship'. With regard to superiors, it would seem that the possession of *de jure* authority is not considered by the ad hoc tribunals as adequate for the finding of command responsibility if it does not epitomise effective control (Bonafe (n. 46), p. 609). As a result, many commanders could not be found responsible for the criminal acts of their subordinates under the doctrine of command responsibility on the grounds that effective control of their troops could not be determined beyond reasonable doubt. For further reference on decisions where commanders were not found accountable, see *Prosecutor* v. *Kunarac*, IT-96-23 and 23/1-T, Judgment, 22 February 2001; *Prosecutor* v. *Kvočka et al.*, IT-98-30/1-T, Judgment, 21 November 2001; *Prosecutor* v. *Blaškić*, IT-95-14-A, Appeal Judgment, 29 July 2004; *Prosecutor* v. *Kordić and Čerkez*, IT-95-14/2-A, Judgment, 17 December 2004; *Prosecutor* v. *Blagojević and Jokić*, IT-02-60-T, Judgment,17 January 2005; *Halilović* (n. 3) and IT-01-48-A, Appeals Judgment, 16 October 2007; *Limaj* (n. 29).

54 *Aleksovski* (n. 29), para. 125.

55 Ibid., para. 76.

56 *Prosecutor* v. *Jean-Pierre Bemba Gombo*, ICC-01/05-01/08-3343, Judgment pursuant to Article 74 of the Statute, 21 March 2016, para. 80.

existence of a superior–subordinate relationship within a transnational terrorist group will need to be inferred from the manner in which terrorist attacks are committed. Support for this proposition comes from the ICTY Appeals Chamber decision in the *Tadić* case which noted that even though the parties to an international armed conflict may no longer be functioning states this does not mean that their officials could not held accountable under the doctrine of command responsibility.[57] Indeed, as discussed in Chapter 2, in some state armed forces and non-state armed groups the superior–subordinate relationship may not be readily apparent from official authorisations and documentation.[58]

The ICC, in determining whether a leader of a transnational terrorist group has committed a crime, will need to examine his/her actual authority within the group. Article 28(1) of the Rome Statute provides that a military superior or a person acting as such will be held criminally accountable for 'acts committed by forces under his or her effective command and control or effective authority and control'.[59] The exact same factors must be taken into account when deciding whether a leader of a transnational terrorist group is criminally accountable for having ordered the execution of criminal acts by their subordinates.[60]

2 *Applicable standards of knowledge*

a Actual knowledge

Leaders of transnational terrorist groups cannot be held accountable for acts committed by their subordinates just because there is evidence of a superior–subordinate relationship.[61] Instead, there must have been a dereliction in duty on the part of the leader.[62] This means either that 'the leader knew, or that the totality of the circumstances . . . establish that the leader must have known that the subordinate was committing, was about to commit or had committed unlawful acts'.[63] The term 'knowledge' essentially indicates an 'awareness as to the existence of a circumstance or awareness of its occurring'.[64] In particular, the *Čelebići* judgment states that 'actual knowledge' of the leader may be, 'established through

57 *Tadić* Appeal (n. 31), para. 166.
58 See p. 29 of this book.
59 Article 28(1) of the Rome Statute.
60 Bemba (n. 56), paras 180–185.
61 For further academic commentary, see Andrew Mitchell, 'Failure to Halt, Prevent or Punish: The Doctrine of Command Responsibility for War Crimes', *Sydney Law Review* 22 (2000) 381–410.
62 Zegveld (n. 21), p. 124. For further reference, see *USA* v. *Wilheim von Leeb et al.* (the *High Command* case) Trials of War Criminals before the Nuremburg Military Tribunals under Control Council Law No. 10 1946–49, Vol. XI 543–544 (US Government Printing Office, Washington, DC, 1950).
63 Zegveld (n. 21), p. 125.
64 Ilias Bantekas, 'The Contemporary Law of Superior Responsibility', *American Journal of International Law* 93 (1999) 573–595, p. 587. ICC Prep-Com, 11–21 February

direct or circumstantial evidence, that his subordinates were committing or about to commit crimes'.[65]

Actual knowledge may also be attributed to leaders where they had:

> in [their] possession information of a nature, which at least, would put [them] on notice of the risk of such offenses by indicating the need for additional investigation in order to ascertain whether such crimes were committed or were about to be committed by [their] subordinates.[66]

Where there is no actual evidence, constructive knowledge of the subordinate's crimes can be inferred from circumstantial evidence.[67] This knowledge can be established by 'examining striking features of subordinate criminal activity and arriving at the inference that the superior who is accused was aware of those crimes'.[68]

This presumption can be made in a number of ways.[69] The UN Commission of Experts, which was in charge of investigating whether there were any violations of international humanitarian law in the former Yugoslavia, stated that commanders 'must have known' about the crimes which were being committed by their subordinates on the grounds that the:

> number, type and scope of illegal acts; the time during which they occurred; the number and type of troops involved; the logistics involved, if any; the geographical location of the acts; their widespread occurrence; the tactical tempo of operations; the *modus operandi* of similar illegal acts; the offenders and staff involved and the location of the commander at that time.[70]

It is interesting to note that Karadžić's actual knowledge of hostage-taking was inferred from his statements that he knew of the incidents.[71] His constructive knowledge was further substantiated by UN Security Council resolutions published at the time,[72] which enabled him to be fully aware of the incidents.[73] There was also

1997, Decisions Taken by the Preparatory Committee, UN Doc. A/AC.249/1997/L.5 Art. H (12 March 1997).

65 *Čelebići* (n. 29), para. 383.

66 Ibid.

67 Bantekas (n. 64), p. 587.

68 Ibid., p. 588.

69 For further reference, see generally Christopher Crowe, 'Command Responsibility in the Former Yugoslavia: The Chances for Successful Prosecution', *University of Richmond Law Review* 29 (1994) 191–233.

70 'Final Report of the Commission of Experts, Established pursuant to Security Council Resolution 780 (1992)', UN SCOR, Annex, UN Doc. S/1994/674, para. 58 (27 May 1994).

71 *Prosecutor* v. *Karadžić and Mladić, Review of the Indictment Pursuant to Rule 61 of the Rules of Procedure and Evidence*, IT-95-5-R61 and IT-95-18-R61, 11 July 1996 reprinted in 108 ILR 86 (1998), para. 72.

72 Ibid.

73 Ibid.

evidence that he was present in the areas when the crimes took place.[74] In the same way, the ICTY in the *Čelebići* case found that the commander of the camp was 'well aware of his sub-commander's proclivity for mistreating detainees, the notoriety of crimes, and proof that there was no possibility that he could have known or heard about them'.[75]

b The 'should have known' standard

Article 28 of the Rome Statute also establishes accountability for failure to act upon information that the commander 'should have known'.[76] The phrase 'should have known' has arguably the same meaning as the phrase 'had information enabling them to conclude' as laid down in Additional Protocol 1 to the Geneva Conventions.[77] Bantekas contends that this 'had reason to know' standard implies that 'commanders who are in possession of sufficient information to be on notice of subordinate criminal activity cannot escape liability by [simply] declaring their ignorance, even if such ignorance of the specific crime is amply established'.[78] This standard establishes an objective negligence test 'which takes into full account the circumstances at the time'.[79]

At the same time, it would seem that a lack of knowledge will provide no defence whatsoever if the leader of a transnational terrorist group did not take the proper steps to ensure that he had all such knowledge.[80] For example, in the *Čelebići* case the ICTY held that leaders will be held responsible if:

> [s]ome specific information was in fact available to him which would provide notice of offences committed by his subordinates. This information need not be such that it by itself was sufficient to compel the conclusion of the existence of such crimes. It is sufficient that the superior was put on further inquiry by the information, or, in other words, that it indicated the need for additional investigation in order to ascertain whether offences were being committed or about to be committed by his subordinates.[81]

The Trial Chamber rejected the contention that the mental standard should include criminal responsibility of a leader for acts committed by his subordinate 'in situations where he should have had knowledge concerning their activities, but where he lacks such information by virtue of his failure properly to supervise his subordinates'.[82]

This mental standard was also applied in the *Aleksovski* case, which involved a leader of an armed group who was in charge of a detention facility which

74 Ibid., para. 80.
75 Bantekas (n. 64), p. 588. For further reference, see *Čelebići* (n. 29), para. 770.
76 Article 28 of the Rome Statute.
77 Article 86(2) of Additional Protocol 1 to the Geneva Conventions.
78 Bantekas (n. 64), p. 589.
79 Ibid.
80 *Čelebići* (n. 29), para. 388.
81 Ibid., para. 387.
82 Zegveld (n. 21), p. 126.

imprisoned Muslims.[83] The ICTY held that the armed conflict was non-international in character and that the Bosnian Croats were an armed group when the alleged crimes took place.[84] The Trial Chamber followed the same reasoning as the *Čelebići* case noting that 'in the absence of direct evidence of the superior's knowledge of the offences committed by subordinates, such knowledge cannot be presumed'.[85] The Tribunal also had to consider whether the geographical and temporal jurisdiction were significant aspects in considering whether the commander had actual knowledge that his subordinates were committing crimes.[86]

The Tribunal concluded that these factors were significant for determining his actual knowledge. Consequentially, 'the physical distance between the crimes and the superior and repetition of the crimes together . . . [could] preclude the responsibility of the leader'.[87] Since the defendant had lived inside the prison for a considerable period of time, the Tribunal deduced that he must have known that the detainees were being mistreated by his subordinates.[88] The ICTY has proposed that customary law on the *mens rea* standard may incorporate a 'should have known' criterion.[89] On this basis, leaders of transnational terrorist groups have a responsibility to attain the necessary knowledge on the activities of his subordinates.[90] As a result, the leader can no longer rely on the defence that he had a lack of knowledge about the activities his subordinates were engaged in.[91]

E The duties of leaders of transnational terrorist groups under the Rome Statute

1 The duty to act

Domestic military law by and large obliges commanders to 'take appropriate action with regard to offences perpetrated by their subordinates'.[92] Article 15 of the United States Uniform Code of Military Justice for example permits

83 Aleksovski (n. 29), para. 46.
84 Ibid.
85 Ibid., para. 80.
86 Ibid.
87 Zegveld (n. 21), p. 127.
88 *Aleksovski* (n. 29), para. 80.
89 *Čelebići* (n. 29), para. 393.
90 Bantekas (n. 64), p. 590.
91 However, Zegveld (n. 21), p. 127 interestingly notes that the principle only applies to: 'military leaders or persons effectively acting as military leaders, not to civilian leaders, for whom the Rome Statute prescribes a different mental standard'. Civilian leaders will only find themselves criminally responsible where they 'either knew or consciously disregarded information which clearly indicated that the subordinates were committing or about to commit' crimes with the jurisdiction of the court (Article 28(2)(a) of the Rome Statute of the International Criminal Court). It would therefore seem that civilian leaders will not be 'under an active duty to inform themselves of the activities of their subordinates' (Zegveld (n. 21), p. 128).
92 Ilias Bantekas, *Principles of Direct and Superior Responsibility in International Humanitarian Law* (Manchester University Press, 2002), p. 115.

commanders to decide whether an incident should be handled administratively or by means of a court trial.[93] Every commander in the chain of command 'possesses independent, yet overlapping discretion, to dispose of offences within the limits of his or her authority'.[94]

International law compels leaders of transnational terrorist groups to properly respect two basic duties with respect to their subordinates: these are the duties to prevent their criminal behaviour and to punish them for crimes committed during terrorist attacks.[95] Leaders of transnational terrorist groups have a pre-existing duty to ensure that the activities of subordinates are lawful, regardless of whether they were ordered by the leader.[96] For instance, the Commentary of the ICRC on Additional Protocol I to the Geneva Conventions notes that '[a] failure to act (omission) consists of failing to do or say something. In a legal sense it consists of failing in a duty to act'.[97]

Similarly, the Trial Chamber of the Special Court for Sierra Leone (SCSL) in the *CDF* and *RUF* cases held that:

> [t]he nature of responsibility pursuant to Article 6(3) is based upon the duty of a superior to act, which consists of a duty to prevent and a duty to punish criminal acts of his subordinates. It is thus a failure to act when under a duty to do so which is the essence of this form of responsibility.[98]

Therefore, responsibility results in the failure to fulfil a pre-existing duty.[99] This is a fundamental development in international criminal law because it was not certain in the early jurisprudence of the ICTY whether a pre-existing duty was a legal requirement for establishing the responsibility of the accused. The term 'duty' is often mentioned in the jurisprudence of both the ICTY and the ICTR but there is very little examination of its content. The same can be said in respect of the ICC. For example, the Pre-Trial Chamber in *Prosecutor* v. *Jean-Pierre Bemba Gombo* referred to a leader of an armed group as 'failing to fulfil his duty' remarking that 'criminal responsibility for omissions is incurred only where there exists a legal

93 10 USC 815.
94 Bantekas (n. 64), p. 115.
95 *USA* v. *von Leeb et al.* (n. 62) X TWC 2. See also American Articles of War, 30 June 1775, Article XII, reproduced in *Journals of the Continental Congress 1774–1779: Volume II* (Government Printing Office, Washington, DC, 1905) 111, p. 114; General Orders No. 130, Headquarters Division of the Philippines, 19 June 1901, as reprinted in Charges of Cruelty to the Natives of the Philippines, 57th Congress, First Session, Senate, Doc. No. 205, Part 2, at 85. For academic commentary, see Georg Schwarzenberger, *International Law, Vol II: The Law of Armed Conflict* (Stevens, 1968), p. 468.
96 Ibid.
97 De Preux (n. 37), p. 1003.
98 *Prosecutor* v. *Fofana and Kondewa*, SCSL-04-14-T, Judgment, 2 August 2007, para. 234; *Prosecutor* v. *Sesay, Kallon and Gbao*, SCSL-04-15-T, Judgment, 2 March 2009, para. 283.
99 *Prosecutor* v. *Mpambara*, ICTR-01-65-T, Judgment, 11 September 2006, para. 27.

obligation to act'.[100] Nevertheless, it did not analyse the parameters of this duty at all.[101]

a Failure to prevent

There are two facets to this ground of criminal accountability. The first relates to situations where the leader of the transnational terrorist group has knowledge that his/her subordinates are about to perpetrate a crime and fails to take the necessary steps to prevent the commission of those acts.[102] The second facet relates to the same factual situation with the distinction that the commander had 'reason to know' instead of actual knowledge that his/her subordinates were about to perpetrate a crime.[103] Article 28(a) (ii) of the Rome Statute clearly states that a leader will be held responsible for criminal wrongdoing if he/she '[f]ailed to take all necessary and reasonable measures within his or her power to prevent or repress their commission or to submit the matter to the competent authorities for investigation and prosecution'.[104] When considering the responsibility of leaders to prevent crimes being committed by their subordinates the characteristics of the transnational terrorist group will have some bearing in determining the extent of superior's duties within this group.[105]

The Rome Statute clearly states that leaders can be held responsible if they fail to take the 'necessary and reasonable measures' to avoid offences being committed.[106] However, it would seem that leaders should only 'be held responsible for failing to take such measures that are within his material possibility'.[107] As a result, the responsibility of leaders of transnational terrorist groups is not as straightforward as a preliminary reading of Article 28 of the Rome Statute suggests. Leaders of transnational terrorist groups can only be held accountable before the ICC if they exercise actual authority over their subordinates and fail to

100 *Decision Pursuant to Article 61(7)(a) and (b) of the Rome Statute on the Charges of the Prosecutor Against Jean-Pierre Bemba Gombo*, ICC-01/05-01/08, Pre-Trial Chamber II, 15 June 2009, para. 407.

101 For further analysis on the history of this pre-existing duty to act, see Alexander Zahar and Goran Sluiter, *International Criminal Law* (Oxford University Press, 2008), p. 259; William Parks, 'Command Responsibility for War Crimes', *Military Law Review* 62 (1973) 1–104; Leslie Green, 'Command Responsibility in International Humanitarian Law', *Transnational Law and Contemporary Problems* 3 (1995) 354.

102 Mirjan Damaska, 'The Shadow Side of Command Responsibility', *American Journal of Comparative Law* 49 (2001) 455–496, p. 461. For further analysis on these two aspects of the duty to prevent, see Damaska (n. 102), p. 461.

103 For further commentary on this 'had reason to know' standard, see Greg Vetter, 'Command Responsibility of Non-Military Superiors in the International Criminal Court (ICC)', *Yale Journal of International Law* 25 (2000) 89–143, p. 114.

104 Article 28(a)(i) of the Rome Statute. See also Article 7(3) of the ICTY Statute and Article 6(3) of the ICTR Statute which is very similar to the wording of Article 28(a)(i) of the Rome Statute.

105 Ibid.

106 Article 86(2) of Additional Protocol 1 to the Geneva Conventions.

107 *Aleksovski* (n. 29), para. 81.

take such measures that are within their power to prevent the commission of a criminal offence.[108]

The duty to prevent the commission of crimes by subordinates begins upon the preparation or planning of the offence by the subordinates.[109] Leaders can also be held accountable for 'failure to prevent [crimes] if they fail to take into account factors such as the age, training, or similar elements that point to obvious conclusions regarding the likelihood that such crimes would be committed'.[110] For example, the wealth of information available to the Israeli Defense Minister, Ariel Sharon, and the Chief-of Staff of the Israeli Defense Forces, indicated that there had been mass killings at Palestinian refugee camps in Lebanon. As a result, the *Final Report of the Kahan Commission* suggested that both individuals were 'indirectly responsible' under a test of anticipated foreseeability lacking direct intent.[111] The two officials had a duty to acknowledge the danger in which these refugees found themselves and to prevent and even stop the massacre by doing everything within their authority to do so.[112]

Leaders of transnational terrorist groups will only be held to have successfully discharged their duty to prevent offences by their subordinates if they make use of every means in their authority to do so.[113] This would also include any opposition the leader may have had to any plan for the commission of a criminal offence even where he/she has no further power to intervene.[114] The duty to prevent has thus far been narrowly interpreted by international tribunals.[115] For example, the ICTR Trial Chamber in the *Akayesu* case, noted whether or not a commander had authority to take measures to prevent the commission of criminal offences by subordinates was completely immaterial if the commander did not make some effort to do so.[116] Trial Chamber III at the ICC arguably made a similar finding in the *Jean-Pierre Bemba Gombo* case[117] and arguably provides an avenue to find commanders of transnational terrorist groups guilty if it has been proven beyond reasonable doubt by the prosecution that they did not take all measures within their authority to prevent terrorist attacks from occurring.

b Duty to punish

The leader of a transnational terrorist group is obliged to take action to punish the commission of a criminal offence after it has occurred.[118] The general rule is that

108 Zegveld (n. 21), p. 129.
109 Bantekas (n. 64), p. 591.
110 Ibid. See also *Canada* v. *Kurt Meyer*, 4 Law Reports (1945) 97.
111 *Final Report of the Kahan Commission* [authorised English translation], 22 ILM 473 (1983).
112 Ibid.
113 *United States* v. *von Weizsaecker*, 14 Trials (1952) 308.
114 Ibid., pp. 496, 518, and 609.
115 Bantekas (n. 64), p. 591.
116 Akayesu (n. 29), p. 46.
117 Bemba (n. 56), paras 202–203.
118 For example, see *USA* v. *Ohlendorf et al.* (the *Einsatzgruppen* case) IV TWC 1 at p. 513. See also Bemba (n. 100), para. 494, where it was noted that Bemba 'specifically

'[a] superior is bound to conduct a meaningful investigation with a view to establish the facts, order or execute appropriate sanctions, or report the perpetrators to the competent authorities in case the superior lacks sanctioning power'.[119] There are two elements to this form of liability. The first element relates to accountability for situations where the leader's failure plays a role in the criminal activity of his subordinates.[120] Damaska contends that it is very easy to see how this could happen 'if . . . [the leader] does not take his aberrant subordinates to task, his troops can interpret the omission as a sign that he condones, perhaps even encourages, the commission of . . . [international] crimes'.[121] Consequently, the leader's failure to punish can be 'linked causally to the subsequent criminal activity of those he did not punish, or of those under his command'.[122] Punishment is therefore intended to deter the commission of future crimes by subordinates.

The first element of the 'failure to punish' standard is arguably the most commonly found within transnational terrorist groups.[123] A leader of a transnational terrorist group who does not suppress the commission of criminal acts by his subordinates can also be held accountable as an accomplice to those crimes. At the same time, if the qualifications for complicity are absent, the commander can still be found accountable for failing to prevent the reverberation of international crimes. In Damaska's view this is because 'he can no longer profess ignorance of criminal propensities among his troops, and because it will be easy for this reason to establish that he failed to take necessary and reasonable measures to prevent these propensities from being acted out again'.[124]

The failure of a leader to punish the criminal acts of subordinates acquires greater significance when one considers the second element of the duty when it is separated from the failure to prevent criminal acts. The element often 'passes unnoticed because of the widespread but faulty assumption that the . . . [failure to prevent and the failure to act] are inseparable'.[125] The two duties often coexist, particularly in prosecutions of persons who held positions of command for a prolonged time period.[126] However, the duty to punish can also be regarded as separate from the duty to prevent. The failure to deter the commission of future

established a commission of enquiry to verify facts relating to alleged crimes committed by MLC soldiers'; Matthew Lippman, 'Humanitarian Law: The Uncertain Contours of Command Responsibility', *Tulsa Journal Comparative and International Law* 9 (2001) 1–93, p. 54.

119 *Limaj* (n. 29), para. 529. See also *Orić* (n. 3), para. 336; *Strugar* (n. 29), para. 376.

120 For further analysis on this point, see Ann Ching, 'Evolution of the Command Responsibility Doctrine in Light of the *Čelebići* Decision of the International Criminal Tribunal for the Former Yugoslavia', *North Caroline Journal of International Law and Commercial Regulation* 25 (1999) 167–205, p. 202.

121 Damaska (n. 102), p. 467.

122 Ibid.

123 Ibid. For further academic commentary see generally Ching (n. 120).

124 Damaska (n. 102), p. 467.

125 Ibid., p. 468.

126 Ibid.

acts is another facet of the duty to punish.[127] It is a 'species of imputed responsibility for an omission and is neither akin to the common law concepts of "accessory after the fact"[128] nor misprision of felony'.[129]

It does not 'require a pre-existing relationship to those who perpetrated the offenses, as this would have been part of the incumbent superior's preventative duty at the time the offences occurred'.[130] The duty to punish when separated from the duty to prevent holds the leader accountable for the criminal acts of his subordinates on the grounds that he failed 'to call them to task after he had learned about what they had done'.[131] There is no requirement to establish that he/she was in any way connected with the commission of the crime. Accordingly, if members of a transnational terrorist group perpetrated crimes against humanity, the leader will also be held accountable for these crimes. The leader's prison sentence will be longer if it can be established that his position exacerbated the perpetration of the crimes.[132]

In view of the severe punishment which the leader of the transnational terrorist group may face if found responsible, the only justification for this standpoint is that the leader's failure to punish 'implies a superior's approval, or subsequent ratification, of his subordinates' transgression'.[133] However, Damaska argues that utilised as a medium for vicarious liability, the approval of a subordinate's criminal act is not in keeping with the central tenets of domestic criminal law.[134] There was a point in time when it was widely accepted that a 'person who condoned a crime ex post ought to be treated as a party to the crime, even if he was in no other way connected to the criminal enterprise'.[135] However, Anglo-American jurisdictions, from which international criminal law is largely drawn, have rejected the concept and do not regard the accessory after the fact as a party to the crime and he cannot be punished for it. As an alternative, the person is treated as having obstructed the course of justice, which is a much less serious offence.

However, attributing accountability to leaders of transnational terrorist groups for simply failing to punish subordinates who committed criminal acts is not in keeping with ordinary understanding either. It is hard for the layperson to understand a legal principle that:

127 Bantekas PDSR (n. 92), p. 119. See also *Blaskić* (n. 29), para. 10, where Trial Chamber I stated that 'failing to punish subordinates inevitably means failing to prevent the recurrence of crimes, whereas by punishing subordinates such recurrence is naturally prevented, with the result that failure to punish alone is sufficient grounds for command responsibility'.
128 Paul Robinson, 'Imputed Criminal Liability', *Yale Law Journal* 93 (1984) 609–676, p. 633.
129 Bantekas (n. 64), p. 591.
130 Ibid.
131 Damaska (n. 102), p. 468.
132 Sandesh Sivakumaran, 'Command Responsibility in Irregular Groups', *Journal of International Criminal Justice* 10 (2012) 1129–1150, p. 1148.
133 Damaska (n. 102), p. 468.
134 Ibid.
135 Ibid., pp. 468–469.

> leads to the branding of an individual as a . . . criminal just because he failed to punish those who actually contributed to its occurrence: the distinction between committing a crime and punishing its perpetrators belongs to a body of distinctions to which ordinary people attach their ideas of just deserts.[136]

However, this ordinary understanding still does not pardon leaders of transnational terrorist groups who fail to punish subordinates who commit criminal acts. Failing to punish criminal acts is not at variance with common moral perceptions.[137] However, friction arises when international law uses this failure to punish as a means for broadening criminal liability, allowing the conviction of a leader of a transnational terrorist group for failing in his duty to punish his subordinates.

In the aftermath of terrorist attacks it may not always be possible for the superior to punish the offending subordinates because he may not be able to sentence a subordinate to a term of imprisonment in a detention facility if the group does not exercise control over territory.[138] At the same time, a leader of a transnational terrorist group ought to be held accountable for failing to take all reasonable steps that are 'within his material possibility'.[139] It would be illogical for leaders of transnational terrorist groups to claim in their defence that they did not have the legal authority to prevent criminal behaviour when they were physically able to do so. In these circumstances, the only appropriate course of action for the leader would be to conduct an investigation into the subordinate's conduct and report his conclusions to his/her own commanding officer.[140] During such an investigation the leader must determine whether offences were committed. If he/she determines that offences were committed, they must take all reasonable steps to prevent future crimes from occurring.[141] This is especially important where leaders are not able to prosecute or discipline a subordinate. If the leader ascertains that subordinates have committed or are in the process of committing a crime, they must notify the appropriate legal authorities.[142]

136 Ibid., p. 469.
137 Ibid.
138 Sivakumaran (n. 132), p. 1145.
139 *Čelebići* (n. 29), para. 395. For further academic commentary, see Robert Cryer et al. (eds), *An Introduction to International Criminal Law and Procedure* (Cambridge University Press, 2010), p. 395.
140 *Aleksovski* (n. 29), para. 81.
141 Bemba (n. 100), para. 494.
142 Ibid., para. 442. For further academic commentary, see Federal Republic of Germany, *Federal Ministry of Defence, Humanitarian Law in Armed Conflict – Manual* (1992). The *German Military Manual*, reflecting Geneva Protocol I, provides in Article 138 a duty to either suppress or 'report to competent authorities breaches of international law'.

F The challenges in prosecuting leaders of transnational terrorist groups under the Rome Statute

State authorities have had major difficulty in prosecuting and obtaining convictions of leaders of transnational terrorist groups in relation to ordinary criminal offences such as murder and grievous bodily harm.[143] This is because it is often 'evidentially impossible to link the leader of a . . . [transnational terrorist group] to any particular crime committed by members of his group'.[144] This explains why prosecuting authorities have often charged members of transnational terrorist groups with terrorism-specific offences such as membership of an illegal organisation instead of the actual crimes the members of the group are alleged to have perpetrated.[145] As a result, the most serious crimes perpetrated by the leaders of transnational terrorist groups are often not put on trial and remain unpunished. In addition, even in cases 'where the prosecuting authorities have charged defendants in terror cases with more traditional offences, such as murder, they have often found it too much of a challenge to conduct successful prosecutions of those ranking higher in terrorist structures'.[146] Therefore, the doctrine of command responsibility would arguably alleviate some of the evidential challenges in determining whether the leader of a transnational terrorist group played a part in the planning and perpetration of terrorist attacks upon the civilian population by subordinates.

Pursuant to the doctrine of command responsibility, the link between the leader and the criminal behaviour of his/her subordinates is in any case once removed from the sort of behaviour that would make him responsible under more conventional forms of liability.[147] Indeed, if the relationship between the leader of the transnational terrorist group and the subordinate who carried out the crime can be established, the doctrine would be a useful tool for the prosecution because there would be no prerequisite to verify the leader's direct participation in the planning and perpetration of these attacks.

However, as noted in the previous paragraph, this particular strategy for holding leaders of transnational terrorist groups accountable is wrought with difficulties. The first concerns the need to demonstrate that there is a superior–subordinate relationship between the individuals who perpetrated the attack and the accused. The doctrine of command responsibility can only be applied to entities that have a

143 For instance, the case against Abu Makar Bashir in Indonesia is a good example of some of the problems. See Christian Walter et al. (eds), *Terrorism as a Challenge for National and International Law: Security Versus Liberty?* (Springer, 2004).

144 Mettraux (n. 4), p. 117.

145 For example, see *Faheem Khalid Lodhi* v. *Regina* [2007] NSWCCA 360, where the Australian authorities charged the defendant with gathering particular documents which were linked with the preparation of an armed attack.

146 Mettraux (n. 4), p. 117. For further academic commentary, see Stefanie Schmahl, 'Specific Methods of Prosecuting Terrorists in National Law', in Christian Walter et al. (eds), *Terrorism as a Challenge for National and International Law: Security versus Liberty?* (Springer, 2004), p. 81.

147 Ibid.

developed chain of command between its superiors and subordinates. However, even if there is an effective superior–subordinate relationship within the transnational terrorist group the capacity of the command of the group to control the use of violence by its subordinate members may be very difficult. In particular, Mettraux notes that '[d]ivergent preference as regard the goals and methods of the organization may certainly limit the ability of the leadership to control its [members]'.[148] The difficulty in establishing the existence of a superior–subordinate relationship within the transnational terrorist group is not only because of the perplexity involved in finding evidence to prove that such a relationship actually exists but also because of the organisational structure adopted by the group in question.

It is often the case that transnational terrorist groups adopt a decentralised organisational structure where there is no clear chain of command in order to protect the leadership of the group.[149] Indeed, as seen in Chapter 1 of this book, some transnational terrorist groups resemble franchised business corporations rather than an armed group.[150] Evidence that the leader of a transnational terrorist group:

> was able to inspire others to commit crimes would not be sufficient to establish that he had effective control over his . . . [subordinates], unless it can be shown that his influence endowed him with the material ability to prevent or punish their crimes.[151]

Therefore, evidence of ideological authority would be insufficient to establish that the leader had effective control.[152] The fact that the leader of the group has goals and purposes similar to those of the subordinates of the group would not be sufficient to prove he had effective control over the group. Indeed, a 'leading organizational role' in conjunction with substantial influence would not in principle meet this standard.[153]

The lack of coordination in transnational terrorist groups may not be the consequence of the manner in which the group is structured but from the corollaries of their terrorist attacks. Efficacious counter-terrorism operations will 'often have the effect of degrading the organization's command and control system as well as its communication network, with the effect of limiting or eliminating altogether

148 Mettraux (n. 4), p. 118. For further commentary on this point, see Wayne Downing and Michael Meese, *Harmony and Disharmony – Exploiting Al-Qaeda's Organizational Vulnerabilities* (United States Military Academy Combating Terrorism Center, 2006), p. 14.
149 See p. 30 of this book; Downing and Meese (n. 148), p. 14.
150 Peter Grier, 'The New Al Qa'ida: Local Franchiser', *Christian Science Monitor*, 11 June 2005.
151 Mettraux (n. 4), p. 118; see also *Čelebići* (n. 29), paras 263 and 266.
152 Guenael Mettraux, *International Crimes and the Ad Hoc Tribunals* (Oxford University Press, 2005), p. 280.
153 *Kunarac* (n. 53), para. 863.

the ability of its leadership to control its . . . [subordinates]'.[154] For example, Justice Murphy in the US Supreme Court decision, *Yamashita*, noted that injustice would arise if the court ignored the interference caused to the hierarchical structure of an organisation while indicting one of its superiors for failing to exercise effective control over his/her subordinates.[155] In particular, he stated that:

> read against the background of military events in the Philippines subsequent to October 9, 1944, these charges [against the defendant] amount to this: 'We, the victorious American forces, have done everything possible to destroy and disorganize your lines of communication, your effective control of your personnel, your ability to wage war. In those respects we have succeeded. We have defeated and crushed your forces. And now we charge and condemn you or having been inefficient in maintaining control of your troops during the period when we were so effectively besieging and eliminating your forces and blocking your ability to maintain effective control. Many terrible atrocities were committed by your disorganized troops. Because these atrocities were so widespread we will not bother to charge or prove that you committed, ordered or condoned any of them. We will assume that they must have resulted from your inefficiency and negligence as a commander. In short, we charge you with the crime of inefficiency in controlling your troops. We will judge the discharge of your duties by the disorganization which we ourselves created in large part. Our standards of Judgment are whatever we wish to make them.' Nothing in all history or in international law, at least as far as I am aware, justifies such a charge against a fallen commander of a defeated force. To use the very inefficiency and disorganization created by the victorious forces as the primary basis for condemning officers of the defeated armies bears no resemblance to justice or to military reality.[156]

Therefore, where the hierarchical structure of the transnational terrorist group has disintegrated to such a degree that control over its members has become ineffective, prosecuting authorities may hesitate to indict an individual under the doctrine of command responsibility.

The second difficulty with prosecuting leaders of transnational terrorist groups under the doctrine of command responsibility is that there can be no assumption that the leader had knowledge of all the criminal acts committed by his subordinates, even if the ideology of the group permits the commission of such acts as a means to achieve its objective. The contention can be made that leaders may not

154 Mettraux (n. 4), p. 119.
155 *In re Yamashita*, Supreme Court of the United States, 4 February 1946, 327 US 1 at pp. 34–35, as published in *Law Reports of Trials of War Criminals, Volume IV* (William S. Hein, 1997), pp. 1ff.
156 Ibid.

have full knowledge of the crimes perpetrated by their subordinates due to the challenges involved in maintaining an effective reporting system.[157] However, the counter argument is that:

> the informed and willing involvement on the part of the accused with an organization that is known to use crime as a means to achieve its goal when combined with a leadership role in that organization would constitute powerful evidence that such a leader had at least some general notice of the criminal activities of his subordinates.[158]

Therefore, according to this line of argument, the doctrine of command responsibility is inadequate for holding leaders of transnational terrorist groups accountable for their role in the planning and perpetration of terrorist attacks because it assumes that leaders of such groups have the capacity to authorise the commission of criminal offences by its subordinates. However, this contention cannot be fully accepted.

The fact that the commission of criminal offences is generally viewed by the transnational terrorist group as a legitimate means of achieving its political objectives does not imply that it has completely relinquished the authorisation of crimes within its ranks. Indeed, Mettraux asserts that the:

> leadership of even the most violent . . . groups would have an interest in maintaining the group's ability to regulate the use of violence to achieve its goals and to prevent the commission of unwanted crimes or to punish those who exceed its instructions even at the cost of the organization's overall efficiency and security.[159]

Nevertheless, the manner in which these groups operate may make it very hard for the leaders of such groups to investigate alleged crimes and to punish subordinates where there is culpable evidence to suggest that such crimes in fact occurred.

The final potential difficulty in the application of the doctrine of command responsibility to transnational terrorist groups is whether successor commanders should be held accountable for failing to punish subordinates for a crime they committed before the leader assumed his command position. For example, in *Prosecutor* v. *Hadžihasanović*, a leader named Kubara assumed his command position after particular crimes had been committed. Nevertheless, he was charged with international crimes that had occurred before his appointment as commander because of his failure to punish his subordinates. The Trial Chamber and the dissenting judges in the case were all of the view that causal contribution was

157 Robert Martinage, *Global War on Terrorism* (Centre for Strategic and Budgetary Assessments, 2008), p. 69.

158 Mettraux (n. 4), p. 120.

159 Ibid.; see also Martinage (n. 157), p. 72.

required to establish accountability.[160] If no causal contribution is required, the individual need not have been in command or even a member of the transnational terrorist group when the crimes occurred.

Instead, responsibility could be attributed to the leader if after taking up his command position he became aware or had reason to know that crimes had been committed in the past and failed to punish the subordinates responsible. On appeal, the ICTY Appeals Chamber rejected the concept of successor commander liability following strong judicial dissent.[161] The majority of the Appeals Chamber concluded that the commander must have been in command of the subordinates at the time the crimes were perpetrated. However, the decision of the Appeals Chamber was not grounded on the culpability principle but instead on the fact that jurisprudence does not support the conviction of successor commanders for crimes committed by their subordinates prior to their assuming their leadership position.[162]

In the aftermath of the ICTY Appeals Chamber decision in the *Hadžihasanović* case, an extensive body of literature emerged which criticised the majority position of the Chamber.[163] Many commentators have argued that the approach of the

160 For further commentary on this particular point, see Judges Shahabuddeen and Hunt in *Hadžihasanović* (n. 1); *Prosecutor* v. *Hadžihasanović*, IT-01-47-T, Judgment, 15 March 2006, para. 65.

161 For further analysis of this dissent, see *Hadžihasanović* (n. 1), paras 53–56 and the dissent of Judge Shahabuddeen, paras 39–41.

162 Ibid., para. 37–56. However, Judges Shahabuddeen and Hunt would have allowed successor commander liability (paras 15–41). For further analysis on this point, see Theodore Meron, 'Revival of Customary Humanitarian Law', *American Journal of International Law* 99 (2005) 817–834, pp. 824–826.

163 For further academic commentary, see Joakim Dungel and Shannon Ghadiri, 'The Temporal Scope of Command Responsibility Revisited: Why Commanders Have a Duty to Prevent Crimes Committed after the Cessation of Effective Control', *University of California Davis Journal of International Law and Policy* 17 (2010) 1–40; Carol Fox, 'Closing a Loophole in Accountability for War Crimes: Successor Commanders' Duty to Punish Known Past Offences', *Case Western Reserve Law Review* 55 (2004) 443–500; Christopher Greenwood, 'Command Responsibility and the *Hadžihasanović* Decision', *Journal of International Criminal Justice* 2 (2004) 598–605; Bing Jia, 'The Doctrine of Command Responsibility Revisited', *Chinese Journal of International Law* 3 (2004) 1–42; Mettraux (n. 4), pp. 190–192; Volker Nerlich, 'Superior Responsibility under Article 28 ICC Statute: For What Exactly is the Superior Held Responsible?', *Journal of International Criminal Justice* 5 (2007) 665–682; Chantal Meloni, 'Command Responsibility: Mode of Liability for the Crimes of Subordinates or Separate Offence of the Superior?', *Journal of International Criminal Justice* 5 (2007) 619; Roberta Arnold and Otto Triffterer, 'Article 28: Responsibility of Commanders and Other Superiors', in O. Triffterer (ed.), *Commentary on the Rome Statute of the International Criminal Court: Observers' Notes, Article by Article* (Beck, 2008, 2nd edn), p. 795; David Akerson and Natalie Knowlton, 'President Obama and the International Criminal Law of Successor Liability', *Denver Journal of International Law and Policy 37* (2009) 615–651, p. 627; Elies van Sliedregt, 'Article 28 of the ICC Statute: Mode of Liability and/or Separate Offence?', *New Criminal Law Review* 12 (2009) 420–432; Bakone Moloto, 'Command Responsibility in International Criminal Tribunals', *Publicist* 3 (2009) 12–25; Stefan Trechsel, 'Command Responsibility as a Separate Offence', *Publicist* 3 (2009) 26–35; Barrie Sander,

ICTY Appeals Chamber fails to embrace the essence of command responsibility. In particular, Fox and Mettraux note that the ICTY has created a 'loophole'[164] whereby wrongdoers can dodge punishment.[165] Both the Trial Chamber of the ICTY and the ICTR have disparaged the majority decision in the *Hadžihasanović* case.[166] For example, the ICTY Trial Chamber in the *Orić* case has noted that:

> it should be immaterial whether he or she assumed control over the relevant subordinates prior to their committing the crime. Since the Appeals Chamber, however, has taken a different view for reasons which will not be questioned here, the Trial Chamber finds itself bound.[167]

The Trial Chamber of the SCSL in *Prosecutor* v. *Brima* has also refused to apply the decision of the ICTY Appeals Chamber.[168] In particular, the SCSL Trial Chamber noted that 'there is no support in customary international law for the proposition that a commander can be held responsible for crimes committed by a subordinate prior to the commander's assumption of command over that subordinate'.[169]

Furthermore, in *Prosecutor* v. *Fofana* the SCSL Trial Chamber noted that:

> [t]he Chamber further endorses the finding of the ICTY Appeals Chamber that an Accused could not be held liable under Article 6(3) of the Statute for crimes committed by a subordinate before the said Accused assumed command over that subordinate.[170]

The ICTY Appeals Chamber nearly overruled the *Hadžihasanović* decision in the *Orić* case.[171] Judge Liu and Judge Schomberg described the decision as 'erroneous'[172] and 'highly questionable'[173] and observed that there 'is a new majority

'Unravelling the Confusion Concerning Successor Superior Responsibility in the ICTY Jurisprudence', *Leiden Journal of International Law* 23 (2010) 105–135; Robert Cryer, 'The Ad Hoc Tribunals and the Law of Command Responsibility: A Quiet Earthquake', in S. Darcy and J. Powderly (eds), *Judicial Creativity at the International Criminal Tribunals* (Oxford University Press, 2010) 159–183, p. 159.

164 Fox (n. 163), p. 423.

165 Akerson and Knowlton (n. 163), p. 645.

166 *Prosecutor* v. *Ndindiliyimana*, ICTR-00-56-T, Judgment, 17 May 2011, paras 1960–1963.

167 *Orić* (n. 3), para. 335.

168 *Prosecutor* v. *Sesay*, SCSL-04-15-T, 2 March 2009, para. 306, where it was held that 'this Chamber is satisfied that the principle of superior responsibility as it exists in customary international law does include the situation in which a Commander can be held liable for a failure to punish subordinates for a crime that occurred before he assumed effective control'.

169 *Prosecutor* v. *Brima*, SCSL-04-16-T, Judgment, 20 June 2007, para. 799.

170 *Prosecutor* v. *Fofana*, SCSL-04-14-T, Judgment, 2 August 2007, para. 240.

171 *Prosecutor* v. *Orić Appeal*, IT-03-68-A, Appeal Judgment, 3 July 2008.

172 Ibid., paras 5 and 8 (per Judge Liu).

173 Ibid.

of appellate thought'.[174] However, the Appeals Chamber refused to overturn the ruling in the *Hadžihasanović* case because the facts in the *Orić* case did not necessitate a ruling on the issue.[175] However, neither the SCSL in the *Forfana* case nor the ICTY Appeals Chamber in the *Orić* case addressed the notion that holding an individual accountable for a crime committed by his subordinates before he/she joined the group is a remarkable departure from the principle of culpability. However, the principle of culpability was not completely ignored in the *Orić* case. Judge Shahabuddeen recognised that in order for an individual to be held liable for criminal conduct he/she must have made a contribution to it.[176]

If a case of a successor commander of a transnational terrorist group comes before the ICC, the Trial Chamber will need to analyse the principle of culpability in conjunction with the doctrine of command responsibility to determine whether he/she can be held accountable for crimes which occurred before he/she assumed his command position. Successor commanders will not have played any role in the planning and perpetration of the crime. However, because they perhaps occupied a subordinate position within the group before they assumed their command position he/she would arguably have knowledge that such crimes were occurring. As a result, he/she could have a duty to punish the subordinates responsible for these crimes. Leaders could be held accountable if they fail to do so. The ICC will need to take these factors into consideration when determining whether the leader is responsible for these crimes. Even though the leader may not have made a physical contribution towards the commission of the crime he/she may still have had knowledge that such crimes were occurring when he was a subordinate member. Ultimately, the ICC would need to weigh up these factors in determining the culpability of the successor commander.

G Conclusion

This chapter examined whether leaders of transnational terrorist groups can be held accountable for terrorist attacks by their subordinates upon civilian populations occurring during non-armed conflict situations. ICTY and ICTR case law was examined in light of the wording of Article 28 of the Rome Statute. There have been very few cases where leaders of non-state armed actors have been charged with crimes committed by their subordinates. The focus of the ICTY and ICTR has very much been on leaders who have some connection or association with the state. The *Aleksovski* and *Bemba* cases are the only cases which have provided some confirmation that the doctrine of command responsibility may also be applied to leaders of non-state armed actors. It remains to be seen how the ICC will apply the doctrine of command responsibility to leaders of a network-based groups, which lack a clear-cut hierarchical command structure in a similar vein.

174 Ibid., para. 3 (per Judge Shahabuddeen).
175 Ibid., para. 167.
176 Ibid., para. 19.

As regards the three conditions which must be present in order for a leader of a transnational terrorist group to be held responsible for offences committed by their subordinates, it is important to bear in mind that the factual characteristics of these groups will have a bearing on how the conditions are applied. The structure of transnational terrorist groups may be difficult to prove; 'the relationship between ranks and responsibilities in these groups may not be as easily determined as within [state armed forces]'.[177] Therefore, the application of the principle of command responsibility will ultimately depend on the facts. In the same way, whether leaders of transnational terrorist groups 'failed to prevent or punish crimes committed by their subordinates depends on their material ability to take appropriate measures'.[178] In turn, this ability will hinge on the organisational structure of the transnational terrorist group of which they are a member. Where the accountability of leaders of transnational terrorist groups is being ascertained, it is essential that the factual circumstances in each case be individually determined.

The accountability of leaders of transnational terrorist groups for acts committed by their subordinates was also explored in this chapter. The ICC is only in the early stages of developing jurisprudence in the area. Nevertheless, an examination of ICTY, SCSL, and ICTR jurisprudence illustrates how leaders of transnational terrorist groups can be held accountable for crimes committed by their subordinates in two situations. First, where the leader has ordered the commission of these crimes, and, second, where the leader of the transnational terrorist group fails to act to prevent or punish the crimes of subordinates where he has not ordered them. However, it can be argued that the prosecution of leaders of transnational terrorist groups before the international criminal tribunals will be rare in any event. A reason for this is that state authorities may be unwilling to cooperate with the court.[179] As a result it is not unreasonable to consider whether any other avenues can be pursued to hold leaders of transnational terrorist groups accountable for international crimes. It should be remembered that international humanitarian law does not necessitate transnational terrorist groups to take legal action against its members for violations of international law.[180] An examination of the conditions which must be met before a leader of a transnational terrorist group can be held accountable for crimes committed by their subordinates was also completed in this chapter. The organisational structure of the group will significantly influence how these conditions are applied. However, the structure of the transnational terrorist group can be difficult to establish. As well as this, the connection between the rank of the leader and his/her responsibilities may not be

177 Zegveld (n. 21), p. 131.

178 Ibid.

179 Manisuli Ssenyonjo, 'Accountability of Non-State Actors in Uganda for War Crimes and Human Rights Violations: Between Amnesty and the International Criminal Court', *Journal of Conflict and Security Law* 10(3) (2005) 405–434; Manisuli Ssenyonjo, 'The International Criminal Court and the Lord's Resistance Army Leaders: Prosecution or Amnesty?', *Netherlands International Law Review* 54(1) (2007) 51–80.

180 Ibid.

as easily identifiable as it is within state armed forces. The application of the doctrine of command responsibility will ultimately turn on the facts of each individual case. The determination of whether leaders failed to prevent or punish the commission of crimes by their subordinates will rely on their capability to exhaust all appropriate channels.

When determining the accountability of leaders of transnational terrorist groups, it is imperative to have regard for the factual circumstances in each individual case. Any problems which arise will be more of a practical nature rather than established on principle. In particular, the manner in which transnational terrorist groups operate may make it very hard for the leaders of such groups to investigate alleged crimes and to punish subordinates where there is culpable evidence to suggest that such crimes in fact occurred. In addition, the doctrine of command responsibility can only be applied to entities that have a developed chain of command between its superiors and subordinates.

However, even if there is an effective superior–subordinate relationship within the transnational terrorist group the capacity of the command of the group to control the use of violence by its subordinate members may be very difficult. Therefore, it must be determined whether any other mechanism can be invoked to hold members of transnational terrorist groups. One possible avenue is the doctrine of co-perpetration under Article 25, which is perhaps a more effective mechanism to bring leaders of transnational terrorist groups to justice. The purpose of the next chapter is to examine the application of this relatively new doctrine to members of transnational terrorist groups by reference to the emerging jurisprudence of the ICC to determine whether it can provide an alternative basis to hold them accountable for their role in the planning and perpetration of terrorist attacks.

6 Holding members of transnational terrorist groups accountable under Article 25 of the Rome Statute

Effectiveness, legitimacy, and impact

A Introduction

Since the aftermath of the Second World War the principle of individual criminal responsibility has challenged and perplexed international courts and tribunals from the International Military Tribunal (IMT) in Nuremberg to the ICTY[1] and the ICC.[2] Indeed, the IMT in Nuremberg held that international crimes can only be 'committed by men, not by abstract entities, and only by punishing individuals who commit such crimes can the provisions of international law be enforced'.[3] The Nuremberg Principles formulated by the International Law Commission (ILC) in 1946 further expanded this central tenet by noting that, 'complicity in the commission of a crime against peace, a war crime or a crime against humanity . . . is a crime against international law'.[4] However, the application of this principle by the ad hoc international criminal tribunals in particular has led to ambiguity on its precise parameters.[5] As noted by Badar, the development of the doctrine of joint criminal enterprise (JCE) at the ICTY has been nicknamed the 'just convict everyone' doctrine because all individuals who participated in the commission of the crime were categorised as perpetrators irrespective of the degree of their participation.[6] If this is the case, is there an

1 Statute of the International Tribunal for the Prosecution of Persons Responsible for Serious Violations of International Humanitarian Law Committed in the Territory of the Former Yugoslavia since 1991, SC Res. 827, UN SCOR 48th session, 3217th mtg, pp. 1–2 (1993); 32 ILM 1159 (1993). See also the Statute of the International Criminal Tribunal for Rwanda, SC Res. 955, UN SCOR 49th session, 3453rd mtg, UN Doc. S/Res/955 (1994); 33 ILM 1598 (1994).

2 Hector Olásolo, *The Criminal Responsibility of Senior Political and Military Leaders as Principals to International* Crimes (Hart, 2009), p. 20; Antonio Cassese, *International Criminal Law* (Oxford University Press, 2008, 2nd edn), p. 33; Elies van Sliedregt, *Individual Criminal Responsibility in International Law* (Oxford University Press, 2012), p. 61; Gerhard Werle, *Principles of International Criminal Law* (TMC Asser Press, 2005).

3 *France et al.* v. *Goering et al.* (1946) 22 IMT 203.

4 Nuremberg Principle VII.

5 Albin Eser, 'Individual Criminal Responsibility', in A. Cassese, P. Gaeta, and J. Jones (eds), *The Rome Statute of the International Criminal Court: A Commentary: Vol. 1* (Oxford University Press, 2002) 767–797, p. 784.

6 Mohamed Badar, '"Just Convict Everyone!" – Joint Perpetration: From *Tadić* to *Stakić* and Back Again', *International Criminal Law Review* 6 (2006) 293–302;

ongoing requirement in the realm of international criminal justice to develop an alternative mode of responsibility to ensure that international criminal law can be applied to new types of entities?

As a counterpart to Badar's belief in the over-expansive nature of the JCE doctrine, one must highlight the risk that the application of an overly restrictive principle of individual criminal responsibility would limit the extent to which members of network-based transnational terrorist groups could be held accountable for crimes before the ICC. In any event, the ICC has arguably sidestepped this dilemma by developing the doctrine of co-perpetration which specifies that an individual can be held responsible for a crime if he or she made an essential contribution towards it commission.[7] So would the doctrine of co-perpetration provide a more sufficient basis upon which to hold members of transnational terrorist groups accountable, or is the adoption of this mode of responsibility merely a re-labelling of the JCE doctrine developed by the ICTY?

It is not possible within the confines of this book to examine in detail the development and conceptual basis for the principle of individual criminal responsibility in general. However, as this chapter discusses the adoption of the doctrine of co-perpetration by the ICC in the *Lubanga* and *Katanga* cases with reference to the organisational structure of the transnational terrorist group, as examined in Chapter 2, it is necessary to understand the specific contribution of each member in the perpetration of the terrorist attack. Each participating member of the group in the terrorist attack may have played a different role in the planning, organisation, coordination, and execution of the crime. Furthermore, this chapter distinguishes between members of transnational terrorist groups which made a contribution

Allison Danner and Jenny Martinez, 'Guilty Associations: Joint Criminal Enterprise, Command Responsibility, and the Development of International Criminal Law', *California Law Review* 93 (2005) 75–169. For a defence of JCE, see Antonio Cassese, 'The Proper Limits of Individual Responsibility under the Doctrine of Joint Criminal Enterprise', *Journal of International Criminal Justice* 5 (2007) 109–133. For examples of case law on the JCE doctrine, see *Prosecutor* v. *Tadić*, IT-94-1-A, Appeal Judgment, 15 July 1999, paras 185ff.; *Prosecutor* v. *Vasiljević*, IT-98-21-A, Appeal Judgment, 25 February 2004, para. 182; *Prosecutor* v. *Krstić*, IT-98-33-A, Appeal Judgment, 19 April 2004, para. 268; *Prosecutor* v. *Laurent Semanza*, ICTR-97-20-T, Judgment of 15 May 2003, paras 408, 410–419; *Prosecutor* v. *Taylor*, Case No. SCSL-03-01-T, Judgment, 18 May 2012, paras 6953 and 6971; *Prosecutor* v. *Charles Ghankay Taylor*, SCSL-03-01-A (10766–11114), Appeal Judgment, 26 September 2013, para. 670. For further academic commentary, see van Sliedregt (n. 2), p. 77; Cassese (n. 2), pp. 324–325; Gerhard Werle, 'Individual Criminal Responsibility in Article 25 ICC Statute', *Journal of International Criminal Justice* 5 (2007) 953–975, p. 955.

7 *Prosecutor* v. *Thomas Dyilo Lubanga, Decision on the Confirmation of Charges*, Pre-Trial Chamber ICC-01/04-01/06 29 January 2007. *Prosecutor* v. *Germain Katanga and Mathieu Ngudjo Chui, Decision on the Confirmation of Charges*, Pre-Trial Chamber, ICC-01/04-01/07, 30 September 2008, para. 525; Claus Roxin, 'Crimes as Part of Organized Power Structures' (trans. B. Cooper), *Journal of International Criminal Justice* 9 (2011) 193.

towards the commission of the attack and the members who had no role whatsoever in the perpetration of the crime.

Since the ICC has not yet had to examine the application of the Rome Statute to members of groups with a network-based organisational structure, the argument I have advanced over the course of this book is that due to the limited development of accountability mechanisms before the ICC the prosecution of transnational terrorist groups will be difficult. On the basis of this understanding, the key question that needs to be asked is: can members of transnational terrorist groups be held accountable under Article 25 of the Rome Statute despite their network-based organisational structure?

As discussed in Chapter 2, some transnational terrorist groups have a network-based organisational structure which makes it difficult to ascertain whether their crimes were committed in pursuance of a joint criminal plan. In order for a member of a transnational terrorist group to be held accountable under Article 25 this chapter needs to ascertain whether their conduct satisfies the constituent elements of the doctrines of direct and indirect co-perpetration as developed by the Pre-Trial and Trial Chambers in the *Lubanga* and *Katanga* cases.[8] While there have been a range of authoritative statements from academics and the judiciary at the ICC on the application of Article 25 to members of groups with a clear-cut hierarchical command structure it is not possible to definitively say that members of some transnational terrorist groups can be held accountable under Article 25 in view of their network-based organisational structure.[9] Even though the doctrine of co-perpetration is an attempt to develop an overall theory of accountability at the ICC this chapter will propose that the concept of control under the doctrine is one-dimensional especially when applied to entities such as transnational terrorist groups which may not have a centralised command. As discussed in Chapters 2 and 5 of the book, it can be difficult to discern who within the transnational terrorist group exercises command, and which subordinates carry out the constituent elements of the crime.

This chapter finds that a more inclusive approach to joint perpetration which includes both objective and subjective elements would be more appropriate for determining the accountability of members of transnational terrorist groups. Relevant factors would include the subordinate member's involvement in the planning of the crime by the transnational terrorist group and his/her own *mens rea*. In particular, it can be difficult to determine the member's contribution towards the commission of the terrorist attacks and the propinquity of his/her contribution to the actual perpetration of the criminal offence. Before considering this question, this chapter will analyse how the ICC has utilised Roxin's control theory of perpetration in its interpretation of Article 25 of the Rome Statute. With reference to the analysis of the organisational structure of transnational terrorist groups conducted in Chapter 2, section B of this chapter will proceed to discuss

8 *Katanga and Chui Confirmation Decision* (n. 7), para. 525; Roxin (n. 7).

9 Jens Ohlin, 'Three Conceptual Problems with the Doctrine of Joint Criminal Enterprise', *Journal of International Criminal Justice* 5 (2007) 69–90; Werle (n. 6), p. 955.

how the Pre-Trial and Trial Chambers' decisions in the *Lubanga* and *Katanga* cases have applied Article 25 to armed groups with clear-cut organisational structures. Section C examines whether the application of Article 25 to transnational terrorist groups is constrained by their network-based organisational structure.

B The principle of individual criminal responsibility under Article 25 of the Rome Statute

Article 25 of the Rome Statute sets out a comprehensive legal framework on criminal responsibility. According to Saland, who chaired the Working Group on General Principles of Criminal Law during the negotiations to establish the ICC, the provision:

> posed great difficulties to negotiate in a number of ways. One problem was that experts from different legal systems took strongly held positions, based on their national laws, as to the exact content of the various concepts involved. They seemed to find it hard to understand that another legal system might approach the issue in another way: e.g.; have a different concept, or give the same name to a concept but with a slightly different content.[10]

Although the initial draft of Article 25 originates from the ILC's Draft Code of Crimes against the Peace and Security of Mankind, the official draft of the provision was proposed by 'an informal group representing various legal systems'.[11] Hence, the official draft of Article 25 is inspired by both domestic criminal law and international legal instruments.[12]

The extensive literature on Article 25 indicates that academics have interpreted the provision on the basis of their own experience and comprehension of criminal liability. For example, Schabas asserts that '[c]oncepts and words in one system . . . [do] not necessarily have the same connotations as they . . . [do] in others'.[13] The *travaux préparatoires* do not distinguish between principal–accessorial liability, nor do they indicate that the modes of liability incorporated in Article 25 should be ranked hierarchically. Although both Ambos and Werle have suggested that Article 25 exemplifies both a differentiated and hierarchical approach to

10 Per Saland, 'International Criminal Law Principles', in R. Lee (ed.), *The International Criminal Court: The Making of the Rome Statute: Issues Negotiations and Results* (Martinus Nijhoff, 1999) 189, p. 198.

11 See generally Working Paper Submitted by Canada, Germany, Netherlands, and the United Kingdom, UN Doc. A/AC.249/1997/WG.2/DP.1.

12 van Sliedregt (n. 2), pp. 64–65.

13 William Schabas, *The International Criminal Court: A Commentary on the Rome Statute* (Oxford University Press, 2010), p. 424; Mahmoud Cherif Bassiouni, *Introduction to International Criminal Law* (Martinus Nijhoff, 2013, 2nd edn), pp. 286–287.

criminal participation,[14] Eser argues that 'it is difficult to find an unambiguous answer' to the question of what modes of criminal participation it incorporates.[15]

1 The judicial approach to interpreting Article 25 in Lubanga *and* Katanga

The ICC Pre-Trial Chamber in the *Lubanga* case developed an alternative approach to interpreting Article 25 based on Roxin's control theory of perpetration.[16] The Chamber analysed the approach of domestic jurisdictions in differentiating between perpetrators and accomplices.[17] In particular, the Pre-Trial Chamber noted that common law jurisdictions such as the UK have adopted an objective approach to perpetration.[18] Pursuant to this approach the perpetrator is described as the person who carried out the *actus reus* of the crime while the individual who provided material support towards its commission is simply defined as an accomplice.[19] However, this leads to a contradictory scenario whereby the commander who orders his/her subordinates to carry out an attack will be convicted as an accomplice because he does not himself physically carry out the attack. A straightforward examination of the events leading up to the perpetration of the attack suggests that the commander of the state armed force or non-state armed actor should be held more culpable than the subordinate who carries out the

14 Kai Ambos, 'Article 25: Individual Criminal Responsibility', in O. Triffterer (ed.), *Commentary on the Rome Statute of the International Criminal Court* (Oxford University Press, 2008) 743–770, p. 743; Werle (n. 6), pp. 956–7; Lachezar Yanev and Tijs Kooijmans, 'Divided Minds in the *Lubanga* Trial Judgment: A Case against the Joint Control Theory', *International Criminal Law Review* 13 (2013) 789–828, p. 804.

15 Eser (n. 5), p. 786.

16 Claus Roxin, *Täterschaft und Tatherrschaft* (de Gruyter, 2006, 8th edn). See generally *Lubanga Confirmation Decision* (n. 7). *Prosecutor* v. *Mathieu Ngudjolo Chui*, Jugement Rendu en Application de l'Article 74 du Statut, Trial Chamber II, ICC-01/04-02/12, 18 December 2012; *Prosecutor* v. *Omar Hassan Ahmad Al-Bashir*, Second Arrest Warrant, Pre-Trial Chamber, ICC-02/05-01/09, 17 July 2010, para. 4. For further academic commentary, see Thomas Weigend, 'Intent, Mistake of Law, and Co-Perpetration in the *Lubanga* Decision on Confirmation of Charges', *Journal of International Criminal Justice* 6 (2008) 471–487, pp. 478–79. See also *Katanga and Chui Confirmation Decision* (n. 7), paras 500–518. See also Defence Brief on Matters the Defence Raised during the Confirmation – Legal Observations, ICC-01/04-01/06-758-Conf, para. 33, where the defence argued that it went 'beyond the clear terms of co-perpetration and indirect perpetration set out in the Statute, and is not supported by either customary international law, or general principles of law derived from legal systems of the world'. See also para. 34 of the brief where the defence contends that the concept of joint control over a crime in German criminal law theory was 'very much predicated on notions of hierarchy and obedience, and were formulated to address the type of systematic criminality which existed in Germany during the Second World War (as exemplified in the *Eichmann* case) and during the communist regime in the GDR'.

17 Ibid., paras 327–332.

18 Ibid.

19 *Lubanga Confirmation Decision* (n. 7), para. 328. For further analysis, see George Fletcher, *Rethinking Criminal Law* (Oxford University Press, 2000), pp. 654–55.

crime. As a result, the 'common law [has] developed numerous doctrinal techniques to mitigate this shortcoming in its jurisprudence, most notably de-emphasising or even collapsing the distinction between principals and accessories'.[20] Hence, UK criminal law provides that accomplices and principals can be held equally culpable and face the same punishment.[21]

The Pre-Trial Chamber in the *Lubanga* case also referred to the 'subjective approach' to perpetration which has been applied by courts in civil law jurisdictions such as Germany.[22] This approach emphasises the *mens rea* of the individual involved in the commission of the crime. Under this approach the commander can be convicted as the principal perpetrator because he exhibits the necessary *mens rea* for the crime to be committed.[23] However, this approach has been criticised because the individual with the requisite *mens rea* may be 'casually, temporally, and geographically removed from the physical commission of the crime – a tenuous connection that some . . . feel is emblematic of the . . . causal connection between the defendant and the resulting crime'.[24] Indeed, as discussed in Chapter 2, some transnational terrorist groups lack a hierarchical structure and are organised in small interconnected but autonomous cells of four to five individuals that may be scattered in a number of different countries.[25] As a result, the question arises whether it is reasonable to classify the commander of a transnational terrorist group as a principal perpetrator given that he/she may have been geographically removed from the location where the crime occurred?

Roxin's control theory of perpetration arguably overcomes this obstacle by proposing a third approach which amalgamated both the objective and subjective approaches to perpetration. Pursuant to this approach the perpetrator is defined as the person who has control of the act and determines whether the crime will be committed. However, the Pre-Trial Chamber in the *Lubanga* case went even further than this and described a perpetrator as the individuals who:

> [p]hysically carry out the objective elements of the offence, but also include those who, in spite of being removed from the scene of the crime, control or mastermind its commission because they decide whether and how the offence will be committed.[26]

20 Ibid.
21 *Davies* v. *DPP* [1954] AC 378.
22 *Lubanga Confirmation Decision* (n. 7), para. 328.
23 Ibid., para. 329.
24 Jens Ohlin, 'Co-Perpetration: German Dogmatik or German Invasion?', in C. Stahn (ed.), *The Law and Practice of the International Criminal Court: A Critical Account of Challenges and Achievements* (Oxford University Press, 2015), p. 57; Cassese (n. 2), p. 191. For further analysis on this point, see Kai Ambos, *Treatise on International Criminal Law* (Oxford University Press, 2013), pp. 2011–12.
25 See p. 30 of this book.
26 *Lubanga Confirmation Decision* (n. 7), para. 330.

Therefore, a 'person who acts through another may be [held] individually criminally responsible, regardless of whether the executor (the direct perpetrator) is responsible [for the crime]'.[27] In domestic criminal cases involving crimes such as murder, the control theory will produce the same result as the subjective and objective approaches combined. This is because the majority of murder cases are perpetrated by just one person who carries out the *actus reus*, possesses the requisite *mens rea*, and ultimately exercises control over the criminal offence. So, if the accused carries out the murder, intends the killing to occur, and displays control over whether the killing does in fact occur, he/she will be classified as the perpetrator.

Nevertheless, international crimes are very different to domestic crimes for a number of reasons. First, international crimes are generally 'perpetrated by a plurality of persons, making co-perpetration . . . crucial to prosecutorial strategy'.[28] Second, and most importantly, the individual in overall control of the group may not necessarily participate in the perpetration of the actual crime. Instead, the individual in control of the crime is usually high up in the hierarchical chain of command while the subordinates carry out the *actus reus*.[29] The *Eichmann Trial* in Israel inspired Roxin to expand his theory to include indirect perpetration and organisation perpetration.[30] With regard to indirect perpetration, Roxin

27 *Katanga and Chui Confirmation Decision* (n. 7), para. 496; Roxin (n. 16), pp. 193–207.

28 Ibid.; Jens Ohlin, 'Joint Intentions to Commit International Crimes', *Chicago Journal of International Law* 11 (2011) 693–753.

29 Ohlin (n. 24), p. 56; Kai Ambos, 'Command Responsibility and Organisationsherrschaft: Ways of Attributing International Crimes to the "Most Responsible"', in A. Nollkaemper and H. van der Wilt (eds), *System Criminality in International Law* (Cambridge University Press, 2009) 127–157, p. 152.

30 *Attorney General of the Government of Israel* v. *Eichmann* (District of Jerusalem) (1961), 36 International Law Reports 5, as reprinted in Elihu Lauterpacht (ed.), *The Eichmann Judgments* (Butterworths, 1968) 16, pp. 29–30. For further academic commentary on the trial, see Hannah Arendt, *Eichmann in Jerusalem: A Report on the Banality of Evil* (Penguin, 2006); Judith Shklar, *Legalism* (Harvard University Press, 1964), pp. 154–155; Mark Osiel, *Mass Atrocity, Ordinary Evil and Hannah Arendt* (Yale University Press, 2001), pp. 61–62; William Schabas, *Genocide in International Law* (Cambridge University Press, 2000), p. 286; Antonio Cassese, *International Criminal Law* (Oxford University Press, 2013, 3rd edn), p. 114; Gary Bass, 'The Adolf Eichmann Case: Universal and National Jurisdiction', in S. Macedo (ed.), *Universal Jurisdiction: National Courts and the Prosecution of Serious Crimes Under International Law* (University of Pennsylvania Press, 2004) 77–90; Leora Bilsky, 'The Eichmann Trial and the Legacy of Jurisdiction', in S. Benhabib (ed.), *Politics in Dark Times: Encounters with Hannah Arendt* (Cambridge University Press, 2010) 198–218, p. 198; Itamar Mann, 'The Dual Foundation of Universal Jurisdiction: Towards a Jurisprudence for the Court of Critique', *Transnational Legal Theory* 1(4) (2010) 485–521; William Schabas, 'The Contribution of the Eichmann Trial to International Law', *Leiden Journal of International Law* 26 (2013) 667–699. For criticism of victims' testimonies in the Eichmann trial, see Stephan Landsman, 'The Eichmann Case and the Invention of the Witness-Driven Atrocity Trial', *Columbia Journal of Transnational Law* 51 (2012) 69–119. For a more general criticism of the reliance on

contended that the accused should be held accountable as a principal perpetrator because despite not performing the *actus reus* of the crime he/she is still an indirect perpetrator who relies on their subordinates to carry out the physical act.[31] Roxin described this as the 'Organisationsherrschaft' which entails the use of an organisation as a means to perpetrate criminal acts.[32] The individual at the very top of the chain of command is the 'Hintermann' who controls the perpetration of the crime by devising the criminal plan to be carried by the subordinates.[33]

Although Roxin's theory was enthusiastically accepted by German legal theorists it was not applied by German courts until three decades later when the *Border Guard* cases were adjudicated.[34] Following the unification of Germany, the state authorities prosecuted border guards for shooting East German civilians as they tried to escape across the Berlin Wall to West Germany. The killings generated fear among East Germans that inhibited them from conducting escape attempts because of the fatal consequences if they failed. It is not remarkable that the German court was reluctant to classify the officials who directed the policy of shoot-to-kill as accomplices and instead tried and convicted them as principal perpetrators. The cases provided German courts with the opportunity to apply Roxin's control theory of perpetration and elevate it from a hypothetical concept to doctrinal actuality.[35]

The Pre-Trial Chamber in *Lubanga* and Trial Chamber II in *Prosecutor* v. *Katanga* utilised Roxin's theory as a guide to interpret Article 25(3)(a) of the Rome Statute.[36] Circumventing the controversial jurisprudence of the ICTY on JCE, the Pre-Trial Chamber concluded that Article 25(3)(a) codifies Roxin's control theory of perpetration.[37] However, Article 25(3)(a) does not refer to the

testimonies of survivors by international tribunals, see Nancy Combs, *Fact-Finding without Facts* (Cambridge University Press, 2010); see generally Roxin (n. 7).

31 Fletcher (n. 19), p. 639.

32 Roxin (n. 7), p.193.

33 Ibid.

34 Bundesgerichtshof (Federal Court of Appeals), Judgment of 26 July 1994, in 40 Entscheidungen des Bundesgerichtshofes in Strafsachen, (1995) 218, p. 236.

35 Ohlin (n. 24), p. 61; Michael Bohlander, *Principles of German Criminal Law* (Hart, 2009), p. 158; *Streletz, Kessler and Krenz* v. *Germany* (Applications No. 34044/96, 35532/97 and 48801/98) 22 March 2001 (European Court of Human Rights, Reports of Judgments and Decisions 2001-II) available at: http://hudoc.echr.coe.int/sites/eng/pages/search.aspx?i=001-59353#{"itemid":["001–59353"]} (date accessed: 31 March 2018). For a useful synopsis on the human rights issues arising in these cases, see Rudolf Geiger, 'The German Border Guard Cases and International Human Rights', *European Journal of International Law* 9 (1998) 540–549.

36 *Lubanga Confirmation Decision* (n. 7), para. 324; Minority Opinion of Judge Christine Van den Wyngaert in *Prosecutor* v. *Germain Katanga*, Jugement Rendu en Application de l'Article 74 du Statut, ICC-01/04-01/07-3436, Trial Chamber II, 7 March 2014, paras 1400–1412.

37 *Lubanga Confirmation Decision* (n. 7), para. 348. However, interestingly the Pre-Trial Chamber did conclude at para. 335 that Article 25(3)(d) 'is closely akin to the concept of joint criminal enterprise or the common purpose doctrine adopted by the jurisprudence of the ICTY'. For further reference, see *Lubanga Confirmation Decision* (n. 7), para. 335.

concept of control whatsoever and merely provides that an individual will be held responsible if he/she '[c]ommits . . . a crime, whether as an individual, jointly with another or through another person'.[38] To add further to the confusion, the Trial Chamber in the *Katanga* case remarked that this was not the only possible interpretation of Article 25, remarking that 'elle estime qu'il n'y a pas lieu de faire cette théorie un élément constitutive incontournable de la commission par l'intermédiaire'.[39] Indeed, Article 25(3)(d) provides that individuals will be held responsible for their contribution to collective crimes. As a result, the scope of application of Articles 25(3)(a) and 25(3)(d) is both ambiguous and broad.[40]

However, the Pre-Trial Chamber in the *Lubanga* case strongly emphasised that '[t]he concept of control over the crime constitutes a third approach for distinguishing between principals and accessories which, contrary to the Defence claim, is applied in numerous legal systems' and is representative of legal cultures worldwide.[41] This is to a certain extent true because the theory has been applied in the legal systems of Latin American states. However, it is an overstatement for the Pre-Trial Chamber to suggest that the theory has been applied worldwide.[42] To support its conclusion, the Chamber referred to Fletcher's book, *Rethinking Criminal Law*, which endorsed Roxin's control theory of perpetration.[43] However, Fletcher's work does not examine the content of criminal law in various legal systems but instead conducts 'a comparative examination of criminal law theory at the normative level'.[44]

Fletcher has stated that his research was only concerned with how criminal law ought to be structured and not with the criminal law doctrine that exists in any particular legal system.[45] Fletcher simply endorsed Roxin's theory.[46] Indeed, Roxin's theory did not have any influence on legal scholarship for a considerable period of time except for a handful of US law review articles.[47] It was only just before the endorsement of Roxin's theory by the

38 Article 25(3)(a) of the Rome Statute of the International Criminal Court.

39 *Katanga Trial Judgment* (n. 36), paras 1400–1412. (Roughly translated: it considered that it was not an indispensable constitutive element of the commission by the intermediary – that is, the intermediary didn't have to commit the offence.)

40 Many academics have attempted to determine the scope of application of both provisions. For example, see Jens Ohlin, 'Joint Criminal Confusion', *New Criminal Law Review* 12 (2009) 406–419; Werle (n. 6). For further reference, see the Concurring Opinion of Judge Christine Van den Wyngaert, *Prosecutor* v. *Mathieu Ngudjolo Chui*, Jugement Rendu en Application de l'Article 74 du Statut, Trial Chamber II, Case No. ICC-01/04-02/12 (18 December 2012), paras 22–30.

41 *Lubanga Confirmation Decision* (n. 7), para. 330.

42 For more on this point, see Kai Ambos, 'The Fujimori Judgment: A President's Responsibility for Crimes against Humanity as Indirect Perpetrator by Virtue of an Organized Power Apparatus', *Journal of International Criminal Justice* 9 (2011) 137–158.

43 *Lubanga Confirmation Decision* (n. 7), para. 330.

44 Ohlin (n. 24), p. 60; Fletcher (n. 19), p. xxiii.

45 George Fletcher, 'Remembrance of Articles Past', in R. Christopher (ed.), *Fletcher's Essays on Criminal Law* (Oxford University Press, 2013) 269, p. 275.

46 Fletcher (n. 19), pp. 655–57.

47 See further Thomas Weigend, 'Sentencing in West Germany', *Maryland Law Review* 42 (1983) 37–89.

ICC in the *Lubanga* case that legal scholars began to critically discuss his hypothesis.[48] Although Fletcher's treatise did disseminate Roxin's theory more widely, the Pre-Trial Chamber's suggestion that the theory has been endorsed by courts worldwide is questionable.

Even though the Chamber made a good attempt to apply the theory, it sidestepped the crucial question of how to align its approach with the sources of applicable law under Article 21 of the Rome Statute.[49] One solution proposed by Ohlin is to:

> liberate international criminal law from its subsidiary status within public international law and recognize that international judges are, fundamentally criminal law judges deciding on the wrongfulness of actions and the culpability of actors appearing before them in a criminal trial.[50]

Due to the ambiguous nature of Article 25 of the Rome Statute the provision is difficult to apply to members of transnational terrorist groups because as discussed in Chapter 2 the network cells operate independently of one another.[51] The absence of a centralised command structure means that the cells perpetrate terrorist attacks in an impromptu manner without receiving orders from a commander. So, it can be difficult to prove whether the terrorist attack was premeditated and who took part. Section C of this chapter considers whether Roxin's theory can clarify some of these ambiguities, especially the criteria for ascertaining the accountability of members of transnational terrorist groups under Article 25.

C The criteria for determining the accountability of members of transnational terrorist groups under Article 25

Article 25(3)(a) of the Rome Statute defines the perpetrator as the individual who commits a crime 'whether as an individual, jointly with another or through another person, regardless of whether that other person is criminally

48 See further Mark Osiel, 'The Banality of Good: Aligning Incentive against Mass Atrocity', *Columbia Law Review* 105 (2005) 1751–1862, pp. 1829–37.

49 George Fletcher, 'New Court, Old Dogmatk', *Journal of International Criminal Justice* 9 (2011) 179–190. For more commentary on the sources of international law, see Malcolm Shaw, *International Law* (Cambridge University Press, 2014, 7th edn), ch. 3; Martin Dixon and Robert McCorquodale, *Cases and Materials in International Law* (Oxford University Press, 2011, 5th edn), ch. 2; Malcolm Evans, *International Law* (Oxford University Press, 2010, 5th edn), pp. 95–121; Thomas Weigend, 'Intent, Mistake of Law and Co-Perpetration in the Lubanga Decision on Confirmation of Charges', *Journal of International Criminal Justice* 6 (2008) 471–487; Mary Fan, 'Visionary Legal Construction: Custom, General Principles and the Great Architect Cassese', *Journal of International Criminal Justice* 10 (2012) 1063–1079; Ferrando Mantovani, 'The General Principles of International Criminal Law: The Viewpoint of a National Criminal Lawyer', *Journal of International Criminal Justice* 1 (2003) 26–38; Fletcher (n. 19).

50 Ohlin (n. 24), p. 62.

51 See p. 30 of this book.

responsible'.[52] The Pre-Trial Chamber in the *Lubanga* case noted that the concept of co-perpetration was premised on 'joint control over . . . [a] crime by reason of the essential nature of the various contributions to the commission of the crime'.[53] The Chamber noted that in cases involving joint perpetration the perpetrators of the crime do not control the commission of the criminal act themselves, since the defining characteristic of co-perpetration is 'the division of essential tasks for the purpose of committing a crime between two or more persons acting in a concerted manner'.[54] Since the perpetration of the crime depends on the successful completion of each participant's contribution, 'they all share control because each of them could frustrate the commission of the crime by not carrying out his or her task'.[55]

1 An agreement or common plan

There must be evidence of an agreement or common plan between the members of the transnational terrorist group to carry out the crime. Indeed, the Pre-Trial Chamber in the *Lubanga* case noted there must be evidence of an 'agreement or common plan between two or more persons'.[56] This agreement or common plan can be implied but must contain an element of criminality, even though it does not need to be aimed explicitly at the perpetration of a crime.[57] If a member of a

52 Article 25(3)(a) of the Rome Statute of the ICC.

53 *Lubanga Confirmation Decision* (n. 7), para. 341; Ambos (n. 14), p. 479. For further commentary on the *Lubanga* case see for example Roman Graf, 'The International Criminal Court and Child Soldiers: An Appraisal of the *Lubanga* Judgment', *Journal of International Criminal Justice* 10 (2012) 945–969; Michael Kurth, 'The *Lubanga* Case of the International Criminal Court: A Critical Analysis of the Trial Chamber's Findings on Issues of Active Use, Age and Gravity', *Goettingen Journal of International Law* 5 (2013) 431–453; Thomas Lieflander, 'The *Lubanga* Judgment at the ICC', *Cambridge Journal of International and Comparative Law* 1 (2012) 191–212.

54 Ibid., para. 342.

55 Ibid. See also Prosecutor v. *Stakić*, IT-97-24-A, 22 March 2006, para. 440.

56 *Lubanga Confirmation Decision* (n. 7), para. 343; *Stakić* (n. 55), paras 470–477, where the ICTY Trial Chamber subdivided the first criterion of co-perpetration into two criteria: (i) an agreement or silent consent and (ii) a common plan. For further analysis of the *Lubanga* case, see Rebecca Brownman, '*Lubanga*, the DRC and the African Court: Lessons Learnt from the First International Criminal Court Case', *African Human Rights Law Journal* 7 (2007) 412–445.

57 *Lubanga Confirmation Decision* (n. 7), paras 343–345; *Prosecutor* v. *Germain Katanga and Mathieu Ngudjolo Chui, Decision on the Confirmation of Charges*, ICC-01/04-01/07, 30 September 2008, paras 522–523; *Prosecutor* v. *Francis Kirimi Muthaura, Uhuru Muigai Kenyatta and Mohammed Hussein Ali, Decision on the Confirmation of Charges*, ICC-01/09-02/11, 23 January 2012, paras 399–400; *Prosecutor* v. *Abdallah Banda Abakaer Nourain and Saleh Mohammed Jerbo Jamus, Decision on the Confirmation of Charges*, ICC-02/05-03/09, 7 March 2011, paras 129–135; *Prosecutor* v. *William Samoei Ruto, Henry Kiprono Kosgey and Joshua Arap, Decision on the Confirmation of Charges*, ICC-01/09-01/11, 23 January 2012, paras 301–304; *Prosecutor* v. *Bahar Idriss Abu Garda, Decision on the Confirmation of Charges*, ICC-02/05-02/09, 8 February 2010, paras 160 and 163–232.

transnational terrorist group participates in the commission of a crime without coordinating with his/her co-perpetrators, that act does not fall within the meaning of Article 25(3)(a) of the Rome Statute.[58] At the same time the Chamber recognised that:

> when the objective elements of an offence are carried out by a plurality of persons acting within the framework of a common plan, only those to whom essential tasks have been assigned – and who, consequently, have the power to frustrate the commission of the crime by not performing their tasks – can be said to have joint control over the crime.[59]

So, the fundamental criterion of joint perpetration is the power to aggravate the commission of an offence 'by not performing their [assigned] tasks'.[60] In view of the fact that this criterion is expressed in negative terms, it would seem that there exists 'no particular affirmative act that a person must perform in order to become a joint perpetrator'.[61]

The Trial Chamber does not require that the common plan must be inherently criminal providing that it contains some element of criminality. The execution of the plan must involve 'a sufficient risk that if events follow the ordinary course, a crime will be committed'.[62] This is a perplexing criterion which does not adequately exclude a plan that is intrinsically non-criminal.[63] The Chamber also dithers between an objective and subjective approach to co-perpetration. At the outset, the Trial Chamber stressed that pursuant to Article 30 of the Rome Statute co-perpetrators must be subjectively cognisant of the risk that the execution of the common plan could lead to the perpetration of a crime.[64] In particular, the Trial Chamber emphasised that 'the mental requirement that the common plan included the commission of a crime will be satisfied if the co-perpetrators knew that, in the ordinary course of events, implementing the plan will lead to

58 *Lubanga Confirmation Decision* (n. 7), para. 343.
59 Ibid., para. 347.
60 *Katanga and Chui Confirmation Decision* (n. 7), para. 525.
61 Jens Ohlin et al., 'Assessing Control Theory', *Leiden Journal of International Law* 26 (3) (2013) 725–746, p. 746.
62 *Prosecutor* v. *Thomas Lubanga Dyilo*, Judgment, ICC-01/04-01/06, 14 March 2012, paras 984–987; Kai Ambos, 'The First Judgment of the International Criminal Court: (*Prosecutor* v. *Lubanga*): A Comprehensive Analysis of Legal Issues', *International Criminal Law Review* 12 (2012) 115–153; Triestino Mariniello, '*Prosecutor* v. *Thomas Lubanga Dyilo*: The First Judgment of the International Criminal Court's Trial Chamber', *International Criminal Law Review* 12 (2012) 137–147.
63 Ambos (n. 62), pp. 139–140.
64 *Lubanga Judgment* (n. 62), para. 986; Jose Rodriguez-Villasante y Prieto, 'Los Principles Generales del Derecho Penal en el Estatuto de la Roma de la Corte Penal Internacional', *Revista espanola de derecho militar* 75 (2000) 417; Donald Piragoff, 'Article 30: Mental Element', in O. Triffterer (ed.), *Commentary on the Rome Statute of the International Criminal Court* (Nomos, 1999) 527–536, p. 534; Elies Van Sliedregt, *The Criminal Responsibility of Individuals for Violations of International Humanitarian Law* (TMC Asser Press, 2003), p. 87.

that result'.[65] Although the Trial Chamber adopted the correct approach, it has been tempered by subsequent formulations which have been supplanted by the requirement that the execution of the plan 'will result in the commission of the relevant crime in the ordinary course of events'.[66]

Judge Fulford, in his dissenting opinion in the *Lubanga* case, proposed an alternative approach which more accurately represented the language of Article 25 and simply requires a common plan between a number of individuals who work together to produce a particular result.[67] Judge Fulford rationalised this approach by observing that:

> [t]his self-evidently necessitates a sufficient meeting of minds, by way of an agreement, common plan or joint understanding. In practice, this will not always be explicit or the result of long-term planning, and the existence of the joint venture may need to be inferred from the conduct of co-perpetrators.[68]

This approach would sidestep the concept of control which is at the very heart of Roxin's theory. The co-perpetration of an international crime would simply require a mutual intention among the co-perpetrators.[69]

Arguably, Judge Fulford's explanation of co-perpetration accurately describes the network-based structure and collective criminality of transnational terrorist groups as examined in Chapter 2 of this book.[70] Despite the fact that the transnational terrorist group may not have a centralised command the cells still have the capacity to reach consensus on the overall short-term and long-term strategy of the group.[71] Indeed, evidence that the accused acquiesced to a criminal plan to carry out terrorist attacks could be inferred from his membership of the transnational terrorist group alone. Since the member either agrees or reaches a mutual understanding with others to commit a crime and wants the result achieved by the group, then the particular action should be attributed to that member for being a participant in the collective action.

a The contribution towards the commission of the crime

Article 25(3)(d) of the Rome Statute does not make any reference to whether the accused must be a member of the transnational terrorist group committing the criminal offence. The provision simply states that an accused will be held accountable if he/she 'contributes to the commission or attempted commission of such

65 Ibid.
66 *Lubanga Judgment* (n. 62), para. 1018.
67 Separate Opinion of Judge Fulford, ICC-01/04-01/06-2842 (14 March 2012), para. 15.
68 Dissenting Opinion of Judge Fulford (n. 67), para. 15.
69 Ohlin (n. 28), p. 742.
70 See p. 31 of this book.
71 Ibid.

crime by a group of persons acting with a common purpose'.[72] The provision further provides that the contribution must be made 'with the aim of furthering the criminal activity or criminal purpose of the group' or 'be made in the knowledge of the intention of the group to commit the crime'.[73] So, on the face of it, there would seem to be no requirement in Article 25 that the accused who is alleged to have made a 'contribution' to the perpetration of a criminal offence by a group must be a member of this group.

However, one should be cautious before reading such a requirement into the provision. Evidence that Article 25(3)(d) does not require that the accused be a member of a transnational terrorist group can be inferred from the contention that the wording of the provision was scrounged from Article 2(3) of the International Convention on the Suppression of Terrorist Bombing 1997 which was open for ratification around the same time the Rome Statute was drafted.[74] Article 2(3) of the Convention provides that an individual can be held responsible if they:

> [i]n any other way contributes to the commission of one of more offences as set forth in paragraph 1 or 2 by a group of persons acting with a common purpose; such contribution shall be intentional and either be made with the aim of furthering the general criminal activity or purpose of the group or be made in the knowledge of the intention of the group to commit the offence or offences concerned.[75]

This interpretation of the term 'contributes' in Article 25(3)(d) of the Rome Statue is not persuasive because Article 2(3)(b) of the International Convention on the Suppression of Terrorist Bombing 1997 provides that an individual is responsible if he/she '[o]rganises or directs others to commit an offence as set forth in paragraph 1 or 2'.[76] This provision in turn clarifies the meaning of Article 2(3)(c) of the Convention which states that an individual will be held liable if he/she '[i]n any other way contributes to the commission of one or more offences as set forth in paragraph 1 or 2 by a group of persons acting with a common

72 Article 25(3)(d) of the Rome Statute of the International Criminal Court; *Lubanga Judgment* (n. 62), paras 346–348; *Katanga and Chui* (n. 57), paras 524–526; *Muthaura, Kenyatta, and Ali* (n. 57), paras 401–406; *Banda and Jerbo* (n. 57), paras 136–149; *Ruto et al.* (n. 57), paras 305–312; *Abu Garda* (n. 57), paras 160 and 180–232.

73 Ibid.

74 International Convention for the Suppression of Terrorist Bombings, GA Res. 164 Article 2(3)(c) at 389, UN GAOR, 52nd session, Supp. No. 49, UN Doc. A/52/49 (8 January 1998); Doug Cassel, 'Corporate Aiding and Abetting of Human Rights Violations: Confusion in the Courts', *Northwestern Journal of International Human Rights* 6 (2008) 304, p. 313.

75 Ibid. The judgment of the ICTY Appeals Chamber noted in the *Tadić* case (n. 6), para. 221 that the drafting history of the Terrorism Convention 'does not shed any light on the reasons behind the adoption of this text'.

76 Article 2(3)(b) of the International Convention on the Suppression of Terrorist Bombing 1997.

purpose'.[77] So it would seem that the contribution can come from outside the group. However, since there is no equivalent provision in Article 25 (3)(d) of the Rome Statute the 'outside contributor' interpretation can be challenged on the grounds that Article 25(3)(b) already prohibits an act of facilitating, aiding and abetting, or assisting in the commission of a crime.

I THE ESSENTIALITY OF THE CONTRIBUTION

The individual's contribution must be essential to ensure the successful commission of the criminal offence. The criterion:

> reflects the value judgment that those who provide vital contributions to the commission of a crime are, in general, more blameworthy than those who remain at the margins of the criminal enterprise and provide only support that the main actors could have done without.[78]

However, the efficacy of the control theory of perpetration advocated by the Pre-Trial Chamber is problematic when applied to transnational terrorist groups. In view of their network-based organisational structure the criteria for determining whether a member's contribution was essential for the successful perpetration of the terrorist attack is ambiguous. Indeed, it can be difficult to discern whether a member made any contribution because as discussed in Chapter 2 the cells of the transnational terrorist groups operate in a clandestine manner.[79]

Nevertheless, the essentiality of the contribution towards the execution of the common criminal plan can be determined from either a subjective or objective approach.[80] However, the determination that a subordinate member's contribution towards the commission of a crime was 'essential' may be more straightforward if one evaluates the individual's contribution from the planning stages of the offence. If this approach was adopted it would be easier to determine whether the member's contribution was valuable but not critical for the successful perpetration of the crime. Indeed, the Trial Chamber in the *Lubanga* case appears to have analysed the accused's contribution from a subjective perspective. In particular, the Trial Chamber noted at paragraph 1000 of its judgment that:

> [t]he determination as to whether the particular contribution of the accused results in liability as a co-perpetrator is to be based on an analysis of the common plan and the role that was assigned to, or was assumed by the co-perpetrator, according to the division of tasks.[81]

77 Ibid.
78 Ibid.
79 See p. 31 of this book.
80 Ibid.
81 *Lubanga Judgment* (n. 62), para. 1000; Weigend (n. 16); Roger Clark, 'Drafting a General Part to a Penal Code: Some Thoughts Inspired by the Negotiations on the Rome Statute of the International Criminal Court and by the Court's First Substantive

The prosecution proposed that co-perpetration requires a subjective approach where the accused must have been 'assigned a central role in the implementation of the plan, [and] it will suffice if in retrospect it appears his or her contribution was substantial, rather than essential'.[82] The ICC Trial Chamber did not embrace this approach and as a result the question remains whether the criteria of joint perpetration should be evaluated from an objective or subjective approach.[83]

If the subjective approach is to be preferred, the judge must accede as binding any error committed by the perpetrators during the commission of the offence. So, if the high-ranking members of a transnational terrorist group decide that the bombing of a supermarket will only succeed if one of the subordinate members of the group provides a vehicle to transport the bomb; this expectation under the subjective approach infers that the member of the group who provided the vehicle is a joint perpetrator. In addition, the subordinate member would still be classified as a joint perpetrator even if the vehicle was not ultimately used to transport the bomb to the location, and instead the bombing was carried out by a different member of the group who transported the bomb to the supermarket on foot in a rucksack.

On the other hand, the objective approach, which would determine whether the member's provision of the vehicle was 'essential' for the successful perpetration of the bombing, would arguably sidestep this difficulty. If the transnational terrorist group actually uses the vehicle provided by the member to transport the bomb to the supermarket, it is uncertain what the result would have been if the member had not provided the vehicle. Perhaps the subordinate members of the transnational terrorist group would have decided not to carry out the bombing, or perhaps they would have found an alternative means of transporting the bomb to the supermarket?

Judge Fulford, in his dissenting opinion, was of the view that the definition of an 'essential' contribution to the criminal plan was too narrow[84] and proposed a more straightforward test for joint perpetration:

> [n]othing in the Statute required that the contribution must involve direct, physical participation at the execution stage of the crime, and instead, an absent perpetrator may be involved. Either way, the use of the word 'commits' simply requires an operative link between the individual's contribution and the commission of the crime.[85]

The application of this alternative test would allow a court to sidestep a hypothetical examination of how the transnational terrorist group was able to commit the terrorist attack without the subordinate's involvement.[86] Judge Fulford concluded

Law Discussion in the Lubanga Dyilo Confirmation Proceedings', *Criminal Law Forum* (2008) 519–552, p. 545; Schabas (n. 13), p. 429.

82 *Lubanga Judgment* (n. 62), paras 990 and 991.

83 Ohlin et al. (n. 61), fn 30.

84 Dissenting Opinion of Judge Fulford (n. 67), para. 15.

85 Ibid.

86 Ibid., para. 17.

that 'the plain text of Article 25(3) does not require proof that the crime would have been committed absent the accused's involvement'.[87] He compares this 'operative link' with causation[88] and suggests that in order to establish co-perpetration there must be 'a causal link between the individual's contribution and the crime'.[89] This in turn raises questions about Judge Fulford's understanding of the phrase 'causal link'.[90] With regard to an act that is pivotal for the commission of a criminal offence, it is unclear whether this act establishes a 'causal link' between it and the commission of the crime.

This is particularly problematic when applied in the context of members of transnational terrorist groups because it is often unclear what specific role the accused played in the commission of the crime because of the group's network-based organisational structure. As discussed in Chapter 2, the lack of communication between the cells of some groups means that a subordinate member may carry out a particular task without realising that he/she has made an 'essential' contribution towards the perpetration of a terrorist attack.[91] Indeed, in the case of the van driver delivering the package to the supermarket he/she may not realise until much later that he/she was in fact delivering a bomb. Unfortunately, Judge Fulford did not consider this question in his dissenting opinion, and, as a result, the parameters of his proposed test are ambiguous and do not specify the precise criteria from which to make a distinction between perpetration and accessorial liability.[92]

At the same time, the Pre-Trial Chamber defined the concept of a perpetrator too broadly. The ICC Trial Chamber agreed with the prosecution's submission that '[i]t is not necessary that the accused physically perpetrated any of the elements of the crimes or that he was present at the crime scene'.[93] It further held that individuals who jointly carry out a crime 'include, *inter alia*, those who assist in formulating the relevant strategy or plan, become involved in directing or controlling other participants or determine the roles of those involved in the offence'.[94] As a result, the prosecution does not need to prove a 'direct or physical link between the accused's contribution and the commission of the crimes'.[95] However, if a distinction is made between the members of the transnational terrorist group who played a central role in the commission of the offence (perpetrators) and the members who merely played a supporting role (accessories) the simplistic criterion of the essentiality of the contribution towards the commission

87 Ibid., para. 15.
88 Ibid., para. 16.
89 Ibid.
90 Ohlin et al. are of the same view (n. 61), p. 154.
91 See p. 27 of this book.
92 Ibid. There is ongoing controversy as to whether there exists a hierarchical grading of liability in Article 25. For further commentary on this point, see Werle (n. 6).
93 *Lubanga Judgment* (n. 62), paras 1003 and 1004.
94 Ibid., para. 1004.
95 Ibid. (emphasis omitted).

of the offence is inadequate because it describes only one aspect of the particular offence.

Judge Van den Wyngaert, in her concurring opinion in the *Chui* case, agreed with the view of Judge Fulford that the control theory advocated by the Pre-Trial Chamber in the *Lubanga* case is inconsistent with Article 25(3)(a) of the Rome Statute.[96] Instead, she proposed that:

> [f]or joint perpetration, there must, in my view, be a direct contribution to the realisation of the material elements of the crime. This follows from the very concept of joint perpetration. Under Article 25(3)(a), only persons who have committed a crime together can be held responsible. The essence of committing a crime is bringing about its material elements.[97]

Similarly to Judge Fulford, she rejected the 'essentiality' criterion concluding that it obliges the judiciary 'to engage in artificial, speculative exercises about whether a crime would still have been committed if one of the accused had not made exactly the same contribution'.[98] Judge Van den Wyngaert also disagreed with Judge Fulford's approach that any individual who provides some causal element towards the commission of the offence will be deemed a perpetrator.[99]

Instead, Judge Van den Wyngaert proposed that the concept of co-perpetration should only be applied to those individuals who directly commit the material elements of the criminal offence.[100] Under this approach a member of a transnational terrorist group could be classified as a direct perpetrator of an attack if he/she plans or organises the commission of the criminal offence. This is because planning, according to Judge Van den Wyngaert, is 'an intrinsic part of the actual execution of the crime'.[101] In *Prosecutor* v. *Germain Katanga* Judge Van den Wyngaert reiterated her position in her dissenting opinion.[102]

Judge Van den Wyngaert's foremost argument in favour of the 'directness' criterion is that it affords equal treatment to both individual perpetrators and joint perpetrators.[103] Both the individual perpetrator and the joint perpetrators can be held accountable if he/she 'brings about' the material elements of the crime.[104] However, the application of the 'directness' criterion to transnational terrorist groups is problematic because as discussed in Chapter 2 the perpetration of an attack by a transnational terrorist group is quite different to the perpetration of the

96 *Concurring Opinion of Judge Christine Van den Wyngaert* (n. 40), paras 41–42. Judge Van den Wyngaert was also of the view that there is no hierarchical ranking of liability in Article 25(3). See further para. 43 of the Concurring Opinion of Judge Van den Wyngaert.
97 Ibid., para. 44.
98 Ibid., para. 42.
99 Ibid.; see also para. 43.
100 Ibid., para. 44.
101 Ibid., para. 47.
102 *Katanga Trial Judgment* (n. 36), paras 277–281.
103 Concurring Opinion of Judge Van den Wyngaert (n. 40), para. 46.
104 Ibid., para. 45.

same attack by an individual acting alone.[105] This is because in a transnational terrorist group the task of planning and carrying out the attack is shared among the subordinate members of the cell whereas an individual acting alone must both plan and execute the act.[106]

The Court would have to infer the 'direct' elements of the offence from the manner in which the terrorist attack occurred.[107] Indeed, these members 'join . . . [together] for the very purpose of relieving each participant of the necessity to "bring about" by himself the result of the criminal plan'.[108] If the trial judges must ascertain what particular action is 'direct', then perhaps, as Judge Fulford suggested, the question whether the accused member of the transnational terrorist group is in fact a perpetrator of the attack should be left to the court to decide. At the same time, if it was essential for each member of the transnational terrorist group 'to individually fulfil each element of the offence definition, the concept of joint perpetration would be superfluous – every participant could be convicted as an individual perpetrator'.[109] The comparison which Judge Van den Wyngaert makes between individual perpetration and joint perpetration sidesteps the very essence of the concept of joint perpetration which is the division of the tasks of planning and carrying out the criminal offence among the participants in the crime.

An alternative approach for prosecuting members of transnational terrorist groups would be to infer these criteria from the *mens rea* of the crime. The prosecution would have to produce evidence that there was a joint plan devised by members of the group to perpetrate international crimes. However, as seen in Chapter 2, evidence that plans were drawn up by the members of the group in advance of the terrorist attack may be difficult for the prosecution to prove in light of the clandestine manner in which transnational terrorist groups operate.[110] Furthermore, inferring the criteria for determining joint perpetration of a terrorist attack from the *mens rea* of the crime would be problematic for two other reasons.

First, it is uncertain whether a comprehensible understanding of the *mens rea* requirement laid down in Article 25(3)(d) in relation to group complicity is conceivable. The wording of the entire provision was not fully conjectured by the drafters of the Rome Statute and was the result of parleyed drafting and negotiations. Article 25(3)(d) on group complicity 'includes complex standards of knowledge or purpose for group complicity, allowing for liability for contributions that are intentional and are made with knowledge of the group's criminality'.[111] There is no mention whatsoever of what standard of knowledge must be established by the prosecution in order to hold an individual accountable under Article 25(3)(b) of the Rome Statute. However, the issue is not whether a different

105 See p. 30 of this book.
106 See p. 31 of this book.
107 Ibid., para. 46.
108 Ohlin et al. (n. 61), p. 265.
109 Ibid.
110 See p. 28 of this book.
111 Ohlin (n. 40), p. 417.

standard of knowledge must be proved in order for terrorist attacks to satisfy the requirements of Article 25(3)(b) but the fact that the provision makes no reference to the necessary standards of knowledge whatsoever. This scenario leads to considerable confusion in determining whether a member of a transnational terrorist group should be classified as a joint perpetrator or an individual perpetrator because there is no definitive stipulation of what standards of knowledge should be applied.

Second, Article 25(3)(d) of the Rome Statute specifically provides that the contribution to the common criminal endeavour must be intentional. An attack by a transnational terrorist group is the result of a common plan where the instigating members of the group work with the perpetrating members during the initial stages of the common plan to intentionally carry out a terrorist attack. Nevertheless, the term 'intentional' in Article 25(3)(d) can be interpreted both broadly and narrowly. If the narrow interpretation of the term is to be preferred, this simply denotes that 'the bare action performed by the complicitous defendant was the product of an intentional decision' and not an accident.[112] The problem with this construal of Article 25(3)(d) is that Article 30 of the Rome Statute states that '[u]nless otherwise provided' the necessary mental element of the Statute is both "intent and knowledge'.[113] So a provision of the Rome Statute must only express this alternative mental element where it is different to the default rule laid down in Article 30.[114]

Nevertheless, Article 25(3)(d) contains the term 'intentional'. It is unclear why it was necessary to include this particular word because Article 30 specifically states that Article 25(3)(d) should only specify the required *mens rea* standard if it wishes to diverge form the default rule.[115] The only explanation is that the drafters utilised the term 'intentional' to distinguish the *mens rea* standard in Article 25(3)(d) from the *mens rea* standard laid down in Article 30. This creates further confusion because the provision should have only specified the required *mens rea* standard if it was different from the *mens rea* standard laid down in Article 30.

Since Article 30 expressly states that 'unless otherwise stated' the required *mens rea* standard is both 'intent and knowledge'[116] it could be in conflict with Article 25(3)(d). In particular, the word 'intentional' in Article 25(3)(d) refers to the nature of the contribution by which the accused 'intends to help the principals, as opposed to a situation where the defendant performs an action that he should reasonably foresee might advance the cause of the principals (even though he does not intend it to do so)'.[117] On the other hand, Article 30 defines the term 'intent' to mean that the 'person means to cause . . . [the] consequence or is aware that it will occur in the ordinary course of events'.[118] As a result, the *mens rea*

112 Ibid.
113 Article 30 of the Rome Statute of the International Criminal Court.
114 Ohlin (n. 40), p. 417.
115 Article 30 of the Rome Statute of the International Criminal Court.
116 Ibid.
117 Ohlin (n. 40), p. 418.
118 Article 30 of the Rome Statute of the International Criminal Court.

requirement laid down in Article 25(3)(d) is arguably the same as the default rule under Article 30. So, the inclusion of the term 'intentional' in Article 25(3)(d) is baffling and is not a sufficient basis from which to derive the criteria for determining whether a member of a transnational terrorist group should be classified as a joint perpetrator or an individual perpetrator on foot of their role in the planning and perpetration of an attack.

An alternative method to the *mens rea* approach for determining the criteria for classifying a member of a transnational terrorist group as a joint perpetrator or an individual perpetrator would be to adopt an objective approach by taking into consideration '[the] element of immediacy, of carrying out a task temporally close to the commission of the material elements of the offence'.[119] Roxin proposed that only the individuals that participated in the commission of the criminal offence after the initial attempt to perpetrate it should be classified as joint co-perpetrators.[120] Although this approach is compelling, it is still problematic because reaching consensus on the definition of an attempt to perpetrate an international crime is difficult. Nevertheless, under the objective approach, the individual's control over the commission of the crime is an essential indicator of joint perpetration.[121]

In general, it is the joint perpetrator who decides 'whether and how the offence is actually perpetrated, either by directly taking part in the *actus reus* or at least by overseeing . . . the commission of the crime by the immediate actors'.[122] It would be possible to classify the leader of the transnational terrorist group as a joint perpetrator of a terrorist attack where there is evidence to suggest that he/she was in contact with the subordinate members by phone at the location of the attack. This would enable the leader to then decide whether the attempt to carry out the terrorist attack should be abandoned when the subordinates report to him/her that there were unforeseen obstacles. As discussed in Chapter 2, transnational terrorist groups because of their network-based structure have developed the capacity to carry out an attack even if the leader is not in close proximity to its geographical location.[123] Therefore, the approach proposed above could enable the ICC to prosecute a leader of a transnational terrorist group under Article 25(3)(b) of the Rome Statute even if he was not in contact with the subordinate members of the group at the location of the proposed attack by phone because he/she has ordered, solicited, or induced the commission of a crime 'which in fact occurs or is attempted'.[124]

Nevertheless, despite the merits of this alternative approach, the concept of control advocated by the ICC Pre-Trial Chamber in the *Lubanga* case is too simplistic. Instead, a more all-inclusive approach to joint perpetration of attacks by transnational terrorist groups which comprises both objective and subjective

119 Ohlin et al. (n. 61), p. 367.
120 Roxin (n. 7), p. 25.
121 Ohlin et al. (n. 61), p. 367.
122 Ibid.
123 See p. 30 of this book.
124 Article 25(3)(b) of the Rome Statute of the International Criminal Court.

elements is necessary. The paradigm of relevant factors includes the subordinate member's involvement in the planning of the attacks and his/her own *mens rea*. Hence, the member's contribution towards the commission of the attacks and the link between his contribution and perpetration of the criminal offence is significant. In any event, it remains a contentious issue whether the ICC should attach greater importance to either objective factors or subjective factors. Perhaps the so-called concept of indirect perpetration may provide a more straightforward approach to prosecuting members of transnational terrorist groups especially in light of their network-based organisational structure?

D The concept of indirect co-perpetration under Article 25 and its application to members of transnational terrorist groups

The ICC Pre-Trial Chamber in *Prosecutor* v. *Katanga and Chui* combined the doctrine of co-perpetration (Mittäterschaft) with the doctrine of indirect perpetration (Täter hinter dem Täter), thereby creating a new controversial mode of liability called the doctrine of indirect co-perpetration (mittelbare Mittäterschaft).[125] There appears to be no foundation for this new mode of liability in Roxin's control theory of perpetration which made no reference whatsoever to the concept of an indirect co-perpetrator.[126] Nevertheless, the Pre-Trial Chamber in the *Katanga and Chui* case described the defendant as an indirect co-perpetrator because he exercised control over an armed group and collaborated with another defendant, who made a significant contribution to the perpetration of attacks on villages.[127]

125 See further *Katanga and Chui Confirmation Decision* (n. 7), para. 492. In this case, the Pre-Trial Chamber held that '[r]ather, through a combination of individual responsibility for committing crimes through other persons together with the mutual attribution among the co-perpetrators at the senior level, a mode of liability arises which allows the Court to assess the blameworthiness of "senior leaders" adequately'. For an analysis on the aptness of combining these two modes of liability, see Thomas Weigend, 'Perpetration through an Organization: The Unexpected Career of a German Legal Concept', *Journal of International Criminal Justice* 9 (2011) 91–111, p. 110; Stefano Manacorda and Chantal Meloni, 'Indirect Perpetration versus Joint Criminal Enterprise: Concurring Approaches in the Practice of International Criminal Law?', *Journal of International Criminal Justice* 9 (2011) 159–178.

126 Neha Jain, 'The Control Theory of Perpetration in International Criminal Law', *Chicago Journal of International Law* 12(1) (2011) 157–200, p. 184. It is also interesting to note that domestic prosecutions that have relied on the control theory of perpetration did not incorporate this principle of indirect co-perpetration. For examples of these domestic cases, see *Fujimori Judgment*, CSJ, Sala Penal Especial, 7 April 2009, Exp. No. AV 19–2001 as referenced in Kai Ambos, 'The *Fjimori* Judgment: A President's Responsibility for Crimes against Humanity as Indirect Perpetrator by Virtue of an Organized Power Apparatus', *Journal of International Criminal Justice* 9 (2011) 137–158, p. 147 (fn 33); *Juntas* Trial Case, Judgment of 9 December 1985, translation reprinted in *International Legal Materials* 26 (1987) 317 as cited by Olásolo (n. 2), p. 127–129.

127 *Katanga and Chui Confirmation Decision* (n. 7), paras 543–545.

Neither the doctrine of indirect perpetration nor the doctrine of co-perpetration could effectively hold both *Katanga* and *Chui* accountable because they controlled two distinct armed groups each of which committed substantial elements of the joint criminal endeavour. Due to 'ethical loyalties within the respective organizations' the two armed groups could not be merged into a single organisation.[128] Therefore, there were two distinct armed groups conducting attacks on villages which were fused at the leadership level.[129] As a result, the 'coordinated essential contribution by each co-perpetrator . . . [resulted] in the realisation of the objective elements of the crime'.[130]

The defence team of *Katanga* challenged the application of this novel mode of liability.[131] Their contention was partly supported by the ICTY Trial Chamber's conclusion in *Prosecutor* v. *Milutinović et al.* that indirect perpetration was not a mode of liability under customary international law before 1992.[132] Nevertheless, the ICC Pre-Trial Chamber in *Katanga* dismissed this argument by stating that Article 25(3)(a) of the Rome Statute made provision for both indirect perpetration and co-perpetration.[133] Although, the wording of Article 25 does not make any reference whatsoever to the concept of indirect co-perpetration the Pre-Trial Chamber made the following flimsy argument to support its conclusion:

> The Chamber finds that there are no legal grounds for limiting the joint commission of the crime solely to cases in which the perpetrators execute a portion of the crime by exercising direct control over it. Rather, through a combination of individual responsibility for committing crimes through other persons together with the mutual attribution among the co-perpetrators at the senior level, a mode of liability arises which allows the Court to assess the blameworthiness of 'senior leaders' adequately.[134]

Judge Van den Wyngaert in her concurring opinion in the *Chui* case[135] disagreed and concluded that the concept was not a mode of liability under Article 25(3)(a) of the Rome Statute.[136]

Nevertheless, the question whether the indirect co-perpetration of a crime is a mode of liability under Article 25 still persists because many of the recent indictments issued by the ICC, including against Saif al-Islam Gaddafi and Abdullah al-Senussi, have accused them of committing crimes as indirect co-perpetrators.[137]

128 Ibid., para. 493.
129 Ibid., para. 548.
130 Ibid., para. 555.
131 Ibid., para. 474; ICC-01/04-01/06-698, para. 16.
132 *Prosecutor* v. *Šainović et al., Decision on Ojdanic's Motion Challenging Jurisdiction: Indirect Co-Perpetration,* IT-05-87, 22 March 2006, para. 37.
133 *Katanga and Chui Confirmation Decision* (n. 7), para. 491.
134 Ibid., para. 492.
135 Concurring Opinion of Judge Van den Wyngaert (n. 40), para. 59.
136 Ibid.
137 Warrant of Arrest for Saif al-Islam Gaddafi, ICC-01/11-14, 27 June 2011, p. 6, available at: www.icc-cpi.int/iccdocs/doc/doc1099329.pdf (date accessed: 14 March

One can understand the appeal of this mode of liability for the prosecution since due to limited resources the ICC has thus far only indicted high-ranking individuals who were generally not present at the scene where the alleged crime took place. By utilising the doctrine of indirect perpetration, the prosecution only needs to establish a connection between the accused and the individuals who actually perpetrated the criminal offence.

It is also similar to the JCE doctrine developed by the ICTY and could be easily utilised in the prosecution of members of transnational terrorist groups.[138] As seen in Chapter 2, it is the network cells of the group that carry out the crime.[139] So the result is the effective distribution of labour among all members of the transnational terrorist group. The doctrine of indirect co-perpetration ensures that the high-ranking members of the group will be held accountable for their role in the perpetration of the attack. Indeed, in the *Katanga and Chui* case the two accused had a joint strategy for their armed groups to effectively conduct attacks on villages.[140] As a result, the prosecution contended that the defendants were not only responsible for the crimes committed by the members of their own armed groups but also the crimes committed by the other armed group.[141]

However, Trial Chamber II in its final judgment in the *Katanga* case dismissed the notion that the modes of liability contained in Article 25 are ordered hierarchically.[142] It also watered down the test for indirect co-perpetration but in so doing caused considerable confusion on the construal of Article 25(3).[143] Overall, the judgment constitutes a significant divergence from the past jurisprudence of the Court and highlights the need to revisit the interpretation of Article 25 in the *Lubanga* Appeal. Judge Van den Wyngaert, in her separate dissenting opinion in the *Katanga* case, dissociated herself from the majority's approach on the grounds that it recategorised the charges against the accused[144] and repeated her opinion in the *Chui* case regarding the correct construal of the provision.[145]

2018; Warrant of Arrest for Abdullah Al-Senussi, ICC-01/11-15, 27 June 2011, p. 6 available at: www.icc-cpi.int/iccdocs/doc/doc1099332.pdf (date accessed: 14 March 2018); *Prosecutor* v. *Francis Kirimi Muthaura and Uhuru Muigai Kenyatta, Decision on Confirmation of Charges*, Pre-Trial Chamber II, ICC-01/09-02/11, 23 January 2012; *Prosecutor* v. *William Samoei Ruto and Joshua Arap Sang*, Decision on Confirmation of Charges, ICC Appeals Chamber, Case No. ICC-01/09-01/11; *Prosecutor* v. *Omar Hassan Ahmad Al Bashir, Decision on Prosecution's Application for a Warrant of Arrest against Omar Hassan Ahmad al Bashir*, Pre-Trial Chamber I, ICC-02/05-01/09, 4 March 2009.

138 Ibid., p. 778.

139 See p. 28 of this book.

140 *Katanga and Chui Confirmation Decision* (n. 7), para. 19.

141 Ibid., para. 484.

142 *Katanga Trial Judgment* (n. 36), paras 1383 and 1384–1388.

143 Ibid., paras 1373, 1384–1388, and 1400–1412.

144 See generally *Katanga Trial Judgment* (Van den Wyngaert Opinion) (n. 36). Judge Van den Wyngaert concluded that the Trial Chamber should have rendered its verdict under Article 25(3)(a) and that Katanga should have been acquitted along with Ngudjolo on 18 December 2012.

145 Ibid., paras 279–281.

Indeed, Judge Van den Wyngaert stressed that the majority's interpretation of Article 25(3)(a) undermined the rationale for importing the control theory of perpetration.[146]

So, the application of the doctrine of indirect co-perpetration to members of transnational terrorist groups is not without its challenges. Article 25(3)(a) of the Rome Statute clearly states that a person will be held accountable for perpetrating a crime 'jointly with another or through another person' but does not explicitly state that these two modes of liability can be combined. Judge Van den Wyngaert in her concurring opinion in the *Chui* case noted that a literal interpretation of the wording of Article 25(3)(a) of the Rome Statute did not convincingly establish that these modes of liability could be combined together.[147] If it did, it could lead 'to a radical expansion of Article 25(3)(a) of the Statute, and . . . a totally new mode of liability'.[148] Furthermore, Judge Van den Wyngaert noted that if this interpretation of Article 25(3)(a) was accepted by the Trial Chamber it would be 'possible to hold the accused responsible for the conduct of the physical perpetrator of a crime, even though he/she neither exercised any direct influence or authority over this person, nor shared any intent with him or her'.[149]

Judge Van den Wyngaert examined whether there are any circumstances in which these two modes of liability could be combined despite the wording of Article 25(3)(a).[150] She held that 'different forms of criminal responsibility under the Statute may be combined, as long as all the elements of each form [of liability] are proven'.[151] However, her conclusion that different forms of criminal responsibility can be combined can be challenged because it conflicts with the wording of the Rome Statute. Judge Van den Wyngaert also did not provide a legal basis for her conclusion or discuss the consequences of the Trial Chamber adopting this approach.

Although high-ranking members of transnational terrorist groups standing trial before the ICC could satisfy the criteria of indirect co-perpetration because of the manner in which their attacks are planned and perpetrated the doctrine entails much more than the simple combination of the concepts of indirect perpetration and co-perpetration. For example, the Pre-Trial Chamber in the *Katanga and Chui Decision Confirmation Decision* held that the two accused were only able to perpetrate attacks on villages after the leaders of both groups agreed on a joint strategy to attack villages.[152] However, the defendants did not fulfil the criteria for either co-perpetration or indirect perpetration. If the defendants had fulfilled the criteria for both forms of liability, the application of the doctrine of indirect co-perpetration would not have been necessary. The prosecution 'could simply have

146 Ibid.
147 Concurring Opinion of Judge Van den Wyngaert (n. 40), paras 60 and 64.
148 Ibid., para. 61.
149 Ibid.
150 Ibid., para. 62.
151 Ibid.
152 *Katanga and Chui Confirmation Decision* (n. 7), para. 33.

selected between co-perpetration and indirect perpetration and could have proceeded with one of these doctrines as their theory of the case'.[153]

If the doctrine of indirect perpetration is to be successfully invoked in the prosecution of members of transnational terrorist groups at the ICC, a clear distinction needs to be made between a defendant who held a command position within the group and exercised control over subordinate members and a defendant who exercised control over the transnational terrorist group as an organisation. The ICC has not yet explored whether control over an organisation rather than mere individual members of an organisation can establish liability under Article 25 of the Rome Statute. The application of the doctrine in this manner could perhaps provide a better basis to hold leaders of transnational terrorist groups accountable for attacks than the doctrine of command responsibility. Indeed, Article 25(3)(a) can be described as the normative approach to participation in an international crime which provides that the principal is the individual with the most responsibility for the crime because he/she has exercised considerable authority over the commission of the crime even though he may have not played any role in actually committing it.

This is in complete contrast to what Ohlin et al., describes as the 'empirical approach to liability' which defines the perpetrator as the individual 'who performs the material elements of the offence and "perpetrates" or "commits" the crime'.[154] Under this approach the accessory is the individual 'who contributes to causing the *actus reus*'.[155] The 'empirical approach to liability' can also be classified as a bottom-up approach to liability.[156] If the empirical approach is applied to a complex organisation such as a transnational terrorist group, one can begin with the subordinate member of the transnational terrorist group who actually carried out the terrorist attack and then move on to the commanders of the group who may have given the orders to the subordinate to carry out the attack.

On the other hand, the normative approach to criminal participation constitutes a top-down approach to liability where the chain of accountability begins with the commander of the transnational terrorist group who ordered the perpetration of the attacks and ends with the lowest ranking members of the group. However, as concluded in Chapter 2, it may be difficult for the prosecution at the ICC to produce evidence that the transnational terrorist group has an overall leader especially if the group is composed of network cells which participate in a consensus decision-making process aimed at developing the overall strategy of the group.[157]

The ICTY has embraced a normative approach to liability. In the *Tadić* case, for example, the ICTY Appeals Chamber described JCE as 'a form of accomplice liability'.[158] Nevertheless, it utilised the terms 'perpetrator' and 'co-perpetrator' to

153 Ohlin et al. (n. 61), p. 367.
154 Ibid., p. 368.
155 Ibid.
156 Ibid.
157 See p. 30 of this book.
158 *Tadić* (n. 6), para. 220.

describe an individual participating in the JCE.[159] The judgment of the ICTY Appeals Chamber in the *Tadić* case led to considerable discussion in the later cases of *Prosecutor* v. *Krstić* [160] and *Prosecutor* v. *Kvočka*. [161] In both cases, some judges believed that it was essential to maintain the distinction between the principal and the accomplice[162] while other members of the judiciary were of the view that such a distinction is irrelevant because it is not until the sentencing stage of the case that the different roles played by the accused becomes important.[163]

Nevertheless, the categorisation of defendants as either principals or accessories has found its footing in the jurisprudence of the ICTY.[164] For example, in *Prosecutor* v. *Odjanić* the majority of the Appeals Chamber held that 'joint enterprise is to be regarded, not as a form of accomplice liability, but as a form of commission'.[165] As a result, aiding and abetting has become a mode of liability that is regarded as less culpable than JCE. Indeed, the Appeals Chamber held in *Prosecutor* v. *Šljivančanin* that 'aiding and abetting is a lower form of liability than ordering, committing, or participating in a joint criminal enterprise and may as such attract a lesser sentence'.[166] Empirical research conducted by Hola et al. would support the conclusion that aiding and abetting is considered less culpable by the ad hoc tribunals than other modes of liability.[167] So the ICTY applies a mitigation principle in relation to aiding and abetting and JCE liability.

It would also appear that a normative approach to liability was applied by the SCSL in the Charles Taylor case where he was found guilty of aiding and abetting both crimes against humanity and war crimes.[168] If Taylor had been convicted of participating in a JCE he would have faced a longer term of imprisonment. Indeed, Judge Lussick held that the prosecution's request that Taylor be sentenced to 80 years' imprisonment was excessive, as the accused had been found guilty of 'a mode of liability [that] generally warrants a lesser sentence than that imposed for more direct forms of participation'.[169] Nevertheless, Taylor was

159 Ibid.

160 *Krstić* (n. 6).

161 *Prosecutor* v. *Kvočka*, Judgment, Trial Chamber I, IT-98-30/1-T, 2 November 2001.

162 Ibid.

163 Ibid.

164 For further academic commentary on this point, see Ciara Damgaard, *Individual Criminal Responsibility for Core International Crimes* (Springer, 2008), pp. 198–212; Elies Van Sliedregt, 'Joint Criminal Enterprise as a Pathway to Convicting Individuals for Genocide', *Journal of International Criminal Justice* 5 (2007) 184–207.

165 *Prosecutor* v. *Milutinović et al., Decision on Dragoljub Ojdanić Motion Challenging Jurisdiction – Joint Criminal Enterprise*, Pre-Trial Chamber, IT-05-87-PT, 22 March 2006, para. 20.

166 *Prosecutor* v. *Šljivančanin*, Judgment, Appeals Chamber, IT-95-13/1-A, 5 May 2009, para. 407.

167 Barbora Hola et al., 'International Sentencing Facts and Figures: Sentencing Practice at the ICTY and ICTR', *Journal of International Criminal Justice* 9 (2011) 411–439, p. 417.

168 *Prosecutor* v. *Charles Taylor, Judgment*, Trial Chamber, SCSL-03-1-T, 26 April 2012, para. 6959.

169 Ibid.

sentenced to 50 years' imprisonment, so, although aiding and abetting is recognised as a lower mode of liability, it does not necessarily imply that the accused will receive a more lenient prison sentence.[170]

The ICC has arguably embraced the normative approach to participation in an international crime developed by the ICTY. In particular, in the Decision on the Confirmation of Charges in the *Lubanga* case the Pre-Trial Chamber noted that the ICC makes a distinction between principals and accessories and also distinguishes between principal liability in Article 25(3)(a) and accessorial liability in Article 25(3)(b–d).[171] Holding members of transnational terrorist groups accountable under Article 25(3)(a) signifies that they played a significant role in the commission of the offence.[172] This is in complete contrast to liability under Article 25(3)(b–d) where individuals categorised as accessories are deemed less responsible. Nevertheless, the application of the normative approach of the control theory at the ICC has caused controversy. Judge Tarfusser, in his dissenting opinion in the Appeals Decision in the Regulation 55 case in *Katanga*, noted that Article 25(3) was 'far from . . . uncontentious or settled'.[173] This in turn illustrates the impact of the normative approach to participation in a joint criminal endeavour.[174] Nevertheless, it may still provide an alternative basis to hold senior members of the transnational terrorist group accountable for their role in planning and ordering a terrorist attack.

1 Indirect control within transnational terrorist groups under Article 25 of the Rome Statute

Significant emphasis is attached to organisations under the doctrine of indirect co-perpetration. However, Judge Van den Wyngaert in her concurring opinion in the *Chui* case expressed concern about this recent development stating that Article 25 of the Rome Statute addresses the indirect control over individuals perpetrating atrocities but not indirect control over organisations committing crimes.[175] Indeed, she held that 'elevating the concept of "control over an organization" to a constitutive element of criminal responsibility under Article 25(3)(a) is misguided'[176] since 'organisations are made up of persons'.[177] Article 25 only concerns the indirect control of individuals even where this control is exerted by means of an organisation, so the question still remains whether organisations such

170 *Taylor* (n. 168), para. 6959.
171 *Lubanga Confirmation Decision* (n. 7), paras 330–335.
172 *Katanga and Ngudjolo Confirmation Decision* (n. 7), para. 518.
173 *Prosecutor* v. *Germain Katanga and Mathieu Ngudjolo Chui, Judgment on the Appeal of Mr. Katanga against the Decision of Trial Chamber II of 21 November 2012 entitled 'Decision on the Implementation of Regulation 55 of the Regulations of the Court and Severing Charges against the Accused Persons'*, Appeals Chamber, ICC-01/04-01/07OA13, 27 March 2013, para. 15.
174 Ohlin et al. (n. 61), p. 368; Olásolo (n. 2), p. 27.
175 Concurring Opinion of Judge Van den Wyngaert (n. 40), para. 52.
176 Ibid.
177 Ibid., para. 53.

as transnational terrorist groups can be afforded any special status under the doctrine of indirect co-perpetration. This is because it is the means by which the defendant is alleged to have directed control over the individuals who physically perpetrated the crime.

Judge Van den Wyngaert noted that 'there is a fundamental difference between the interaction among individuals, even within the context of an organisation, and the exercise of authority over an abstract entity such as an "organisation"'.[178] Consequently, by undermining the relationship between the indirect perpetrator and the actual perpetrator who committed the crime 'the control over an organisation concept dilutes the level of personal influence that the indirect perpetrator must exercise over the person through whom he or she commits a crime'.[179] As a result, Judge Van den Wyngaert was of the opinion that there is no basis for the concept of the organisation in Article 25 of the Rome Statute.[180]

However, Judge Van den Wyngaert's finding can be challenged. Roxin's theory of control highlights how organisational control is essential to establish liability because it is the subordinate members which carry out the orders of the commander.[181] If the ICC wants to utilise the doctrine of indirect co-perpetration in the prosecution of members of transnational terrorist groups, it needs to develop a principle that explains how the indirect perpetration of a terrorist attack upon a civilian population through a transnational terrorist group is in keeping with the wording of Article 25 and its clear reference to 'persons'.[182]

One explanation would be that the transnational terrorist group is simply a vessel through which the defendant exercises control over the members of the group who physically perpetrate the attack. Pursuant to this approach, the indirect co-perpetrator can be charged with an offence under the Rome Statute if the offence is committed by another person within the group. In other words, the transnational terrorist group provides the medium through which the indirect co-perpetrator can order the actual perpetrator to carry out the offence. Accordingly, the doctrine of indirect co-perpetration may be an effective mechanism for holding high-ranking members of transnational terrorist groups accountable even if the group is composed of network cells operating without a centralised command. As discussed in Chapter 2, this is because the high-ranking members can utilise the organisational structure of the group to their advantage to perpetrate highly coordinated terrorist attacks aimed at civilian populations in different jurisdictions.[183]

However, this approach is not without significant shortcomings, because the ICC in the past has relied on the ambiguous concept of *dolus eventualis*. Despite the ambiguity as to whether the concept is akin to recklessness, the majority of definitions recognise that the concept means 'liability for foreseeing the mere

178 Ibid.
179 Ibid.
180 Ibid.
181 Roxin (n. 7).
182 See generally Article 25 of the Rome Statute of the International Criminal Court.
183 See p. 30 of this book.

possibility of future events'.[184] The ICTY expanded criminal liability to individuals who did not unequivocally foresee the harmful consequences of his/her conduct by relying on JCE III whereby 'a participant [can be] . . . held responsible for any reasonably foreseeable act of any other participant done in furtherance of the joint enterprise'.[185] JCE III permits individuals to be convicted as principals for crimes carried out by co-perpetrators which fall outside the joint criminal plan. In the *Lubanga* case, the Trial Chamber refused to apply the JCE doctrine, instead opting for the control theory of perpetration.

However, an analysis of the doctrine of indirect co-perpetration when liability for *dolus eventualis* is enforced reveals how similar it is to JCE III liability.[186] The Pre-Trial Chamber in *Prosecutor* v. *Jean Pierre Bemba Gombo* concluded that *dolus eventualis* 'is not captured by Article 30 of the Statute'.[187] It also noted that '[t]his conclusion is supported by the express language of the phrase "will occur in the ordinary course of events"'.[188] However, the Pre-Trial Chamber in the *Lubanga* case reached the opposite conclusion and affirmed that *dolus eventualis* is in keeping with Article 30 of the ICC Statute.[189] Indeed, the Pre-Trial Chamber went as far as to state that when *dolus eventualis* is combined with the doctrine of indirect co-perpetration it produces a result that is analogous to the JCE III doctrine developed by the ICTY.[190]

So, if *dolus eventualis* is combined with the doctrine of indirect co-perpetration, the defendant can be held accountable even if the crimes committed by the transnational terrorist group were not part of the criminal endeavour agreed by the members in command of the group. The Pre-Trial Chamber in the *Lubanga* case noted that the only restriction in applying the combined *dolus eventualis* and indirect co-perpetration doctrine is that the accused was 'aware of the risk that the objective elements of the crime may result from his or her actions or omissions, and . . . accepts such an outcome by reconciling himself or herself with it or consenting to it'.[191]

This is in keeping with the reasoning of the ICTY Trial Chamber in *Prosecutor* v. *Milomir Stakić* which affirmed that '[t]he technical definition of *dolus eventualis* is the following: if the actor engages in life-endangering behaviour, his . . . [action] becomes intentional if he "reconciles" himself or "makes peace" with the likelihood of death'.[192] The *Lubanga* Pre-Trial Chamber further noted that 'if the risk of bringing about the objective elements of the crime is low, the suspect must

184 Ohlin et al. (n. 61), p. 127.
185 Ibid.
186 *Tadić* (n. 6), para. 224.
187 *Prosecutor* v. *Jean-Pierre Bemba Gombo. Decision Pursuant to Article 61(7)(a) and (b) of the ICC Statute on the Charges of the Prosecutor against Jean-Pierre Bemba Gombo*, ICC-01/05-01/08, Pre-Trial Chamber II, 15 June 2009, para. 360.
188 Ibid. For a more in-depth analysis of the Pre-Trial Chamber's reasoning for this conclusion, see paras 360ff..
189 *Lubanga Confirmation Decision* (n. 7), paras 352–353.
190 Ibid.
191 Ibid., para. 352.
192 *Stakić* (n. 55), para. 587.

have clearly or expressly accepted the idea that such objective elements may result from his or her actions or omissions'.[193] Therefore, the subordinate and high-ranking members of the transnational terrorist group can be held accountable under Article 25 of the Rome Statute even if he/she did not want a crime to occur but nevertheless apprehended that such a crime could occur if a terrorist attack was carried out.

At the same time, however, it is unclear whether *dolus eventualis* is in keeping with the *mens rea* standard underlying Article 30 of the Rome Statute which states that 'unless otherwise provided' the required mental elements of a criminal offence is intent and knowledge.[194] These two elements necessitate that the consequences of the criminal conduct occur 'in the ordinary course of events'.[195] Clark asserts that *dolus eventualis* is not included in Article 30[196] and has even gone as far as to state that '*dolus eventualis* and its common law cousin, recklessness, suffered banishment by consensus [during the drafting process] at Rome'.[197] The draft report of the 1996 Preparatory Committee supports Clark's contention[198] because it initially included a section on *dolus eventualis* and recklessness which was subsequently deleted.[199]

The ICC would need to thread carefully when applying *dolus eventualis* to cases involving members of transnational terrorist groups who are accused of being indirect co-perpetrators to ensure that it is in keeping with the fundamental principle of individual criminal responsibility. Chapter 2 deciphered that some transnational terrorist groups are composed of network cells with no centralised command.[200] In addition, organisational theory on armed groups as propounded by Marighella and Stepanova illustrates that high-ranking members of transnational terrorist groups may be unaware that the subordinate members are planning and perpetrating terrorist attacks outside the nexus of the joint criminal plan.[201] Therefore, a high-ranking member of a transnational terrorist group who stands accused of being an indirect co-perpetrator could be held responsible under Article 25 for terrorist attacks which he did not actually command or direct. With regard to *dolus eventualis*, the accused does not wish to carry out attacks but does foresee that such acts could cause serious bodily injury and death. It is unclear what this individual's degree of responsibility should be under the Rome Statute.

193 *Lubanga Confirmation Decision* (n. 7), para. 354. The Trial Chamber in *Stakić* (n. 55), para. 587 stated that '[i]f the killing is committed with "manifest indifference to the value of human life", even conduct of minimal risk can qualify as international homicide'. See further *Stakić* (n. 55), para. 587.

194 Article 30(1) of the Rome Statute of the International Criminal Court.

195 Ibid., Article 30(2)(b).

196 Roger Clark, 'Elements of Crimes in Early Decisions of Pre-Trial Chambers of the International Criminal Court', *New Zealand Yearbook of International Law* (2009) 209, p. 231. Professor Schabas has reached a similar conclusion (n. 13), p. 476.

197 Ibid.

198 Chairman's Text, UN Doc. A/AC.249/1997/WG.2/CRP.4.

199 Ibid.

200 See p. 30 of this book.

201 See p. 27 of this book.

In view of the fact that the doctrine of indirect co-perpetration is not definitively categorised as a mode of liability under the Rome Statute, the ICC needs to ascertain whether such a categorisation is justified.

E Limitations of Article 25 of the Rome Statute in prosecutions of members of transnational terrorist groups

The newly formulated control theory of co-perpetration is an attempt to develop an overall theory of liability at the ICC, but is ambiguous in terms of its application and scope to transnational terrorist groups. Since it does not offer any guidance on the limitation of liability under Article 25 of the Rome Statute, the foundations of the doctrines of co-perpetration and indirect perpetration are ambiguous. In addition, the concept of 'control' under the control theory of co-perpetration advocated by the ICC Trial Chambers in the *Lubanga* and the *Katanga* cases is one-dimensional. As an alternative, a more inclusive approach to joint perpetration which includes both objective and subjective factors would be more appropriate for prosecuting members of transnational terrorist groups. Relevant factors would include the subordinate member's involvement in the planning of the attacks by the transnational terrorist group and his/her own *mens rea*, and the propinquity of his contribution to the actual perpetration of the criminal offence is also important.

A leader can be held responsible for the indirect co-perpetration of an international crime even if he/she did not play any physical role in the commission of the offence or were not at the location where the actual perpetrators committed the crime. It is the concept of 'control' that links the defendant to the actual perpetrator of the crime.[202] However, there seems to be no legal basis for this mode of liability in Roxin's control theory of co-perpetration. Neither can it be inferred from the wording of Article 25 of the Rome Statute. Nevertheless, the ICC Pre-Trial Chamber in the *Katanga and Chui* case defined the accused as indirect co-perpetrators because they exercised control over armed groups, and collaborated with each other to perpetrate attacks on villages.[203]

If this doctrine is to be applied in prosecution of members of transnational terrorist groups, it needs to make a distinction 'between individuals who control distinct organizations but deploy them towards a common cause and individuals who jointly exercise combined authority over a single vertical organization'.[204] The latter would represent a more simplistic application of the doctrine of indirect co-perpetration to one single organisation, while the former would institute joint perpetration by means of several organisations. Unfortunately, the ICC has not had the opportunity to examine the application of the doctrine of co-perpetration in this manner, so it remains to be seen what approach it will adopt.

202 Jens Ohlin, 'Second-Order Linking Principles: Combining Vertical and Horizontal Modes of Liability', *Leiden Journal of International Law* 25 (2012) 771–797.
203 *Katanga and Chui Confirmation Decision* (n. 7), paras 543–545.
204 Ibid.

Finally, the ICC needs to be cautious when applying *dolus eventualis* in prosecutions of members of transnational terrorist groups who are accused of being indirect co-perpetrators to guarantee that it is in conformity with the fundamental principle of individual criminal responsibility. A member of a transnational terrorist group who stands trial before the ICC on charges of being an indirect co-perpetrator could be held responsible for attacks perpetrated by an organisation which he/she does not actually command or direct. However, this individual's degree of responsibility under the Rome Statute remains unclear. Since the doctrine of indirect co-perpetration is not definitively categorised as a mode of liability under the Rome Statute, the ICC needs to ascertain whether such a categorisation is justified.

F Conclusion

This chapter has shown there is considerable divergence of opinion among the judiciary at the ICC on the application of Article 25 of the Rome Statute because the concept of control developed by the ICC is not explicitly mentioned in the provision. Yet, despite the ongoing significance of the concept of control in the jurisprudence of the ICC, not many would contest that applying the provision to transnational terrorist groups with a network-based organisational structure would be even more challenging, since it is not always clear who within the group planned and carried out the terrorist attack and thus had control over the crime. In addition, determining whether the leader had control over the attack is also difficult in view of the fact that the subordinate may not have received specific orders to plan and carry out a particular attack, and instead may only have a general instruction to perpetrate an attack whenever the opportunity presents itself. So perhaps a looser definition of the term 'control' needs to be applied to entities such as transnational terrorist groups which have a looser organisational structure. So, the efficacy of Article 25 in the prosecution of members of transnational terrorist groups can be questioned. Perhaps it is worth considering whether international criminal law should shift its focus from the accountability of individuals to the accountability of the transnational terrorist group as a collective entity as well.

7 The accountability of transnational terrorist groups as a collectivity

Quandaries for the jurisdiction of the ICC

A Introduction

This chapter examines a complicated question: should we hold the transnational terrorist group as a collective entity accountable under international criminal law, and if so, how? The prevalence of non-state armed groups in the twenty-first century would suggest that international criminal law should have already grappled with this question. However, from its inception, international criminal law has had very little if anything to do with collective entities, how to think about them, and how to hold them accountable for international crimes.[1] This is without doubt because of international criminal law's focus on individuals and is even more important now as questions emerge about how the non-state armed group as a collective entity can be brought within international criminal law's ambit.[2] As discussed in Chapter 2, many transnational terrorist groups are structurally complex, consisting of dynamic networks of interactions, with a loosely organised command structure. As a result, it can often be difficult to pinpoint which individuals within the group are responsible for the planning and commission of international crimes. This is in direct contrast to other types of collective entities such as state armed forces that are generally determinant closed systems with a clear-cut hierarchical organisational structure. The lack of a hierarchical command structure and a centralised leadership exercising direct control over subordinates within some transnational terrorist groups enables them to change their *modus operandi* quite easily and thus complicates the task of bringing members of these entities to justice.

1 Gerhard Werle, *Principles of International Criminal Law* (TMC Asser Press, 2005), p. 35.

2 Andrew Clapham, 'Extending International Criminal Responsibility Beyond Individuals to Corporations and Armed Opposition Groups', *Journal of International Criminal Justice* 6 (2008) 899–926; Annyssa Bellal and Stuart Casey-Maslen, 'Enhancing Compliance with International Law by Armed Non-State Actors', *Goettingen Journal of International* Law 3(1) (2011) 175–197; Jann Kleffner, 'The Collective Accountability of Organized Armed Groups in System Crimes', in A. Nollkaemper and H. van der Wilt (eds), *System Criminality in International Law* (Cambridge University Press, 2009) 238–269.

This dilemma raises questions about whether it is still appropriate for international criminal law to remain focused on the pursuit of individual members of transnational terrorist groups or whether we should also be pursuing the accountability of the collective entity as well. We need then to clarify our thinking on the issue and this chapter proposes to examine the methodologies developed by sociologists to make sense of this question – specifically that we should look to systems theory to inform our analysis of prospects for holding transnational terrorist groups accountable under international criminal law. In particular, this chapter examines whether it makes a difference for international criminal law if its applicants are complex adaptive systems, a concept derived from complexity theory.

Although Andrew Clapham and others have written on the prospects for holding the non-state armed group as a collective entity accountable under international criminal law, this growing interest in non-state armed groups lacks any contextual analysis and understanding of the environment in which their crimes are planned and perpetrated.[3] This chapter provides that foundation. It is the first dedicated piece of research to examine systems theory's implications for the accountability of the transnational terrorist group as a collective entity under international criminal law. It focuses on particular strands of collective entity responsibility to determine whether systems theory has anything to contribute and also provides an interesting study of international criminal law at a critical juncture in its development.

Systems theory is inconsistent with the principle of individual criminal responsibility, but it also highlights another irresolvable problem for it. The gap between the transnational terrorist group and the latent interactions from which it has emerged correlates to a gap that is starting to become more apparent in international criminal law. This gap separates the responsibility the transnational terrorist group has to ensure its compliance with international humanitarian law (IHL) norms from its accountability for violations of those same norms. International criminal law tends to overlook the significance of this element and has put aside questions about the ontology of collective entities; therefore, it would appear insignificant whether a transnational terrorist group is a complex adaptive system. Nevertheless, despite the practical and conceptual advantages of separating law from ontology there is a practical and conceptual toll as well. It is natural persons who must bear the burden of responsibility under international criminal law and certainly, if there is a legal and ontological segregation between the collective entity and the individual member, it is debatable why only individual members should bear that responsibility. Particular reforms could be made to international criminal law to tackle this problem; however, it could also be the case that the gap

3 Clapham (n. 2); Bellal and Casey-Maslen (n. 2); Kleffner (n. 2), p. 238; Liesbeth Zegveld, *Accountability of Armed Opposition Groups in International Law* (Cambridge University Press, 2002); Marco Sassòli, 'Possible Legal Mechanisms to Improve Compliance by Armed Groups with International Humanitarian Law and International Human Rights Law' (paper presented at the Armed Groups Conference, Vancouver, 13–15 November 2003) (on file with author).

between the conduct of transnational terrorist groups and its individual members who are ultimately held accountable for it will never be fully overcome.[4] If so, international criminal law's distribution of responsibility for international crimes to individuals only is deficient. Thus, systems theory imparts an ontological elucidation of why the dilemma of distributing criminal responsibility to the individual is so problematic.

This chapter contributes to the exploration of this argument in three sections. Section B considers the friction between the objective of international criminal law to investigate and prosecute those most responsible for international crimes on the one hand and its failure to address collective entities on the other.[5] International criminal law pays very little attention to this accountability distribution dilemma, and therefore the chapter looks to the literature on moral responsibility for guidance. A preliminary analysis of this literature suggests that there are rationales for holding the transnational terrorist group as a collective entity responsible for the conduct of its members. But even though this literature does lay some foundations, which would justify the imposition of such culpability, it is not beyond reproach, and there are considerable differences between moral and legal norms for such rationales to be challenged. Section C introduces systems theory to explain why the problem has been so difficult to resolve. As will be explored, the theory argues that as a complex adaptive system the transnational terrorist group is not always reducible to its individual members. One consequence is that it will be difficult to explain international criminal law's distribution of responsibility for international crimes to individuals only, particularly if the crimes were planned and perpetrated by the emergent group. This is clearly problematic, and the chapter thus responds to the literature that encourages that ontology be set aside and that a consideration of purely legal conceptions of the transnational terrorist group be embraced.

B The transnational terrorist group and the dilemma of collective entity responsibility in international criminal law

1 Contextualising the dilemma

An effective international legal system endeavours to impose repercussions for breaches of the norms it seeks to protect. This was the premise behind the Articles

4 For further academic commentary on the concept of collective responsibility, see the seminal works of Hans Kelsen, 'Collective and Individual Responsibility in International Law with Particular Regard to the Punishment of War Criminals', *California Law Review* 31(5) (1942) 530–571; 'Collective and Individual Responsibility for Acts of State in International Law', *Jewish Yearbook of International Law* 1 (1948) 226; Shane Darcy, *Collective Responsibility and Accountability under International Law* (Brill, 2007); Daryl Levinson, Collective Sanctions, *Stanford Law Review* 56 (2003) 345–428.

5 Clapham (n. 2), p. 899; Mark Chinen, 'Complexity Theory and the Horizontal and Vertical Dimensions of State Responsibility', *European Journal of International Law* 25(3) 703–732.

on the Responsibility of States for Internationally Wrongful Acts of 2001 adopted by the ILC, which to a significant extent codified customary international law.[6] It took the best part of 50 years for the ILC to conclude its work on the draft. However, scholars have been highly critical of it since by the time it was adopted it was already out of date with regard to contemporary challenges.[7] Indeed, in a globalised world with many different types of actors the state-centric system of responsibility has proven itself to be ill-equipped to address breaches of international norms by them.[8] This dilemma has also spilled over into international criminal law. Only individuals can be prosecuted for international crimes and so international criminal courts and tribunals do not have jurisdiction over collective entities such as states and their organs, non-state armed groups, or corporations.[9] This is perplexing since international crimes are archetypically perpetrated by collective entities.[10] Indeed '[w]here the organization of the social whole largely determines the character and conduct of its parts, exclusive attention to these constituent components risks missing everything of significance to moral judgment and social understanding'.[11] This has led commentators to raise concerns about the potential for discord between international criminal law's objective to bring those most responsible for international crimes to justice on the one hand and its perceived failure to address collective entities on the other.[12]

The underlying issue is not new, but has become more salient because of one key development in international law. It is now a given that transnational terrorist groups are obliged to comply with and, to some extent, further IHL.[13] Among the rules that transnational terrorist groups must obey when conducting hostilities, they are prohibited from carrying out direct and indiscriminate attacks against civilians and must take all feasible precautions to avoid civilian casualties as far as possible. Duties are not always absolute, and in particular under the Geneva Conventions the application of some are limited by the resources available during

6 Draft Articles on the Responsibility of States for Internationally Wrongful Act with Commentaries, *Yearbook of the International Law Commission*, 2001, vol. II, pt 2. For a seminal analysis of the Draft Articles, see James Crawford, *The Law of International Responsibility* (Oxford University Press, 2010).

7 Edith Brown Weiss, 'Invoking State Responsibility in the Twenty-First Century', (2002) 96 *American Journal of International Law* 96 (2002) 798–816, p. 799.

8 Jutta Brunnée, 'International Legal Accountability Through the Lens of the Law of State Responsibility', *Netherlands Yearbook of International Law* 36(1) (2005) 21–56, p. 23.

9 Clapham (n. 2).

10 George Fletcher, 'The Storrs Lectures: Liberals and Romantics at War: The Problem of Collective Guilt', *Yale Law Journal* 111 (2002) 1499–1573; Larry May, 'Collective Punishment and Mass Confinement', in T. Isaacs and R. Vernon (eds), *Accountability for Collective Wrongdoing* (Cambridge University Press, 2011), pp. 170–171.

11 Mark Osiel, *Making Sense of Mass Atrocity* (Cambridge University Press, 2009), p. 188.

12 Clapham (n. 2), p. 899.

13 Christopher Greenwood, 'Scope of Application of Humanitarian Law', in D. Fleck (ed.), *The Handbook of Humanitarian Law in Armed Conflict* (Oxford University Press, 2007, 2nd edn) 45–78, p. 76.

hostilities. Nevertheless, such duties continue to evolve; some non-state armed groups have endeavoured to adopt them as part of their internal rules of operations and the feasible precautions principle implies that duties can take on a harder cast as such resources do in fact become more available.[14]

The growth of IHL has accompanied a more general concern about how transnational terrorist groups can be held accountable for breaches of humanitarian norms since there continues to be no formal international judicial mechanism with jurisdiction to investigate and prosecute them.[15] This is reflected in criticisms about the reality deficit in international criminal law, as well as the critique by some scholars that international criminal law has been used to impose particular political structures on the international community, with resulting doubts about international criminal law's legitimacy. Focusing on the concerns set out here, scholars have voiced their disquiet about the possible impact of only prosecuting individuals for crimes arising from the conduct of the non-state armed group. Andrew Clapham, in particular, notes that:

> [w]hile the practice concerning criminalization of individual members of rebel groups under international law is now well-established (with regards to inter alia war crimes and crimes against humanity), the question of whether the groups as such can be said to have violated international criminal law remains, however, under explored.[16]

So international criminal law's failure to embrace collective guilt needs to be re-examined and the *modus operandi* by which international crimes are planned and perpetrated acknowledged.[17]

That is all well and good, but what precisely is impeding the extension of international criminal law to collective entities such as transnational terrorist groups? One argument is that modes of collective entity responsibility that have been adopted in domestic law systems have not garnered universal acceptance and as a result, have not been included in international criminal law.[18] Of course, international criminal law can from time to time be quite innovative but an understanding of why this inventiveness has not expanded to embrace the

14 Anna Brennan, 'Exploring the Accountability of Leaders of Armed Opposition Groups under International Law', *The Hague Yearbook of International Law* 23 (2010) 223, p. 236.

15 The Uppsala Conflict Data Program has estimated that the number of armed conflicts worldwide has increased by nearly 20 per cent from 41 in 2014 to 50 in 2015. Of these 50 armed conflicts only one can be described as purely international in character (India–Pakistan).

16 Clapham (n. 2), p. 920.

17 Mark Drumbl, 'Collective Violence and Individual Punishment: The Criminality of Mass Atrocity', *Northwestern University Law Review* 99 (2005) 539–610, p. 570.

18 Shachar Eldar, 'Exploring International Criminal Law's Reluctance to Resort to Modalities of Groups Responsibility: Five Challenges to International Prosecutions and their Impact on Broader Forms of Responsibility', *Journal of International Criminal Justice* 11 (2013) 331–349, p. 335.

accountability of collective entities such as transnational terrorist groups needs to be explored. Is it the case that individual criminal responsibility is so deeply entrenched in international criminal law that there is no room for collective entity responsibility? Or are there broader political reasons, which have impeded the development of a doctrine of collective entity responsibility? If there are, does this ultimately hinder international criminal law's objective to investigate and prosecute those most responsible for international crimes?

One practical manifestation of this theoretical dilemma is the lack of a comprehensive definition of the term 'transnational terrorist group' due to the intricacies of modern warfare and the ambiguity about whether they should satisfy a minimum set of criteria with regard to their size, organisation, and power to qualify as international legal subjects. There is also the apprehension that recognising a doctrine of collective entity responsibility under international criminal law would somehow place the transnational terrorist group on an equal legal footing with states and give their political/quasi political objectives legitimacy.[19] Despite these concerns the potential for international criminal law to be utilised to prosecute them has been explored in a piecemeal fashion.[20]

Prompted by Article 9 of the Charter of the International Military Tribunal at Nuremberg, which criminalised organisations such as the Leadership Corps of the Nazi Party, the Gestapo, and the SS, the ICC Working Group did consider the possibility of prosecuting corporations, political parties, and even racist groups. But according to James Owen '[t]he French and the Soviets had grave concerns [during the Nuremberg Trials] about such corporate and retrospective declarations of guilt'.[21] Thus, the ICC Working Group rejected the proposal since declarations that particular organisations are criminal could be utilised to prosecute individuals by virtue of their membership of the entity.[22] In particular, Bassiouni was of the view that:

> [t]o impose international criminal responsibility merely for passive responsibility in an organization stretches the generally accepted principles of criminal responsibility found in most legal systems. Such a proposition would be

19 For more general commentary on this point, see Daragh Murray, *Human Rights Obligations of Non-State Armed Groups* (Hart, 2016), ch. 3.

20 Clapham (n. 2), p. 920.

21 James Owens, *Nuremberg: Evil on Trial* (Headline Review 2006), p. 13.

22 In particular, the IMT held that, '[a] criminal organisation is analogous to a criminal conspiracy in that the essence of both is cooperation for criminal purposes. There must be a group bound together and organized for a common purpose. The group must be formed or used in connection with the commission of crimes denounced by the Charter. Since the declaration with respect to the organisations and groups will, as has been pointed out, fix the criminality of its members, that definition should exclude persons who had no knowledge of the criminal purposes or acts of the organisation and those who were drafted by the State for membership, unless they were personally implicated in the commission if acts declared criminal by Article 6 of the Charter as members of the organisation. Membership alone is not enough to come within the scope of these declarations.'

tantamount to guilt by association which most legal systems reject as fundamentally unfair.[23]

As will be discussed further below, it must be questioned what benefits if any would be derived from extending international criminal law to the transnational terrorist group? They are not legally incorporated, and generally do not have assets or financial resources in their name. Neither are they very concerned about reputational damage if allegations are made that they have breached humanitarian norms and in any event their activities are likely to already be prohibited under the domestic laws of the state in which they are in conflict.[24]

Even if Article 25 of the Rome Statute was amended to include collective entity accountability how would the trial of a transnational terrorist group proceed? What rules of evidence and procedure would apply and would members, in particular those who are high-ranking, be permitted to attend the trial and also give evidence without fear of being arrested? And, finally, how would an international criminal court or tribunal punish a transnational terrorist group if it is found guilty? It would seem on the face of it that the concerns of Bassiouni and the ICC Working Group are jurisprudentially reasonable. However, it seems nevertheless justified from a moral standpoint since the group may be condoning and inciting the individual member to carry out crimes.[25] As Kleffner contends 'organized armed groups regularly succeed to create a climate in which crimes are perceived to be in conformity with, rather than a deviation from, standards of behaviour accepted within such a group'.[26] International bodies such as the UN Security Council and the Special Representative of the UN Secretary General for Children in Armed Conflict rely on naming and shaming non-state armed groups when they breach international law.[27] The prosecution of the transnational terrorist group could perhaps 'enable better implementation of international law . . . by calling on the group to change its practice rather than simply punish the individual and it could be encouraged to develop training and structures to prevent and punish [future] violations'.[28]

23 Mahmoud C. Bassiouni (ed.), *International Criminal Law: Volume 1: Crimes* (Transnational, 1999, 2nd edn), p. 24; Andrea Bianchi, 'Security Council's Anti-Terror Resolutions and their Implementation by Member States', *Journal of International Criminal Justice* 4 (2006) 1044–1073, p. 1053.

24 Antonio Cassese, 'The Status of Rebels under the 1977 Geneva Protocol on Non-International Armed Conflicts', *International and Comparative Legal Quarterly* 30 (1981) 424–439; Clapham (n. 2), p. 921.

25 Annyssa Bellal, 'Establishing the Direct Responsibility of Non-State Armed Groups for Violations of International Norms: Issues of Attribution', in N. Gal-Or, M. Noortmann, and C. Ryngaert (eds), *Responsibilities of the Non-State Actor in Armed Conflict: Theoretical Considerations and Empirical Findings* (Brill, 2014) 304–322, p. 305.

26 Kleffner (n. 2), p. 246.

27 Clapham (n. 2), p. 921.

28 Bellal (n. 25), p. 306. For more commentary on this point, see Andrew Clapham, 'Non-State Actors', in Daniel Moeckli et al. (eds), *International Human Rights Law* (Oxford University Press, 2013, 2nd edn), ch. 26; Mark Drumbl, 'Collective

At present, international criminal law does not address these issues. Instead, it ignores the collective entity and only pays attention to its individual members. This focus on the individual when determining whether an international crime has been committed corresponds perhaps to a similar focus when remedies are being crafted. Where it is proven beyond a reasonable doubt that an individual has committed an international crime, two consequences may follow: first, the individual can be sentenced to a term of imprisonment; second, they may also have to provide reparation to the victims for the injury caused by their crimes. Pursuant to Article 75 of the Rome Statute, reparation can take the form of restitution, compensation, and rehabilitation or some combination of all three. As discussed above, the Rome Statute does not consider the role that a collective entity may have played in the planning and commission of an international crime. Under Article 75, '[t]he Court may [only] make an order directly against a convicted person specifying appropriate reparations'; thus, there seems to be no basis for an argument that a transnational terrorist group's role in the perpetration of the international crime can be a factor in that calculus. There would also appear to be no limit to reparation: a convicted individual is required to make restitution even if it is materially impossible for them to do so and even if it would constitute a burden which is out of proportion to the benefit deriving from restitution instead of compensation.

A reading of Article 75 would also infer that a convicted individual is not excused from providing reparation even if the injury suffered was instigated at the group level. Considerations of equity and reasonableness are not factored into the provision leading to concerns that the burden of reparation on the defendant is somewhat arbitrary since the crimes may have been planned and committed by numerous members of the transnational terrorist group and not the defendant alone. In any event, the implementation of reparation orders against individuals is exceptionally challenging since past studies show that defendants often claim destitution.[29] Since other forms of responsibility are not provided for in the Rome Statute, it was considered necessary to implement an alternative means of ensuring reparation for victims who would otherwise be reliant on the financial solvency of the accused. So, Article 79 was adopted with the aim of establishing a trust fund for the benefit of victims and their relatives, which is independent of the Court and overseen by the Assembly of State Parties.

The Rome Statute does not provide guidance on how the fund is to be administered aside from stating that the Court is permitted to order the money and property collected through fines and forfeiture to be handed over to the Trust Fund. But what is interesting is that the Assembly of State Parties has subsequently clarified that the Trust Fund may receive voluntary contributions from states, international organisations, individuals, and other entities and this would

Responsibility and Post-Conflict Justice', in T. Isaacs and R. Vernon (eds), *Accountability for Collective Wrongdoing* (Cambridge University Press, 2011) 23–60, p. 23.

29 William Schabas, *An Introduction to the International Criminal Court* (Cambridge University Press, 2004, 2nd edn), p. 175.

potentially seem to include non-state armed groups such as transnational terrorist groups as well.[30] Yet, no repercussions follow for transnational terrorist groups when they commit breaches of international law. Since the Rome Statute does not have jurisdiction over non-natural persons, a transnational terrorist group is excused from providing reparation even if there is a finding that one of its members has committed a breach of IHL. It is clear that these limitations are significant when it comes to the question of accountability. No provision of international law necessitates or permits an international court or tribunal to make determinations about a transnational terrorist group's responsibility for violations of IHL.

2 A legal breakdown of the dilemma

a Accounting for collective entity responsibility in international criminal law

The ambiguity concerning a transnational terrorist group's responsibilities under international law is not just becoming important because of the challenges just explored, but the dilemma of juggling a transnational terrorist group's responsibilities for its members' conduct with its obligations towards other subjects of international law is not new. It would seem that the drafters of the ILC Articles were somewhat cognisant of this issue. In 1956 the first special rapporteur for the ILC, Garcia-Amador contended that:

> It is no longer true, as it was for centuries in the past, that international law exists only for, or finds its sole raison d'etre in, the protection of the interests and rights of the States; rather its function is now also to protect the rights and interests of its other subjects who may properly claim its protection.[31]

Garcia-Amador's comments formed part of a discussion that states have a responsibility to guarantee that foreign nationals have the same rights as their own citizens. However, they also suggest that the Commission was of the view that the Articles were to be construed in their broader context in which all subjects enjoy rights and protections under international law. This wider perspective makes room for considering not only the rights and interests of transnational terrorist groups but also their duties and the extent to which they can be held accountable for international crimes.

Indeed, the ILC Articles distinguish between primary obligations that derive from specific treaties, customary international law, and other sources of

30 Gilbert Bitti and Gabriela Gonzalez Rivas, 'The Reparations Provisions for Victims under the Rome Statute of the International Criminal Court', in *Redressing Injustices through Mass Claims Processes, Innovative Responses to Unique Challenges* (Permanent Court of Arbitration, 2006), pp. 315–316.

31 'Report on International Responsibility', by F. Garcia-Amador, Special Rapporteur (1956) ii *ILC Yearbook* 174, at p. 184 (para. 57).

international law on the one hand and secondary obligations that stem from the law of state responsibility on the other. Reconciling a transnational terrorist group's responsibilities under international law could happen at either a primary or secondary level. Their obligations could be accounted for and enshrined within international law among the primary rules of state responsibility, as international courts and tribunals demarcate the specific obligations of transnational terrorist groups and construct remedies for their wrongful acts. There is some evidence that this is beginning to happen: international courts and tribunals have given consideration to the obligations of non-state armed groups under international law. Judges have harnessed the Geneva Conventions as they considered the minimum conditions for ascertaining the duties of non-state armed groups in armed conflict situations. These include, among others: defining the degree of organisation a non-state armed group must possess in order for the Geneva Conventions to apply to their conduct; their control over territory; their capacity to gain access to weapons and training; their ability to develop a coherent military strategy; and their capability to generally act as one unit and negotiate agreements such as ceasefires and peace accords.[32] As a result, judges have been cognisant that non-state armed groups have not only 'recognised and respected the international treaties of the United Nations and conventions on war'[33] but also 'issued communiqués assuming responsibility for . . . attacks'.[34]

In particular, Bilkova argues that the *Case Concerning Military and Paramilitary Activities in and Against Nicaragua*, supports her claim that the rules on responsibility for internationally wrongful acts can be extended to non-state armed groups; she points out that 'violations of primary rules binding on . . . [non-state armed actors] by a conduct attributable to them would constitute internationally wrongful acts entailing responsibility with its classical content'.[35] However, Bilkova's argument is flawed since she does not outline exactly how a principle of collective entity responsibility could be introduced in international law or how international courts and tribunals, in particular the ICC could approach claims against non-state armed groups such as transnational terrorist groups. The *Nicaragua* case may imply that non-state armed groups must comply with IHL, but the decision also perhaps supports a separate argument that the decision-maker declined to adjudicate on the precise parameters of the duties of non-state armed groups in international law perhaps for lack of competence or because he/she is limited by terms of reference or by the primary rules themselves.

32 *Prosecutor* v. *Ramush Haradinaj*, Case No. IT-04-84-84-T, Judgment (Trial Chamber), 3 April 2008, para. 60; *Prosecutor* v. *Jean Paul Akayesu*, ICTR-96-4-T, Judgment, 2 September 1998, para. 619.

33 Ibid., para. 69.

34 Ibid., para. 91.

35 Veronika Bilkova, 'Armed Opposition Groups and Shared Responsibility', *Netherlands International Law Review* 62 (2015) 69–89, p. 76.

This is a trend that has been followed by other international courts and tribunals as well.[36] While they have readily accepted that non-state armed groups must comply with IHL, they have so far parked any further elaboration about their precise obligations. It is perhaps understandable that decision-makers would be apprehensive about applying rules that were originally designed for states. The legal personality of non-state armed groups like transnational terrorist groups is likely to be limited since they generally only exist for a short time period, either because they are suppressed by the state and are disbanded; or they succeed in seizing power and form a new government, or they create a new state. Such groups thus cannot enjoy rights akin to the permanent nature of international actors; but also perhaps do not have the capacity to fulfil legal obligations either. So, what would be the impact of a finding that a transnational terrorist group as a collective entity has committed an international crime? Bilkova posits that a non-state armed group should most probably be held responsible for the conduct of its members and constituent organs acting on its behalf but she does not outline how to implement this or acknowledge that the organisational structure of some non-state armed groups such as transnational terrorist groups can be so ambiguous that it is difficult to ascertain whether these individuals are members of the group in the first place.[37] Thus, determining whether the individual member's conduct can be attributed to the transnational terrorist group will at times be difficult to ascertain.

A decision-maker could follow an approach suggested by the ICRC called the 'continuous function' test; he/she could take into account whether 'a person assumes a continuous function for the group involving his or her direct participation in hostilities' as a decisive criterion for ascertaining individual membership of the group.[38] This test, however, relegates to the background the contemporary realities of transnational terrorist groups and the fact that the ambiguous organisational structure of some transnational terrorist groups means that it can be difficult to pinpoint whether an individual member performs a continuous function for the group. Under this approach, the principle of individual criminal responsibility could run the risk of being ignored as a matter of substance or at best becoming part of a spasmodic mishmash of law in which the genesis of how international crimes are perpetrated plays a significant role in some modes of liability and a lesser role in others. No doubt the challenges of consistency and legitimacy caused by multiple competing legal principles are much broader than the particular concerns raised here, but in this context a prosecutor could find him/herself stuck between a regime that prioritises individual criminal responsibility and another that impedes it, thus running the risk of not only slowing down, but also even forestalling, investigations into alleged crimes and prosecutions.

36 *Prosecutor* v. *Ramush Haradinaj* (n. 32), para. 60; *Prosecutor* v. *Jean Paul Akayesu* (n. 32), para. 619.

37 Bilkova (n. 35), p. 76.

38 Nils Melzer, *Interpretive Guidance on the Notion of Direct Participation in Hostilities under International Humanitarian Law* (International Committee of the Red Cross, 2009), p. 33.

C Attributing responsibility to collective entities and ethics theory: prospects for international criminal law

The issue of distributing responsibility for international crimes to collective entities has been somewhat under-explored in international criminal law,[39] but there is emerging scholarly work on this issue in ethics, which may provide some guidance here.[40] Much of the literature focuses on whether a collective entity can be the subject of moral responsibility or whether the collective entity's members are the proper bearer instead. Other questions arise about what type of collective entity can bear responsibility, or if it is even pertinent for criminal responsibility to be distributed to individual members at all. Moreover, if an individual member is held responsible for an international crime but there is evidence to suggest that it was instigated by the transnational terrorist group why are the consequences of that crime only borne by the individual members and not by the group which facilitated its perpetration?

Although this question has repercussions for group responsibility, the literature tends to agree that 'judgments about the moral responsibility of [a collective entity's] members are not logically derivable from judgments about the moral responsibility of a collectivity'.[41] So, moral judgements about a collective entity can only be made after an individual member must have committed a wrongful act. This implies that the best justification for having individual members shoulder the responsibility of the collective entity is that they are inculpated in the collective entity's wrongful act. A number of reasons have been put forward to support this proposition. First of all, some commentators are of the view that if the individual members have committed themselves to the objectives of the group, then they must bear responsibility for its acts.[42] Others argue that membership itself is a basis for holding an individual directly responsible for what the collective entity

39 For academic commentary, see Shane Darcy, *Collective Responsibility and Accountability under International Law* (Martinus Nijhoff, 2006).

40 Peter French, *Collective and Corporate Responsibility* (Columbia University Press, 1984); Joel Feinberg, 'Collective Responsibility', in J. Feinberg (ed.), *Doing and Deserving: Essays in the Theory of Responsibility* (Princeton University Press, 1970) 222–251, p. 222; Steven Lukes, *Power: A Radical View* (Palgrave Macmillan, 2005, 2nd edn); William Connolly, *The Terms of Political Discourse* (D. C. Heath, 1974); Hannah Arendt, 'Collective Responsibility', in J. Bernhauer (ed.), *Amor Mundi* (Nijhoff, 1987) 43–50; Benjamin Martin, 'Can Moral Responsibility Be Collective and Non-Distributive?', *Social Theory and Practice* 4 (1976) 93–106; David Copp, 'What Collectives Are: Agency, Individualism and Legal Theory', *Dialogue* 23 (1984) 253–269; Christopher Kutz, *Complicity: Ethics and Law for a Collective Age* (Cambridge University Press, 2000); Sanford Levinson, 'Responsibility for Crimes of War', in M. Cohen et al. (eds), *War and Moral Responsibility* (Princeton University Press, 1974) 104–133, p. 104.

41 Virginia Held, 'Can a Random Collection of Random Individuals Be Morally Responsible?', *Journal of Philosophy* 67 (1970) 471–481, p. 475; Seumas Miller, 'Collective Moral Responsibility: An Individualist Account', *Midwest Studies in Philosophy* 30 (2006) 176–193.

42 Chinen (n. 5), p. 716.

does.[43] This is because membership insinuates a commitment to the collective entity and its members and a commitment to face the consequences for the collective entity's wrongful acts in recognition that the collective entity 'is his as well as theirs'.[44]

However, another approach would be to focus on the transnational terrorist group as well as the individual member. The transnational terrorist group would be responsible for wrongful acts committed by each member as a matter of course. So, when one member of the collective entity commits a wrong, the collective entity as a whole is held responsible for that wrong since 'each member of the community is an expression of its moral center'.[45] Pursuant to this approach, if the collective entity is our fundamental concern, any misgivings about individual members must be confined to the sidelines. But, whether a transnational terrorist group should bear the consequences of a wrongful act committed by individual members will ultimately depend on the purpose of the punishment and whether the punishment fulfils that purpose.[46]

Establishing what type of punishment should be imposed on transnational terrorist groups and whether it will be effective in fulfilling its purpose will be particularly challenging in view of the characteristics of the transnational terrorist group and the fact that it is only individual members who have thus far borne the brunt of punishments for the perpetration of crimes. Therefore, it is necessary to strike a balance between the aim of punishing the transnational terrorist group as a collective entity and the consequences this may have for individual members' future behaviour within the group. The type of punishment enforced on the group is of considerable importance. Realistically, the transnational terrorist group could only be subjected to a pecuniary punishment; it is not conceivable to imprison the entire membership of the group by virtue of the fact that they are members.[47] Liability would therefore not be based on the culpability of the group but instead on the sense that an individual who has suffered harm as a result of its wrongdoing should be provided compensation or another form of reparation or restitution.[48]

Research on moral responsibility can provide some guidance to international criminal law on this dilemma. This can be readily observed by considering the rationales for holding transnational terrorist groups responsible for the wrongdoing of its members; the possible arbitrariness of the individual being the sole

43 Amy Sepinwell, 'Citizen Responsibility and the Reactive Attitudes: Blaming Americans for War Crimes in Iraq', in T. Isaacs and R. Vernon (eds), *Accountability for Collective Wrongdoing* (Cambridge University Press, 2011) 231–260, p. 241.

44 Ibid.

45 Mark Reiff, 'Terrorism, Retribution and Collective Responsibility', *Social Theory and Practice* 34 (2008) 209–242, p. 209.

46 Garrett Hardin, 'The Tragedy of the Commons', *Science* 162 (1968) 1243–1248.

47 Chandra Sriram, *Globalizing Justice for Mass Atrocities: A Revolution in Accountability* (Routledge, 2010), p. 66.

48 Avia Pasternak, 'The Distributive Effect of Collective Punishment', in T. Isaacs and R. Vernon (eds), *Accountability for Collective Wrongdoing* (Cambridge University Press, 2011) 210–220, p. 213.

focus of international criminal law; the group's enjoyment of the benefit derived from the individual member's wrongful conduct; and the group as a system in condoning and inciting the individual to carry out crimes. Could all these constitute rationales for holding the transnational terrorist group as a collective entity accountable under international criminal law? The next subsection will consider each of these rationales in turn.

1 The individual member as the principal unit of concern for international criminal law

A contention can be made that it is fully conceivable that the individual member of the transnational terrorist group be regarded as the main focus of international criminal law and it therefore follows logically that collective entities are not prosecutable before the ICC. Therefore, it could be argued that the individual-centric focus of international criminal law should be retained in its current form. When theorising the dilemma of distributing responsibility for international crimes, it could be said that questions about the collective entity fade into oblivion because as discussed above, without the principle of individual criminal responsibility international criminal law would be defunct. This argument has undeniable merit; but even if the natural person continues to be the primary subject of international criminal law it does not follow as either a moral or legal matter that the transnational terrorist group as a collective entity should be excluded from international criminal justice.

If international criminal law is supposed to concern itself with the dynamics of how international crimes are committed in reality, it is unclear why it does not concern itself with the accountability of collective entities or support reparation for their crimes or at a minimum concede to them. Malle posits that 'humans have no trouble reasoning about the actions and minds of groups and have the desire to blame and punish them when they act immorally'.[49] So, it would seem that the same theories are utilised when attributing blame to individuals as they do to collective entities. At the same time, there would appear to be considerable repugnance to guilt by association, holding collective entities responsible for wrongdoing seems to be widely acceptable but less so for individual members of collective entities. But the capacity and effectiveness of international criminal law to punish transnational terrorist groups is very limited.[50] Prior to the Nuremberg trials there was a clear decision to eschew collective responsibility, but, in doing so, international criminal law perhaps runs the risk of being ineffective if it is not cognisant of these normative values and fundamental conceptions of morality. Without additional clarification, it is hard to elucidate why collective entities should not bear at least some of the burden of responsibility for crimes that emanate from the group itself.

49 Bertram Malle, 'The Social and Moral Cognition of Group Agents', *Journal of Law and Policy* 19(1) (2010) 95–136, p. 136.

50 Ibid.

2 The transnational terrorist group as the beneficiary of the individual member's act

One further justification for distributing responsibility for international crimes to collective entities is that they benefit directly from the acts of individual members and should therefore shoulder the burden of accountability. There are persuasive arguments that transnational terrorist groups benefit from the conduct of individual members because the crime is often perpetrated in pursuance of the aims and objectives of the group. If an individual's conduct brings about these benefits, it is perhaps reasonable to assume that the group as a collective entity should bear some responsibility as well. This contention is further bolstered if the group's recruitment of the individual as a member of the group involves some sort of acquiescence to be responsible for that member's actions.

This argument is persuasive for a number of reasons. The benefits of imposing accountability on the transnational terrorist group as a collective entity may far outweigh the costs of putting an accountability mechanism in place to prosecute every individual member who played a role in the commission of the international crime, and in most cases the transnational terrorist group directly benefits from the conduct of the individual member since they were formed to accomplish a particular strategic goal which is achieved through the individual member's conduct. Moreover, by virtue of the individual's membership, the transnational terrorist group has an expectation of return. But in view of the differences in the genesis of transnational terrorist groups the benefits accrued from an individual member's conduct may not slot very easily into a transnational terrorist group–individual member, benefit–burden paradigm. In addition, given differences in the aims and objectives of transnational terrorist groups, it is difficult to compare the benefits enjoyed by one transnational terrorist group from the conduct of an individual member with those of another group. Last but not least, the content of a transnational terrorist group's obligations under international law is highly contested, and, in any event, the transnational terrorist group does not ordinarily commit itself to being held jointly responsible for its individual member's conduct.

Even if this rationale for rerouting responsibility from individual members to the group did not have such shortcomings, in order to be enforceable in law it would need to be developed into a body of legal principles used to ascertain how and when a transnational terrorist group should be held accountable as a collective entity for international crimes. This raises the dilemma of commensurability: it is not clear-cut whether the benefits of an individual member's conduct in fulfilling the aims and objectives of the group should extend liability to the transnational terrorist group as a collective entity. Moreover, a body of legal principles based on the proposition that recruitment by the transnational terrorist group necessitates a commitment to some form of joint liability with the individual member would perhaps require international law to move beyond its focus on the criminal responsibility of individuals to the duties the transnational terrorist group owes to them. Of course, some international instruments already make some reference to the responsibilities of some types of non-state armed groups, and perhaps some of the dilemmas raised in this chapter will incentivise their articulation.[51] Even if this were the case, it is not clear whether an elaboration of a transnational terrorist group's responsibilities at the international level should include a principle that a transnational terrorist group as a collective entity be held responsible alongside its individual members for that individual's actions. This would be tantamount to committing a transnational terrorist group to a form of direct criminal liability, even though in some instances it would be difficult to prove a link between the crime and the transnational terrorist group because as discussed below and in Chapter 2 some groups have such an ambiguous organisational structure that it can be difficult to pinpoint whether the individual member received orders from the centralised command.

3 The transnational terrorist group as a system in the planning and commission of international crimes

Some scholars would argue that a transnational terrorist group, which provides material support for the wrongdoing of a member should be held accountable for that member's conduct.[52] However, international criminal law does not account for this: a transnational terrorist group which infringes an international norm cannot be held responsible for that infringement, even if an individual member was acting in an official capacity with its authority. More importantly is the question whether the distribution of responsibility to the collective entity is necessary when it is the individual members who ultimately commit the international crime in the first place. In a group, members are deemed to act on its behalf. So, when a transnational terrorist group commits an international crime, this is not a question of collective responsibility because individual criminal responsibility can be invoked instead. Nevertheless, the organisational structure and *modus operandi* of transnational terrorist groups vary greatly. On the one hand, there are a small number of groups that function as quasi-states,[53] while on the other hand, there are groups which do not have state-like features, but nevertheless are highly organised and have the capacity to assert control over vast swathes of territory and the civilian population within it.

Nevertheless, that the transnational terrorist can comprise the environment in which violations of IHL can be committed is recognised by the legal framework governing the conduct of hostilities. IHL has not merely bound non-state armed groups such as transnational terrorist groups since the adoption of Common Article 3 to the Geneva Conventions 1949 but breaches of this law also entail individual criminal responsibility of the group's members. A snapshot of ongoing hostilities in Syria, Afghanistan, Iraq, the Democratic Republic of Congo, Nigeria,

51 See in particular Common Article 3 to the Geneva Conventions as supplemented by Additional Protocol II.

52 Lee McConnell, *Extracting Accountability from Non-State Actors in International Law* (Routledge, 2011); Bellal (n. 34), p. 305.

53 For further academic commentary on this point, see Jochen Frowein, 'De facto Regime', *EPIL* 1 (1992) 966.

and Mali showcases how war crimes are not just the purview of states. This is abundantly established by the systematic operation orchestrated by ISIS in Syria and Iraq of deliberately spreading terror among the civilian population, the perpetration of sexual slavery, rape, mutilations, collective punishment, the recruitment and use of child soldiers, and so on; the widespread killing of civilians and taking of hostages by Boko Haram in Nigeria; the policy of the Union of Congolese Patriots (UOC) and Patriotic Forces for the Liberation of Congo (FPLC) to forcefully recruit and use children in armed conflict; the indiscriminate use of landmines, booby traps, and other improvised explosive devices intended to cause widespread devastation and civilian casualties by the National Union for the Total Independence of Angola (UNITA), or the summary executions of civilians by the Revolutionary United Front (RUF) in Sierra Leone.

Besides war crimes, the law on crimes against humanity has also been expanded to encapsulate transnational terrorist groups. Although it had been contended for a number of decades that such crimes could only be committed in pursuance of a governmental policy, this is no longer the case. This is acknowledged in the Rome Statute of the International Criminal Court, the case law of the ad hoc tribunals, and customary international law. In particular, the Trial Chamber of the International Criminal Tribunal for the Former Yugoslavia in *Prosecutor* v. *Duško Tadić* held that crimes against humanity can be perpetrated by 'forces which, although not those of the legitimate government, have *de facto* control over, or are able to move freely within, defined territory'.[54] However, Werle has posited that territorial requirement is not necessary and that this category of international crime can be perpetrated by any group of individuals if it has the capacity to commit a widespread and systematic attack against a civilian population.[55] In any event, it is generally recognised that the system which provided the material support for the perpetration of the crimes may either be a state or a non-state armed group. The conviction of Alex Brima, Brima Kamara, and Santigie Kanu who were members of the Armed Forces Revolutionary Council (AFRC) for crimes against humanity before the Special Court for Sierra Leone provides ample evidence for this actuality.[56]

There is also nothing within the law on genocide which implies that this crime can only be perpetrated by a state and its organs and officials. The Genocide Convention 1948 is silent on the matter of non-state armed groups since it is only concerned with state responsibility and individual criminal responsibility. Although the most prominent instances of genocide in the twentieth century, the holocaust perpetrated by the Nazis and the Rwandan genocide of 1994 concerned state systems, the judgment of the International Court of Justice in the *Case Concerning the Application of the Convention on the Prevention and Punishment of the*

54 *Prosecutor* v. *Duško Tadić*, IT-94-1, Judgment, Trial Chamber (7 May 1997), para. 654.

55 Werle (n. 1), p. 228.

56 *Prosecutor* v. *Alex Tamba Brima, Brima Bazzy Kamara and Santigie Borbor Kanu*, SCSL-04-16-T, Trial Judgment (20 June 2007).

Crime of Genocide (Bosnia and Herzegovina v. *Serbia and Montenegro)* demonstrate that acts committed by non-state armed groups which can be attributed to a state can be classified as genocide if the conditions laid down in Article II of the Genocide Convention 1948 are fulfilled.[57] This further strengthens the argument that non-state armed groups such as transnational terrorist groups can perpetrate the crime of genocide.

Indeed, in recent months it has been alleged that ISIS has deliberately killed members of the Yazidi group, a Kurdish ethno-religious group, with the intent to destroy the group in whole or in part. It may very well be the case that non-state armed groups will more frequently perpetrate crimes of genocide since they may have the material and personnel capacity necessary to do so. Thus, transnational terrorist groups can be regarded as systems that can plan, commit, and repeatedly perpetrate system crimes whether they are war crimes, crimes against humanity, or genocide. For now, however, international criminal law does not take into account whether non-state armed groups including transnational terrorist groups have the capacity to perpetrate international crimes, despite the overwhelming empirical evidence to the contrary. The idea that only members of a transnational terrorist group should bear responsibility for those crimes is abstract, given the socio-political realities of how such crimes are planned and committed. As discussed in Chapter 2, the ambiguous organisational structure of some groups provides a platform through which individual members can argue that their prosecution is arbitrary and unjust.[58] If this is true, the argument that the non-state armed group has approved an individual member's actions, and therefore has consented to bear the cost of that responsibility becomes tenuous.

D Systems theory: the repercussions for the responsibility of transnational terrorist groups for international crimes

1 The transnational terrorist group as a complex adaptive system

I have contended in section C that the literature on moral responsibility indicates a number of reasons why international criminal law should be expanded to distribute punishment for international crimes to the transnational terrorist group as a collective entity. However, none of those propositions are entirely satisfying because of the ontology of the transnational terrorist groups, which systems theory postulates as a complex adaptive system. Systems theory does not constitute a single body of thought but instead has emerged from different traditions and approaches.[59] It concerns the study of individuals' interactions and the system-wide effects they produce. As a theory, it has created two ways of responding to

57 *Bosnia and Herzegovina* v. *Serbia and Montenegro, ICJ Case Concerning the Application of the Convention on the Prevention and Punishment of the Crime of Genocide,* Judgment (26 February 2007) General List No. 91, paras 278–97.

58 See p. 31 of this book.

59 Sylvia Walby, 'Complexity Theory, Globalisation and Diversity' (British Sociological Association Conference, University of York, April 2003) 3 available at: www.leeds.ac.

the matter of change and diversity. First, where the small interactions of individuals lead to bifurcations and new self-sustaining phenomena emerge which the individuals could not have reasonably predicted themselves.[60] The ant colony is a frequently cited example; the individual ant placed on a flat surface will walk around in circles to the point of exhaustion; however, a colony of ants programmed to work together and follow simple instructions can construct amazingly complex nests with underground passages and chambers that are essential for survival.[61] With the ant colony, it is the microscopic interactions between the individual ants that leads to this complex behaviour. Such behaviour can also emerge from the interaction of individuals and the adaptation of a system.

The second way is that from time to time an emergent phenomenon like the colony of ants will endure in its environment as a complex adaptive system. Mitchell suggests that a complex system is one 'in which large networks of components with no central control and simple rules of operation give rise to complex collective behaviour, sophisticated information processing, and adaptation via learning or evolution'.[62] She also alternatively proposed that it is 'a system that exhibits nontrivial emergent and self-organizing behaviours'.[63] Pursuant to the theory, the human body, the environment, and the economy can all be regarded as complex adaptive systems since they are distinct from the entity from which they first emerged.[64] So the key component of systems theory is its anti-reductionist analytic strategy, which is inextricably linked to a vital re-examination of the nature of systems, in order to more sufficiently conceptualise the dynamic and systematised interrelationship between phenomena.[65]

However, systems theory also has its limitations in that the concept of 'system' is entangled within outmoded conceptions of a self-balancing equilibrium. This

uk/sociology/people/swdocs/Complexity%20Theory%20realism%20and%20path%20dependency.pdf (date accessed: 14 March 2018).

60 Ibid.

61 The ant colony as a complex adaptive system has been examined considerably in the literature. See for example Carl Anderson and Daniel McShea, 'Individual versus Social Complexity, with Particular Reference to Ant Colonies', *Biological Reviews of the Cambridge Philosophical Society* 76(2) (2001) 211–237; Walter Gutjahr, 'First Steps to the Runtime Complexity Analysis of Ant Colony Optimization', *Computers and Operations Research* 35(9) (2008) 2711–2727; Judith Innes and David Booher, 'Consensus Building and Complex Adaptive Systems: A Framework for Evaluating Collaborative Planning', *Journal of the American Planning Association* 65(4) (1999) 412–423; Stuart Kauffman, *The Origins of Order: Self-Organization and Selection in Evolution* (Oxford University Press, 1993); Stuart Kauffman, *At Home in the Universe: The Search for Laws of Self-Organization and Complexity* (Viking, 1995).

62 Melanie Mitchell, *Complexity: A Guided Tour* (Oxford University Press, 2009), p. 13.

63 Ibid.

64 See for example Eric Beinhocker, *The Origin of Wealth: Evolution, Complexity and the Radical Remaking of Economics* (Random House, 2006); Simon Levin, *Fragile Dominion: Complexity and the Commons* (Perseus, 1999); Robert Sawyer, *Social Emergence: Societies as Complex Systems* (Cambridge University Press, 2005).

65 Walby (n. 59), p. 3; David Bryne, *Complexity and the Social Sciences: An Introduction* (Routledge, 1998), p. 15.

has led to some difficulty in delineating the precise boundaries of the modern complex system. As a result, a conceptually cogent theory of a complex system was difficult to ground in reality.[66] However, new theorisations of the system within the theory have reshaped the concept so that it can now be applied to the most dynamic and irregular emergent phenomena. Some of these modifications are the culmination of 'simple conceptualisations, such as replacing the conception of parts and wholes with the notion that each system takes all other systems as its environment, while others are more complex conceptions of the relations between systems as well as dynamic conceptions of their uneven, non-linear transformations'.[67]

Nevertheless, there are still considerable theoretical and empirical questions about systems theory, especially whether it can clarify how transnational terrorist groups work or if the concept can only apply by analogy. If correct, the theory provides an insight into the transnational terrorist group and its consequences for the matters examined here. The theory suggests that the transnational terrorist group is a complex adaptive system that has emerged from the interactions of individuals and the variety of conceptual and social tools such as law, ethics, language, culture, and religion that bolster cohesion among significant numbers of individuals that may share a common objective. The transnational terrorist group as a complex adaptive system has causal effects in its environment, on its members, and the interactive processes from which it has emerged.[68] As such, the transnational terrorist group is greater than its total members since it is has the capacity to achieve far more than one individual acting alone.

2 *Conceptualising the responsibility of the transnational terrorist group as a collective entity*

The ontology of complex adaptive systems has considerable ramifications for the responsibility of the transnational terrorist group as a collective entity in general and for the principle of individual criminal responsibility more importantly. Since it enforces the actuality of complex adaptive systems, systems theory arguably supports the claim that collective entities are ontologically distinct and separate from their individual members. Responsibility necessitates that there is an actor upon which responsibility can be imposed. Systems theory implies that the transnational terrorist group can be regarded as such an actor because it has causative effects that cannot be devolved into integral components. International criminal law ignores the central premise of systems theory: that the transnational terrorist group is an appropriate entity to which criminal responsibility should be attributed on the grounds that it is an extension of the individual.

66 Steven Manson, 'Simplifying Complexity: A Review of Complexity Theory', *Geoforum* 32 (2001) 405–414, p. 411.

67 Walby (n. 59), p. 3.

68 Jean-Jacques Fresard, *The Roots of Behaviour in War: A Survey of the Literature* (International Committee of the Red Cross, 2004), p. 46.

That said, the ontology of the complex adaptive system indicates that the aperture between the transnational terrorist group and the individual is still significant for two reasons. First, systems theory substantiates that rather anodyne conduct has superfluous consequences at group level. In particular, Bella asserts that '[t]o merely blame individuals . . . is to avoid . . . the essential claim of emergence: that the character of wholes should not be reduced to the character of parts . . . [Therefore] outcomes can emerge through the efforts of normal competent and well adjusted people much like ourselves'.[69] Take, for example, the members of a transnational terrorist group whose role is to follow the instructions of the centralised command and manufacture improvised explosive devices. The interactions of individuals following straightforward rules or instructions could result in the catastrophic loss of civilian life. If Bella's contention is correct, then systems theory helps to support the idea that the transnational terrorist group must be a focal point of responsibility under international criminal law as a collective entity.

Nevertheless, the 'non-linear relationship between the complex interactions of individuals and the phenomena that emerge from those interactions means that in most cases it will be impossible to trace direct connections between an individual and the complex adaptive system from which it is a part and the impacts that system may have in the world'.[70] Considering how systems theory would posit that the perpetration of an international crime generally stems from the interactions of multiple individuals, it is difficult to delineate why an individual member should shoulder responsibility for that crime alone when numerous other individuals may have contributed towards its commission as well. This implies that even if an individual member conforms with the complex system's behaviour, there may still be no consequential link between that conformity and the crimes that system has committed. The non-linearity between the individual members and the transnational terrorist group infers that the distribution of responsibility requires a link no matter how tenuous between the group and its members. So, systems theory can perhaps help explain why the distribution of responsibility for international crimes can be difficult to elucidate.

Systems theory also has consequences for the concept of responsibility. Under international criminal law, it is deemed pertinent that individuals should bear responsibility for a crime where he/she understood the potential consequences and, nevertheless, committed the act anyway. Juarrero posits that '[s]elf-organization . . . counsels for a wider denotation for the term cause, one reconceptualised in terms of "context-sensitive constraints" to include those causal powers that incorporate circular causality, context-sensitive embeddedness, and temporality'.[71] Klaus Mainzer also supports this argument stating that in a linear model causation 'the extent of an

69 David Bella, 'Emergence and Evil', *Emergence: Complexity and Organization* 8(2) (2006) 102–115, p. 103.

70 Chinen (n. 5), p. 723.

71 Alicia Juarrero, 'On Philosophy's "To Rethink" List: Causality, Explanation and Ethic', *Ecological Psychology* 20 (2008) 278–282, p. 280.

effect is believed to be similar to the extent of the cause. Thus a legal punishment of a punishable action can be proportional to the degree of damage effected.'[72]

However, according to systems theory, phenomena can emerge from random events, so the principle of proportionate responsibility can be questioned. Systems theory presupposes that most issues have non-linear characteristics. Indeed, Juarrero asserts that '[a]s the ecological, economic, and political problems of mankind have become global, complex, nonlinear, and random, the traditional concept of individual responsibility is questionable'.[73] The same can be said of collective entities such as transnational terrorist groups: the acts they commit in the short term can result in consequences that are felt by the wider international community in the long term. Thus, regard should be had to the context in which responsibility is being applied. While in the short term the individual member of the transnational terrorist group will retain some element of control over the effects of their actions for which they can be held accountable, they are also restricted by their environment and the internal dynamics which leads to the emergent behaviour of the group.[74] These limitations have led some commentators to be sceptical about whether a member of a transnational terrorist group has much autonomy. For instance, Kelly contends that (individuals):

> are shaped by environment, genetics, and experience in a way that affects what we perceive as reasons and narrows the horizon of possibilities for action. Environmental, genetic and psychological factors all shape what count as reasons for a person. Recognising this should challenge our confidence that a given wrongdoer was morally capable of doing better.[75]

This is precisely why some scholars who wish to retain some semblance of the concept of responsibility argue that it should be constructed. In particular, Schütz states how responsibility 'does not exist prior to its assignment'.[76]

For the purposes of this chapter, the question whether a transnational terrorist group has enough autonomy, or some other characteristics, to rationalise the assignment of responsibility to it does not need to be immediately determined. But it is my view that the ontology of complex systems, such as transnational terrorist groups, implies that when the entity commits an international crime there is no way to sidestep the criticism that its individual members are unfairly bearing the brunt of accountability for it.

72 Klaus Mainzer, *Thinking in Complexity: The Computational Dynamics of Matter, Mind and Mankind* (Springer, 1997, 5th edn), p. 435.

73 Ibid.

74 William Frederick, 'Emergent Management Morality: Explaining Corporate Corruption', *Emergence* 5 (2003) 5–35, p. 5.

75 Erin Kelly, 'Reparative Justice', in T. Isaacs and R. Vernon (eds), *Accountability for Collective Wrongdoing* (Cambridge University Press, 2011) 193–209, p. 194.

76 Anton Schütz, 'Desiring Society: Autopoiesis Beyond the Paradigm of Mastership', *Law and Critique* 5 (1994) 149–164, p. 160.

3 *The transnational terrorist group: an ontology or a legal concept?*

It would appear that systems theory and its ontology of the complex adaptive system has not been able to answer all our questions. If this is the case, why should we pay any attention to it especially since international law seems to yearn for us to set questions about the ontology of the transnational terrorist group to one side? Indeed, the ILC's Articles on the Responsibility of States for Internationally Wrongful Acts would suggest that '[c]ontemporary international law is clearly the work of states, every last word conforms to their wishes. States jealously safeguard their constitutional attribute of independent sovereignty and thereby affirm their monopoly over both national and international matters.'[77] So there would seem to be very little leeway for transnational terrorist groups in this quandary. At the same time, prosecuting the transnational terrorist group as a collective entity under international criminal law would imply that they are international legal subjects, but as discussed in section B, there is no clear-cut definition of transnational terrorist groups and this is clearly illustrated in the myriad of terms that have been used to describe them.

Contemporary international law would posit that the transnational terrorist group does not have 'a legal status attaching to a certain set of affairs by virtue of certain rules or practices'.[78] Portmann contends that international practice is cognisant of, first, a formal conception of international personality where legal rules delineate the criteria for legal personality, and, second, an 'actor conception' in which legal personality is composed of actors who take part in and contribute to the creation of international law.[79] He suggests that it is futile to 'recognise certain entities as international persons: [because] such status in itself does not entail any international legal rights, duties or capacities whatsoever'.[80] It is for international norms to bestow legal rights and obligations upon entities and not the mere fact of international legal personality. On the basis of these amalgamated constructs, even if transnational terrorist groups could be described as having a legal status they 'do not automatically possess so-called fundamental rights and duties nor are they automatically authorized to formally contribute to the creation of international law'.[81]

Of course, the idea that international law should regard the transnational terrorist group as a legal concept would be quite appealing, if only because it sidesteps the difficulties with construing the transnational terrorist group as a sociopolitical object. It has further significance for the issue of responsibility itself. As discussed in the previous section, the majority of the literature has strived to

77 Agnes Lejbowicz, *Philosophie du droit international: l'impossible capture de l'humanité* (PUF 1999), p. 292 (ICRC translation).

78 James Crawford, *The Creation of States in International Law* (Cambridge University Press, 2006, 2nd edn), p. 5.

79 Roland Portmann, *Legal Personality in International Law* (Cambridge University Press, 2010), p. 176.

80 Ibid.

81 Ibid., p. 177.

answer whether a collective entity can ever be subject to moral judgement since it is unclear whether the tools we utilise to make moral judgements about individuals can also be applied to entities such as transnational terrorist groups. Developing a legal conception of the transnational terrorist group would do very little to alleviate the problem, since transnational terrorist groups are regarded as incapable of fulfilling their duties under international law, so it could be said that international law is still not comfortable with regarding a transnational terrorist group as having the capacity to bear legal responsibility for its wrongful conduct, preferring instead to distinguish them from states under the law and treat its members as mere domestic criminals. As Portmann provides: 'the only consequence directly stemming from international personality is the capacity to invoke international responsibility and to be held internationally responsible'.[82]

Classifying a transnational terrorist group as a legal concept would also have ramifications for the principle of individual criminal responsibility under international criminal law. A transnational terrorist group needs individuals to act for it. In turn, if the transnational terrorist group could be held accountable under international criminal law as a collective entity the member's conduct could be imputed to the collective entity. As a result, the member would not always face the consequences for their role in the perpetration of the international crime. This was also a dilemma recognised by Roberto Ago, the second rapporteur for the ILC, with regard to states. However, he averred that the entity to which the individual's actions are imputed must be a legal one and not a sociopolitical entity. The same can be contended with regard to transnational terrorist groups:

> There are no activities of the . . . [transnational terrorist group] which can be called 'its own' from the point of view of natural causality as distinct from that of legal attribution . . . In describing the . . . [transnational terrorist group] as a real entity . . . like any other legal person – one must nevertheless avoid the error of giving an anthropomorphic picture of the collective phenomenon, in which the individual-organ would have his personality absorbed and annulled in the whole world and would be an inseparable part of it, rather like an organ of the human body.[83]

So, there would be conceptual difficulties with holding a transnational terrorist group accountable as a collective entity under international criminal law.

In particular, there would be difficulties in utilising the principle of individual criminal responsibility under the Rome Statute if the transnational terrorist group is regarded as an entity that subsumes the individual member. Indeed, how would the principle of individual criminal responsibility exist alongside a

82 Ibid., p. 275.

83 'Second Report on State Responsibility', by Roberto Ago, Special Rapporteur, *ILC Yearbook* ii (1970) 177, p. 190 at para. 39 (n. 4).

principle of collective entity responsibility? From an evidential point of view, pursuing the transnational terrorist group as a collective entity would perhaps be a more straightforward option for the Office of the Prosecutor than pursuing individual members. As a result, members of the group who played a crucial role in the planning, ordering, and commission of international crimes would potentially evade justice, thereby fostering a culture of impunity. It would be essential for international criminal law to preserve some degree of autonomy and responsibility for individuals who act on behalf of transnational terrorist groups, in particular high-ranking members who may have ordered or failed to prevent the commission of international crimes. Realistically, the only way such autonomy could be preserved is to dismiss the concept of the transnational terrorist group as a collective entity that can subsume the individual member's conduct.

Thus, analysing the transnational terrorist group in legal terms has its benefits, but also its limitations. The idea that a transnational terrorist group becomes a legal subject of international law by meeting certain pre-existing legal criteria which it had no role in creating or developing would be a major bone of contention for them. Indeed, many transnational terrorist groups refuse to be bound by laws that were created by what they perceive to be the 'enemy state'. One could retort by contending that at least some fundamental international legal principles preceded the existence of states, so why not for non-state armed groups such as transnational terrorist groups as well? Law existed before the Treaty of Westphalia in 1648 but at the same time it is 'shorthand for the processes in which law and social-political entities interacted well before 1648 and thereafter, not just a single event'.[84] Of course, the debate about whether law or sociopolitical entities existed first is incessant, but modern-day international practice has certainly taken the stance that one precedes the other.

So perhaps it is crucial to reconsider James Crawford's use of the phrase 'state of affairs' to figure out its legal implications. As Chinen points out '[t]erritory, population, government, and the ability to engage in international relations are legal terms . . . but they also purport to say something meaningful about the socio-political and geographic state of affairs to which legal analysis applies'.[85] One could posit that as an autopoietic system international criminal law views the world with reference to its own terms. But, even so, the state of affairs should not be relegated to the back burner. As with the relationship between law and ethics, if legal categorisations depart from reality, a number of challenges ensue. There is a danger that international criminal law could become ineffective either because it cannot sufficiently address this reality or it hazards becoming pointless for this same reason. Both levy a price on international criminal law's legitimacy. As explored above, the reality is that individual members bear the brunt of responsibility for international crimes. But if we recognise that the state of affairs is an important component in any analysis of international criminal law,

84 Chinen (n. 5), p. 727.
85 Ibid.

ontology can perhaps be brought within the fold. With regards the sociopolitical entity that is the transnational terrorist group, systems theory would suggest that ontology is one of an entity with a membership, individuals who must unfairly shoulder the burden of accountability for international crimes which emanate from the group itself. It is long overdue for international criminal law to embrace this reality.

E Conclusion

As stated in the introduction, international criminal law has so far had very little to do with the accountability of the transnational terrorist group as a collective entity and this chapter has examined a fundamental consequence of that actuality. It has explored the potential impact of certain ideas from systems theory on international criminal law, in particular the challenges that arise from the distribution of criminal responsibility within a transnational terrorist group to individual members. Systems theory highlights how international criminal law does not adequately capture where accountability should lie for transnational terrorist groups in view of how international crimes are planned and orchestrated within the group in reality. Systems theory contributes to this discussion by providing an ontology of the transnational terrorist group that complicates international criminal law's focus on the individual; it is an entity that is not differentiable from its individual members. So, if international criminal law is to be effective and achieve its objective to thwart impunity and deter future crimes it must deal with the transnational terrorist group itself as well. However, the theory also helps to elucidate that any attempt to interlink individual and group conduct is rife with difficulty: as a complex adaptive system, the transnational terrorist group could not exist without the interactions of its individual members, but the transnational terrorist group is also more than the aggregate of its members. Thus, the relationship between the individual member and the transnational terrorist group is more challenging to delineate than the principle of individual criminal responsibility allows. Unfortunately, international criminal law continues to overlook this ontology thereby risking incoherence. This conclusion does not exclude group responsibility as such, but does make it difficult to account for it, and makes the job of distributing accountability upwards from the individual members to the transnational terrorist group more difficult.

Efforts to hold the transnational terrorist group accountable for the behaviour of its individual members have been and will continue to be challenging at best because of the non-linear connection between the group and the individual member. This chapter could thus seem quite dispiriting: like a lot of research it endeavours to illustrate why a particular dilemma in international criminal law recurs perennially, and why any possible strategies to overcome it are likely to fail. Nevertheless, the consequences of only distributing responsibility for international crimes to individual members of the transnational terrorist group are far-reaching, especially since for the most part it is the group as a whole who may be condoning and inciting the individual member to carry out crimes. Therefore, it is at the very least useful to consider whether the benefits ensuing from holding individual members of the transnational terrorist group accountable outweigh those negative consequences and whether there is any means to overcome those impacts, in particular because there may be no rational means to vindicate them.

8 Conclusion

There have been numerous developments in the international law on terrorism since the inception of international criminal justice. However, the inclusion of terrorism as a crime within the subject-matter jurisdiction of the ICC could also realise justice for victims of transnational terrorist groups and end impunity. This book has endeavoured to flesh out the meaning of terrorism and its prosecution as a crime before the ICC. However, one of the major challenges of prosecuting members of transnational terrorist groups under international criminal law (ICL) is to respond effectively and meaningfully through a single court to international crimes. As a result, international criminal justice will encounter structural barriers, as well as political ones, owing to the contentious nature of terrorism, which could lead to further tension with the intervention of the international community in domestic affairs. The previous chapters expose the difficulties in holding members of transnational terrorist groups accountable before the ICC. This conclusion will bring together the key themes discussed in this book, as well as outlining the key findings and recommendations, before ending with some final remarks.

A Accountability for crimes by transnational terrorist groups

The ICC has made a number of innovations since its inception in particular with regard to the development of a principle of direct and indirect co-perpetration. The first 15 years of the Court's existence has also involved 11 situations and 25 cases, though all have focused on crimes concerning either state armed forces or non-state armed groups with a clear-cut hierarchical command structure. The failure of the ICC to intervene in situations involving alleged crimes by transnational terrorist groups has considerably undermined the credibility of the Court. In particular, its failure to investigate alleged crimes committed by all sides to the armed conflicts in Iraq and Syria, including ISIS, has showcased the structural weaknesses of the Court from both a legal and political perspective. As such, the ICC can be seen to have little influence on states in recognising the importance of bringing members of transnational terrorist groups to justice for international crimes. The difficulty also remains in developing the constituent elements of an international crime of terrorism that takes into consideration the unique organisational structure of transnational terrorist groups. Using systems theory to understand the organisational structure of transnational terrorist groups in Chapter 2, this book makes four findings: (1) the role of the ICC in achieving justice for victims of transnational terrorist groups is limited and unlikely to ever be fully realised; (2) the international crimes of genocide, war crimes, and crimes against humanity may not encapsulate violence perpetrated by transnational terrorist groups; (3) no crime of transnational terrorism currently exists under ICL; and (4) the principle of individual criminal responsibility will be difficult to apply to members of network-based transnational terrorist groups.

1 Accountability of members of transnational terrorist groups before the ICC is limited

First, there is a deep scepticism regarding the capacity of the ICC to be an effective accountability mechanism to prosecute members of transnational terrorist groups.[1] This can be seen from Chapter 3 where it was found that there is a need for legal clarity on the classification of their attacks as an international crime within the subject-matter jurisdiction of the Court in view of their network-based organisational structure.[2] This includes clarity for affected states and the Office of the Prosecutor so they can ensure an adequate response to potential challenges in prosecuting members of these types of groups including, the type of evidence needed at trial to prove the constituent elements of each crime. The widespread and inconsistent academic commentary on whether attacks by transnational terrorist groups constitute an international crime, linked as it is to the ongoing impasse on a definition of terrorism, reflects the evolving nature of interpretations underway within the international community on the appropriate methods and normative standing of such a definition.[3]

In the absence of an authoritative definition, this book first utilised network theory to examine whether the organisational structure of transnational terrorist groups is fundamentally different to that of other types of non-state armed actors such as armed opposition groups, and, second, to explore how the Rome Statute would apply to members of transnational terrorist groups.[4] As this book suggests the Office of the Prosecutor at the ICC continues to be focused on prosecuting members of state and non-state armed actors with a clear-cut hierarchical organisational structure and has so far sidestepped the investigation and prosecution of more ambiguously organised groups such as ISIS despite considerable international pressure. Thus, the question that has emerged from this book is whether the ICC is best equipped to fulfil its mandate to hold those most responsible for international crimes accountable. It follows that the ICC has the legal tools

1 Michael Lawless, 'Terrorism: An International Crime', *International Journal* 63(1) (2007–2008) 19–159, p. 139; Aviv Cohen, 'Prosecuting Terrorists at the International Criminal Court: Re-Evaluating an Unused Legal Tool to Combat Terrorism', *Michigan State International Law Review* 20(2) (2012) 219–257.

2 See p. 60 of this book.

3 See p. 66 of this book.

4 See p. 30 of this book.

necessary to prosecute members of state armed forces and non-state armed actors with traditional clear-cut hierarchical organisational structures but arguably the same cannot be said of transnational terrorist groups with a network-based organisational structure. There is a growing need for a coordinated international approach to reconsider the Rome Statute as a mechanism for bringing members of transnational terrorist groups to justice that will also provide support and guidance to states and intergovernmental organisations on how best to ensure ICL can evolve in the complex context of transnational terrorist groups. The ICC needs to encourage states to pursue the accountability of members of transnational terrorist groups for international crimes, overcome its juridical limitations, and realise redress for victims of terrorist attacks.

2 The international crimes of genocide, war crimes, and crimes against humanity may not encapsulate violence perpetrated by transnational terrorist groups

An apparent issue throughout this book has been the difficulties of constructing an accountability mechanism for members of network-based non-state armed actors. The trouble with ICL is its limited jurisdiction and selective prosecution of crimes. The majority of terrorist attacks cannot be categorised as crimes under the Court's current subject-matter jurisdiction. As discussed in Chapter 3, the constituent elements of international crimes distinguish them from domestic crimes. From a legal perspective, in order for a terrorist attack to be classified as an international crime, it must fall within the definition of genocide, war crimes, or crimes against humanity. However, from a systems theory approach attacks by transnational terrorist groups do not fit neatly into the present categories of international crimes. Although Chapter 4 has shown that ICL can be adapted through case law and practice, this process is gradual and inherently slow. The current legal categories of international crimes exclude sporadic one-off violence by a non-state armed group, which does not rise to the definition of a non-international armed conflict, or acts such as rape, sexual slavery, or disappearances that do not fulfil the requirement of 'widespread' or 'systematic'. As such, victims are denied recognition and justice, despite suffering serious violence by transnational terrorist groups which should be of serious concern to the international community. In order for members of transnational terrorist groups to be brought within the jurisdiction of the ICC, an amendment of the Rome Statute to include a crime of transnational terrorism is imperative.

Indeed, since the majority of attacks by transnational terrorist groups, occurring in non-armed conflict situations, are one-off and sporadic, they cannot be classified as a crime against humanity under Article 7 of the Rome Statute since it would be difficult to prove that they were committed as part of a widespread or systematic attack.[5] Utilising the analysis of the organisational structure of transnational terrorist groups in Chapter 2, it is clear that some transnational terrorist groups have

5 See p. 59 of this book.

a network-based structure composed of cells that do not directly communicate with each other.[6] As a result, it is difficult to ascribe the acts of an individual member or cell to the overall 'organisation'.[7] Network cells of some transnational terrorist groups do not receive any direct orders from a centralised command, and carry out attacks autonomously.[8] So, it would be difficult to not only prove that the transnational terrorist group is a collectivity, established to achieve a common purpose but also that their attacks were committed as part of a widespread or systematic attack directed against a civilian population.[9] As discussed in Chapter 3, there is a disquieting propensity to apply a narrow interpretation of a 'widespread or systematic attack' in the jurisprudence of the ICC.[10] If the Court continues to apply this approach, it will exclude many definitive cases of crimes against humanity by transnational terrorist groups.

There are other serious concerns from a critical perspective of the politicisation of violence and victims of transnational terrorist groups: why investigate and prosecute crimes in Nigeria, Iraq, Afghanistan, and the Democratic Republic of Congo but not Syria or Sri Lanka? Victims have suffered immensely at the hands of members of ISIS and other groups, but because a state has not signed the Rome Statute, or the UN Security Council has declined to refer the situations to the ICC, there is an incongruence in justice. If terrorist attacks constitute a threat to international peace and security and are of concern to the international community, it should mandate justice for victims. The political and strategic interests of states have superseded this mandate and denied justice to victims. A systems theory approach to international crimes would suggest that states should recognise the Rome Statute as the minimum yardstick of international criminal justice, as other violence which does not fall within the subject-matter jurisdiction of the ICC should be tackled by states, due to the serious harm it inflicts on victims. Such serious suffering necessitates substantive accountability mechanisms of truth, justice, reparation, and reconciliation.

3 No crime of transnational terrorism exists under ICL

The lack of an unequivocal provision criminalising transnational terrorism is to be lamented, and any concerted attempt to include such a contentious provision into the Rome Statute would be opposed by many members of the Assembly of State Parties. Yet the inclusion of an operative provision on transnational terrorism would serve as a timely reminder to the Assembly of State Parties that holding members of transnational terrorist groups accountable before the ICC where states are unwilling or unable to do so themselves would serve to combat impunity. But, as discussed in Chapter 4, the definition of terrorism is highly contested, so even if a provision criminalising transnational terrorism is agreed upon by the

6 See p. 30 of this book.
7 Ibid.
8 Ibid.
9 Article 7 of the Rome Statute of the International Criminal Court.
10 See p. 58 of this book.

Assembly of State Parties, member states may be hesitant to ratify it.[11] One must also bear in mind the fact that states in which transnational terrorist groups carry out the majority of terrorist attacks, in particular Iraq, Pakistan, and Syria have not yet ratified the Rome Statute. So, questions arise as to how more states can be encouraged to ratify the Rome Statute particularly those that are most impacted by transnational terrorist groups.

Following on from this, the book examined whether a customary crime of transnational terrorism has emerged in international law in light of the interlocutory decision of the Special Tribunal for Lebanon in 2011 and how it could be prosecuted before the ICC.[12] Despite the conclusion of the Special Tribunal for Lebanon, that there is a customary crime of transnational terrorism under international law, this book has concluded that at this moment in time there is no identifiable crime of transnational terrorism under ICL.

Notwithstanding my negative finding as to the existence of a crime of transnational terrorism under international law at present, it is possible to discern that a crime of transnational terrorism is beginning to take root in international law. Yet, international institutions, most notably UN human rights bodies, have been remarkably slow to specifically identify a crime of transnational terrorism. Building on the definition of transnational terrorism proposed by the UN High Level Panel on Threats, Challenges and Change in its report 'A More Secure World: Our Shared Responsibility',[13] the non-binding definition of terrorism laid down in UN Security Council Resolution 1566 (2004)[14] and the inclusion of the crime of terrorism in the International Law Commission's Draft Statute for an International Criminal Court, there is an increasing awareness of the need to ensure that members of transnational terrorist groups are brought to justice for their role in committing terrorist attacks.[15] The potential exists for the crystallisation of such a crime through an amendment of Article 5 of the Rome Statute, subject to a comprehensive definition of transnational terrorism being agreed upon by the state parties to the Rome Statute.

4 The principle of individual criminal responsibility will be difficult to apply to members of network-based transnational terrorist groups.

The concept of the network-based organisation set out in this book was introduced as a means of understanding the evolving body of law and practice relating

11 See p. 67 of this book.
12 See pp. 67–70 of this book. *Interlocutory Decision on the Applicable Law: Terrorism, Conspiracy, Homicide, Perpetration, Cumulative Charging* (Appeals Chamber) STL-11-01/I, 16 February 2011, para. 85.
13 UN High Level Panel on Threats, Challenges and Change, 'A More Secure World: Our Shared Responsibility' (2004) available at: www.un.org/en/peacebuilding/pdf/historical/hlp_more_secure_world.pdf (date accessed: 14 March 2018).
14 UN Security Council Resolution 1566 (2004).
15 International Law Commission, Draft Statute for an International Criminal Court (2005) available at: http://legal.un.org/ilc/texts/instruments/english/draft%20articles/7_4_1994.pdf (date accessed: 14 March 2018).

specifically to the prosecution of members of transnational terrorist groups before the ICC, as a result of crimes committed in either an armed conflict situation or a non-armed conflict situation. Therefore, at the conclusion of this book, it is worthwhile speculating how the accountability of transnational terrorist groups before the ICC may progress. Furthermore, it is important to consider whether prosecuting members of transnational terrorist groups before the ICC would be beneficial for states, international organisations, or the victims of terrorist attacks.

First, it is clear from the emerging jurisprudence of the ICC, reinforced by academic commentary, that there is deep scepticism regarding the utilisation of the ICC as a mechanism to prosecute members of transnational terrorist groups.[16] Prosecuting members of transnational terrorist groups before the ICC will be difficult due to the network-based organisational structure of the group, which will have a significant bearing on how the Rome Statute is applied to them. As discussed in Chapter 3, it follows that if members of transnational terrorist groups are prosecuted before the ICC, there is a need for legal clarity on the classification of their attacks as an international crime within the subject-matter jurisdiction of the Court.[17] This includes clarity for affected states and the Office of the Prosecutor so they can ensure an adequate response to potential challenges in prosecuting members of these types of groups including, the type of evidence needed at trial to fulfil the constituent elements of each crime. Nevertheless, the widespread and inconsistent academic commentary on whether attacks by transnational terrorist groups constitute an international crime, linked as it is to the ongoing impasse on a definition of terrorism, reflects the evolving nature of the transnational interpretations underway within the international community on the appropriate methods and normative standing of such a definition.[18]

Similarly, it is important for states and non-governmental organisations to recognise that such attacks constitute an international crime as well as their obligations to bring those responsible to justice. In the absence of an authoritative definition, this book utilised network theory to first examine whether the organisational structure of transnational terrorist groups is fundamentally different to that of armed opposition groups, and, second, to explore how the Rome Statute would apply to members of transnational terrorist groups.[19] Indeed, the Office of the Prosecutor at the ICC continues to be focused on prosecuting members of state and non-state armed actors with a clear-cut hierarchical organisational structure, in particular their high-ranking commanders. So, the question that has emerged from this book is whether the ICC is best equipped to fulfil its mandate to hold those most responsible for international crimes accountable, when the Rome Statute does not adequately apply to transnational terrorist groups with a network-based organisational structure? It follows that the ICC has the legal tools necessary to prosecute members of state armed forces and non-state armed actors

16 Lawless (n. 1); Cohen (n. 1).
17 See p. 61 of this book.
18 See p. 94 of this book.
19 See p. 30 of this book.

with traditional clear-cut hierarchical organisational structures but arguably the same cannot be said of transnational terrorist groups with a network-based organisational structure. So there is a growing need for a coordinated international approach to reconsider the Rome Statute as a mechanism for bringing members of transnational terrorist groups to justice that will also provide support and guidance to states and intergovernmental organisations on how best to ensure ICL can evolve in the complex context of transnational terrorist groups.

As seen in Chapter 5, since transnational terrorist groups lack a clear chain of command due to their network-based organisational structure the principle of individual criminal responsibility will be difficult to apply.[20] One possible way to overcome this challenge is to prosecute members of transnational terrorist groups under the doctrine of co-perpetration as enunciated by the Pre-Trial Chamber in *Prosecutor* v. *Lubanga.* [21]Chapter 6 found that the doctrine of co-perpetration is clearly an attempt by the ICC to develop a new theory of liability.[22] A member of a transnational terrorist group can be held responsible for the perpetration of a criminal offence even if he/she did not play any physical role in the commission of the offence and also enables individuals to be held accountable before the ICC even if they were not present at the location where the actual perpetrators committed the crime.[23] It is the concept of 'control' that links the accused to the actual perpetrator of the crime.[24] The foundation for this mode of liability can be found in the *Lubanga* case where the Pre-Trial Chamber noted that a co-perpetrator is the individual who exercises 'control over the crime'.[25]

The doctrine may provide a more effective basis upon which to hold members of transnational terrorist groups accountable in view of the challenges in prosecuting them under the Rome Statute. Nevertheless, a distinction needs to be made between members that possess the capacity to exert control over the transnational terrorist group but 'deploy them towards a common cause and individuals who jointly exercise combined authority over a single vertical organization'.[26] The latter would constitute the most straightforward application of the doctrine of indirect co-perpetration to transnational terrorist groups. The ICC has not yet considered the application of the doctrine of indirect co-perpetration in this manner, but one can deduce that high-ranking members especially could be brought to justice even where they did not direct their subordinates to orchestrate the attack.

Since the ICC has repeatedly invoked the concept of *dolus eventualis* in its interpretation of the doctrine of indirect co-perpetration, it must be careful when

20 See p. 123 of this book.
21 *Prosecutor* v. *Thomas Dyilo Lubanga, Decision on the Confirmation of Charges*, Pre-Trial Chamber ICC-01/04-01/06 29 January 2007.
22 See p. 157 of this book.
23 Ibid.
24 Jens Ohlin, 'Second-Order Linking Principles: Combining Vertical and Horizontal Modes of Liability', *Leiden Journal of International Law* 25 (2012) 771–797.
25 *Lubanga Decision on Confirmation of Charges* (n. 21), para. 340.
26 Ibid.

applying the concept to prosecutions involving members of transnational terrorist groups.[27] This is to ensure that the doctrine of indirect co-perpetration is in conformity with the fundamental principle of individual criminal responsibility underlying Article 25 of the Rome Statute. In particular, a member accused of being an indirect co-perpetrator could be held responsible for terrorist attacks perpetrated by an organisation which he does not actually command or direct. This is particularly the case for leaders of transnational terrorist groups who do not have knowledge of the activities of his/her subordinates because of the organisational structure of the group into decentralised network cells which as discussed in Chapter 5 makes it problematic to prosecute them under Article 28 of the Rome Statute.[28]

However, considering the ongoing emphasis placed on the concept of control in the jurisprudence of the ICC, it would be difficult for members of transnational terrorist groups to be successfully prosecuted before the ICC in view of the network-based organisational structure of the group. As explored in Chapter 2, the network cells in some transnational terrorist groups act autonomously and do not comply with orders from a centralised command.[29] As a result, it is unclear who within the group directs or controls the perpetration of terrorist attacks. Until a case involving a transnational terrorist group comes before the ICC, it remains to be seen how the judiciary will actually apply the Rome Statute to indicted members of these groups. Thus, this book makes a number of recommendations which try to bridge the gap between the theory of accountability for members of transnational terrorist groups and the emerging practice of the ICC. Such an approach is about moving justice for victims of transnational terrorist groups at the ICC from a symbolic function to a more effective accountability mechanism that will assist the Court in ending impunity for transnational terrorism.

B Recommendations

1 Facilitate a re-evaluation of the crimes that may potentially be perpetrated by members of transnational terrorist groups

It is incumbent upon human rights monitoring and legal accountability mechanisms, as represented at the international level by UN human rights bodies and the ICC, to proactively examine the possible crimes which may be committed if an attack is perpetrated by a transnational terrorist group. By clarifying the ICL applicable to terrorist attacks, states will be provided key guidance on how to protect the rights of individuals affected by transnational terrorist groups, while simultaneously receiving clarity on their own obligations to investigate and prosecute them under ICL. True and effective accountability of members of transnational terrorist groups requires an explanation of how ICL applies to them. Thus,

27 See p. 158 of this book.
28 See p. 157 of this book.
29 See p. 28 of this book.

an examination of how the principle of individual criminal responsibility applies to members of an entity composed of autonomous network-based cells would provide an avenue for bolstering justice and redress. The developing jurisprudence of the ICC regarding the accountability of leaders of armed opposition groups, in particular, the successful conviction of the commander-in-chief of the Forces patriotiques pour la libération du Congo (FPLC), Thomas Lubanga Dyilo, provides just one example of how it is possible for members of non-state armed actors to be brought to justice under ICL.[30]

If ICL prohibits attacks by transnational terrorist groups committed in non-armed conflict situations, there is a need for legal clarity on the obligations of these actors. This includes clarity for affected states, so they can ensure an adequate legal response to terrorist attacks. Nevertheless, the widespread, inconsistent state practice on the legal response to transnational terrorist groups in the aftermath of attacks highlights the evolving nature of the interpretations of the international community on the appropriate methods of addressing terroristic activity.[31] Indeed, the use of alternative means by some states to address the activity of transnational terrorist groups such as secret detention provides an unfortunate reminder that states can wittingly or unwittingly undermine the rule of law. Thus, the ICC would provide an additional accountability mechanism for prosecuting members of transnational terrorist groups where states are unwilling or unable to do so.

2 Amend the Rome Statute to include a crime of transnational terrorism

In addition, the extensive level of ratification of international treaties and the broadly authoritative pronouncements made by the UN Security Council and General Assembly provides a strong impetus for the inclusion of transnational terrorism as a crime within the Rome Statute.[32] While the ICC may face particular challenges in bringing members of transnational terrorist groups to justice due to

30 *Lubanga Decision on Confirmation of Charges* (n. 21). See also *Prosecutor* v. *Thomas Lubanga Dyilo*, ICC-01/04-01/06, Judgment, 14 March 2012, paras 984–987.

31 See p. 65 of this book.

32 With regard to international treaties, see for example Convention on Offences and Certain Other Acts Committed on Board Aircraft, 14 September 1963, entered into force 4 December 1969; Convention for the Suppression of Unlawful Seizure of Aircraft, 16 December 1970, entered into force 14 October 1971; Convention for the Suppression of Unlawful Acts against the Safety of Civil Aviation, 23 September 1971, entered into force 26 January 1973; Convention on the Prevention and Punishment of Crimes against Internationally Protected Persons, including Diplomatic Agents, 14 December 1973, entered into force 20 February 1977; International Convention against the Taking of Hostages, 17 November 1979, entered into force 3 June 1983; Convention on the Physical Protection of Nuclear Material, 26 October 1979, entered into force 8 February 1987; Convention for the Suppression of Unlawful Acts against the Safety of Maritime Navigation, 10 March 1988, entered into force 1 March 1992. With regard to UN Security Council and General Assembly Resolutions, see UN Security Council Resolution 1373 (2001).

states' lack of cooperation with the Court's investigations and subsequent proceedings, the amendment of the Rome Statute to include a provision criminalising transnational terrorism would clarify that states have a duty under international law to investigate and prosecute suspected members of transnational terrorist groups for their role in perpetrating a terrorist attack.[33] It would also signal to states that there is an international mechanism to bring members of these groups to justice where they fail to do so.

However, the pressures of workload and limited resources available to the ICC may act as a concerted brake on opening investigations into the activity of transnational terrorist groups and in turn on developing jurisprudence on the application of ICL to them. Nevertheless, the recognition of terrorism as a threat to international peace and security by the UN Security Council in the aftermath of the 9/11 attacks and its establishment of the UN Counter-Terrorism Committee coincides with a resolute effort by the international community to strengthen the overall monitoring and reporting of states' obligations to prosecute individuals suspected of participating in terroristic activity.[34] Likewise, the key focus on human dignity within the ILC draft ICC Statute reinforces the requirement for a broader debate on how best to embed an effective and practical legal provision criminalising transnational terrorism into the Rome Statute. While some state parties have insisted on a provision criminalising terrorism in the Rome Statute, there is a growing need for a coordinated approach to recognise and enumerate the constituent elements of a crime of transnational terrorism and to provide practical support and guidance to states on how best to ensure that all provisions of the Rome Statute are respected in the complex context of terrorist attacks.

So, while numerous thematic human rights issues demand the attention of international bodies, the current UN-led draft definition of terrorism combined with the development of the ILC draft ICC Statute provides an important opportunity for debate and discussion to occur as to how best to address the accountability of members of transnational terrorist groups for their role in committing international crimes. While the ILC draft ICC Statute provided a clear and authoritative basis for the inclusion of a crime of terrorism within the Court's subject-matter jurisdiction, the challenge now is to amend the Rome Statute to include this crime. By marrying a state's obligation to bring members of transnational terrorist groups to justice with regular reporting and monitoring by the UN Counter-Terrorism Committee, the international community can help to ensure the accountability of these groups.

3 Foster an ICL framework for transnational terrorist groups

The first ten years of the Court's existence has seen the investigation of eight situations and 21 cases, though all have focused on the prosecution of members of state and non-state armed actors with a clear-cut hierarchical structure. If the ICC is to prosecute members of transnational terrorist groups, the Assembly of State

33 See p. 63 of this book.
34 UN Security Council Resolution 1373 (2001).

Parties must still decide what the final form and function of a draft article on the crime of transnational terrorism will be. To date, one draft article has been discussed but there is no guarantee that the proposal in its current format will be retained.[35] So would the current draft text provide a formula for the successful prosecution of members of transnational terrorist groups before the ICC? Or should the draft provision focus primarily on a detailed and specialised definition of transnational terrorism? Would the state parties to the Rome Statute be more likely to acquiesce to a provision which does not include a non-technical definition of terrorism such as the definition in UN Security Council 1566 (2004) which does not attempt progressive development of state responsibility for terrorist attacks? Yet, should the Assembly of State Parties adopt the draft provision on terrorism proposed by the ILC or should they formulate an alternative?

An international legal framework for prosecuting transnational terrorism is still in its infancy. So, a new provision within the Rome Statute criminalising terrorism will not act as a panacea for the thousands of victims of terrorist attacks each year. More to the point, the evidence for analysing whether the insertion of a provision into the Rome Statute is the most effective means of achieving the accountability of members of transnational terrorist groups is not available. Therefore, one must proceed on the assumption that the state parties to the Rome Statute will work together to form an agreed understanding of the definition of terrorism which will in turn lead to a means of legal redress for the victims of a transnational terrorist attack. This implies an interconnection and synthesis of national, regional, and international legal responses to transnational terrorist groups.

The conclusion of a provision criminalising transnational terrorist attacks under the Rome Statute would be a major achievement and could potentially pave the way for an effective mechanism to prosecute members of transnational terrorist groups where states are unwilling or unable to do so. By formulating a definition of transnational terrorism, the Assembly of State Parties may be able to balance the different approaches to transnational terrorism: binding/non-binding and universal/regional. An amendment would also provide the compromise required to facilitate international cooperation and the efficiency of state responses to terrorist attacks by transnational terrorist groups like ISIS. Yet, history shows that reaching consensus on the definition of transnational terrorism has been difficult.[36] The inclusion of a provision criminalising transnational terrorism into the Rome Statute would perhaps feed directly into other institutional and substantive initiatives at both an international and domestic level aimed at ensuring the effective accountability of members of transnational terrorist groups.

Moreover, the creation of a principle of collective entity responsibility which would operate in tandem with the principle of individual criminal responsibility under Article 25 of the Rome Statute would be a welcome development. Indeed, by harnessing systems theory this book has provided an ontology of the transnational terrorist group which frustrates ICL's focus on the individual. As a theory, it

35 See p. 93 of this book.
36 See p. 67 of this book.

highlights how the transnational terrorist group is difficult to differentiate from its individual members. Ultimately, if the ICC is to be effective in achieving its objective to thwart impunity and deter future crimes, it must focus on the accountability of the transnational terrorist group as well. However, systems theory also underlines how any efforts to interlink individual and group behaviour will be challenging: as a complex adaptive system, the transnational terrorist group could not exist without the interactions of its individual members, but the transnational terrorist group is also more than the aggregate of its members. Hence, the relationship between the individual member and the transnational terrorist group is more challenging to demarcate than the principle of individual criminal responsibility allows. If ICL continues to overlook this ontology, it risks incoherence. The implications of only distributing responsibility for international crimes to individual members of the transnational terrorist group are far-reaching, especially since for the most part it is the group as a whole who may be condoning and inciting the individual member to carry out crimes. So, it is important to consider whether the benefits ensuing from holding individual members of the transnational terrorist group accountable outweigh those negative consequences, and whether there is any means to overcome those impacts, in particular because there may be no rational means to vindicate them.

C Reflections on the state-centric system of the ICC and its implications for the accountability of transnational terrorist groups

Considering how the Rome Statute is supposed to place 'State and non-State actors side-by-side in the international arena'[37] one of the contested flaws with the ICC in the prosecution of transnational terrorist groups is its jurisdiction to enforce which 'is paltry, at best'.[38] In contrast to the ICC's jurisdiction to prescribe and adjudicate, its jurisdiction to enforce is far from effective because it almost completely relies on State Party cooperation to accomplish even the most rudimentary of judicial functions such as the execution of search warrants.[39] While there is nothing wrong with having a state-dependent enforcement structure, the Rome Statute offers very little incentive to State Parties to comply with its provisions and does not include penalties for failure to do so. Since states have the power to undermine the ICC's enforcement mechanism, the ICC's jurisdiction to prosecute members of transnational terrorist groups is entirely at the whim of states.[40]

As examined in this book, the drafters of the Rome Statute are responsible for these structural and substantial flaws because they sought to reach a compromise

37 Leila Sadat, *The International Criminal Court and the Transformation of International Law: Justice for the New Millennium* (Martinus Nijhoff, 2002), p. 8.
38 Ibid., p. 11.
39 Sadat (n. 37), p. 120–122; Bruce Broomhall, *International Justice and the International Criminal Court* (Oxford University Press, 2003), pp. 151–162.
40 Stephen Rademaker, 'Unwitting Part to Genocide: The International Criminal Court is Complicating Efforts to Save Darfur' (*Washington Post*, 11 January 2007) A25.

between two competing interests: sovereignty and the international rule of law.[41] So, as the workload of the ICC gradually increases, these flaws will mature into mammoth barriers to prosecutions not only of members of transnational terrorist groups but all state and non-state armed actors. At the same time, perhaps the most valuable contribution of the Rome Statute drafters was their understanding of how a permanent international criminal court should be conceptually structured in light of the Westphalian legal order. Even though some assert that the Westphalian legal order still persists, there is a widely held belief that globalisation, the increasing recognition of human rights, and the legitimacy of international law have increased the influence of multinational corporations and other non-state actors in the international arena, and likewise eroded the authority of sovereign states.[42] However, others believe this is a mischaracterisation of the reality on the ground which is that a state-centred conception of ICL continues to prevail at the ICC.[43] Indeed, some would argue that 'there are few signs that the tension between the international order' rationale of ICL and the state-centric character of the "Westphalian" system is likely to abate in the foreseeable future'.[44] Nevertheless, the principle of individual criminal responsibility is at the very heart of the ICC and the Rome Statute compels states to turn over members of transnational terrorist groups to the ICC to face trial. Thus, the structures of ICL are not confined by a continuing Westphalian legacy and instead the ICC merely lacks the legal props necessary to bring members of transnational terrorist groups to justice.

Although some states may be unwilling to cooperate with an ICC that investigates and prosecutes members of transnational terrorist groups where there is a risk that a trial could lead to an increase in terrorist attacks. This was especially the case following the ICC's indictment of Joseph Kony, the commander-in-chief of the Lord's Resistance Army (LRA) in Uganda. Following the issuance of a warrant for his arrest, the number of attacks carried out by his group increased in an attempt not only to thwart the ICC's efforts to bring him to justice but also to pressurise the Ugandan government to enter into peace talks and grant him amnesty. Nevertheless, the fundamental mandate of the ICC is to deter future crime, so states must cooperate with the Court once a situation involving a transnational terrorist group has been referred to it.

41 Broomhall (n. 39), pp. 56 and 68.

42 Daphne Josselin and William Wallace (eds), *Non-State Actors in World Politics* (Palgrave, 2001); Christyne Vachon, 'Sovereignty versus Globalization: The International Court of Justice's Advisory Opinion on the Threat or Use of Nuclear Weapons, *Denver Journal of International Law and Policy* 26 (1998) 691–724.

43 Gene Lyons and Michael Mastanduno, 'State Sovereignty and the International Intervention: Reflection on the Present and Prospects for the Future', in G. Lyons and M. Mastanduno (eds), *Beyond Westphalia? State Sovereignty and International Intervention* (John Hopkins University Press, 1995) 250, pp. 250–251; Duncan Hollis, 'Why State Consent Still Matters – Non-State Actors, Treaties and the Changing Sources of International Law', *Berkeley Journal of International Law* 23 (2005) 137–174, pp. 145–174.

44 Broomhall (n. 39), p. 58.

The dilemma with holding members of transnational terrorist groups accountable before the ICC is that the Rome Statute in its current form does not adequately capture non-state armed actors with a network-based organisational structure. So, prosecutions of members of transnational terrorist groups are highly unlikely in the near future. The lack of an explicit provision criminalising transnational terrorism in the current text of the Rome Statute is disappointing. Ensuring that such a provision is implemented would provide a more fruitful way of bringing members of transnational terrorist groups to justice for their role in perpetrating terrorist attacks than relying on the contentious parameters of Article 7. However, proposals to amend the Rome Statute have been repeatedly rejected due to a lack of a definition of terrorism and fear that it would lead to the politicisation of the ICC.[45] Yet, despite the ongoing attempts to define the term, few would contest that the ICC should play an important role in the prosecution of members of transnational terrorist groups where states are unwilling to do so. Such prosecutions would potentially have a deterrent effect by sending a message to transnational terrorist groups that even though some states may be unwilling or unable to investigate and prosecute their crimes there is a judicial mechanism at international level with the necessary resources to do so.

D Final remarks

Even though the ICC has existed for nearly 15 years, the international community has yet to take the first steps in providing an accountability mechanism for victims of transnational terrorist groups. The inclusion of a provision on terrorism in the draft Rome Statute in 1998 was of course innovative on paper, but during negotiations states decided that more time was needed to agree on a comprehensive definition of terrorism. Issues remain about the constituent elements of a proposed international crime of terrorism and how reparations would be made to victims.

The Office of the Prosecutor at the ICC has yet to launch a formal investigation into the Syria situation where there are widespread allegations that crimes have been perpetrated by members of ISIS and other non-state armed groups. An examination of other situations before the ICC reveals that the Syrian situation is not unique, as other states have not delivered justice for victims of transnational terrorist groups. The ICC and the State Parties to the Rome Statute need to reassess why this is the case; is the objective of holding those most responsible for international crimes unrealistic or mere rhetoric? This perhaps reflects the political environment both internationally and domestically which hinders the work of the ICC. For now, the ICC is only symbolic of potential justice for victims of transnational terrorist groups.

45 Assembly of State Parties to the Rome Statute of the International Criminal Court, 8th Session at Annex II, at paras. 40–51 and Appendix III at 65–66. The ILC has recommended the amendment of the Rome Statute to include the crime of terrorism. See further Article 20 of the ILC Draft Statute for an International Criminal Court.

The ICC has so far not had the opportunity to end impunity and provide justice to victims of transnational terrorist groups, but this does not mean that this can never be the case. Although there would be serious challenges facing the ICC in bringing prosecutions, innovative solutions are required to bring international criminal justice up to date by realising the accountability of members of network-based groups. The ICC cannot be expected to achieve justice for victims of these groups by utilising the Rome Statute which was drafted with only state and non-state armed actors with a clear-cut hierarchical organisational structure in mind. Key to ensuring this is for State Parties to complement the Court by including a provision that addresses the accountability of members of organisations that are network based.

This book has examined the ICC and its potential to provide justice for victims of transnational terrorist groups, and, in doing so, has made a few recommendations to bridge the gap between the two. But, due to the complexity of international crimes and the organisational structure of transnational terrorist groups, there is no remedial touchstone. The ICC is just over 15 years old: it needs to reflect on its experiences so far, not to neglect situations such as Syria, and learn how to better achieve justice for crimes committed by members of transnational terrorist groups, and end their impunity. Numerous disagreements and divergent approaches remain at the international level to address crimes by transnational terrorist groups, underlining the need for a uniform approach in the pursuit of their accountability. If we are serious about ending the impunity of transnational terrorist groups and addressing their international crimes, we have to start by outlining a legal model that takes stock of their unique organisational structure. Fundamental to this is recognising that the accountability of transnational terrorist groups begins with the state; the ICC must always be a court of last resort.

Bibliography

AdamsonF., 'International Terrorism, Non-State Actors, and Transnational Political Mobilization: A Perspective from International Relations', in T. Biersteker et al. (eds), *International Law and International Relations: Bridging Theory and Practice* (Routledge, 2006) 79–92.

AkehurstM., 'Custom as a Source', *British Yearbook of International Law* 47(1) (1975) 1–53.

AkersonD. and KnowltonN., 'President Obama and the International Criminal Law of Successor Liability', *Denver Journal of International Law and Policy* 37(2009) 615–651.

AllainA., 'The Legacy of Lockerbie: Judicial Review of the Security Council Actions or the First Manifestations of "Terrorism" as a Threat to International Peace?', *Indian Journal of International Law* 44(1) (2004) 74–112.

AllenC., 'Armed Groups and the Law', in J. Norwitz (ed.), *Armed Groups: Studies in National Security, Counterterrorism and Counterinsurgency* (US Naval College, 2008) 87–112.

AmbosK., 'Article 25: Individual Criminal Responsibility', in O. Triffterer (ed.), *Commentary on the Rome Statute of the International Criminal Court* (Oxford University Press, 2008) 743–770.

AmbosK., 'Command Responsibility and Organisationsherrschaft: Ways of Attributing International Crimes to the "Most Responsible"', in A. Nollkaemper and H. van der Wilt (eds), *System Criminality in International Law* (Cambridge University Press, 2009) 127–157.

AmbosK., 'Judicial Creativity at the Special Tribunal for Lebanon: Is There a Crime of Terrorism under International Law?', *Leiden Journal of International Law* 24 (2011) 655–675.

AmbosK., 'The First Judgment of the International Criminal Court (Prosecutor v. Lubanga): A Comprehensive Analysis of the Legal Issues', *International Criminal Law Review* 12 (2012) 115–153.

AmbosK., 'The *Fjimori* Judgment: A President's Responsibility for Crimes against humanity as Indirect Perpetrator by Virtue of an Organized Power Apparatus', *Journal of International Criminal Justice* 9 (2011) 137–158.

AmbosK., *Treatise on International Criminal Law* (Oxford University Press, 2013).

AndersonC. and McSheaD., 'Individual versus Social Complexity, with Particular Reference to Ant Colonies', *Biological Reviews of the Cambridge Philosophical Society* 76(2) (2001) 211–237.

Andreu-GueranR., 'Terrorisme et droits de l'homme', *Review of the International Commission of Jurists* (2002) 31, UN Doc.A/CONF.183/C.1/L.27.

ArceD. and SandlerT., 'An Evolutionary Game Approach to Fundamentalism and Conflict', *Journal of Institutional and Theoretical Economics* 159 (2003) 132–154.

ArendtH., 'Collective Responsibility', in J. Bernhauer (ed.), *Amor Mundi* (Nijhoff, 1987) 43–50.

ArendtH., *Eichmann in Jerusalem: A Report on the Banality of Evil* (Penguin, 2006).

ArnoldR., 'The Prosecution of Terrorism as a Crime against Humanity' (Max-Planck-Institut für ausländisches öffentliches Recht und Völkerrecht, 2004) available at: www.zaoerv.de/64_2004/64_2004_4_a_979_1000.pdf (date accessed: 14 March 2018).

ArnoldR. and TrifftererO., 'Article 28: Responsibility of Commanders and Other Superiors', in O. Triffterer (ed.), *Commentary on the Rome Statute of the International Criminal Court: Observers' Notes, Article by Article* (Hart, 2008, 2nd edn) 795. ArsanjaniM., 'The Rome Statute of the International Criminal Court', *American Journal of International Law* 93 (1999) 22–43.

AustA., *Handbook on International Law* (Cambridge University Press, 2010, 2nd edn).

BabcockH., 'Democracy's Discontent in a Complex World: Cab Avalanches Sandpiles and Finches Optimize Michael Sandel's Civic Republican Community?', *Georgetown Law Journal* 85(1996–1997) 2085–2103.

BadarM., '"Just Convict Everyone!" – Joint Perpetration: From Tadić to Stakić and Back Again', *International Criminal Law Review* 6(2006) 293–302.

BalesE., 'Torturing the Rome Statute: The Attempt to Bring Guantanamo's Detainees within the Jurisdiction of the International Criminal Court', *Tulsa Journal Comparative and International Law* 16(2009) 173–191.

BantekasI., 'The Contemporary Law of Superior Responsibility', *American Journal of International Law* 93 (1999) 573–595.

BantekasI., *Principles of Direct and Superior Responsibility in International Humanitarian Law* (Manchester University Press, 2002).

BarbozaJ., 'Liability: Can We Put Humpty-Dumpty Together Again?', *Chinese Journal of International Law* 1(2002) 499–526.

BassG., 'The Adolf Eichmann Case: Universal and National Jurisdiction', in S. Macedo (ed.), *Universal Jurisdiction: National Courts and the Prosecution of Serious Crimes under International Law* (University of Pennsylvania Press, 2004) 77–90.

BassiouniM., *Introduction to International Criminal Law* (Martinus Nijhoff, 2013, 2nd edn).

BassiouniM., 'Legal Control of International Terrorism: A Policy-Oriented Assessment', *Harvard International Law Journal* 43 (2002) 83–104.

BasuchoudharyA. and ShughartW., 'On Ethnic Conflict and the Origins of Transnational Terrorism', *Defence and Peace Economics* (2010) 65–87.

BeckC., 'The Contribution of Social Movement Theory to Understanding Terrorism', *Sociology Compass* 2(2008) 1565–1581.

BeckT., *The Normality of Civil War: Armed Groups and Everyday Life in Angola* (Campus, 2012).

BeckerT., *Terrorism and the State: Rethinking the Rules of State Responsibility* (Hart, 2006).

BeinhockerE., *The Origin of Wealth: Evolution, Complexity and the Radical Remaking of Economics* (Random House, 2006).

BellJ., *A Time of Terror: How Democratic Societies Respond to Revolutionary Violence* (Basic Books, 1978).

BellaD., 'Emergence and Evil', *Emergence: Complexity and Organization* 8(2) (2006) 102–115.

BellalA., 'Establishing the Direct Responsibility of Non-State Armed Groups for Violations of International Norms: Issues of Attribution', in N. Gal-Or, M. Noortmann, and

C. Ryngaert (eds), *Responsibilities of the Non-State Actor in Armed Conflict: Theoretical Considerations and Empirical Findings* (Brill, 2014) 304–322.

BellalA., 'The 2009 Resolution of the Institute of international Law on Immunity and International Crimes', *Journal of International Criminal Justice* 9(2011) 227–241.

BellalA. and Casey-MaslenS., 'Enhancing Compliance with International Law by Armed Non-State Actors', *Goettingen Journal of International Law* 3(1) (2011) 175–197.

BernholzP., 'International Political System, Supreme Values and Terrorism', *Public Choice* 128 (2006) 221–231.

BettiS., 'The Duty to Bring Terrorists to Justice and Discretionary Prosecution', *Journal of International Criminal Justice* 4(5) (2006) 1104–1116.

BianchiA. (ed.), *Enforcing International Law Norms against Terrorism* (Hart, 2004).

BianchiA., 'Security Council's Anti-Terror Resolutions and their Implementation by Member States', *Journal of International Criminal Justice* 4(2006) 1044–1073.

BianchiA. and NaqviY., *International Humanitarian Law and Terrorism* (Hart, 2011).

BilkovaV., 'Armed Opposition Groups and Shared Responsibility', *Netherlands International Law Review* 62(2015) 69–89.

BilskyL., 'The Eichmann Trial and the Legacy of Jurisdiction', in S. Benhabib (ed.), *Politics in Dark Times: Encounters with Hannah Arendt* (Cambridge University Press, 2010) 198–218.

BittiG. and Gonzalez Rivas G., 'The Reparations Provisions for Victims under the Rome Statute of the International Criminal Court', in International Court of Arbitration (ed.), *Redressing Injustices through Mass Claims Processes, Innovative Responses to Unique Challenges* (Oxford University Press, 2006) 299–322.

BohlanderM., *Principles of German Criminal Law* (Hart, 2009).

BonafeB., 'Command Responsibility between Personal Culpability and Objective Liability: Finding a Proper Role for Command Responsibility', *Journal of International Criminal Justice* 5(3) (2007) 599–618.

BoyleK., *A Voice for Human Rights: Mary Robinson* (University of Philadelphia Press, 2006).

BrandJ., 'Crimes against Humanity and the Nuremburg Trials', *Oregon Law Review* 28 (1949) 93–119.

BrennanA., 'Exploring the Accountability of Leaders of Armed Opposition Groups under International Law', *The Hague Yearbook of International Law* 23 (2010) 223–268.

BroomhallB., *International Justice and the International Criminal Court* (Oxford University Press, 2003).

BrownB., 'U.S. Objections to the Statute of the International Criminal Court: A Brief Response', *New York Journal of International Law and Policy* 31(1999) 855–891.

BrownmanR., 'Lubanga, the DRC and the African Court: Lessons Learnt from the First International Criminal Court Case', *African Human Rights Law Journal* 7(2007) 412–445.

Brown WeissE., 'Invoking State Responsibility in the Twenty-First Century', *American Journal of International Law* 96 (2002) 798–816.

BrunnéeJ., 'International Legal Accountability Through the Lens of the Law of State Responsibility', *Netherlands Yearbook of International Law* 36(1) (2005) 21–56.

BryneD., *Complexity and the Social Sciences: An Introduction* (Routledge, 1998).

BurgoonB., 'On Welfare and Terror: Social Welfare Policies and Political–Economic Roots of Terrorism', *Journal of Conflict Resolution* 50(2) (2008) 176–203.

CarlineA. and PearsonZ., 'Complexity and Queer Theory Approaches to International Law and Feminist Politics: Perspectives on Trafficking', *Canadian Journal of Women and the Law* 19 (2007) 73–118.

CarnahanB., 'Lincoln, Lieber and the Laws of War: The Origins and Limits of the Principle of Military Necessity', *American Journal of International Law* 92 (1998) 213–231.

CasselD., 'Corporate Aiding and Abetting of Human Rights Violations: Confusion in the Courts', *Northwestern University Journal of International Human Rights Law* 6 (2008) 304–326.

CasseseA., 'On the Use of Criminal Law Nations in Determining State Responsibility for Genocide', *Journal of International Criminal Justice* 5 (2007) 875–887.

CasseseA., 'Terrorism as an International Crime', in A. Bianchi and Y. Naqvi (eds), *Enforcing International Law Norms Against Terrorism* (Hart, 2004) 213–225.

CasseseA., 'Terrorism Is also Disrupting Some Crucial Legal Categories of International Law', *European Journal of International Law* 12(2001) 993–1001.

CasseseA., 'The Multifaceted Criminal Notion of Terrorism in International Law', *Journal of International Criminal Justice* 4 (2006) 933–958.

CasseseA., 'The Proper Limits of Individual Responsibility under the Doctrine of Joint Criminal Enterprise', *Journal of International Criminal Justice* 5 (2007) 109–133.

CasseseA., 'The Status of Rebels under the 1977 Geneva Protocol on Non-International Armed Conflicts', *International and Comparative Legal Quarterly* 30 (1981) 416–439.

CastellsM., *The Information Age: Economy, Society and Culture: Vol. 1: The Rise of the Network Society* (Blackwell, 2000, 2nd edn).

CharneyJ., 'The Persistent Objector Rule and the Development of Customary International Law', *British Yearbook of International Law* 56 (1985) 1–24.

ChinenM., 'Complexity Theory and the Horizontal and Vertical Dimensions of State Responsibility', *European Journal of International Law* 25(3) (2014) 703–732.

ChingA., 'Evolution of the Command Responsibility Doctrine in Light of the *Čelebići* Decision of the International Criminal Tribunal for the Former Yugoslavia', *North Carolina Journal of International Law and Commercial Regulation* 25 (1999) 167–205.

ChristopherR. (ed.), *Fletcher's Essays on Criminal Law* (Oxford University Press, 2013) 269.

ClaphamA., 'Extending International Criminal Responsibility beyond Individuals to Corporations and Armed Opposition Groups', *Journal of International Criminal Justice* 6 (2008) 899–926.

ClaphamA., 'Non-State Actors', in D. Moeckli et al. (eds), *International Human Rights Law* (Oxford University Press, 2013, 2nd edn) 561–582.

ClarkR., 'Drafting a General Part to a Penal Code: Some Thoughts Inspired by the Negotiations on the Rome Statute of the International Criminal Court and by the Court's First Substantive Law Discussion in the Lubanga Dyilo Confirmation Proceedings', *Criminal Law Forum* 19(3–4) (2008) 519–552.

ClarkR., 'Elements of Crimes in Early Decisions of Pre-Trial Chambers of the International Criminal Court', *New Zealand Yearbook of International Law* (2008) 209.

CombsN., *Fact-Finding without Facts* (Cambridge University Press, 2010).

ComerfordR., *The Fenians in Context: Irish Politics and Society: 1848–82* (Wolfhound Press, 1985).

ConnollyW., *The Terms of Political Discourse* (D. C. Heath, 1974).

CoppD., 'What Collectives Are: Agency, Individualism and Legal Theory', *Dialogue* 23 (1984) 249–269.

CornG., 'Hamdan, Lebanon and the Regulation of Hostilities: The Need to Recognise a Hybrid Category of Armed Conflict', *Vanderbilt Journal of Transnational Law* 40(2) (2007) 295–355.

CornG. and TalbotJ., 'Transnational Armed Conflict: A "Principled" Approach to the Regulation of Counter-Terror Combat Operations', *Israel Law Review* 42(1) (2009) 46–79.

CrawfordJ., *I. Brownlie: Principles of International Law* (Oxford University Press, 2012, 8th edn).

CrawfordJ., *The Creation of States in International Law* (Cambridge University Press, 2006, 2nd edn).

CrawfordJ., *The Law of International Responsibility* (Oxford University Press, 2010).

CroninA., 'Behind the Curve: Globalisation and International Terrorism', *International Security* 27(3) (2002–2003) 30–58.

CroweB., 'Command Responsibility in the Former Yugoslavia: The Chances for Successful Prosecution', *University of Richmond Law Review* 29 (1994) 191–233.

CryerR., 'The Ad Hoc Tribunals and the Law of Command Responsibility: A Quiet Earthquake', in S. Darcy and J. Powderly (eds), *Judicial Creativity at the International Criminal Tribunals* (Oxford University Press, 2010) 159–183.

CryerR. and WilmhurstE., 'Introduction: What Is International Criminal Law?', in R. Cryer et al. (eds), *An Introduction to International Criminal Law and Procedure* (Oxford University Press, 2010) 1–21.

D'AmatoA., *The Concept of Custom in International Law* (Cornell University Press, 1971).

DamaskaM., 'The Shadow Side of Command Responsibility', *American Journal of Comparative Law* 49 (2001) 455–496.

DamgaardC., *Individual Criminal Responsibility for Core International Crimes* (Springer, 2008).

DannerA. and MartinezJ., 'Guilty Associations: Joint Criminal Enterprise, Command Responsibility, and the Development of International Criminal Law', *California Law Review* 93 (2005) 75–169.

DarcyS., *Collective Responsibility and Accountability under International Law* (Brill, 2007).

LevinsonD., 'Collective Sanctions', *Stanford Law Review* 56 (2003) 345–428.

DavenportC., 'Human Rights and the Democratic Proposition', *Journal of Conflict Resolution* 43(1) (1999) 92–116.

de BrichambautM., 'The Role of the United Nations Security Council in the International Legal System', in M. Byers (ed.), *The Role of International Law in International Politics* (Oxford University Press, 2001) 269–276.

de GuzmanM., 'Article 21', in O. Trifterrer (ed.), *Commentary on the Rome Statute of the International Criminal Court: Observers' Notes, Article by Article* (Hart, 2008, 2nd edn) 932–948.

de LondrasF., 'Terrorism as an International Crime', in W. Schabas and N. Bernaz (eds), *Routledge International Book of Criminal Law* (Routledge, 2010) 169–180.

de MesquitaE., 'Conciliation, Counterterrorism and Patterns of Terrorist Violence', *International Organization* 59(1) (2005) 145–176.

De PreuxP. et al., *Commentary on the Additional Protocols of 8 June 1977 to the Geneva Conventions of 12 August 1949* (International Committee of the Red Cross, 1987).

Di FiliippoM., 'Terrorist Crimes and International Co-operation: Critical Remarks on the Definition and Inclusion of Terrorism in the Category of International Crimes', *European Journal of International Law* 19(3) (2008) 533–570.

DickinsonL., 'Using Legal Process to Fight Terrorism: Detentions, Military Commissions, International Tribunals and the Rule of Law', *Southern California Law Review* 75 (2001) 1407–1492.

DixonM. and McCorquodaleR., *Cases and Materials in International Law* (Oxford University Press, 2011, 5th edn).

DixonR., 'Prosecuting the Leaders: The Application of the Doctrine of Superior Responsibility before the United Nations International Criminal Tribunals for the Former

Yugoslavia and Rwanda', in A. Vogelaar et al., *NL Arms Netherlands Annual Review of Military Studies* (Gianotten, 1998) 109.

Donnedieu de VabresH., 'La répression internationale du terrorisme – Les conventions de Genève (16 Nov. 1937)', *Revue de droit international et législation comparée* 62(1938) 45.

DonohueL., 'Terrorism and Counter-Terrorist Discourse', in V. Ramraj, M. Hor, and K. Roach (eds), *Global Anti-Terrorism Law and Policy* (Cambridge University Press, 2005) 13–36.

DownesC., 'Targeted Killings in an Age of Terror: The Legality of the Yemen Strike', *Journal of Conflict and Security Law* 9(2) (2004) 277–294.

DowningW. and MeeseM., *Harmony and Disharmony – Exploiting Al-Qaeda's Organizational Vulnerabilities* (United States Military Academy, 2006).

DruckerP., 'Introduction', in A. Sloan, *My Years with General Motors* (Doubleday, 1963).

DrumblM., 'Collective Responsibility and Post-Conflict Justice', in IsaacsT. and VernonR. (eds), *Accountability for Collective Wrongdoing* (Cambridge University Press, 2011) 23–60.

DrumblM., 'Collective Violence and Individual Punishment: The Criminality of Mass Atrocity', *Northwestern University Law Review* 99 (2005) 539–610.

DrumblM., 'Judging the 11 September Terrorist Attack', *Human Rights Quarterly* 24 (2002) 323–360.

DungelJ. and GhadiriS., 'The Temporal Scope of Command Responsibility Revisited: Why Commanders Have a Duty to Prevent Crimes Committed after the Cessation of Effective Control', *University of California Davis Journal of International Law & Policy* 17 (2010) 1–40.

EldarS., 'Exploring International Criminal Law's Reluctance to Resort to Modalities of Groups Responsibility: Five Challenges to International Prosecutions and their Impact on Broader Forms of Responsibility', *Journal of International Criminal Justice* 11 (2013) 331–349.

EserA., 'Individual Criminal Responsibility', in A. Cassese, P. Gaeta, and J. Jones (eds), *The Rome Statute of the International Criminal Court: A Commentary: Vol. 1* (Oxford University Press, 2002) 767–797.

EubankW. and WeinbergL., 'Terrorism and Democracy: Perpetrators and Victims: Terrorism and Political', *Violence* 13(1) (2001) 155–164.

Evans A. and J. Murphy (eds), *Legal Aspects of International Terrorism* (American Society of International Law, 1978).

EvansM., *International Law* (Oxford University Press, 2010, 5th edn).

FanM., 'Visionary Legal Construction: Custom, General Principles and the Great Architect Cassese', *Journal of International Criminal Justice* 10 (2012) 1063–1079.

FassbenderB., 'Reflections on the International Legality of the Special Tribunal for Lebanon', *Journal of International Criminal Justice* 5(5) (2007) 1091–1105.

FeinbergJ., 'Collective Responsibility', in J. Feinberg (ed.), *Doing and Deserving: Essays in the Theory of Responsibility* (Princeton University Press, 1970) 222–251.

Fernández-SánchezP. (ed.), *International Legal Dimension of Terrorism* (Nijhoff, 2009).

FletcherG., 'New Court, Old Dogmatik', *Journal of International Criminal Justice* 9 (2011) 179–190.

FletcherG., *Rethinking Criminal Law* (Oxford University Press, 2000).

FletcherG., 'The Storrs Lectures: Liberals and Romantics at War: The Problem of Collective Guilt', *Yale Law Journal* 111 (2002) 1499–1573.

FootR., 'The United Nations, Counter Terrorism, and Human Rights: Institutional Adaptation and Embedded Ideas', *Human Rights Quarterly* 29 (2007) 489–514.

FoxC., 'Closing a Loophole in Accountability for War Crimes: Successor Commanders' Duty to Punish Known Past Offences', *Case Western Reserve Law Review* 55 (2004) 443–500.

FrancoA., 'Armed Non-State Actors', in D. Malone (ed.), *The UN Security Council: From Cold War to the 21st Century* (Lynne Rienner, 2004) 117.

FrederickW., 'Emergent Management Morality: Explaining Corporate Corruption', *Emergence* 5(1) (2003) 5–35.

FreestoneD., 'International Cooperation against Terrorism and the Development of International Law Principles of Jurisdiction', in R. Higgins and M. Flory (eds), *Terrorism and International Law* (Routledge, 1997) 50.

FrenchP., *Collective and Corporate Responsibility* (Columbia University Press, 1984)

FresardJ. -J., *The Roots of Behaviour in War: A Survey of the Literature* (International Committee of the Red Cross, 2004).

FreyB. et al., 'Calculating Tragedy: Assessing the Costs of Terrorism', *Journal of Economic Surveys* 21(1) (2007) 1–24.

FreytagA., KrügerJ., MeierrieksD., and SchneiderF., 'The Origins of Terrorism: Cross-Country Estimates on Socio-Economic Determinants of Terrorism' (CIE Working Paper 2009–01, University of Paderborn, 2008).

FrolichR., 'Prosecutor v. Callixte Mbarushimana: Judgment on the Appeal of the Prosecutor against the Decision of Pre-Trial Chamber I of 16 December 2011 Entitled "Decision on the Confirmation of Charges": Introductory Note', *International Legal Materials* 52(2) (2013) 417–439.

FroweinJ., 'De facto Regime', *EPIL* 1 (1992) 966.

GaetaP. (ed.), *A. Cassese: International Criminal Law* (Oxford University Press, 2013).

GaetaP., 'Genocide d'état et responsabilité pénale individuelle', *Revue general de droit international public* 111 (2007) 272.

GaetaP., 'International Criminalisation of Prohibited Conduct', in A. Cassese (ed.), *The Oxford Companion to International Criminal Justice* (Oxford University Press, 2009) 63–74.

GanorB., 'Terrorism as a Strategy of Psychological Warfare', in Y. Danieli et al. (eds), *The Trauma of Terrorism: Sharing Knowledge and Shared Care: An International Handbook* (Haworth Press, 2013) 33.

GarvenJ., 'Les crimes l'humanité', *Recueil des cours* 76 (1950–1951) 433–607.

GasserH., 'Armed Conflict within the Territory of a State', in W. Haller et al. (eds), *Im Dienst and der Gemeinschaft* (Helbing und Lichtenhahn, 1989).

GeartyC., 'The Superpatriotic Fervour of the Moment', *Oxford Journal of Legal Studies* 28 (1) (2008) 183–200.

GeigerR., 'The German Border Guard Cases and International Human Rights', *European Journal of International Law* 9 (1998) 540–549.

GerlachL., 'Protest Movements and the Construction of Risk', in B. Johnson and V. Costello (eds), *The Social and Cultural Construction of Risk: Essays on Risk Selection and Perception* (Reidel, 1987) 103–145.

GerlachL. and HineV., *People, Power, Change: Movements of Social Transformation* (Bobbs-Merrill, 1970).

GilbertN. (ed.), *Researching Social Life* (Sage, 2001, 2nd edn).

Giles-CarneroR., 'Terrorist Acts as Threats to International Peace and Security', in P. Fernández-Sanchez (ed.), *International Legal Dimension of Terrorism* (Martinus Nijhoff, 2009) 55–71.

GilletM. and SchusterM., 'Fast Track Justice: The Special Tribunal for Lebanon Defines Terrorism', *Journal of International Criminal Justice* 9 (2011) 989–1020.

GoldrickD., *From '9–11' to the 'Iraq War 2003': International Law in an Age of Complexity* (Hart, 2004).

GoldstoneJ., 'Towards a Fourth Generation of Revolutionary Theory', *Annual Review of Political Science* 4(1) (2001) 139–187.

GoldstoneR. and SimpsonJ., 'Evaluating the Role of the International Criminal Court as a Legal Response to Terrorism', *Harvard Human Rights Journal* 16 (2003) 13–26.

GrafR., 'The International Criminal Court and Child Soldiers: An Appraisal of the *Lubanga* Judgment', *Journal of International Criminal Justice* 10 (2012) 945–969.

GreenL., 'Command Responsibility in International Humanitarian Law', *Transnational Law and Contemporary Problems* 3 (1995) 354.

GreenL., *The Contemporary Law of Armed Conflict* (Manchester University Press, 1993).

GreenwoodC., 'Command Responsibility and the *Hadžihasanović* Decision', *Journal of International Criminal Justice* 2 (2004) 598–605.

GreenwoodC., 'Scope of Application of Humanitarian Law', in D. Fleck (ed.), *The Handbook of Humanitarian Law in Armed Conflict* (Oxford University Press, 2007, 2nd edn) 45–78.

GuevaraE., *Guerrilla Warfare* (University of Nebraska Press, 1985).

GunaratnaR., *Inside Al Qaeda: Global Network of Terror* (Hurst, 2002).

GurrT., 'The Political Origins of State Violence and Terror: A Theoretical Analysis', in M. Stohl and G. Lopez (eds), *Government Violence and Repression: An Agenda for Research* (Greenwood, Press, 1986) 45–71.

GurrT., *Why Men Rebel* (Princeton University Press, 1970).

GutjahrW., 'First Steps to the Runtime Complexity Analysis of Ant Colony Optimization', *Computers and Operations Research* 35(9) (2008) 2711–2727.

HaerR., *Armed Group Structure and Violence in Civil Wars: The Organizational Dynamics of Group Killing* (Routledge, 2015).

HallingM., 'Push the Envelope Watch It Bend: Removing the Policy Requirement and Extending Crimes against Humanity', *Leiden Journal of International Law* 23(4) (2010) 827–845.

HardinG., 'The Tragedy of the Commons', *Science* 162 (1968) 1243–1248.

HeldV., 'Can a Random Collection of Random Individuals be Morally Responsible?', *Journal of Philosophy* 67 (1970) 471–481.

HeymannP., *Terrorism and America: A Common-Sense Strategy for a Democratic Society* (MIT Press, 1998).

HigginsR. and FloryM. (eds), *Terrorism and International Law* (Routledge, 1997).

HobsbawmE., *The Age of Capital: 1848–1875* (Vintage, 1996).

HoffmanB., 'The Confluence of International and Domestic Trends in Terrorism', *Terrorism and Political Violence* 9(2) (1997) 1–15.

HoffmanB., *Inside Terrorism* (Columbia University Press, 1998).

HolaB. et al., 'International Sentencing Facts and Figures: Sentencing Practice at the ICTY and ICTR', *Journal of International Criminal Justice* 9 (2011) 411–439.

HollisD., 'Why State Consent Still Matters – Non-State Actors, Treaties and the Changing Sources of International Law', *Berkeley Journal of International Law* 23 (2005) 137–174.

HwangP., 'Defining Crimes Against Humanity in the Rome Statute of the International Criminal Court', *Fordham International Law Journal* 22 (1998) 457–504.

InnesJ. and BooherD., 'Consensus Building and Complex Adaptive Systems: A Framework for Evaluating Collaborative Planning', *Journal of the American Planning Association* 65 (4) (1999) 412–423.

JainN., 'The Control Theory of Perpetration in International Criminal Law', *Chicago Journal of International Law* 12(1) (2011) 157–200.

JallohC., 'What Makes a Crime against Humanity a Crime against Humanity', *American University International Law Review* (2013) 381–441.

JenningsR. and Watts, A. (eds), *Oppenheim's International Law* (Longman, 1992, 9th edn).

JiaB., 'The Doctrine of Command Responsibility Revisited', *Chinese Journal of International Law* 3 (2004) 1–42.

JohnsF., 'Guantanamo Bay and the Annihilation of the Exception', *European Journal of International Law* 16(4) (2005) 613–635.

JonesG., 'Dynamical Jurisprudence: Law as a Complex System', *Georgia State University Law Review* 24 (2008) 884–911.

JonesS., 'The Changing Nature of Jemaah Islamiyah', *Australian Journal of International Affairs* 59(2) (2005) 169–178.

JosselinD. and WallaceW. (eds), *Non-State Actors in World Politics* (Palgrave, 2001).

JuarreroA., 'On Philosophy's "to Rethink" List: Causality, Explanation and Ethic', *Ecological Psychology* 20 (2008) 278–282.

JurovicsY., 'Article 7: crimes contre l'humanité', in J. Fernandez and X. Pacreau (eds), *Statut de Rome de la Cour pénale international: commentaire article par article* (Pedone 2012) 417–478.

Kahn-FreundO., 'Comparative Law as an Academic Subject', *Law Quarterly Review* 82 (1966) 40–61.

KaldorM., *New and Old Wars: Organised Violence in a Global Era* (Stanford University Press, 1999).

KammerfhoferJ., 'The Uncertainty in the Formal Source of International Law: Customary International Law and Some of Its Problems', *European Journal of International Law* 15 (2004) 523–553.

KaplanJ., 'Leaderless Resistance', *Terrorism and Political Violence* 9(3) (1997) 80–95.

KastF. and RosenzweigJ., 'General Systems Theory: Applications for Organizations and Management', *Academic of Management Journal* 15(4) (1972) 446–466.

KauffmanS., *At Home in the Universe: The Search for Laws of Self-Organization and Complexity* (Viking, 1995).

KauffmanS., *The Origins of Order: Self-Organization and Selection in Evolution* (Oxford University Press, 1993).

KeijzerN., 'Terrorism as a Crime', in W. Heere (ed.), *Terrorism and the Military: International Legal Implications* (Asser Press, 2003) 115–132.

KellyE., 'Reparative Justice', in IsaacsT. and VernonR. (eds), *Accountability for Collective Wrongdoing* (Cambridge University Press, 2011) 193–209.

KelsenH., 'Collective and Individual Responsibility for Acts of State in International Law', *Jewish Yearbook of International Law* 1 (1948) 226.

KelsenH., 'Collective and Individual Responsibility in International Law with Particular Regard to the Punishment of War Criminals', *California Law Review* 31(5) (1942) 530–571.

KelsenH., *The Law of the United Nations: A Critical Analysis of its Fundamental Problems* (Law Book Exchange, 2000).

KeohaneR. and NyeJ., 'World Politics and the International Economic System', in C. Bergsten (ed.), *The Future of the International Economic Order: An Agenda for Research* (Lexington Books, 1973) 115–179.

KilcullenD., 'Counter-Insurgency Redux', *Survival: Global Politics and Strategy* 48 (2006) 111–130.

KirschS. and OehmichenA., 'Judges Gone Astray', *Durham Law Review* 1 (2011) 1–20.

KittichaisareeK., *International Criminal Law* (Oxford University Press, 2001).

Kleffner, J. 'The Collective Accountability of Organized Armed Groups in System Crimes', in A. Nollkaemper, and H. van der Wilt (eds), *System Criminality in International Law* (Cambridge University Press, 2009) 238–269.

KleinP., 'Le droit international à l'épreuve du terrorisme', *Recueil des cours* 321 (2006) 203.

KohH., 'The Case against Military Commissions', *American Journal of International Law* 96 (2002) 337–344.

KolbR., 'Universal Criminal Jurisdiction in Matters of International Terrorism: Some Reflections on Statutes and Trends in Contemporary International Law', *Revue hellenique droit international* 1 (1997) 43–88.

KontorovichE., 'A Guantanamo on the Sea': The Difficulty of Prosecuting Pirates and Terrorists', *California Law Review* 98(1) (2010) 243–276.

KovacsP., 'La Société des Nations et son action après l'attentat contre Alexandre, roi de Yougoslavie', *Journal of the History of International Law* 6 (2004) 65–77.

KrebC., 'Some Reflections on the International Legal Framework Governing Transnational Armed Conflicts', *Journal of Conflict and Security Law* 15 (2010) 245–274.

KreigerT. and MeierricksD., 'What Causes Terrorism?', *Public Choice* 147 (2011) 3–27.

KressC., 'International Criminal Law', in R. Wolfman (ed.), *The Max Planck Encyclopaedia of Public International Law* (2008), available at www.mpwpil.com, at paras 6ff. (date accessed: 14 March 2018).

KruegerA. and MaleckovaJ., 'Education, Poverty and Terrorism: Is there a Causal Connection?', *Journal of Economic Perspectives* 17(4) (2003) 119–144.

Kurrild-KlitgaardP., JustesenM., and KlemmensenP., 'The Political Economy of Freedom, Democracy and Transnational Terrorism', *Public Choice* 128 (2006) 289–315.

KurthM., 'The *Lubanga* Case of the International Criminal Court: A Critical Analysis of the Trial Chamber's Findings on Issues of Active Use, Age and Gravity', *Goettingen Journal of International Law* 5 (2013) 431–453.

KutzC., *Complicity: Ethics and Law for a Collective Age* (Cambridge University Press, 2000).

LambertJ., *Terrorism and Hostages in International Law: A Commentary on the Hostages Convention 1979* (Grotius, 1990).

LandsmanS., 'The Eichmann Case and the Invention of the Witness-Driven Atrocity Trial', *Columbia Journal of Transnational Law* 51 (2012) 69–119.

LaqueurW., *No End to War: Terrorism in the Twenty-First Century* (Bloomsbury, 2003).

LauterpachtH., *The Development of International Law by the International Court* (Cambridge University Press, 1958).

LawlessM., 'Terrorism: An International Crime', *International Law Journal* 63 (2007–2008) 139.

LeeR. et al. (eds), *The International Criminal Court: Elements of Crimes and Rules of Procedure and Evidence* (Transnational, 2001).

LejbowiczA., *Philosophie du droit international: l'impossible capture de l'humanité* (PUF, 1999).

LevinS., *Fragile Dominion: Complexity and the Commons* (Perseus, 1999).

LevinsonD., 'Collective Sanctions', *Stanford Law Review* 56 (2003) 345–428.

LevinsonS., 'Responsibility for Crimes of War', in CohenM. et al. (eds), *War and Moral Responsibility* (Princeton University Press, 1974) 104–133.

LieflanderT., 'The *Lubanga* Judgment at the ICC', *Cambridge Journal of International and Comparative Law* 1 (2012) 191–212.

LippmanM., 'Humanitarian Law: The Uncertain Contours of Command Responsibility', *Tulsa Journal of Comparative and International Law* 9 (2001) 1–93.

LippmanM., 'The New Terrorism and International Law', *Tulsa Journal of Comparative and International Law* 10 (2003) 297.

LivingstonN., *The War against Terrorism* (Heath Lexington, 1982).

Luban, D., 'Fairness to Rightness: Jurisdiction, Legality, and the Legitimacy of International Criminal Law', in S. Besson and J. Tasioulas (eds), *The Philosophy of International Law* (Oxford University Press, 2010) 569–588.

LukesS., *Power: A Radical View* (Palgrave Macmillan, 2005, 2nd edn).

LyonsG. and MastandunoM., 'State Sovereignty and the International Intervention: Reflection on the Present and Prospects for the Future', in G. Lyons and M. Mastanduno (eds), *Beyond Westphalia? State Sovereignty and International Intervention* (John Hopkins University Press, 1995) 228–249.

LyonsG., BaldwinD., and McNemarD., 'The Politicization Issue in the UN Specialized Agencies', in D. Kay (ed.), *The Changing United Nations: Options for the United States* (Praeger, 1977) 81–92.

McAdamD., *Political Process and the Development of Black Insurgency: 1930–1970* (University of Chicago Press, 1982).

McConnellL., *Extracting Accountability from Non-State Actors in International Law* (Routledge, 2011) 169–192.

McDougalH. et al. (eds), *Studies in World Public Order* (Yale University Press, 1960).

McKeyF., 'U.S. Unilateralism and International Crimes: The International Criminal Court and Terrorism', *Cornell International Law Journal* 36 (2004) 455–471.

MacGibbonI., 'Customary International Law and Acquiescence', *British Yearbook of International Law* 33 (1957) 115–145.

MainzerK., *Thinking in Complexity: The Computational Dynamics of Matter, Mind and Mankind* (Springer, 1997, 5th edn)

MalleB., 'The Social and Moral Cognition of Group Agents', *Journal of Law and Policy* 19 (1) (2010) 95–136.

Maloney-DunnK., 'Humanizing Terrorism through International Criminal Law: Equal Justice for Victims, Fair Treatment of Suspects, and Fundamental Human Rights at the ICC', *Santa Clara Journal of International Law* 8 (2010) 69–86.

ManacordaS., 'The Principle of Individual Criminal Responsibility: A Conceptual Framework', *Journal of International Criminal Justice* 5 (2007) 913–916.

ManacordaS. and MeloniC., 'Indirect Perpetration versus Joint Criminal Enterprise: Concurring Approaches in the Practice of International Criminal Law?', *Journal of International Criminal Justice* 9 (2011) 159–178.

MannI., 'The Dual Foundation of Universal Jurisdiction: Towards a Jurisprudence for the Court of Critique', *Transnational Legal Theory* 1(4) (2010) 485–521.

MansonS., 'Simplifying Complexity: A Review of Complexity Theory', *Geoforum* 32 (2001) 405–414.

MantovaniF., 'The General Principles of International Criminal Law: The Viewpoint of a National Criminal Lawyer', *Journal of International Criminal Justice* 1 (2003) 26–38.

MaotogoJ., 'Countering Terrorism: From Wigged Judges to Helmeted Soldiers – Legal Perspectives in America's Counter-Terrorism Responses', *San Diego International Law Journal* 6 (2005) 243–294.

MarighellaC., *Mini-Manual of the Urban Guerrilla* (Paladin, 1975), available at: www.marxists.org/archive/marighella-carlos/1969/06/minimanual-urban-guerrilla (date accessed: 14 March 2018).

MarinielloT., '*Prosecutor* v. *Thomas Lubanga Dyilo*: The First Judgment of the International Criminal Court's Trial Chamber', *International Criminal Law Review* 12 (2012) 137–147.

MarschikA., 'The Security Council's Role: Problems and Prospects in the Fight against Terrorism', in G. Nesi (ed.), *International Cooperation in Counter-Terrorism: The United Nations and Regional Organisations in the Fight against Terrorism* (Ashgate, 2006) 69–80.

MarstonG., 'Early Attempts to Suppress Terrorism: The Terrorism and International Criminal Court Conventions of 1937', *British Yearbook of International Law* 73 (2002) 293–313.

MartinB., 'Can Moral Responsibility be Collective and Non-Distributive? Social Theory and Practice', 4 (1976) 93–106.

MartinJ., *Les règles internationales relatives à la lutte contre le terrorisme* (Bruylant, 2006).

MartinezL., 'Prosecuting Terrorists at the International Criminal Court: Possibilities and Problems', *Rutgers Law Journal* 34 (2002) 1–62.

MartingeR., *Global War on Terrorism* (Centre for Strategic and Budgetary Assessments, 2008).

MayL., 'Collective Punishment and Mass Confinement', in T. Isaacs and R. Vernon (eds), *Accountability for Collective Wrongdoing* (Cambridge University Press, 2011).

MégretF., 'The Case for a General International Crime against the Environment', in S. Jodoin and M. Cordonier Segger (eds), *Sustainable Development, International Criminal Justice and Treaty Implementation* (Cambridge University Press, 2013) 50.

MeloniC., 'Command Responsibility: Mode of Liability for the Crimes of Subordinates or Separate Offence of the Superior?', *Journal of International Criminal Justice* 5 (2007) 619–637.

MelzerN., *Interpretive Guidance on the Notion of Direct Participation in Hostilities under International Humanitarian Law* (International Committee of the Red Cross, 2009).

MeronT., 'Revival of Customary Humanitarian Law', *American Journal of International Law* 99 (2005) 817–834.

MettrauxG., *International Crimes and the Ad Hoc Tribunals* (Oxford University Press, 2005).

MettrauxG., *The Law of Command Responsibility* (Oxford University Press, 2009).

MilanovićM., 'Is the Rome Statute Binding on Individuals? (And Why Should We Care)', *Journal of International Criminal Justice* 9(1) (2011) 25–52.

MillerS., 'Collective Moral Responsibility: An Individualist Account', *Midwest Studies in Philosophy* 30 (2006) 176–193.

MitchellA., 'Failure to Halt, Prevent or Punish: The Doctrine of Command Responsibility for War Crimes', *Sydney Law Review* 22 (2000) 381–410.

MitchellM., *Complexity: A Guided Tour* (Oxford University Press, 2009) 13.

MolotoB., 'Command Responsibility in International Criminal Tribunals', *Publicist* 3 (2009) 12–25.

MorrisM., 'Arresting Terrorism: Criminal Jurisdiction and International Relations', in A. Bianchi and Y. Naqvi (eds), *Enforcing International Law Norms against Terrorism* (Hart, 2004) 65.

MuchC., 'The International Criminal Court (ICC) and Terrorism as an International Crime', *Michigan State Journal of International Law* 14 (2006) 121–138.

MulajK. (ed.), *Violent Non-State Actors in World Politics* (Columbia University Press, 2010).

MundisD., 'The Use of Military Commissions to Prosecute Individuals Accused of Terrorist Acts', *American Journal of International Law* 96 (2002) 320–328.

MurrayD., *Human Rights Obligations of Non-State Armed Groups* (Hart, 2016).

NagleL., 'Terrorism and Universal Jurisdiction: Opening a Pandora's Box?', *Georgia State University Law Review* 27 (2011) 339–378.

NerlichV., 'Superior Responsibility under Article 28 ICC Statute: For What Exactly is the Superior Held Responsible?', *Journal of International Criminal Justice* 5 (2007) 665–682.

NisselA., 'Review of Tal Becker, Terrorism and the State: Rethinking the Rules of State Responsibility', *Journal of International Criminal Justice* 5 (2007) 245–249.

NiworuS., 'Boko Haram Sects: Terrorists or a Manifestation of the Failed Nigerian State', *Journal of Politics and Law* 245–250.

NohriaN. et al. (eds), *Networks and Organizations: Structure, Form and Action* (Harvard Business School, 1992).

NorbergN., 'Terrorism and International Criminal Justice: Dim Prospects for a Future Together', *Santa Clara Journal of International Law* 8 (2010) 11–50.

O'BrienB., *Long War: IRA and Sinn Féin 1985 to Today* (Syracuse University Press, 1999).

O'BroinL., *Revolutionary Underground: The Story of the Irish Republican Brotherhood: 1858–1924* (Gill & Macmillan, 1976).

O'ConnellM.-E., 'Enhancing the Status of Non-State Actors through a Global War on Terror?', *Columbia Journal of Transnational Law* 43 (2005) 435–458.

OhlinJ. et al., 'Assessing Control Theory', *Leiden Journal of International Law* 26(3) (2013) 725–746.

OhlinJ., 'Co-perpetration: German Dogmatik or German Invasion?', in C. Stahn (ed.), *The Law and Practice of the International Criminal Court: A Critical Account of Challenges and Achievements* (Oxford University Press, 2015) 57.

OhlinJ., 'Joint Criminal Confusion', *New Criminal Law Review* 12 (2009) 406–419.

OhlinJ., 'Joint Intentions to Commit International Crimes', *Chicago Journal of International Law* 11 (2011) 693–753.

OhlinJ., 'Second-Order Linking Principles: Combining Vertical and Horizontal Modes of Liability', *Leiden Journal of International Law* 25 (2012) 771–797.

OhlinJ., 'Three Conceptual Problems with the Doctrine of Joint Criminal Enterprise', *Journal of International Criminal Justice* 5 (2007) 69–90.

OlásoloH., *The Criminal Responsibility of Senior Political and Military Leaders as Principals to International Crimes* (Hart, 2009).

OsielM., 'The Banality of Good: Aligning Incentive against Mass Atrocity', *Columbia Law Review* 105 (2005) 1751–1862.

OsielM., *The End of Reciprocity: Terror, Torture, and the Law of War* (Cambridge University Press, 2009).

OsielM., *Mass Atrocity, Ordinary Evil and Hannah Arendt* (Yale University Press, 2001).

Ould MohamedouM., 'Al-Qaida: une guerre non linéaire', *Revue interdisciplinaire de sciences sociales* 3(2) (2005) 130–170.

OwensJ., *Nuremberg: Evil on Trial* (Headline Review, 2006).

ParksW., 'Command Responsibility for War Crimes', *Military Law Review* 62 (1973) 1–104.

PasternakA., 'The Distributive Effect of Collective Punishment', in IsaacsT. and VernonR. (eds), *Accountability for Collective Wrongdoing* (Cambridge University Press, 2011) 210–220.

PaustJ., 'Individual Criminal Responsibility for Human Rights Atrocities and Sanction Strategies', *Texas International Law Journal* 33 (1999) 631.

PaustJ., 'Superior Orders and Command Responsibility', in C. Bassiouni (ed.), *International Criminal Law: Vol III* (Transnational, 1999) 73.

PauwelynJ., 'At the Edge of Chaos? Emergence and Change in International Investment Law', *ICSID Review* 29(2) (2014) 372–418.

PearlmanW., *Violence, Non-Violence and the Palestinian National Movement* (Cambridge University Press, 2011).

PejicJ., 'The Protective Scope of Common Article 3: More than Meets the Eye', *International Review of the Red Cross* 93(881) (2011) 189–225.

PetropoulosN., 'Defining and Combating Terrorism: International and European Legislative Efforts', in G. Andreopoulos (ed.), *Policing Across Borders: Law Enforcement Networks and the Challenges of Crime Control* (Springer, 2013) 123.

PiragoffD., 'Article 30: Mental Element', in O. Triffterer (ed.), *Commentary on the Rome Statute of the International Criminal Court* (Nomos, 1999) 534.

PlattnerD., 'The Penal Repression of Violations of International Humanitarian Law Applicable in Non-International Armed Conflicts', *International Review of the Red Cross* 30 (1990) 409–420.

PortmannR., *Legal Personality in International Law* (Cambridge University Press, 2010).

PostJ., *The Mind of the Terrorist: The Psychology of Terrorism from the IRA to Al-Qaeda* (Palgrave MacMillan, 2007).

ProulxV., *Transnational Terrorism and State Accountability: A New Theory of Prevention* (Hart, 2012).

QinJ. et al., 'Analysing Terrorist Networks', *Intelligence and Security Informatics Lecture Notes in Computer Science* 3495 (2005) 287–304.

RapportD., 'The Fourth Wave: September 11 and the History of Terrorism', *Current History* (2001) 419–424.

RatnerS. and AbramsJ., *Accountability for Human Rights Atrocities in International Law: Beyond the Nuremburg Legacy* (Oxford University Press, 2001).

RawlinsonG. (ed.), *The History of Herodotus* (Appleton, 1885), vol. III, bk 4.

ReiffM., 'Terrorism, Retribution and Collective Responsibility', *Social Theory and Practice* 34 (2008) 209–242.

ReudyJ., *Modern Algeria: The Origins and Development of a Nation* (Indiana University Press, 2005, 2nd edn).

RichardsonL. (ed.), *The Roots of Terrorism* (Routledge, 2006).

RiedelB., *The Search for Al Qaeda: Its Leadership, Ideology and Future* (Brookings Institution, 2010).

RobinsonD., 'Defining Crimes Against Humanity at the Rome Conference', *American Journal of International Law* 93 (1999) 43–57.

RobinsonP., 'Imputed Criminal Liability', *Yale Law Journal* 93 (1984) 609–676.

Rodriguez-Villasante y PrietoJ., 'Los principles generales del derecho penal en el estatuto de la Roma de la Corte penal internacional', *Revista espanola de derecho militar* 75 (2000) 417.

RosandE., 'Resolutions 1373 and the CTC: The Security Council's Capacity-Building', in G. Nesi (ed.), *International Cooperation in Counter-Terrorism: The United Nations and Regional Organisations in the Fight against Terrorism* (Ashgate, 2006) 81–88.

RosandE., 'Security Council Resolution 1373, the Counter-Terrorism Committee, and the Fight Against Terrorism', *American Journal of International Law* 97 (2003) 333–341.

RossJ., 'The Primary Grievance of a Structural Cause of Oppositional Political Terrorism: Comparing Al-Fatah, FARC and PIRA', in D. Canter (ed.), *The Faces of Terrorism: Multidisciplinary Perspectives* (Wiley, 2009) 75–96.

RossJ. and GurrI., 'Why Terrorism Subsides: A Comparative Study of Canada and the United States', *Comparative Politics* 21(4) (1989) 405–426.

RoxinC., 'Crimes as Part of Organized Power Structures' (trans. B. Cooper) *Journal of International Criminal Justice* 9 (2011) 193.

RoxinC., 'Straftaten im Rahmen Organisatorischer Machtapparate', in H. Grüntzer (ed.), *Goltdammer's Archiv für Strafrecht* (Deckers, 1963).

RoxinC., *Täterschaft und Tatherrschaft* (de Gruyter, 2006, 8th edn).

RuhlJ. B., 'Complexity Theory as a Paradigm for the Dynamical Law-and-Society System: A Wake-up Call for Legal Reductionism and the Modern Administrative State', *Duke Law Journal* 45 (1995–1996) 849–927.

RuhlJ. B., 'Law's Complexity: A Primer', *Georgia State University Law Review* 24 (2007–2008) 885–911.

RussellC. and MillerB., 'Profile of a Terrorist', *Terrorism* 1(1) (1977) 17–34.

SadatL., *The International Criminal Court and the Transformation of International Law: Justice for the New Millennium* (Martinus Nijhoff, 2002).

SalandP., 'International Criminal Law Principles', in R. Lee (ed.), *The International Criminal Court: The Making of the Rome Statute: Issues Negotiations and Results* (Martinus Nijhoff, 1999) 189.

SanderB., 'Unravelling the Confusion Concerning Successor Superior Responsibility in the ICTY Jurisprudence', *Leiden Journal of International Law* 23 (2010) 105–135.

SandlerT. and SiqueiraK., 'Global Terrorism: Deterrence versus Pre-emption', *Canadian Journal of Economics* 39(4) (2006) 1370–1387.

SantoriV., 'The UN Security Council's (Broad) Interpretation of the Notion of the Threat to Peace in Counter-Terrorism', in G. Nesi (ed.), *International Cooperation in Counter-Terrorism: The United Nations and Regional Organisations in the Fight against Terrorism* (Ashgate, 2006) 89–111.

SassóliM., 'Transnational Armed Groups and International Humanitarian Law' (HPCR Occasional Paper Series, 2006).

SaulB., 'The Curious Element of Motive in Definitions of Terrorism: Essential Ingredient or Criminalizing Thought?', in A. Lynch, E. MacDonald, and G. Williams (eds), *Law and Liberty in the War on Terror* (Federation Press, 2007) 28–38.

SaulB., *Defining Terrorism in International Law* (Oxford University Press, 2008).

SaulB., 'The Legal Response of the League of Nations to Terrorism', *Journal of International Criminal Justice* 4(1) (2006) 78–102.

SaulB., 'Legislating from a Radical Hague: The United Nations Special Tribunal for Lebanon Invents an International Crime of Transnational Terrorism', *Leiden Journal of International Law* 24 (2011) 677–700.

SaulB., 'Terrorism and International Humanitarian Law', in B. Saul (ed.), *Research Handbook on International and Terrorism* (Edward Elgar, 2014) 208–231.

SawyerR., *Social Emergence: Societies as Complex Systems* (Cambridge University Press, 2005).

SchabasW., 'The Contribution of the Eichmann Trial to International Law', *Leiden Journal of International Law* 26 (2013) 667–699.

SchabasW., *Genocide in International Law* (Cambridge University Press, 2000).

SchabasW., *The International Criminal Court: A Commentary on the Rome Statute* (Oxford University Press, 2010).

SchabasW., 'State Policy as an Element of International Crimes', *Journal of Criminal Law and Criminology* 98 (2008) 953–982.

Schachter, O., 'The Quasi-Judicial Role of the Security Council and the General Assembly', *American Journal of International Law* 58 (1964) 960–965.

ScharfM., 'Defining Terrorism as the Peacetime Equivalent of War Crimes: Problems and Prospects', *Case Western Reserve Journal of International Law* 36 (2004) 359–374.

ScharfM., 'Special Tribunal for Lebanon Issues Landmark Ruling on Definition of Terrorism and Modes of Participation' (4 March 2011) *ASIL Insights*, available at: www.asil.org/insights110304.cfm (date accessed: 14 March 2018).

ScharfM. and NewtonM., 'Terrorism and Crimes against Humanity', in L. Sadat (ed.), *Forging a Convention for Crimes against Humanity* (Cambridge University Press, 2011) 262–278.

SchmahlS., 'Specific Methods of Prosecuting Terrorists in National Law', in C. Walter et al. (eds), *Terrorism as a Challenge for National and International Law: Security versus Liberty?* (Springer, 2004) 81.

SchmidA., 'Terrorism and Democracy, *Terrorism and Political Violence* 4(4) (1992) 14–25.

SchmidA. and JongmanA., *Political Terrorism: A New Guide to Actors, Authors, Concepts, Databases, Theories and Literature* (North Holland, 2005).

SchrijverN., 'Responding to International Terrorism: Moving the Frontiers of International Law for "Enduring Freedom"?', *Netherlands International Law Review* 49 (2001) 271–291.

SchützA., 'Desiring Society: Autopoiesis Beyond the Paradigm of Mastership', *Law and Critique* 9 (1994) 149–164.

SchwarzenbergerG., *International Law, Vol II: The Law of Armed Conflict* (Stevens, 1968).

ScobbieI., 'Lebanon 2006', in E. Wilmshurst (ed.), *International Law and the Classification of Armed Conflicts* (Oxford University Press, 2012) 387.

SepinwellA., 'Citizen Responsibility and the Reactive Attitudes: Blaming Americans for War Crimes in Iraq', in IsaacsT. and VernonR. (eds), *Accountability for Collective Wrongdoing* (Cambridge University Press, 2011) 231–260.

ShawM., *International Law* (Cambridge University Press, 2014, 7th edn).

ShklarJ., *Legalism* (Harvard University Press, 1964).

ShubikM., 'Game Theory, Complexity and Simplicity Part II: Problems and Applications', *Complexity* 3(3) (1998) 36–45.

ShumateB., 'New Rules for a New War: The Applicability of the Geneva Conventions to Al Qaeda and Taliban Detainees in Afghanistan', *New York International Law Review* 18 (2005) 1–79.

SillimanS., 'On Military Commissions', *Case Western Reserve Journal of International Law* 34 (2004) 529–540.

SimpsonG., 'Terrorism and the Law: Past and Present International Approaches', *SIPRI* (2003) 23, available at: www.sipri.org/yearbook/2003/files/SIPRIYB03E1.pdf (date accessed: 14 March 2018).

SinaiJ., 'How to Define Terrorism', *Perspectives on Terrorism* 2(4) (2008) available at: www.terrorismanalysts.com/pt/index.php/pot/article/view/33/html (date accessed: 14 March 2018).

SivakumaranS., 'Command Responsibility in Irregular Groups', *Journal of International Criminal Justice* 10 (2012) 1129–1150.

SkyttnerL., 'Systems Theory and the Science of Military Command and Control', *Kybernetes* 74(7–8) (2005) 1240–1260.

SluiterG., *International Criminal Law* (Oxford University Press, 2008).

SriramC., *Globalizing Justice for Mass Atrocities: A Revolution in Accountability* (Routledge, 2010).

SsenyonjoM., 'Accountability of Non-State Actors in Uganda for War Crimes and Human Rights Violations: Between Amnesty and the International Criminal Court', *Journal of Conflict and Security Law* 10(3) (2005) 405–434.

SsenyonjoM., 'The International Criminal Court and the Lord's Resistance Army Leaders: Prosecution or Amnesty?', *Netherlands International Law Review* 54(10) (2007) 51–80.

StarkeJ., 'The Convention for the Prevention and Punishment of Terrorism', *British Yearbook of International Law* 19 (1938) 214.

SteinT., 'The Approach of the Different Drummer: The Principle of the Persistent Objector in International Law', *Harvard International Law Journal* 26 (1985) 457–482.

StepanovaE., *Terrorism in Asymmetrical Conflict: Ideological and Structural Aspects* (Oxford University Press, 2008).

SternJ., *The Ultimate Terrorist* (Harvard University Press, 1999).

StohlM., 'Is the Past Prologue? Terrorists and WMD', *International Studies Review* 7(1) (2005) 146–148.

StromsethJ., 'The Security Council's Counter-Terrorism Role: Continuity and Innovation', *American Society of International Law Proceedings* 97 (2003) 41–45.

Sukru HaniogluM., *The Young Turks in Opposition* (Oxford University Press, 1995).

SuyE., 'The Meaning of Consensus in Multilateral Diplomacy', in R. Akkerman, P. Van Krieken, and C. Pannenborg (eds), *Declarations on Principles: A Quest for Universal Peace* (Springer, 1977) 259–272.

SzaszP., 'The Security Council Starts Legislating', *American Journal of International Law* 96 (2002) 901–905.

TalmonS., 'The Security Council as World Legislature', *American Journal of International Law* 99(1) (2005) 175–193.

TrappK., *State Responsibility for International Terrorism* (Oxford University Press, 2011).

TrechselS., 'Command Responsibility as a Separate Offence', *Publicist* 3 (2009) 26–35.

TsoukasH. and KnudsenC. (eds), *The Oxford Handbook of Organisation Theory* (Oxford University Press, 2005).

VachonC., 'Sovereignty versus Globalization: The International Court of Justice's Advisory Opinion on the Threat or Use of Nuclear Weapons', *Denver Journal of International Law and Policy* 26 (1998) 691–724.

VagtsD., 'Which Courts Should Try Persons Accused of Terrorism?', *European Journal of International Law* 14(2) (2003) 313–326.

Van KriekenP., *Terrorism and the International Legal Order* (Asser Press, 2002).

Van SliedregtE., 'Article 28 of the ICC Statute: Mode of Liability and/or Separate Offence?', *New Criminal Law Review* 12 (2009) 420–432.

Van SliedregtE., *The Criminal Responsibility of Individuals for Violations of International Humanitarian Law* (TMC Asser Press, 2003).

Van SliedregtE., *Individual Criminal Responsibility in International Law* (Oxford University Press, 2012).

Van SliedregtE., 'Joint Criminal Enterprise as a Pathway to Convicting Individuals for Genocide', *Journal of International Criminal Justice* 5 (2007) 184–207.

VärkR., 'State Responsibility for Private Armed Groups in the Context of Terrorism', *Juridica International* 11 (2006) 184–193.

VenturaM., 'Terrorism According to the STL's Interlocutory Decision on the Applicable Law', *Journal of International Criminal Justice* 9 (2011) 1021–1042.

VetterG., 'Command Responsibility of Non-Military Superiors in the International Criminal Court (ICC)', *Yale Journal of International Law* 25 (2000) 89–143.

Voltaire, *Questions sur les miracles à M. Claparede, professeur de théologie à Genève, par un proposant: ou extrait de diverses lettres de M. de Voltaire* (Penguin, 2005).

Von HebelH. and RobinsonD., 'Crimes within the Jurisdiction of the Court', in R. Lee (ed.), *The International Criminal Court: The Making of the Rome Statute* (Martinus Nijhoff, 1999) 92–103.

WalkinsonP., *Terrorism and the Liberal State* (Halstead, 1997).

WalterC. et al. (eds), *Terrorism as a Challenge for National and International Law: Security Versus Liberty?* (Springer, 2004).

WaltersF., *A History of the League of Nations* (Oxford University Press, 1969).

WebbJ., 'Law, Ethics and Complexity: Complexity Theory and the Normative Reconstruction of Law', *Cleveland State Law Review* 5(2) (2005) 227–242.

WebbT., 'Tracing an Outline of Legal Complexity', *Ratio Juris* 27 (2014) 477–495.

WeberM., *The Theory of Social and Economic Organisation* (Free Press, 1947).

WeigendT., 'Intent, Mistake of Law, and Co-Perpetration in the *Lubanga* Decision on Confirmation of Charges', *Journal of International Criminal Justice* 6 (2008) 471–487.

WeigendT., 'Perpetration through an Organization: The Unexpected Career of a German Legal Concept', *Journal of International Criminal Justice* 9 (2011) 91–111.

WeigendT., 'Sentencing in West Germany', *Maryland Law Review* 42 (1983) 37–89.

WeinbergL., PerdzhurA., and Hirsch-HoeflerS., 'The Challenge of Conceptualizing Terrorism', *Terrorism and Political Violence Journal* 16 (2004) 777–794.

WerleG., 'Individual Criminal Responsibility in Article 25 ICC Statute', *Journal of International Criminal Justice* 5 (2007) 953–975.

WerleG., *Principles of International Criminal Law* (TMC Asser Press, 2005).

WerleG., and BurghardtB., 'Do Crimes Against Humanity Require the Participation of a State or a "State-like" Organization?', *Journal of International Criminal Justice* 10(5) (2012) 1151–1170.

WheatleyS., 'The Emergence of New States in International Law: The Insights from Complexity Theory', *Chinese Journal of International Law* 15(1) (2016) 579–606.

WilliamsJ., 'Carlos Marighella: The Father of Urban Guerrilla Warfare', *Terrorism* 12(1) (1989) 1–20.

WilmshurstE., 'Transnational Crimes, Terrorism and Torture', in R. Cryer et al. (eds), *An Introduction to International Criminal Law and Procedure* (Cambridge University Press, 2010, 2nd edn) 344.

WolfkeK., *Custom in Present International Law* (Martinus Nijhoff, 1993, 2nd edn).

YanevL. and KooijmansT., 'Divided Minds in the Lubanga Trial Judgment: A Case against the Joint Control Theory', *International Criminal Law Review* 13 (2013) 789–828.

YezdaniO., SanzogniL., and PoropatA., 'Theory of Emergence: Introducing a Model-Centred Approach to Applied Social Science Research', *Prometheus: Critical Studies in Innovation* 33(3) (2015) 305–322.

ZappaláS., 'Do Heads of State in Office Enjoy Immunity from Jurisdiction for International Crimes? The Ghaddafi Case before the French Cour de Cassation', *European Journal of International Law* 12(3) (2001) 595–612.

ZegveldL., *The Accountability of Armed Opposition Groups under International Law* (Cambridge University Press, 2002).

ZlataricB., 'History of International Terrorism and Its Legal Control', in M. Bassiouni (ed.), *International Terrorism and Political Crimes* (Charles C. Thomas, 1975) 474–484.

Index

For Product Safety Concerns and Information please contact our EU representative GPSR@taylorandfrancis.com
Taylor & Francis Verlag GmbH, Kaufingerstraße 24, 80331 München, Germany

www.ingramcontent.com/pod-product-compliance
Ingram Content Group UK Ltd.
Pitfield, Milton Keynes, MK11 3LW, UK
UKHW011006180926
475701UK00004B/595

* 9 7 8 0 3 6 7 5 8 8 1 0 6 *